Business Research

To Kelli, for your love, support, and courage.

Courage is not simply one of the virtues,
but the form of every virtue at
the testing point.

—C. S. Lewis

Sara Miller McCune founded SAGE Publishing in 1965 to support the dissemination of usable knowledge and educate a global community. SAGE publishes more than 1000 journals and over 800 new books each year, spanning a wide range of subject areas. Our growing selection of library products includes archives, data, case studies and video. SAGE remains majority owned by our founder and after her lifetime will become owned by a charitable trust that secures the company's continued independence.

Los Angeles | London | New Delhi | Singapore | Washington DC | Melbourne

Business Research

A Guide to Planning, Conducting, and Reporting Your Study

Donald R. Cooper

Los Angeles | London | New Delhi
Singapore | Washington DC | Melbourne

FOR INFORMATION:

SAGE Publications, Inc.
2455 Teller Road
Thousand Oaks, California 91320
E-mail: order@sagepub.com

SAGE Publications Ltd.
1 Oliver's Yard
55 City Road
London EC1Y 1SP
United Kingdom

SAGE Publications India Pvt. Ltd.
B 1/I 1 Mohan Cooperative Industrial Area
Mathura Road, New Delhi 110 044
India

SAGE Publications Asia-Pacific Pte. Ltd.
3 Church Street
#10–04 Samsung Hub
Singapore 049483

Acquisitions Editor: Robert Farrell
Content Development Editor: Darcy Scelsi
Editorial Assistant: Alexandra Randall
Production Editor: Bennie Clark Allen
Copy Editor: Christina West
Typesetter: C&M Digitals (P) Ltd.
Proofreader: Eleni Maria Georgiou
Indexer: Jean Casalegno
Cover Designer: Rose Storey
Marketing Manager: Rob Bloom

Printed in the United States of America

Library of Congress Cataloging-in-Publication Data

Names: Cooper, Donald R., author.

Title: Business research : a guide to planning, conducting, and reporting your study / Donald R. Cooper.

Description: First Edition. | Thousand Oaks : SAGE Publications, [2018] | Includes bibliographical references and index.

Identifiers: LCCN 2018016816 | ISBN 9781544307824 (pbk. : alk. paper)

Subjects: LCSH: Business—Research. | Research—Methodology.

Classification: LCC HD30.4 .C6548 2018 | DDC 650.072—dc23 LC record available at https://lccn.loc.gov/2018016816

This book is printed on acid-free paper.

SUSTAINABLE FORESTRY INITIATIVE

Certified Chain of Custody
Promoting Sustainable Forestry
www.sfiprogram.org
SFI-01268

SFI label applies to text stock

18 19 20 21 22 10 9 8 7 6 5 4 3 2 1

BRIEF CONTENTS

DETAILED CONTENTS

LIST OF EXHIBITS

PREFACE

*B*usiness Research: A Guide to Planning, Conducting, and Reporting Your Study provides an in-depth view of the research process and design. It connects the learning objectives of these topics with *how to write a research report*. The goal of the book is to give you the necessary background to start a term project or research paper with confidence. It is a reference designed for business students and managers but is also useful for allied disciplines that teach research methodology at upper undergraduate and graduate levels with statistics as a prerequisite. The book aspires to mirror its title. It was designed to function as a *guide* through the research process and to unburden students of digesting a full-length text *before* starting the *planning*, *conducting*, and *writing* of their report. That goal comes with risks. It places inordinate faith that students are motivated to use the references, in-text URLs, examples, appendices, tutorials, and cases that show them how to craft an exemplary academic project or business report. Although quantitative research receives ample coverage, I value and voice the ascendency of qualitative research, mixed designs, and their contribution to business research.

DESIGN AND PHILOSOPHY

The aim of this guide is *minimalism* because this aesthetic enhances the flow of the text. "Less is more." Scientific evidence (psychological associations and neurological research) calls the current mantra of designers and the preoccupation with the "visual learner" a "neuromyth" seized upon by zealous but misguided educators. Yet it remains pervasive in books cluttered with photos on each page, boxes and sidebars, marginal notes, and other features that have the opposite of the intended effect—they disconnect the reader from the learning point. The exhibits and images in this guide are basic but try to limit distractions by providing information that amplifies the text in a connected and simple way.

If you are naturally curious, you will likely become skilled at research and enamored by the power of data. I hope this book creates a passion for data-driven solutions. I am reminded of Google's former Senior Vice President for Product Management, Jonathan Rosenberg, who elevated data from sexy to Samurai. Rosenberg wrote an internal e-mail for Google employees, which he posted on the official Google blog, stating "When every business has free and ubiquitous data, the ability to understand it and extract value from it becomes the complimentary scarce factor. It leads to intelligence, and the intelligent business is the successful business, regardless of its size. ...Data is the sword of the 21st century; those who wield it well, the Samurai."

Data will make or break 21st-century businesses, especially ones that rely on the Internet. Indeed, customers are already there and many companies have discovered algorithms that not only understand their shopping behaviors but also predict future ones. Pew Research reported in 2018 that 77% of Americans own smartphones, while the number of mobile devices in the world is over 7 billion. Data changes not only the face of research in business but also the knowledge, vision, and creative capacity required to be a problem-solver in management. Old ways of collecting, processing, interpreting, and integrating data will be revolutionized faster than anyone imagines— much to the chagrin of traditional methodologists. So keep your mind open as you read this book, knowing that it is intentionally limited to some topics and a little edgy on others. It too must evolve in a rapidly changing environment.

PURPOSE

This book intends to lessen the anxiety surrounding complex research assignments, particularly term projects. It pursues ways to help new researchers become more self-reliant and enjoy the research experience. Conversations with faculty, students, and new managers explain *why* doing research and producing a report causes so much apprehension. They say that the teaching of research can be imbalanced because of too much time spent on favored techniques or endless philosophical diatribes on the superiority of a preferred worldview. Students add that data analysis modules quickly become a statistics course. This impedes the student's ability to obtain critical information on assignments *in advance* of due dates.

Every student has experienced the time constraints of classes; there is seldom time enough to acquire course content and the skills to create a successful term project. Although projects frequently make up a large percentage of the grade in a course, insufficient attention is devoted to them because of the pressure of mastering a 600-page textbook. One answer to this dilemma is to make the research process, design, and writing the report more approachable with more concise information. It must have content that is current, technically accurate, and accessible. A simple analogy calls attention to this need. We all use manuals for technological consumer products that are thick instructional booklets with a myriad of topics from installation to troubleshooting, regulatory compliance, repair, and warranty. As extensive references, they do not get users up-and-running speedily because of the massive amount of detail. The sheer size frustrates and potentially intimidates the reader.

In contrast, a *"quick-start guide"* is a relatively short, simple introduction to get users acquainted with basic operations and functions without delay. The Apple product guides describe essential features in few paragraphs per topic. Similarly, self-learning programs on the Internet have quick-start guides with a few pages on enrolling, logging in, purchasing access, and then adapting to your learning needs. Adaptation and accessibility are this book's goals to respond to your demanding schedules.

ORGANIZATION OF THE GUIDE

Editors like to "advise" authors about writing a Preface so that readers know how to approach their book, but that is really for advertising and readers are perceptive enough to know what they want from a book. This book's structure will be clear in a moment. For an immediate response, let me use a quote from Chapter 3 by Booth et al. in *The Craft of Research* (2008): "And no matter how carefully you plan, research follows a crooked path, taking unexpected turns, sometimes up blind alleys, even looping back on itself... When you can manage its parts, you can manage the often intimidating whole and look forward to doing more research with greater confidence." Read my book in any sequence that appeals to you! Perhaps you'll seek out just the "parts" but remember that although the whole of the research process may seem like a fuzzy sequence, it has a purposeful logic.

Each chapter consists of a set of learning objectives, the content that supports them, a summary, key terms, and discussion questions. Learning objectives perform a vital role in reducing student anxiety. They tell students what they should be able to do, promote fairness in assessment, and help instructors create courses that distinguish between knowledge, attitude, and skill objectives.

Chapter 1 provides compelling reasons to study business research and reveals the need for research skills by presenting the disparity between employers' assessments of what students demonstrate on the job and students' perceptions of their success. It introduces what it takes to become an accomplished researcher, the most practical of which is evaluating and conducting quality research and producing a respectable report on your own. The chapter establishes what business research is and is not. To prepare for selecting a project topic or managerial problem, I explore the scope of business research "purposes" including reporting, exploring, describing, explaining, predicting, and changing (or action research). Chapter 1 also clarifies the continuum of research from basic to applied and offers a detailed description of what comprises *good* research. The latter serves as a checklist to evaluate your interim project decisions, to apply to the selection of sources for your literature review, and to assess each activity until the completion of your study. The last section describes research orientations (philosophical perspectives) that affect how researchers approach problems (quantitative, qualitative, or both). A graphic "road map" for the book and the phases of the research process conclude Chapter 1. The road map is intuitive and you will want to refer to it on occasion for orientation.

Chapter 2 explains and outlines the role of scientific inquiry. Every form of reasoning contributes to qualitative and quantitative research. The chapter emphasizes the importance of reasoning soundly using deduction, induction, abduction, and the Toulmin Model of argumentation and logic. The latter has considerable implications for writing your report because it shows you how to generate evidence for your claims and support your arguments. A case expands this section as a detailed example. And, to establish a comfort level with this book, the chapter defines the terms and principles that researchers use every day. The terms constitute the vocabulary you need to understand the language of this book, to conduct a study, and to communicate its results. Definitions and examples clarify the nature of concepts, constructs, definitions, variables, propositions, hypotheses, and theory. They may sound intimidating now, but you will use them later with ease.

Chapters 3, 4, and 5 provide a *detailed* outline, the roadmap, of the research process. The research process model is a seven-phase sequence composed of exploring, planning, creating, conducting, collecting, analyzing, and reporting (writing the report). Collectively, there are 17 elements or activities linked to the major phases of this model. At first glance, it looks complicated and overwhelming. But if you follow the steps one at a time, it soon becomes quite simple. By taking baby steps, a psychological principle used with exposure therapy to reduce stress and anxiety, you do one difficult thing each day. Likewise, with this process, one step will build upon another and soon you will have mastered 17 activities giving you a broad learning experience in doing research.

I describe each activity by connecting it to your research project. The elements or activities are introduced in Exhibit 3.2. The ones related to the research *problem* or *questions* receive expanded treatment. For example, many students have a perennial question: How do I select a topic? I cover topic sources for your project along with ways to frame, define, and translate a topic into a research question. The remaining 16 steps are described prescriptively to guide you through each aspect of your study. You will not find this level of detail on the research process elsewhere. At the beginning of each process chapter, there is a graphic that orients you to where you are and highlights the activities to be presented. Chapter 3 deals with exploring and planning your research; it has eight activities. Chapter 4 concentrates on creating and conducting and features six elements. Chapter 5 takes you into the home stretch with data collection and processing, analysis and interpretation, and an introduction to report writing—which adds another three activities. There are also appendices that illustrate the learning points for various chapters and provide tools and skill-building tutorials.

Chapters 6, 7, and 8 deal with difficult research decisions: what design to select, what separates one design from another, and what distinguishes a design from a method. These three chapters discuss nonexperimental quantitative designs, qualitative and mixed designs, and experimental designs, respectively. When you compare the designs, you will discover their relative advantages and how to apply them to business research. The types of design appear in a graphic that is certain to be more visually intuitive than exposition alone. Representative studies from the business literature (organized by the study's objective and time dimension of data collection) illustrate various designs so you can design a study by example.

You will understand the necessity to cover research design in separate chapters when you see the number of designs, explanations, and applications. Practically, you will find many options to create a blueprint for connecting a design to the problem you have chosen, including using the synergy of the mixed design, which is very underrated.

Chapter 9 is the climactic point of the book. It is the summit you reach after all your planning, perspiration, and execution; and you finally come to reporting your study. Because it was designed to be practical, this chapter is the jewel of the guide for students. Several reviewers enthusiastically claimed they would adopt the textbook for this chapter alone. Chapter 9 helps you prepare each section of your research report using numerous "how-to" examples. Over 25 illustrations are used that were derived from articles and other sources created by students and business professors. You will discover that you can devise a proper title, write an abstract, develop your introduction, and describe the problem and its setting. You will add to that your literature review, hypotheses, design, method(s), and procedures for collecting and analyzing your data. Finally, by presenting the results, discussing their implications, and stating your conclusions, you will complete a report that provides a sense of satisfaction and achievement. If it's a management report, it may also help solve a pressing problem for your organization and simultaneously elevate your credibility.

The sources of information for this guide are legendary but *relevant*. I try to balance traditional coverage of theory and practice with *contemporary* contributions from books, journal articles, and online sources. You will see the influence of distinguished researchers by observing the substantial quantity and diversity of references in each chapter. It is easy to criticize an experienced textbook writer for failing to paraphrase; however, it is far more advantageous to hear from authorities in their own words. Cognitive biases cause a lot to get lost in translation. This approach may persuade readers to seek more information from experts directly. For the benefit of student researchers and to honor the authors, this guide is heavily referenced with more than 600 citations to help readers pursue topics of interest in greater depth and detail.

We must omit specific topics because this book is a problem-focused, report-oriented guide. For example, I do not show you *how* to oversee or physically conduct an experiment, distribute or administer a questionnaire, create an interview guide to do an intercept, become a participant observer, assess the construct validity of a measuring instrument, or calculate sample size (well, maybe there is some help for that in Chapter 9). All of these topics are covered extensively in specialty books or statistics texts. And they are discussed in those sources at a level of detail that is not manageable here. However, there are three tutorials in the Appendix, one of which takes you step-by-step through the creation of an online questionnaire and considers question wording and measurement scales.

DIGITAL RESOURCES

Instructor Teaching Site (Password Protected)

SAGE edge for Instructors supports your teaching by making it easy to integrate quality content and create a rich learning environment for students. Instructors can access these resources at **https://edge.sagepub.com/cooperresearch**.

- **Test banks** provide a diverse range of pre-written options as well as the opportunity to edit any question and/or insert your own personalized questions to effectively assess students' progress and understanding.

- **Sample course syllabi** for semester and quarter courses provide suggested models for structuring your courses.

- Editable, chapter-specific **PowerPoint®️ slides** offer complete flexibility for creating a multimedia presentation for your course.

- **Multimedia content** includes original SAGE videos that appeal to students with different learning styles.

- **Lecture notes** summarize key concepts by chapter to help you prepare for lectures and class discussions.

- **Course cartridge** for easy LMS integration is included.

- **Author-selected video, cases, and data sets** from SAGE Business Research are provided.

Student Study Site (Open Access)

SAGE edge for Students provides a personalized approach to help students accomplish their coursework goals in an easy-to-use learning environment.

- Mobile-friendly **eFlashcards** strengthen understanding of key terms and concepts.

- Mobile-friendly practice **quizzes** allow for independent assessment by students of their mastery of course material.

- **Chapter summaries** with **learning objectives** reinforce the most important material.

- Exclusive! Access to full-text **SAGE journal articles** that have been carefully selected to support and expand on the concepts presented in each chapter is included.

ACKNOWLEDGMENTS

I would like to thank many colleagues and friends who offered advice about coverage and audience while others contributed valuable materials. The editorial assistance, proof-reading, and design ideas were invaluable. My wife, Kelli, encouraged me during the absence of creativity and craft. I am grateful for her perseverance.

This work is not *prima creatura* or as Voltaire put it, "Originality is nothing but *judicious* imitation. The most original writers borrowed one from another." Therefore, I am especially obliged to my colleagues for inspiring my ideas. In reaction to my prior books, they shared their impressions and materials unselfishly. I worked with brilliant undergraduate and graduate students in diverse places during my years of teaching research and statistics in business and other disciplines. I am grateful to my doctoral students who have taught me much over the years and supported my teaching and writing.

Robert J. Farrell, III, is the editor of this book and the Executive Editor responsible for operations management, business analytics, and international business at SAGE. He shepherded this work from his first reading through various obstacles and remained a true champion of its concept, content, and style. Other members at SAGE that should be recognized are Alexandra Randall (editorial assistant), Bennie Clark Allen (production editor), and Christina West (copyeditor).

I am indebted to R. Burke Johnson, Professor of Professional Studies at the University of Southern Alabama, for permission to use and modify his elegant design typology. I am thankful to William J. Lammers, Professor of Psychology at the University of Central Arkansas, for writings such as *Fundamentals of Behavioral Research,* an example of expositional clarity; I am also grateful for his permission to use the statistical decision trees in Appendix D to help students make sound and less complicated statistical choices. I also thank Dr. Adam Lund of the Laerd Statistics Team and Lund Research Ltd., for permission to use materials from their comprehensive website for portions of the SPSS® analytical write-up in Chapter 9. John W. Creswell was my authority for qualitative and mixed designs. He is a world-renowned scholar in mixed methods and is Co-Director of the Michigan Mixed Methods Research and Scholarship Program in the Department of Family Medicine at University of Michigan Medical School. He inspired the theme for Chapter 7, which is based on the fourth edition of *Qualitative Inquiry and Research Design: Choosing Among Five Approaches.* I also benefited from the work of Professor Paul C. Price, a cognitive psychologist at California State University, Fresno. I admire his straightforward writing, minimal digressions, and diverse examples.

Other valued contributors include Rafik Elias, Professor of Accounting at California State University, Los Angeles, for his gracious permission to use excerpts from his *SBAJ* journal article in Chapter 9. I thank S. Srinivasan, Dean, JHJ School of Business, Texas Southern University, and Editor-in-Chief of *SBAJ*, for permissions. Michelle LeMenager, Human Research Protections Office, University of Pittsburgh, provided permission for the use of their Institutional Review Board's Exemption Application (Appendix B), which is especially useful for business students.

Galina Biedenback, Associate Professor in Marketing at the Umeå School of Business and Economics, Umeå University, Sweden, facilitated permission for her advisees, Anna Fanoberova and Hanna Kuczkowska's Master's thesis. Thank you, Hanna and Anna, for the instructive examples that you shared with students. As this book crystallized, journal articles and the thesis were envisioned as the ways to illustrate how to help students prepare their term project even before they started writing.

Google, Inc., gave their permission to use Google Forms screenshots in a tutorial showing the creation of an online questionnaire in Appendix A. Adriano Ferrari allowed me to use his ingenious software app, *Gingko Tree*, to teach students how to turn their outlines into connected pieces of text through a hierarchical card structure that lets them visualize and organize a paper by seeing the parts and their relation to the whole (Appendix G).

I also acknowledge the many reviewers who suggested improvements.

Farrukh Abbas, *Barani Institute of Information Technology, Pakistan*

Joseph F. Adamo, *Cazenovia College*

Zara Ambadar, *Carlow University*

Sherryl Berg-Ridenour, *University of California, Riverside*

Sharon Didier, *St. Joseph's College*

Brian J. DiVita, *Aquinas College*

Diane R. Edmondson, *Middle Tennessee State University*

Ina Freeman, *Rockford University*

Mary Goebel-Lundholm, *Peru State College*

Ronald E. Goldsmith, *Florida State University*

Drake S. Mullens, *Tarleton State University*

Pushkala Raman, *Texas Woman's University*

Scott D. Roberts, *University of the Incarnate Word*

Elizabeth Robinson, *Champlain College and Metropolitan State University*

Marcel M. Robles, *Eastern Kentucky University*

Sarah Tanford, *University of Nevada, Las Vegas*

Haibo Wang, *Texas A&M International University*

Jun Yu, *Emporia State University*

Nan Zhang, *North Carolina Central University*

Peter D. Lindblom, author of *English Fundamentals* (16th edition), offered editorial insights. Summer Leverette created the original cover design.

Finally, I pay homage to my mentors. I first became interested in research methodology as a doctoral student conversing with the late eminent scholar John R. Platt, a physicist and biophysicist and professor at the University of Chicago and the University of Michigan. He was also a visiting scholar at the Salk Institute for Biological Studies, Harvard, and MIT. At the time of my dissertation research, he channeled me from psychophysics to complex systems methodology with extraordinary insight and encouragement that would later further my academic and consulting careers. Equally, the late James G. Coke (a Harvard-trained political scientist and systems theorist) and Steven R. Brown (the guru of Q methodology and a skilled general research methodologist) were remarkable research mentors.

ABOUT THE AUTHOR

 **Donald R. Cooper's** specialty is research methods, statistics, and organizational behavior. He has taught for over 30 years in masters (MBA, Executive MBA, and MPA programs) and doctoral programs in business and public administration. Dr. Cooper started his doctorate at the University of Colorado, Boulder, and completed his PhD in an interdisciplinary curriculum (Communication Studies, Business-OB, and complex systems methodology) at Kent State University. At various institutions, his administrative assignments included Associate Dean of the Business School and director of a research center. Dr. Cooper is a recipient of grants and has produced articles, books, and monographs. He also received several teaching awards.

Among his publications, Dr. Cooper and his coauthor produced a market-leading MBA textbook on research methods, used on four continents, in nine international editions, and in four languages for 25 years. That work and its derivations have been cited by over 24,200 researchers (according to Google Scholar) as they wrote in academic journals, books, theses, and dissertations. As a methodologist, Dr. Cooper's colleagues at IBM engaged him to join a small team in Europe as a visiting scholar. Together they created IBM's first desktop computer, Ambra, which later became Aptiva in North America. He also established IBM's first customer satisfaction program for EMEA (Europe, Middle East, and Africa). Currently, he serves as the managing director of the Cooper Research Group, a consultancy specializing in customer satisfaction, loyalty, and market segmentation research. He has consulted in the Americas, Europe, and Asia-Pacific regions. A recent assignment in strategic planning for the Canadian investment community resulted in prediction studies from the sentiment side of stock price movement and the development of metrics for stockholder confidence. Before his academic career, Dr. Cooper was responsible for executive recruitment at a Fortune 500 company and served as a Captain in an SAS unit of the U.S. Air Force during 4 years of active duty.

FROM THE RESEARCH JITTERS TO EMPLOYERS' MOST-WANTED SKILLS

LEARNING OBJECTIVES

Performance Objective

Use the book's guidance to acquire skills in selecting a topic, crafting a research question, finding sources in print and on the Internet, choosing a suitable design and pairing it with a method for data collection, analyzing data, and producing a report of your results.

Enabling Objectives

1. Evaluate the three reasons to study business: diversity of disciplinary choices, career variety, and salary expectations.

2. Become sensitive to the gap that exists between what students think they know, the level of analytical and research skills they possess, and what they demonstrate to employers on the job. Evaluate and expand the research skills you need to fast track your career: making sound decisions, contributing to executive research, buying research services, and becoming a research specialist.

3. Define business research from the perspective of problem-solving for business decisions.

4. Distinguish among the purposes of business research: reporting, exploring, describing, explaining, predicting, and changing (action research).

5. Provide examples to differentiate basic, practical, and applied research.

6. Outline eight defining characteristics for judging a research report: ethical issues, the research purpose, design, procedures, data and instrumentation, findings, researcher qualifications, and outcomes.

7. Discuss how philosophical orientations influence research strategy, namely the choice of quantitative or qualitative research.

8. Become familiar with the road map metaphor for the research process as its phases take you from exploring, planning, creating, conducting, collecting, and analyzing to ultimately writing your report.

Are you intimidated when you open the syllabus for your Business Research Methods class or another course in a research-oriented curriculum? Do you feel panic when you see a requirement for a major research paper or term project that accounts for a substantial percentage of your grade? Employees with minimal research training encounter the same anxiety when their managers ask them on short notice to produce a study to solve a problem or chart a course of action.

You may have purchased an expensive, exhaustive textbook on research methods that appears daunting. Often, the book cannot be covered in one semester because it was designed to give professors latitude in selecting chapters that match their instructional approach, or it contains three to five chapters on statistics that should be taught in a separate course. By the time you reach the end of the book, you will find one or two chapters on written reports and presentations.

On syllabi I am familiar with, these readings are typically assigned during the last few weeks of class when you should be proofreading your paper. You may be fortunate because some instructors coach you to develop modules for your project incrementally throughout the term and that work can help reduce your apprehension about a term project. Nevertheless, I know how challenged you feel when you are assigned a substantial research assignment.

This text, *Business Research: A Concise Guide to Planning, Conducting, and Reporting Your Study*, was designed for business students and managers. It is also a resource for students and managers in fields that are management oriented, such as public administration, hospitality management, sports, entertainment and performing arts management, nonprofit management, and others. You may have a business career now or aspire to work in a city, county, state, or federal government agency; or you may want to advocate for a nongovernmental organization (NGO) like Médecins Sans Frontières, Red Cross, or CARE International. Maybe you are committed to managing a healthcare or pharmaceutical company or an educational organization. This book should be a part of the preparation for your goals.

Managerial opportunities are everywhere: veterans' affairs, conservation groups, medical foundations, museums, churches, and so on. This guide prepares you to report the results of your research in business, public, and nonprofit organizations and in NGOs and elsewhere. I hope you will keep it as a reference on your bookshelf for future projects. This book covers the essentials of the *research process* comprehensively and accelerates your progress toward achieving a respectable research report.

What should you expect from this guide? First, it is practical. As Sir Peter Medawar said, "The art of research [is] the art of making difficult problems soluble by devising means of getting at them."[1] This book will explain all aspects leading to and including the writing process, thereby giving you sufficient understanding in dealing with difficult problems and the confidence to carry out an assignment successfully. It will provide you with direct paths to obtain information often obscured by the layout of other books. You will also receive guidance on selecting a topic, crafting a research question, finding sources in print and on the Internet, choosing a suitable design and pairing it with a method for collecting data, analyzing data, and producing a report of your results.

The topics for this chapter are as follows:

- Reasons to Study Business

- What Recruiters Say About Research Skills

- Research Fast-tracks Your Career

- Business Research Defined

- The Scope of Business Research

- Basic, Practical, and Applied Research

- Good Research Is . . .

- Research Orientations

- The Roadmap

REASONS TO STUDY BUSINESS

There are three good reasons to study business. The first is the diversity of disciplinary choices. At the undergraduate level, there are many study options from at least a dozen fields that range from highly specialized to interdisciplinary. The MBA and Executive MBA programs mentor students with more work experience. Their orientation is skill building and professional development. The second reason is career variety. When you combine preferences for organizational size, mission, and type, including entrepreneurial start-ups, nonprofits, and NGOs, the choice becomes vast. Third, many business students are motivated by the earnings potential. Since that is not the least important of these reasons, let's look at salary expectations.

The Pew Research Center conducted its most recent iteration of a longitudinal study on educational attainment in higher education and the rising value of a college degree. The data, collected in 1979, 1986, 1995, and 2013, used a nationally representative sample of 2,002 people. The U.S. Census Bureau and Bureau of Labor Statistics supplemented the data. Overall, Pew concluded that "college-educated millennials are outperforming their less-educated peers on virtually every economic measure" from personal earnings to job satisfaction and percentage of full-time employment.[2]

There are four findings of interest to business majors:

1. Your college major matters: 72% of business majors said that their current job is "very closely" or "somewhat closely" related to their undergraduate or graduate school major. In comparison, 60% of social science, liberal arts, and education majors agree.

2. A college education is worth more today: College graduates ages 25 to 32 working full time make $17,500 a year *more* than their peers with a high school diploma.

3. Career progress: 86% of millennials with a bachelor's degree say they have a career or career-track position.

Good reasons to study business include the diversity of disciplinary choices, career variety, and earnings potential. When you combine the career preferences for organizational size, mission, and type, including entrepreneurial start-ups, nonprofits, and NGOs, the choice of jobs becomes vast.

4. The millennial cohort says the cost was worth it: For what they and their families paid for their undergraduate education, 62% say it "has paid off" and 26% say "it will pay off"—in other words, 88% are satisfied.

For those curious about *starting salaries* in business fields, the National Association of Colleges and Employers (NACE) benchmark survey revealed actual starting salary data for business majors. The average starting salary for the Class of 2018 was $56,720, up from $49,500 in 2015. NACE's "2018 Salary Survey" reported that top-paid business majors at the baccalaureate level had an average starting salary (in order) of $62,634 for marketing majors, followed by MIS, actuarial science, economics, logistics/supply chain, finance, international business, accounting, administration/management, hospitality management, sales, and human resources at $52,322. With a master's degree, the top-paid majors had an average starting salary of $78,332 for business administration/management, followed by sales, marketing, human resources, MIS, actuarial science, finance, economics, logistics/supply chain, and international business at $58,600.[3]

PayScale's "2017–2018 College Salary Report" ranks the best universities and colleges for *salary potential*. The median salary of the top three ranked schools for business majors with bachelor's degrees (alumni with 0–5 years of experience) was $77,800 and the median for mid-career pay (≥10 years of experience) was $152,900.[4]

WHAT RECRUITERS SAY ABOUT RESEARCH SKILLS

While salary potential is enticing, it is because high-paid performance correlates with high-level skills. But a gap exists between what students think they know, the skills they possess, and what they demonstrate on the job. To discover the disconnect between missing job skills among recent graduates joining the workforce and the skills they acquired in school, PayScale, the compensation information company, recently surveyed 63,924 managers and 14,167 recent graduates. The survey results showed that "60% of managers claim the new graduates they see taking jobs within their organizations do not have the critical thinking and problem-solving skills they feel are necessary for the job."[5] Only 25% of grads agreed they were "*extremely* prepared" for their new jobs, while 8% of managers felt that way.

Forbes, citing a study on the 10 skills employers want most, used an NACE survey of 260 large companies.[6] Among the 10 are three research-related skills:

- Ability to obtain and process information

- Ability to analyze quantitative data

- Ability to create and/or edit written reports

A study by Hart Research Associates for the Association of American Colleges and Universities shows the value of a research paper, term project, or senior thesis. In the results from 400 employers and 613 students surveyed, 91% of employers agreed on the importance of "a candidate's demonstrated capacity to think critically, communicate clearly, and solve complex problems for career success. . . . Eighty-eight percent think it is important for colleges to ensure that ALL students are prepared with skills/knowledge needed to complete *a significant applied learning project*."[7] But just 14% of the employers said that most students have the skills to do so. The disparity between employers' evaluations of what students demonstrate they have learned and students' perceptions of their success is astounding. Interestingly, employers' desired outcomes follow the skill set needed to conduct research on the job successfully, but their assessment of students' possession of these skills is low. Students, on the other hand, consistently overestimate what they offer and how they think it translates to on-the-job performance (Exhibit 1.1).

Shutterstock/Rawpixel.com

PayScale, a compensation information company, in a recent survey revealed that 60% of managers claim that new graduates they see taking jobs in their organizations do not have the critical thinking and problem-solving skills they feel are essential for the job.

As part of the Bloomberg research ranking of 122 top MBA programs, 1,320 recruiters from more than 600 companies responded to a list of 14 sought-after characteristics.[8] From the 14, they were asked to pick five qualities that are *most important* in hiring MBAs and five that are *hardest to find*. Among their top picks are the following research-related skills:

- Analytic thinking
- Creative problem-solving
- Quantitative skills

EXHIBIT 1.1 ■ Employer-Student Perception of Skills

Skill-based Learning Outcomes	Skills Employers vs. Students Believe They Have Acquired	
	Employers	Students
Analyzing/solving complex problems	24%	59%
Locating, organizing, and evaluating information	29%	64%
Critical/analytical thinking	26%	66%
Working with numbers, statistics	28%	55%
Written communication	27%	65%

These studies reveal the discrepancy between skills that employers seek and students are missing. Ironically, the findings also target skills that are taught in rarely required, often-avoided research courses. Accrediting bodies of business schools spend little time advocating research methods courses but rather refer to "Documented improvements in learning outcomes that result from *teaching innovations* that incorporate research methods from learning/pedagogical research projects."[9] Does this mean stand-alone research courses (their requirement dropped over 20 years ago), modules in a course syllabus, literature reviews, or a comprehensive class research project? Vagueness will not likely impress the 88% of employers who want students to experience the completion of a rigorous learning project, a project that embodies specific performance criteria and prepares students with behavioral skills necessary for doing research successfully in their chosen fields.

RESEARCH FAST-TRACKS YOUR CAREER

The three good reasons to study business—discipline choices, career variety, and salaries—do not address the question about research skills. You read the feedback from recruiters and employers. There are unmet curriculum goals, courses that are avoided, and aversions to applied learning projects. These are barriers to success.

Business research provides the knowledge and expertise needed to solve problems and meet challenges in daily decision-making. Courses in business research are recognition that students in all functional areas of business, nonprofit, and public organizations need research skills for successful decision-making.

In addition to aspiring to high quality in business education, there are other ways you can profit from acquiring research skills:

- Managers need credible information on which to base sound decisions. Research-based information represents the pinnacle of support for decision-making. Your options are limited if there is no one to whom you can delegate the research task. You can do it yourself or base the decision on intuition and experience, not research.

Shutterstock/Peshkova

Courses in business research are recognition that students in all functional areas of business, nonprofit, and public organizations need research skills for successful decision-making.

- Early-career employees may be called upon to do a study and present the findings to high-level executives. The C-suite is a demanding research audience. Executives seek and rely on the advice of experts. Their peers are often audience members, and their opinions about how you defend the quality of your research count, too. They expect the findings of well-conducted research to be presented in a highly focused fashion, appropriate for their responsibilities and ruthless schedules. They insist on concrete, measurable outcomes and courses of action that justify their time[10] and create a value proposition for the firm. This opportunity can be career changing and, handled well, can allow you to gain credibility in the organization.

- At some point in your career, you may need to buy research services through outsourcing. The outsourcing of research occurs when firms need to (a) add a significant amount of new knowledge to innovate, (b) overcome obstacles in early-stage projects, (c) limit spending and risk when the industry does not protect intellectual property, and (d) provide a competitive edge in project management using their prior outsourcing experience.[11] You may also be required to evaluate research that was conducted internally by colleagues. If you can visualize the problem, possess the terminology and tools to understand the endeavor, and can work through the stages of the research process, you can assess trustworthy designs and judge the quality of the finished product.

- Finally, you may seek a position or a career as a research specialist. A research specialty offers attractive opportunities and prestige. About 15% of seniors from a recent Harvard class went into consulting after graduation, according to the Harvard *Crimson's* senior survey.[12] In 2016, that percentage increased to 21%. However, the motives for recent graduates accepting a position in finance, technology, or consulting (the "big three") appear to center on finding "a good place to learn." Only a fraction of the original 53% expected to continue their career path after 10 years.[13] Here is where experience makes a difference. For experienced MBAs with research skills in their portfolio, if you know *where* you want to be (Fortune 500 companies, Wall Street, marketing, multinationals), you will find specialized programs at various universities that match your career path. For example, consider Amazon—Ross (Michigan), McKinsey—Kellogg (Northwestern), Apple—Fuqua (Duke), private equity—(Stanford), luxury goods—HEC (Paris), Global Network (Yale), and so on.[14] Research competence hastens your ascent in an organization and enables your organization to remain competitive and innovate more quickly than the competition.

BUSINESS RESEARCH DEFINED

Research answers questions and solves problems through systematic inquiries that provide information. Intuition, creativity, and speculation play a part in suggesting or directing research, but they do not constitute research. Research is *not* merely gathering and classifying facts; it is *not* an exercise in the application of a technique or tool; and it is *not* a study that draws no conclusions.

Business research is a systematic and objective process that provides information to solve problems and guide business decisions. This process includes collecting, recording, analyzing, and interpreting data. But the data must be evaluated objectively, requiring the researcher to be free from bias in all phases of the study, thereby ensuring the accuracy of the decision. This standard applies to all fields and functions of business, nonprofit, and public organizations.

THE SCOPE OF BUSINESS RESEARCH

An understanding of business research obliges one to grasp its scope. The range of business research is broad. Studies differ by design and many other factors, but that is a topic for later chapters. In this section, I will describe six primary *purposes* of business research: reporting, exploring, describing, explaining, predicting, and changing (action research). These purposes, their definitions, and concrete examples should accomplish two goals: (1) give you a sense of the breadth of the field and (2) reinforce the context for defining what business research is and what it does.

Reporting

Reporting studies perform the most basic purpose of research: delving into an issue or topic " . . . to provide an account of something, for example, of an event or a situation. In business settings, reports provide advice and information designed to aid decision-making . . . including financial reports, annual reports, feasibility reports, incident reports, impact reports, project reports, research reports, and so on."[15]

Reporting involves a substantial use of secondary information sources (existing data originally collected by others) such as public records, journals, and online sources on such topics as accountability and social issues. Less often, the information sought may require a reliance on rigorous fact-checking using primary sources (original research conducted by you). This process involves quantitative or qualitative methods (conclusions derived numerically versus interpretative, non-numerical analysis).

For example, reporting may investigate an industry's policies or specific businesses for a nonacademic audience. Reporting may also detect changes in the business environment through an assessment of economic, political, and cultural trends that are of interest to a client, a company, or the public. A study of Irish financial institutions and their web-sites was used to demonstrate the extent of social reporting (voluntary social disclosure) in company annual reports compared with four European "best practice" institutions. The findings showed that the Irish banks were well behind leading European banks in both quality and quantity of social disclosure in their annual reports.[16] On the theme of corporate responsibility, an investigation of leading companies in four countries (United States, United Kingdom, Australia, and Germany) examined corporate social reporting. The report found that business commitment to social reporting varies widely in these countries. Furthermore, industry and country-specific factors determined which issues companies promoted and which ones they tended to emphasize less.[17]

A reporting project does not need to be complex for it to be useful. Investigative report-ing revealed Volkswagen's diesel emissions deception and exposed the business tactics of pharmaceutical CEO, Martin Shkreli, who increased the price of a 62-year-old HIV drug by 5,000% and, at another firm, hiked the cost of a pill for children with an incur-able kidney disease by 2,000%. Then there was Well Fargo's creation of unauthorized accounts and customer accusations of insurance fraud, and the *New York Times* reve-lations of Amazon's cut-throat corporate culture. The misuse of resources from politics to Wall Street requires reporting research. Extensive in-depth interviews and thorough fact-finding are the basis for many investigative techniques. Qualitative reporting exposes similar details through the "lived stories" of teams, departments, and companies.[18]

Exploring

Exploratory studies are conducted to identify, diagnose, and explore a problem. They clarify a problem's nature or find new ideas. They are often used to define preliminary key issues and variables or suggest propositions and hypotheses for further research. In many instances, there is little information, and existing theories do not shed light on the prob-lem. As a prelude to a structured research design, exploration can assess the feasibility of a more comprehensive study when perspective is lacking. Exploration may help researchers find and screen methods, procedures, and types of measurement that will be productive in subsequent research, but exploration is not a research design. As Gerring notes, "Path-breaking research is, by definition, exploratory." The appellation "path-breaking" results from the discovery of a new idea or novel view of a problem. However, the results are sub-ject to later, more rigorous confirmatory research designed "to verify or falsify a preexisting hypothesis or a set of hypotheses."[19] Exploration does not offer final solutions to existing questions or create results that are necessarily useful for high-level management decisions. When the focus is on a discovery, drawing definitive conclusions is inappropriate.

However, the benefit of an exploratory study is a clearer insight into the problem by incorporating multiple research techniques (e.g., literature searches, focus groups, experience surveys, observations, in-depth interviews, critical incident techniques, case studies, histor-ical analysis, content analysis, or pilot studies). A researcher explored customer-switching behavior in service industries, which at the time was virtually unmapped. Her critical incident study, a set of procedures for gathering direct observations of behaviors, revealed 800 critical behaviors of service companies (n > 500 customers) that, when condensed, produced eight reasons or critical behaviors for customers switching services.[20]

Describing

Descriptive studies attempt to discover answers to the questions of who, what, when, and where. Descriptive studies do not answer the question why. They may be quantitative or qualitative. The researcher's purpose is to describe or define a subject by creating a profile of a group of problems, people, or events. Such studies use frequency distributions or summary statistics such as the number of times we observe a variable or the relationship among variables. They rely on instrumentation for observation and measurement. Descriptive studies rarely provide the power for drawing inferences. When researchers use them for that purpose, they do not meet the criteria for inferences, particularly strong ones.[21] Description investigates such issues as quantity, adequacy, cost, and efficiency.

The descriptive study is prevalent in business research because of its versatility across fields of study. For example, in an older but frequently cited article that describes the process of new venture creation, the author countered prior findings that all entrepreneurs are alike and all venture creation is the same. He described the complexity and variation in the formation of new ventures. His framework proposed integrating four perspectives of entrepreneurship: (1) the psychological and demographic characteristics of those who start the venture, (2) the variables that nurture the organization to come into existence, (3) the 20 or more environmental factors affecting success of the new venture, and (4) the process of starting a new venture (business opportunity, resources, marketing, production, organization building, and response to government and society).[22]

Additional examples of descriptive studies include a study prepared for the Intellectual Property Office in the United Kingdom. One finding on piracy indicated that 17% of e-books are consumed online illegally, which amounts to 4 million e-books.[23] Other examples include studies on consumer satisfaction of those who purchased products in a specific category on eBay in the last month and descriptive policy studies used by charitable organizations to plan and evaluate campaigns. Instructor/course evaluation surveys are familiar to students; the results induce them to gravitate to particular instructors while avoiding others. Universities use them for curriculum planning, faculty assignment, and tenure or promotion decisions.

Explaining

Explanatory studies (causal experimental and nonexperimental) go beyond a description of phenomena to explain *how* and *why* an event occurs, depending on the level of causal inference demanded and the degree of control exerted by the researcher. Under ideal conditions, explanation is defined causally and *explanatory modeling* is "the use of statistical models for testing causal explanations."[24] In practice, association-based statistical models such as regression, confirmatory factor analysis, path analysis, structural equation models, and partial least squares models are commonly used to model observational data when experiments or other causal inference methods are not available.[25]

With explanatory studies, the use of theories, designs, hypotheses, and strong inference try to account for the forces that cause a phenomenon.

Strong inference consists of applying the following steps to every problem in science, formally, explicitly, and regularly: (1) devising alternative hypotheses; (2) devising a crucial experiment (or several of them), with alternative possible outcomes, each of which will, as nearly as possible, exclude one or more of the hypotheses; (3) carrying out the experiment so as to get a clean result; and (4) recycling the procedure, making subhypotheses or sequential hypotheses to refine the possibilities that remain, and so on.[26]

Flight crews, of which there are over 124,800 U.S. pilots and 115,000 flight attendants, are classified as "radiation workers" by the Centers for Disease Control and Prevention (CDC).[27] This means that they are consistently exposed to radiation, especially on high-latitude routes. It also implies that they are exposed annually to more radiation than nuclear plant workers.[28] The Federal Aviation Administration (FAA) has published documents, issued recommendations for crew education, and stated risks but has not issued dose limits. And the aviation industry has not voluntarily adopted dose-monitoring programs like the nuclear power industry.[29] The National Aeronautics and Space Administration (NASA) continues to research the effects of radiation from solar particle events (SPEs) and cosmic particles (cosmic rays or cosmic ionizing radiation) on pilots and crews.[30] Future research to build on NASA's studies concerns the radiation risks for flight crews. One rationale for these studies would be the World Health Organization's claim that ionizing radiation causes cancer. The CDC's focus is *cosmic* ionizing radiation that may result in causal links to cancer and reproductive problems.[31]

An explanatory causal study on this problem would likely be multivariate in that the relationships among numerous variables would be modeled: altitude (as altitude increases, radiation doubles with every 6,000 feet), flight duration, geomagnetic latitude (Arctic circle proximity), time of year, time in the 11-year cycle of galactic cosmic radiation intensity, SPEs, and aircraft shielding (aluminum, titanium, graphite-epoxy composite, and polyethylene).[32] This quickly becomes complex because relationships among these variables, or their interactions, could explain radiation risks and health outcomes. This study produces knowledge of the reasons and causes of the occurrence (the how and why questions). This problem can also pose experimental problems because some pilots and crews will be exposed to radiation and others will not. Another group of researchers created a predictive model of heliocentric potential based on the monthly

Flight crews receive consistent exposure to radiation, especially on high-latitude routes. They are exposed annually to more radiation than nuclear plant workers. There is a need for future research to build on NASA's studies on the radiation risks for flight crews, especially with the CDC's concern that cosmic ionizing radiation may result in causal links to cancer and reproductive problems.

sunspot number. This model is very valuable for real-time space-weather operations[33] and also improves the *explanation* of radiation risks for aircrews.

Predicting

Predictive studies attempt to anticipate future performance before it occurs, usually with regression-based statistics and advanced modeling techniques. Greener suggests that "Surprisingly few research methods textbooks contain sections on forecasting trends."[34] She contends that this is because predicting and forecasting are risky and most academic researchers do not see their job as predicting the future, since rigorous research tries to avoid high-risk strategies. However, with research *in* business rather than academic research *about* business, forecasting affects a company's future.[35]

Prediction studies in business evaluate future courses of action or make forecasts: production planning, financial and revenue analysis, sales forecasts, product development, and environmental scanning are daily activities for firms. They enhance a manager's ability to determine, acquire, and allocate resources, thereby exploiting future opportunities. Prediction looks at antecedent conditions in historical or current data to see if those patterns are likely to occur in the future. Prediction includes temporal forecasting to produce future values, point and interval estimates, predictive regions, and distributions. A "**predictive model** is any method that produces predictions, regardless of its underlying approach: Bayesian, . . . parametric or nonparametric, data mining algorithm or statistical model, etc."[36] Specific applications include time-series forecasting, qualitative scenario writing, and the quantitative technological forecasting from the Delphi Method.[37]

In an interesting predictive study for students, "Student Success Rating 2016," researchers used institutional data from more than 1,100 U.S. institutions to discover which colleges and universities are beating the retention odds. By comparing predicted retention rates based on academics, affordability, and social factors with actual rates, the researchers could create overall institutional scores, along with variations on scores for performance, retention trends, graduation trends, and others.

The authors examined 4-year public and not-for-profit institutions with data from 2004 to 2014.[38] The methodology used regression models where the dependent variable was a "student success score," an index created from first-year retention and 6-year graduation rates. The predictors included demographic, academic, social, and financial variables from the Integrated Postsecondary Education Data System (IPEDS). In addition, they produced 10-year trend rates for absolute change in first-year retention and 6-year graduation. You may be interested in discovering how your institution ranked.

Changing

Action research (AR) and one of its many variations, participatory action research, "are powerful tools for people in business, nonprofits, and public administration who seek to *create change* in complex situations for the sake of sustainable improvement."[39] Contrary to those who confuse collaborative research with consulting, "AR is an approach to research that aims both at taking action and creating knowledge or theory about action."[40]

Action research combines research of organizational systems with the dynamics of organizational change—the research knowledge reveals how an organizational system perceives the need for change, articulates the desired outcome, and collaboratively plans and implements how to achieve a future goal. Students who have completed a course in organizational development will know the origins and evolution of AR through Kurt Lewin, Wendell French, Cecil Bell, Chris Argyris, Peter Senge, and others. Lewin defined and legitimized AR "as a way in which researchers could bridge the gap between practice and theory."[41] In business, we find AR studies in marketing, product development, manufacturing, engineering, operations management, accounting, small business, and management development.[42]

Primary characteristics of AR include the following:

- Research in action, but not simply *about* action—researchers are not merely observing and documenting but working to make change happen.

- Participation—cooperation between researchers and clients who act as collaborators and co-researchers.

- Concurrency with action—conducted in real time similar to the way a "live case" in qualitative research unfolds and provides continuous adjustment with new information.

- An approach to problem-solving in an event sequence—since organizations are dynamic sociotechnical systems, the researcher is required to transition freely between structure, technical processes, and informal subsystems of people.

- The use of methods and data collection techniques, which are formal and informal, quantitative and qualitative.[43]

The AR process is cyclical, alternating between action and critical reflection: (1) data-gathering through observations and active involvement in the proposed change; (2) data feedback to decision makers, stakeholders, and the client system; (3) collaborative data analysis linked to the research purpose; and (4) participative action planning to include the nature and types of change required, organizational subsystems involved, support from and buy-in by management, commitment from those who will implement the change, and the management of resistance. AR concludes with client implementation followed by evaluation.[44] Poza and colleagues describe four thought-provoking case examples of changing family businesses through action research and Boyle describes five "best practice" examples.[45]

THE CONTINUUM OF BASIC, PRACTICAL, AND APPLIED RESEARCH

"The snobbish idea that pure science is in some way superior to applied science dates to antiquity, when Plutarch says of Archimedes: 'Regarding the business of mechanics and every utilitarian art as ignoble and vulgar, he gave his zealous devotion only to those subjects whose elegance and subtlety are untrammeled by the necessities of life.'"[46] Plutarch's remark about Archimedes as an elitist researcher is now considered a snarky criticism because Archimedes was not only the most prominent mathematician of antiquity, but also a creative inventor. His observations of physical phenomena allowed him to recognize the source of buoyancy and discover fluid physics. I am not sure why textbook authors dwell on the old shibboleth—the basic-applied dichotomy—when it is a continuum. (Translation: Archimedes understood 2,200 years ago that there was a confluence of discovery knowledge and pragmatic problem-solving, but we can't catch on.)

Archimedes (287 BC–212 BC, Syracuse, Sicily) was a Greek physicist, engineer, astronomer, inventor, and one of the most-famous mathematicians in classical antiquity. The Fields Metal, described as the mathematician's "Nobel Prize" and mathematics highest honor worldwide, carries the image of Archimedes and a carving of his proof on the sphere and the cylinder. His understanding of the confluence of discovery knowledge and pragmatic problem-solving is the foundation for this section. Building bridges of cooperation and collaboration between pure and applied researchers serves the research community.

Basic research (pure, fundamental, or conceptual) examines issues of a theoretical nature that have deferred impact on action, performance, or policy. Its primary emphasis is expanding the human and scientific knowledge base by better "understanding" a perplexing problem. Thus, academic researchers are more likely to investigate basic research problems because academic agendas weigh in. The focus is on theories, models, constructs, or concepts. Basic research seeks controlled conditions, particularly with experiments, thereby enhancing the *internal validity* of the project by discerning whether the study's findings imply cause while other explanations are ruled out. However, controlled conditions also have the disadvantage of alerting participants to the fact that deviations they perceive in their environment are researcher induced. Thus, they may behave differently. As an example of basic research, cognitive scientists thought that cell phones would lead to a higher frequency of automobile accidents. Although envisioned in an entirely different way, it seems like an applied problem. The researchers did not hypothesize that accidents occurred because drivers steered the car with one hand but that the attention requirements of phone use might cause accidents. Improving the understanding of "limited attention capacity" was their basic research problem.[47]

Practical research fits somewhere in the middle of the continuum between basic and applied research and is more common in business because the solutions tell managers "what to do." That is, the solutions are action oriented and provide an answer to the question that helps managers know "what to do to change or fix some troublesome or at least improvable situation."[48] Practical research questions may interest academic researchers whose research agenda involves organizational problems but are compelling for managers. While basic research is somewhat context general or independent of context, practical research is usually context specific; it focuses on a company-specific set of circumstances and issues. Many writers say applied research is designed to solve *practical* problems of the modern world. But the tautology of practical and applied research defeats the purpose of making a useful distinction regarding "action." Applied research has a larger purview that affects much more than business research.

Applied research has a problem-solving emphasis but contains the element of "understanding" before knowing what to do. "Often we are aware we must do *something* to solve a … problem, but before we can know what that is, we must do research to understand the problem better."[49] Immediate real-world problems call for applied research when a decision is needed. They encompass those studies that are a step toward solutions or make decisions to provide solutions on issues that exceed action and extend to performance or policy. The results of applied research elevate themselves to immediate relevance because of their closeness to managerial decision-making. For this reason, companies and public and nonprofit organizations engage in applied research.

Applied research is ideally conducted in the ordinary course of events so that participants perceive little variation from their daily lives or do not attribute observed changes to the researcher. That is, applied research is more often more valuable when performed in the field rather than in the laboratory. This advantage affects **external validity** or whether a found causal relationship generalizes across persons, places, and times.[50] This topic is covered in greater detail in Chapter 8. For example, a bank might use actual applicants for a mortgage to evaluate the benefits of offering online applications. This research seeks to discover advantages for the firm, such as converting more customers, convenience, reduced time to acceptance, 24/7 access, anonymity, financing flexibility, and lower rates and fees than traditional lenders.

GOOD RESEARCH IS…

Before you venture into the remainder of this book and start planning your term project, you should know what standards authorities suggest to judge great (even celebrated) research.[51] These characteristics are the pillars of your research knowledge and the basis for a stellar research report. Understanding these characteristics also enables you to become an informed consumer of research. Good quantitative research follows various scientific approaches. They are systematic, empirically based procedures for generating replicable research and solving problems. That does not say that qualitative research is not real, beneficial, or good (as Chapter 7 shows), only that it has different criteria by which to judge it. Research reports differ in their focus. They can be quantitative, qualitative, or mixed. They also vary by problem,

There are at least eight defining criteria that you should look for in evaluating research. Some are elevated in importance because the study is for a scholarly journal or a report for a business executive committee. Class projects should contain similar qualities but at a level suited for their purpose.

design, method, and intended audience. A paper written for a class project should contain the characteristics of good research but at a level different from a report for a business executive or a scholarly journal article. Here are eight defining criteria, from a list of many, that you should look for in evaluating research, whether yours or others. Many criteria apply to qualitative research as well. They provide a summary of what exemplifies basic scholarly research as well as carefully constructed applied business research.

Ethical Issues

1. Good research anticipates ethical problems and selects the environment, design, procedures, data collection, and other protocols to protect participants who volunteer for the research.[52] Researchers must assess if the project should be undertaken based on the risks and benefits of the proposed study. "No one should participate in research unless [an] independent review concludes that the risks are reasonable in relation to the potential benefits."[53] In the United States, Canada, and the European Union, an Institutional Review Board, or similarly titled entity, is the primary authority responsible for implementing laws on human participants in research. Research must have a value for society. Researchers must communicate risks that could result in physical, psychological, or social harm to the participants, so they know that safeguards are in place.

    Voluntary participation, the requirement for informed consent, means that individuals will not be coerced to participate. They are fully informed and "understand" the purpose, procedures, and risks of the research, as well as its duration. Thus, they either participate willingly or decline involvement. They may also discontinue once the investigation has started. Protecting their collected data and keeping their contribution confidential from anyone not involved in the study safeguards the participants' privacy. Anonymity conceals the participants' identity so that demographics, geographical location, and organizational membership cannot be used to identify them. In some cases, participants are anonymous even to the researchers. In Chapter 4, there is a section devoted to describing the federal laws that have been implemented through the National Research Act to safeguard the rights and welfare of human participants in research. It also covers the foundational principles of Institutional Review Boards at universities, hospitals, and private research facilities. "Research is a public trust that must be ethically conducted, trustworthy, and socially responsible if the results are to be valuable. All parts of a research project—from the project design to submission of the results for peer review—have to be upstanding in order to be considered ethical."[54]

Purpose

2. An explicitly stated problem reflects the purpose of business research that is grounded in a theoretical framework. This framework applies existing theory, or at least well-documented relevant studies, to the new problem. It, therefore, builds on previous findings. The statement of the problem should be delineated clearly. The research problem or research question should include subproblems or investigative questions that reflect the critical parts or facets of the original problem. As required by the chosen design, the researcher should select the number of subproblems judiciously, since these will be the basis for hypotheses (and measurement) and they will be used to identify variables in the study.

    The terminology that frames the research problem (concepts, constructs, and variables) should be operationally defined (as described in Chapter 2). An explicitly stated problem also includes the assumptions the researcher accepts to be true or plausible as they bear on the problem, delimitations that explain what the research does not contain, possible limitations or weaknesses that reveal expected flaws, and the importance or benefits that justify doing the study in the first place. Stating the problem's components reflects the credibility of the researcher as well as the value of the study.[55]

Design

3. The design of research is structured logically (i.e., its priority is the evidence to be collected to answer the research question). Subsequently, the process has specific guidelines or procedures that occur in a sequence based on the rules of a method matched to the design. After the design's structure is logically connected to the problem, it finally becomes a carefully controlled blueprint for obtaining required data (Chapters 6, 7, and 8). When selecting among competing designs, the researcher chooses the one that is feasible and achievable in the investigative setting within the time and resources available. The design should also do a better job than its rivals because it minimizes bias and confounding effects but maximizes the reliability and validity of the collected data.

    The results from the design should be reproducible in future research to verify the findings—a principle of the scientific method. The selection of a design should reveal familiarity with the features of available designs. For example, one should not use a descriptive retrospective survey, in which the researcher must go back in time, if biases are suspected (participant selection, recall, or misclassification of observations). The evidence sought might be more reliable from a study in the present, a *meta-analysis* (combining data from multiple studies), or a "stand-alone literature review" (see Chapter 3). While control is the *sine qua non* of experiments, the selection of other designs should explain how threats to internal validity (the power of the independent variable to produce an effect) and external validity (generalizing beyond the sample findings to the population) are applicable.[56]

Procedures

4. The research procedures should contain enough information about the execution of the method to repeat the study. Procedures are usually unique to the chosen method, but many procedures and techniques have versatile protocols. In an experiment, the report states precisely the structure, the selection of variables to control, and sources of contamination. You should look for an identification of the method of selection and preparation of participants in the experiment or nonexperiment. Procedures also cover the determination of sample size and the administration of the instrument. Procedures explain how participants were recruited and found eligible, and they state that the individuals agreed to participate and signed informed consent forms. The study reveals the number and demographics of the participants who completed the study and have data included in the report. An accurate description of the data collection instruments and the environmental conditions under which the data collection occurred is essential.

   The sampling plan includes information about the reasons for choosing a probability sample (simple random, systematic, strata, cluster, etc.) or a nonprobability sample and if the choice will affect the generalizability of the study. The information may suggest that generalizability is irrelevant for the type of study being conducted. This information helps the reader judge whether the sample represents the population or representation is not essential (as in the case of some qualitative studies). Procedures also cover how the sample size was decided so that it neither overestimates nor underestimates the number of participants needed for statistical conclusions. In addition, there should be a convincing argument for using a population versus a sample when the population is small.

Data and Instrumentation

5. The researcher's commentary on data and instrumentation should describe the needed data for solving the problem and its subproblems (investigative questions or support for *a priori* hypotheses). Subproblems or hypotheses and the issues

they pose usually mirror the findings of the literature and problem statement. Information about the materials, instruments, measures, scales, observational protocols, and apparatus reveals how they are acceptable (operational) definitions of the variables and why their measurement characteristics are ideal for the intended purpose. In quantitative studies, empirical evidence is the basis for reliability and validity of the measures. This evidence includes commonly used tests, literature citations, or advanced researcher activities, such as pilot studies or statistics that support the writer's claim of reliability or validity. It is imperative to organize and present the sequence of activities clearly.

The researcher also explains the procedures for data collection, coding, editing, and dealing with missing data. The overall analytical approach chosen reveals how it fits the research question and the data to be analyzed. Exploratory and descriptive statistics are used to summarize the data set, and inferential statistics facilitate testing and inference making from sample data. Statistical procedures that are unfamiliar to readers are described as well as how you or other researchers met the requirements for their use. Diagnostics to examine the data before use of statistical techniques are described.

Findings

6. Findings are stated in simple, straightforward, and unpretentious language and are connected to the problem and subproblems. The tone of the writing reinforces the readers' impression of comprehensive coverage and objectively reported results. Each insight generated by the method, procedures, and data analysis should parallel definitive conclusions about the original problem. The findings and conclusion of the research demark the end of statistical interpretation. Thus, a return to speculating about an interesting but unrelated statistical result is misplaced. Conjecture about how findings might apply beyond the population is unwarranted. Good researchers do not read more into the conclusions than the evidence supports. However, unexpected findings pertinent to the problem, as well as results revealed that do not support the hypotheses, deserve discussion. Reiterate weaknesses or limitations mentioned previously in the study if they affect a conclusion. This transparency strengthens the readers' confidence.

Some research reports (e.g., short research notes in journals, client projects, and research for managerial decision makers) do not have space for complete sections on results, discussion, and conclusions. Longer reports appropriately delve into the meaning of the research, comment on gaps in the literature, discuss implications of the findings, and identify areas for further study. For applied and scholarly research, conclusions should help the reader understand how the research makes a material difference in solving the management or academic dilemma. At the least, answering the "so what?" question helps the reader understand the importance and tangible benefits.

Qualifications of the Researcher

7. When research reports contain evidence about the reputation and qualifications of the researcher, the reader has greater assurance that a well-trained, competent person has conducted the study. Managers and sponsors of research want to know more about the credentials of researchers responding to a Request for Proposal and students are not likely to know which scholars in their field have the best reputation as thought leaders. Author qualifications are essential for evaluating materials for a project's literature review, methods, and procedures. Unfortunately, all research reports are not configured to display details about researcher qualifications. Technical and grant reports for state and federal government agencies and the military have a section on previous work of researchers and their collaborators. Other lengthy reports to management or sponsors contain appendices that will serve that purpose. In most scholarly journals, the investigator's name, degree, position, rank, and institutional affiliation are about all that appear in the article. However, there are databases and tracking systems to assess a researcher's influence and impact although individual sources are not exhaustive. The primary means of evaluation are citation counts, journal impact factors, and article-level metrics. Studies frequently link researcher reputation to citation counts of publications. A single article, monograph, or book widely cited by other authors leads to what is called a "reputation boost"[57] and reflects author influence. You can track citations in Google Scholar, Scopus, and Web of Science, along with several other compilers but remember that articles are cited for both positive and negative reasons. Moreover, *counts* from different sources are not comparable. *Journal Citation Reports* gauge journals for their *impact* in the worldwide research community. "In each specialty, the best journals are those in which it is most difficult to have an article accepted, and these are the journals that have a high impact factor."[58] The term impact factor has evolved to describe journal and author impact although using it for individual authors is controversial. There are at least a dozen indices for journal impact, which makes journal evaluation impractical for managers and students. *Article-level metrics* "capture ways in which articles are disseminated throughout in the expanding scholarly ecosystem, and reach beyond the scope of traditional trackers and filters."[59] Finally, a researcher's books and book chapters can be found through Scopus, WorldCat, and Google Books. All of these methods are useful for benchmarking in the same field, comparing authors at the same career point, or determining an author's productivity in comparison to previous years.[60] The importance of evaluating a researcher's

qualifications confirms the necessity for high quality in academic publishing (researchers are cited more frequently for work that is ground-breaking and moves the field forward than work that merely adds a line to their vitae).

Outcomes

8. Good research communicates the findings, produces evidence of usefulness, and evaluates impact. In academic research, the student project is disseminated in different ways, such as presenting to a class or professor-facilitated corporate sponsor, writing a thesis, or giving talks and presenting posters at professional meetings. Students interested in an academic career will have goals such as giving a conference presentation and refining their work for a peer-reviewed journal. Regardless of the venue, but especially important to corporations, your communication should not just recite findings but recommend what should happen next. This is the critical thinking and creative piece that employers believe students lack. One benefit ". . . of communicating through journals is that being peer-reviewed enables decisionmakers to access quality research whose methodological merits have been thoroughly scrutinized."[61] Publishing in a peer-reviewed journal also has liabilities when you are trying to reach decision makers beyond an academic audience. "Micro level decision makers often complain about lack of access to such journals, and about the lack of practical guidance in how to operationalize the findings in a service delivery program."[62] Decision makers, policy makers, and implementers can be hard to reach without donor-sponsor assistance. A well-thought-out plan includes media coverage, policy briefs, and newsletters designed for granting agencies, advocacy groups, and legislators.

    In addition to communication, usefulness is critical. The utilization stage of *practical* or action research should inform decision makers of what to do; and, in applied research, implementation is successful when there is a continuing dialog between researchers, decision makers, implementers, and end-users. "Alliances between researchers and stakeholders will enable researchers to examine the problem from the perspective of the decision makers and implementers, think about the practicality of scaling up of research findings, *planning actions required at [an] operational level*, and address some of the macro contextual barriers to implementation."[63]

    The last part of the trilogy is evaluation of impact. "It is important to see the distinction between evaluating the impact of research and evaluating its quality. Traditional academic checks on the quality of basic research . . . have sometimes been found to be remote for donors and policy makers, and there is a view that the process of quality assurance should be more systematic for applied research."[64] Evaluation of impact addresses whether it works in practice and the cost-benefit for the resources expended. Some of these issues are unique to basic, practical, and applied research studies and may not be addressed in each one. At a minimum, you should look for implications of the findings as practical implications and suggestions for future research or action.

WHICH RESEARCH ORIENTATION IS RIGHT FOR YOU?

Which philosophical perspective should prevail in directing how research ought to be conducted? Whereas the underlying philosophy that legitimizes a particular stance should be *pragmatic*, it often reflects the beliefs of researchers or the views of an academic discipline. This is an important topic because it determines not only which research questions and methods are perceived legitimate but also how they are selected, constructed, and correspond with researchers' assumptions about which design, method, or techniques should be chosen. Such assumptions also affect research funding even though this is not publicly expressed.

Recognizing this problem sheds light on many disagreements about research strategy. To illustrate, please refer to Exhibit 1.2, which is adapted from the metaphor of the "Research Onion" by Mark Saunders.[65] Each layer reveals more detail about the research process, previewing the progression of topics in this book. In the first layer, the term worldview is encountered. **Worldview** means a point of view, mindset, philosophy, or conception of the world that shapes one's view of "knowing." It also affects how researchers approach a problem (quantitative, qualitative, or mixed). It is frequently an extensive philosophical system guiding how to tackle research and methodology, as well as an attitude about life in general. You will find various writers using the terms worldview, paradigm, and *Weltanschauung* (a German word) depending on the degree of precision they want to convey.

A **paradigm**, used by Thomas Kuhn in *The Structure of Scientific Revolutions*, is a set of assumptions or a belief system shared by members of a scientific community. These assumptions are pervasive, assumed to be true, but often untested. Paradigms not only include key theories and laws but "the applications of those theories in the solution of important problems, along with the new experimental or mathematical techniques."[66] According to Kuhn, a paradigm serves three functions: it suggests (1) new puzzles, (2) approaches to solving those puzzles, and (3) the standards by which the quality of a proposed solution can be measured.[67] This is comparable to determining the nature, type, and structure of the research questions asked; authenticating what is studied and how; and governing the ways the results should be interpreted.

The researcher's preferred paradigm influences the design, method, sampling plan, data collection, and analysis approach selected. One argument centers on the objective/empirical versus interpretive/naturalistic ways of knowing. Does a phenomenon (e.g., gender discrimination in business) possess an independent existence that is objective? Or does it only exist in the minds of those who communicate about it (qualitative)? Can it be studied empirically or do we interpret its meaning from what individuals say?[68]

EXHIBIT 1.2 ■ The "Research Onion" as a Metaphor for the Research Process

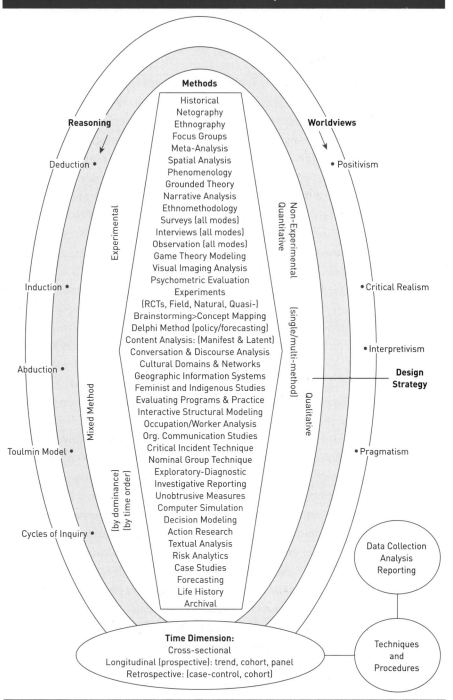

Source: Adapted from Saunders, Mark N. K., Philip Lewis, and Adrian Thornhill, *Research Methods for Business Students*, 7th ed. (Essex, UK: Pearson Education Ltd., 2016), 124, Figure 4.1.

When quantitative research is dominant (an objective/empirical perspective), derived from the **positivist/post-positivist worldview**, researchers are preoccupied with the scientific method because it emphasizes the most objective methods to achieve the closest estimate of empirical reality.[69] Sir Karl Popper (1902–1994) suggested that post-positivism "… retains the positivist notion of an objective truth and its emphasis on the scientific method."[70] Researchers with this worldview prefer quantitative studies where direct observation and manipulation of variables and their measurement explain how variables interact, shape events, and "cause" outcomes.[71] By combining deductive logic with precisely worded questionnaires, standardized instruments, or scaled observations of participants' behavior, quantitative studies describe how variables differ in amount or magnitude. They also develop and test statistically explanatory and predictive theories using large samples. "The nature of social reality for positivists is: empirical facts exist apart from personal ideas or thoughts; they are governed by laws of cause and effect; patterns of social reality are stable, and knowledge of them is additive."[72]

Qualitative researchers subscribe to an **interpretivist worldview** (or **constructivist/naturalistic**). They reject the positivist position that there is a concrete reality or an objective truth. "Instead, constructivists believe that people construct an image of reality based on their own preferences and prejudices and their interactions with others."[73] The qualitative researcher's purpose is to understand individuals' interactions with each other and how they react to their experiences in the context of the wider society. This reveals an awareness of the subjective meanings of phenomena. Among their tools are case studies, narratives, life story, in-depth interviews, observations, historical analysis, and recorded media that reveal the meaning of everyday occurrences and problematic moments in individuals' lives.[74] Qualitative methodologies are inductive; they seek to discover a deeper understanding of the problem in its context, with less concern for generalizing findings from samples to populations.[75] Qualitative studies are (1) theoretically driven, credible, and rigorous; (2) complement quantitative research by revealing how social phenomena occur in "real time"; and (3) are as much about social practice as experience.[76]

Another worldview embraced by some researchers is **realism**. Realism is somewhat similar to positivism in that "reality exists independent of the mind and that what a researcher's senses show her or him is the truth, although the researcher is influenced by worldviews and their own experiences."[77] For example, the realist argues that the existence of macroscopic objects and their properties is independent of the mind. The existence of "tables, rocks, the moon, and so on, all exist, as do the following facts: the table's being square, the rock's being made of granite, and the moon's being spherical and yellow."[78] But the interpretation of their meaning is processed by the mind, which filters our perceptions conceptually, experientially, linguistically, and based on our value system. Thus, the practitioner of realism is likely to seek both quantitative and qualitative design strategies, the latter to grasp a better understanding of what lies beneath the surface.

The final philosophy or worldview mentioned here is pragmatism. **Pragmatism**, "when regarded as an alternative paradigm, sidesteps the contentious issues of truth and reality, accepts, philosophically, that there are singular and multiple realities that are open to empirical inquiry and orients itself toward solving *practical* problems in the 'real world.'"[79] As such, pragmatists reject a forced choice of design strategies that dichotomize quantitative versus qualitative. Pragmatism "debunks concepts such as 'truth' and 'reality' and focuses instead on 'what works' as the truth regarding the research questions under investigation … [and] advocates for the use of mixed methods in research, and acknowledges that the values of the researcher play a large role in interpretation of results."[80] From a logical standpoint (see Chapter 2, Reasoning), pragmatism "can be used as a guide not only for top-down deductive research design but also for grounded inductive or abductive research."[81] Researchers who advocate pragmatism "also consider the research question to be more important than either the method they use or the paradigm that underlies the method (the 'dictatorship of the research question')."[82] That is, to be pragmatic is to be more focused on the research question and not align oneself with a single, exacting research approach or philosophy. This makes sense for business researchers when you consider "grounded theories" in marketing and consumer behavior (see Chapter 7), research in advertising, the ethnographic culture of brands, projective methods, focus groups in marketing, and researching *sensitive topics*.

The qualitative researcher's purpose is to discover and understand individuals' experiences, perceptions, and interactions and to make sense of and interpret the derived meanings from their thoughts, actions, and events in the wider context of inquiry. These experiences may be everyday occurrences or problematic (even traumatic) instances that give meaning to individuals' lives. In-depth interviews, shown here, are among their tools.

Justin Kase zninez/Alamy Stock Photo

The next layer of Exhibit 1.2 is reasoning. Here you see the terms deduction, induction, abduction, the Toulmin Model of Argumentation, and combined approaches (i.e., cycling from one reasoning approach to another). This is a central topic in Chapter 2, so I will only provide enough background to interpret the exhibit. *Deduction* is a form of reasoning that claims to be conclusive—the conclusions must necessarily follow from the reasons (premises) given. The premises are said to imply the conclusion; if those reasons are successful in "warranting the conclusion" (i.e., they are true premises), then the argument is deductively valid and represents a proof. In deductive research, you would start with a theory, immerse yourself in the literature on the topic, and develop a design to answer your question.

Inductive reasoning moves from specific instances into a generalized conclusion. Induction begins with observations and draws a conclusion from one or more specific facts or pieces of evidence. If the premises are strong enough to be true, it would be *improbable* that you would produce a false conclusion. In short, induction needs to increase the probability of a correct conclusion. This is similar to starting with the collection of data to research an incident or event; discover themes, patterns, or relationships; and then construct an explanatory framework.

Abduction, referred to as inference to the "best explanation," is a form of inference making in which one selects the hypothesis that would best explain the relevant evidence if that evidence were true. Abduction starts with "surprising facts" or "puzzles" and the research process is devoted their explanation.[83] The researcher seeks facts and infers the simplest, most probable, explanation. Literature and observations are often the starting point to generate the most obvious hypothesis. Whereas true premises and a valid form guarantee a true conclusion in deduction, abductive premises do not. The initial abductive hypothesis is often the equivalent of an educated guess, but it is a guess that must be tested and subsequently corrected. Abduction "informs" the process of the scientific method by developing the construction of explanatory theory.

The *Toulmin Model* is a structure for constructing decisive arguments containing six components that evaluate the pros and cons of the topic and the effectiveness of rebuttals. The structure is based on the legal system, in which the litigant (1) makes a claim, (2) gives data to support that claim, and (3) backs the data or evidence with a warrant. These three elements—claim, data, and warrant—are present in every argument. Three additional elements of the model may be added as necessary: a backing (for the warrant), rebuttals, and qualifier(s). The diagram in Chapter 2, Exhibit 2.6, explains this process with an extended example of Wells Fargo.

In Exhibit 1.2, *Cycles of Inquiry* refer to the complementary nature of these various forms of reasoning that are beneficial to researchers who design projects with the idea of using them together for a more comprehensive picture of the study. Often, a researcher plans to focus on one approach and then discovers during the study that new questions emerge that the other approaches help to clarify.

The next three layers of the exhibit are design strategy, methods, and the time sequence for the project. Although they appear self-explanatory, there is ample discussion of each one in Chapters 3 through 8. There are a multitude of methods, which cover not only business and management applications but also those that may be adapted from the social, behavioral, and physical sciences to solve business problems.

THE ROAD MAP

To find your way from A to B, you use phones, tablets, and other electronic devices with Google or Apple Maps or you may prefer your car's navigation system. But the images they produce are just sophisticated versions of an old paper road map, except with highlighted movement and often with three-dimensional graphics. My approach to this book, and especially the research process, is like a *road map* that directs you from point to point like lines for roads and dots for cities. The *research process* is composed of seven phases: exploring, planning, creating, conducting, collecting, analyzing, and writing. There are *17 activities* or specific elements associated with constructing the various *phases* of your research. The line is the path that you follow, and the dots are the waypoints or milestones along the way. In Exhibit 1.3, you will see much of the book's content and the research process illustrated as a map. The process chapters (Chapters 3, 4, and 5) represent your "departure," "journey," and "arrival"— and may parallel your emotions about the experience. In these chapters, there is a process diagram for each chapter to locate your position and highlight the activities to be covered.

I will try not to overwhelm you with detail about the height and contours of mountains or where to stop at a favorite restaurant along the way. Some detail is necessary, however, and it is a means to learn the "ropes to skip and the ropes to know." Like Ritti and Levy,[84] who wrote a clever book of that title, this guide seeks to provide you with the essentials and a few of the nuances.

EXHIBIT 1.3 ■ The Road Map for This Guide and the Research Process

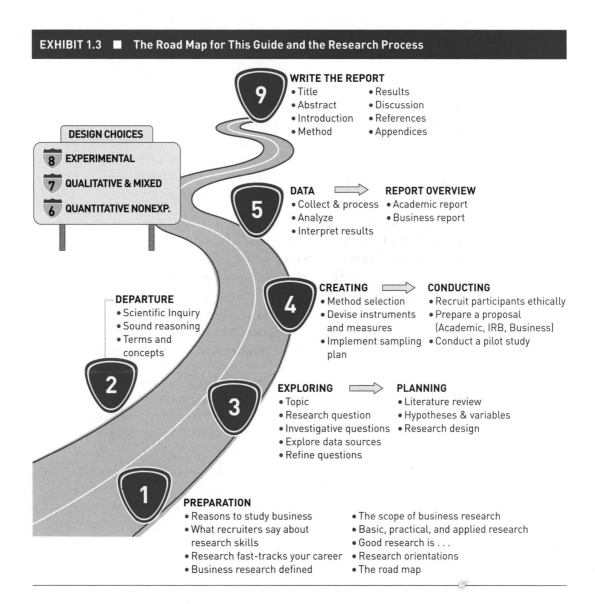

Chapter Summary

- This chapter presented good reasons for studying the various fields of business, including the diversity of disciplinary choices, career variety, and earnings potential. You saw the disparities between how students perceive their financial worth and why employers disagree—as it pertains to the learning outcomes of your curriculum and the knowledge and skills you obtain. Recent research from recruiters and employers revealed what skill sets they expect.

- This chapter examined the ways to fast track your career and how research competence is a necessary part of that process. As to research skills, business research provides the knowledge and expertise needed to solve problems and meet challenges in daily decision-making. Those skills coincide with helping managers frame business problems, conduct the research, and communicate the findings. The skills also enable managers to assess the research contributions of other providers. I offered evidence of official recognition for research competence and its importance in attaining the highest level of business education, which in turn increases managerial skills and leads to career opportunities.

- Other reasons to profit from research skills include the following: (1) Research-based information represents the pinnacle of support for decision-making. (2) Early-career employees may be called upon to do a study and present the findings to a high-level executive, and this opportunity may be career changing. (3) During your career, you may need to buy research services through outsourcing or evaluate research that was conducted internally by others.

- (4) Finally, you may seek a prestigious career as a research specialist in an organization or a position as a consultant.

- A definition for business research was presented and the continuum from basic to applied business studies described.

- In establishing a broad context for business research and your student project or managerial problem, I explored six different "purposes" of research including reporting, exploring, describing, explaining, predicting, and changing (action research).

- Eight characteristics of good research, the pillars of your research knowledge and the basis for an excellent research report, are the standards by which to judge good research. They include ethical issues, the research purpose, design, procedures, data and instrumentation, findings, researcher qualifications, and outcomes. They exemplify the best qualities of basic scholarly research as well as carefully constructed applied business research.

- In examining research orientations, you discovered that philosophical perspectives often prevail in determining the research strategy. Whereas the underlying philosophy that legitimizes a particular stance should be *pragmatic*, it often reflects the beliefs of researchers or the views of an academic discipline. This was illustrated with Exhibit 1.2, from the metaphor of the "Research Onion."

- A "Road Map" with waypoints showed critical events in the book's content and, particularly, the activities along the route of the research process. It is intended to help you navigate this book.

Key Terms

action research

applied research

basic research (pure, conceptual, or fundamental)

business research

descriptive study

explanatory study (causal experimental and nonexperimental)

exploratory study

external validity

interpretivist/naturalistic worldview

paradigm

positivist/post-positivist worldview

practical research

pragmatism worldview

predictive model

predictive study

realism worldview

reporting study

strong inference

worldview

Discussion Questions

1. List three reasons to study business. Add others that are important to you in the pursuit of your major.

2. Define business research. How might business research differ from research in other disciplines (e.g., psychology, sociology, anthropology)?

3. Distinguish between basic, practical, and applied research. Do companies use all varieties of research or focus on only one? Provide some examples.

4. List the characteristics of "good research." Are they universal or unique to the business environment? Why would you use these characteristics to evaluate a research paper or journal article?

5. Do developments in technology suggest that future research will be of higher quality or utility than past research or simply swift but superficial? Explain. (e.g., Here are some examples: Pew Research increased their surveys to 75% *mobile*; do-it-yourself (DIY) approaches for simple corporate research projects; artificial intelligence integration of data on brand, customer sentiment/behavior, and social media; "agile" research—speed over depth and methodological rigor; microsurveys; and instant MROCs—market research online communities.)

6. What is a worldview or paradigm? Why does the way a researcher perceives the world affect his or her view of what constitutes legitimate research?

7. How do the "purposes" of business research reflect a spectrum of typical studies in business? Could some of the purposes become study designs that describe, explain, and predict? Are there other candidates?

8. What are the seven phases of the research process? How does the road map metaphor establish the activities along the route to completion of a student research project or managerial report?

SELF-DEFENSE
TOOLS FOR RESEARCH

Preparation, Reasoning, and Terminology

LEARNING OBJECTIVES

Performance Objective

Demonstrate your ability to apply a scientific approach in conjunction with the principles of reasoning and types of argument to investigate phenomena, obtain new knowledge, integrate previous knowledge, and acquire systematically the language and mindset needed to *communicate* your research and justify its results.

Enabling Objectives

1. Defend and criticize why the method of science distinguishes itself from other ways of knowing, but the doing of research is a frame of mind and not just a recipe or series of steps.

2. Understand how deduction, induction, abduction, and the Toulmin Model are tools the researcher uses to build cases, reason, and derive conclusions.

3. Practice the Toulmin Model to develop informal and research arguments in preparation for constructing your research report later in the term.

4. Become familiar with the new jargon of research and understand that practice masters its nuances.

5. Define by example concepts, constructs, definitions, hypotheses, propositions, and theories.

Several years ago, I was consulting for a multinational technology company whose European headquarters was on the 28th floor of Tour Pascal (Pascal Tower). With a spectacular view of Paris' Grande Arche, the Paris-La Défense business district was an exciting place to work. As I got off the elevator one morning, a half dozen staffers were scurrying about assembling a research presentation for a group of executives. From their conversation (all spoke English as a second language), it was apparent that their research vocabulary was limited. They were throwing around words like novice martial arts students would throw stars. The wall absorbed most of the impact, not their colleagues with whom they were desperately trying to communicate. A debate ensued about whether to use the word "theory" or "model" on a slide. Other disagreements arose. What was the difference between the research problem and a hypothesis? Are the conclusions obtained by induction or deduction? Realizing that time was getting away from them, I stepped in to help.

This chapter's title is rather odd. People do not usually equate research with the martial arts. But the parallels are interesting. Many students are uncomfortable with their research knowledge and skills. They lack practice and discipline, and they can't wade through the impenetrable jargon. This chapter builds your confidence by discussing the researcher's essential tools and their influence on research practice. As Confucius

Student interns assemble a research presentation for a group of executives.

said, "A workman bent on good work will first sharpen his tools."[1]

As used in this book, the phrase *scientific inquiry* applies a body of techniques in conjunction with principles of reasoning to investigate phenomena, acquire new knowledge, or correct and integrate previous knowledge.[2] Scientific inquiry requires preparation and practice. Like the martial arts, research requires new skills, focus, persistence, and situational awareness.

Sound reasoning is a hallmark of outstanding research. How you reason improves the way you make research decisions and also influences your daily communication. How well do you defend your positions on important issues? Understanding reasoning results in improved mental conditioning and the self-discipline required for success. In the *Laws*, Plato addresses self-discipline: "to conquer yourself is the first and best victory of all. . . ."[3] In this chapter, I cover the use of reasoning to obtain reliable conclusions with four essential types of argument: deduction, induction, abduction, and the Toulmin Model.

Finally, the chapter concludes with definitions of *research terminology*. The unknown vocabulary of any field is intimidating and makes you feel like an outsider. It may sound kitschy, but students who are anxious about learning a new language can transform their worries through a different optic. Fighting through uncertainty means "I'm not merely surviving this, I am conquering it. And in doing so, I'm increasing my skills." I help you decipher the technical jargon and the mindset needed to *communicate* what you are doing and your results with examples of concepts, constructs, definitions, variables, hypotheses, and theory.

SCIENTIFIC INQUIRY

The **scientific method** is a system for originating and developing knowledge. The scientific method is considered the dominant method for making useful and valuable contributions to human knowledge. The tenets of the scientific method are comprehensive:

- Direct observation of phenomena

- Clear definition of variables, methods, and procedures

- Empirical tests of hypotheses

- Exclusion of rival hypotheses

- Statistical rather than linguistic justification of conclusions

- Self-correcting processes

An indispensable term in this list is *empirical*. **Empirical testing** of hypotheses means that we make "observations and propositions based on sensory experience and/or derived from such experience by methods . . . including mathematics and statistics."[4] These tenets are reflected in what many books call the steps of the scientific method.

In antiquity, Aristotle, in his introduction to the *Metaphysics*, said that all men by nature desire to know. In Athens, Aristotle's lectures continued that theme when he articulated a system that is likely a precursor to the scientific method. It included stating the idea or problem, defining the terms, examining the thinking of others, and using arguments based on the correspondence of ideas with observations to derive conclusions.

American philosophers Charles Sanders Peirce (1839–1914) and John Dewey (1859–1952) influenced the elaboration of the scientific method. Almost any research textbook will discuss the role and scope of science in conjunction with Dewey's work on reflective thinking and his concept of inquiry (*How We Think*, 1910, 1933). Occasionally, you run across Peirce's work on the four methods of settling opinion; the most prominent is the method of science (*The Fixation of Belief*, 1877). Dewey's contribution to formulating the scientific method is better characterized as understanding the process of inquiry, yet he liked to refer to it as "the scientific method."

In this chapter, you should not conclude that the scientific method is a superior way of knowing or that "doing" research is only accomplished through a series of steps. To the contrary, it is a way of thinking about the study of phenomena. We could equally look to the writings of Gottfried Wilhelm Leibniz, Immanuel Kant, or Georg Wilhelm Friedrich Hegel or even the principles of Sun Tzu as applied to business strategy. There are alternative systems of inquiry when the scientific method is ill suited to tackle specific problems.

From distinguished scientists, we see a more skeptical view of "science as method." For example, Joel H. Hildebrand, a prize-winning chemist said:

Scientific method is often defined as if it were a set procedure, to be learned, like a recipe, as if anyone could like a recipe, as if anyone could become a scientist simply by learning the method. This is absurd . . . [so I shall not] discuss scientific method, but rather the methods of scientists. We proceed by common sense and ingenuity. There are no rules, only the principles of integrity and objectivity, with a complete rejection of all authority except that of fact.[5]

The Nobel Laureate, Steven Weinberg, a legend of 20th-century physics, declared:

The fact that the standards of scientific success shift with time does not only make the philosophy of science difficult; it also raises problems for the public understanding of science. We do not have a fixed scientific method to rally around and defend.[6]

Exhibit 2.1 shows scientific inquiry as a process. It is a viable way of knowing, but the words "sequence" and "steps" distort how it is done. Researchers who resist template-like approaches know this. The unique qualities of the research problem determine if the ideas presented in Exhibit 2.1 are expanded or eliminated. We must also oppose the notion that the scientific method is only useful for the natural or physical sciences and has limited application in business. As Karl Pearson cautioned, "The scientific method of examining

---

EXHIBIT 2.1 ■ Reflective Inquiry: The Systematic Reasoning Process

A felt difficulty; an unexpected meeting with curiosity, doubt, suspicion, or obstacle.

⇓

Wrestling to state the problem to be solved: ask questions, contemplate existing knowledge, gather facts, and move from an emotional to an intellectual confrontation with the problem.

⇓

The use of one suggestion after another as a leading idea or hypothesis to explain the facts; to initiate and guide observation and other operations in the collection of factual evidence.

⇓

Form hypotheses; deduce outcomes or consequences to discern what happens if the results are opposite the predicted direction, or if the results support expectations.

⇓

Formulate several rival hypotheses.

⇓

Devise and construct a decisive (empirical) test with various possible outcomes, each of which selectively excludes one or more hypotheses.

⇓

Draw a conclusion, an inductive inference, based on acceptance or rejection of the hypotheses.

⇓

Reflective thinking involves a look into the future, a forecast, anticipation, or a prediction; feeding information back into the original problem, modifying it according to the strength of the evidence. ↵

Source: See Dewey, John, *How We Think* (Lexington MA: D. C. Heath, 1910), 72; and Dewey, John, *The Collected Works of John Dewey, 1852–1953*, ed. Jo Ann Boydston, citation published in the *Later Works, 1925–1953*, vol. 8 (Carbondale: Southern Illinois University Press, 1991), 200, 208.

facts is not peculiar to one class of phenomena and to one class of workers; it is applicable to social as well as to physical problems, and we must carefully guard ourselves against supposing that the scientific frame of mind is a peculiarity of the professional scientist."[7]

Although the method of science may distinguish it from other ways of knowing and understanding, the doing of research is more than a recipe—it is a frame of mind. Whereas a method implies an algorithm for answering questions, curiosity leads to asking questions. Curiosity and suspicion characterize the nature of scientists. The researcher is observant, always on the lookout for discrepancies, unusual occurrences, or oddities, which suggest new possibilities. Suspicion is the uneasiness with the answers that current paradigms provide us. Many of these aspects will be apparent in Exhibit 2.1.

REASONING TO SOUND CONCLUSIONS

Many of us are familiar with the TV series *Elementary*, which presents a contemporary update of Sherlock Holmes, Sir Arthur Conan Doyle's character, leaving London for present-day Manhattan. In the opening scene of the book, *The Sign of the Four*, Doyle uses a conversation between Sherlock Holmes and Dr. Watson to demonstrate the importance of precise reasoning and careful observation to solve problems and unravel mysteries. Watson provides the test by handing Holmes a watch and asking for an opinion on the character or habits of the late owner. After a few moments of examination, Holmes's observations lead to facts from which he correctly infers that Watson's careless and untidy elder brother was the owner of the watch, a man who had inherited wealth, treated his prospects foolishly, and died a drunkard. The speed of the conclusion is startling, but the trail of his reasoning from small facts to conclusions, which Watson subsequently confirms, is a standard thought process for detectives and researchers alike.

Let's expand on the events from Holmes's observations. Initials on the watch back suggest Watson's last name. The date of the watch was 50 years back—thus made for the last generation. Jewelry of the time descended to the eldest son, Watson's brother. The lower part of the watch was dented and marked by keeping other hard objects in the same pocket, thus carelessness. He was well provided for in other respects, as evidenced by inheriting the watch, yet there were a pawnbroker's pinpoints scratched in four places. We can infer that the brother had pawned the watch four times, yet he had occasional bursts of prosperity so

A conversation between Sherlock Holmes and Dr. Watson reveals the importance of precise reasoning and careful observation to solve problems and unravel mysteries.

he could reclaim it. The inner plate containing the keyhole had thousands of scratches around the hole, thus revealing that the brother, a drunkard, wound the watch at night, leaving traces of his unsteady hand.[8]

The next sections describe types of argument such as deduction, induction, abduction, and the Toulmin Model. Sherlock Holmes rarely uses deduction, in the proper sense of the word. Occasionally he will apply induction, using specifics (facts) from the past to predict future behavior or make a generalization. But he is best at abduction, moving from accepted facts to infer the most probable or "best explanation." Notice that reasoning from factual descriptions of the watch (e.g., its date, dents and marks, pawnbroker's scratches, and the inner plate) could all have led to different conclusions, but connecting those facts to Watson's brother was the most obvious and basic hypothesis.

Exposition and argument are essential tools of the researcher. Deduction, induction, abduction, and the Toulmin Model are the types of argument used to build cases, reason, and derive conclusions. You will find the latter to be a very intuitive and practical approach to logical writing and speaking.

Deduction

Deduction is a form of reasoning that claims to be conclusive—the conclusions must necessarily follow from the reasons given. Deduction is an argument in which the reasons (premises) are said to imply the conclusion and if those reasons are successful in "warranting the conclusion" (i.e., they are true premises, the argument is deductively valid and represents a proof). The premises are assumptions that the researcher takes tentatively to be true. For a deduction to be correct, it must be both true and valid. The premises given for the conclusion must agree with the real world (be true). In addition, the arrangement of premises follows such a form that the conclusion must "necessarily follow from the premises": There are many valid forms. One deductive argument is called *modus ponens*, with which you are familiar: (1) If P, then Q. (2) P. (3) Therefore, Q.

> Because deductive arguments are those in which the truth of the conclusion is thought to be completely *guaranteed* and not just *made probable* by the truth of the premises, if the argument is a sound one, then the truth of the conclusion is said to be "contained within" the truth of the premises; that is, the conclusion does not go beyond what the truth of the premises implicitly required.[9]

For example, consider this simple deduction of **premises** and conclusion from years of inner-city health research designed to improve health care and care delivery among disadvantaged urban populations:

- Premise 1: Cooperation of inner-city participants in follow-up studies is challenging because of their mobility and the use of pseudonyms.[10]

- Premise 2: This study requires re-contacting the study's original inner-city participants.

- Conclusion: Participant cooperation in this study will be challenging.

If we know that the sample requirement of this follow-up study involves substantial re-contact of the original study's participants, we might think this is a sound deduction. But the conclusion cannot be accepted unless the argument form is valid and the premises are both true. The form is valid, and in this case, you can confirm both premises. The deductive approach begins with a theory, develops hypotheses from that theory, and gathers and analyzes data to test those hypotheses.[11]

Induction

Induction is different. The relationship between premises and conclusions is not the same. **Induction**, as classically defined, draws a conclusion from one or more particulars (specific facts or pieces of evidence). The premises are intended to be strong enough that if they were true, it would be *improbable* that you would produce a false conclusion. In short, induction needs to increase the probability of a correct conclusion. The conclusion explains the facts and the facts support the conclusion.

Induction begins with observations. For example, you are working on a time-sensitive project when you meet with your boss and other managers for updates on the team's progress. After the meeting, you ask your boss about the absolute deadline, and your boss says 3 weeks. From colleagues who are also managers, you know authoritatively that the time limit is 5 weeks away. Your boss was untruthful.[12] This is a fact—you ask the critical timing question and get an answer that is false. Why is that? One likely answer is that your boss is under pressure from his manager to perform well. This conclusion is an induction. We know from experience that this organization places such undue pressure on managers that they will risk the loyalty of their staff to save themselves.

The nature of induction, however, is that the conclusion is a hypothesis. It is one explanation, but there are others that fit the fact equally well. Perhaps your boss answered quickly, without thinking, that completion ahead of the deadline would make him look good, that the team had a reputation for slowness in delivering on time-sensitive projects, or that he wanted to boost the department's reputation; on the other hand, he might have a pathological disorder. Deviant and destructive behaviors are not uncommon in organizations.[13]

The essential nature of induction in this example is that the inductive conclusion is an inferential jump beyond the evidence presented. While one conclusion explains the fact of the lie and has a chance of being true, we might have more confidence in others that can also explain the fact. It may also be that none explain the manager's response. The researcher's task is to determine the nature of the evidence needed and to find methods that discover and measure it. This strategy, in turn, rules out hypotheses that do not explain the phenomenon. The inductive approach begins with a set of empirical observations, attempts to find patterns in those observations, and then theorizes about them.[14]

The complementary nature of these methods of reasoning is beneficial to researchers who design research with the idea of using induction and deduction together for a more comprehensive picture of the study. Often, a researcher plans to focus on an inductive or deductive approach and then discovers during the study that new questions emerge that the other approach helps to clarify.

Abduction

Abductive reasoning is one of the three types of inference. **Abduction**, referred to as inference to the "best explanation," is a form of logical inference in which one chooses the hypothesis that would best explain the relevant evidence if that evidence were true. Abduction starts from accepted facts and infers the simplest, most probable, explanation. Whereas true premises and a valid form guarantee a true conclusion in deduction, abductive premises do not. Without practice, it is sometimes difficult to distinguish between induction and abduction:

> The mere fact that an inference is based on statistical data is not enough to classify it as an inductive one. You may have observed many gray elephants and no non-gray ones, and infer from this that all elephants are gray, *because that would provide the best explanation for why you have observed so many gray elephants and no non-gray ones.* This would be an instance of an abductive inference. It suggests that the best way to distinguish between induction and abduction is . . . [that in both forms] the conclusion goes beyond what is (logically) contained in the premises . . . but in abduction there is an implicit or explicit appeal to explanatory considerations, whereas in induction there is not.[15]

Peirce, mentioned earlier, introduced abduction. According to Peirce, "abduction consists in studying the facts and devising a theory to explain them."[16] Abduction may take different forms. It can postulate the existence of previously unknown objects, such as a new planet, or it may rely on past hypotheses to produce new ones.[17] It is thus a form of hypothetical reasoning that leads to adopting a tentative explanatory hypothesis on the basis of observations.[18] Although Peirce says that abduction is reasoning, he also questions how close it comes to *intuition*, insight, sensations, emotions, guessing, instinct, and perceptual judgment.[19]

In scientific reasoning, one of the first tasks is to state the facts that explain a curiosity, doubt, or problem (Exhibit 2.1). This involves an explanatory hypothesis or abduction. Then, there is a crucial test using inductive and deductive processes. The initial abductive hypothesis is often the equivalent of an educated guess, but it is a guess that must be tested and subsequently corrected. Although Aristotle and philosophers who came after him abandoned abduction,

Wikimedia Commons/Light show

> Peirce, however, for whom abduction is the only *ars inveniendi* [art of invention that], integrates it again among effective scholarly procedures and thus allows for a moment of *creativity and mere guessing* in the process of controlled scientific reasoning.[20]

Albert Einstein was convinced that insight was not the product of logic or mathematics, but rather it arises from intuition and inspiration, similar to artists.

"When I examine myself and my methods of thought, I come close to the conclusion that the gift of imagination has meant more to me than any talent for absorbing absolute knowledge."—Albert Einstein

> "When I examine myself and my methods of thought, I come close to the conclusion that the gift of imagination has meant more to me than any talent for absorbing absolute knowledge." Explaining his assertion, he said, "All great achievements of science must start from intuitive knowledge. I believe in intuition and inspiration. . . . At times I feel certain I am right while not knowing the reason." Thus, his famous statement that, for creative work in science, "Imagination is more important than knowledge."[21]

Exhibit 2.2 presents a diagram of the three logical processes and describes Peirce's famous bean example.

These three forms of reasoning are complementary operations of the human mind: "Deduction infers a *result* (conclusion) that is certain; induction produces a *rule* (conclusion) that is valid until a contrary instance is found; abduction produces a *case* (conclusion) that is always uncertain (i.e., merely plausible)."[22]

You might find a stock market scenario interesting. The NASDAQ Stock Exchange consists of approximately 4,000 companies.[23] Its primary index is the Nasdaq Composite. Nasdaq movements sometimes signal broader market activity in the overall U.S. stock market. The Nasdaq-100 Index is a weighted, market-capitalization index that tracks the 100 most valuable large-cap growth, nonfinancial stocks. Their weights give some companies a disproportionate influence on the Nasdaq-100's value. Thus, when the Nasdaq loses value, it may be because all markets are under pressure or significant selling is occurring in leading companies of an important sector of the Nasdaq-100, such as technology. (Technology accounts for over 50% of the market-cap weight.) When the Nasdaq-100 peaked, 11 stocks were down between 40% and 54%.[24] I will take a representative subset for our example, which I will call *S*; it is a subset of the 11 losing stocks. See Exhibit 2.3.

EXHIBIT 2.2 ■ Peirce's Triangle and Three Forms of Argument

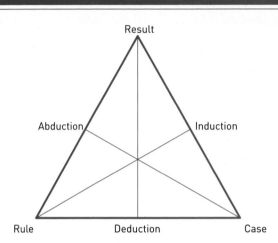

Peirce proposes the following:

> Suppose I enter a room and there find a number of bags, containing different kinds of beans. On the table there is a handful of white beans; and, after some searching, I find one of the bags contains white beans only. I at once infer as a probability, or as a fair guess, that this handful was taken out of that bag. This sort of inference is called *making a hypothesis*. It is the inference of a *case* from a *rule* and a *result*. We have, then[a]:

Deduction	Induction	Abduction
Rule: All the beans from this bag are white.	Case: These beans are from this bag.	Rule: All the beans from this bag are white.
Case: These beans are from this bag.	Result: These beans are white.	Result: These beans are white.
Result: These beans are white.	**Rule**: All the beans from this bag are white.	**Case**: These beans are from this bag.

Source: Peirce's triangle adapted from "Reasoning Patterns," The Pennsylvania State University, Eberly College of Science, Forensic Statistics, 2016, https://online.science.psu.edu/frnsc297a_sandbox_2391/node/2402, as cited in Sebeok, Thomas A., "One, Two Three Spells UBERTY," *The Sign of Three: Dupin, Holmes, Peirce*, ed. Umberto Eco and Thomas A. Sebeok (Bloomington: Indiana University Press, 1983), 1–10. Also see Kim, Joohoan, "From Commodity Production to Sign Production: A Triple Triangle Model for Marx's Semiotics and Peirce's Economics" (Presentation at the 79th Annual Convention of the Speech Communication Association, Miami, FL, November 18–21, 1993), Figure 2.

Note: [a]Peirce, C. S., *Collected Papers (1931–1958)*, vols. 1–8, ed. C. Hartshorne, P. Weiss, and A. Burks (Cambridge, MA: Harvard University Press: 1934), vol. 2, § 623.

EXHIBIT 2.3 ■ Forms of Reasoning Illustrated With the NASDAQ Example

Deduction
When *S* is selling off, the Nasdaq loses value. *S* is selling off. Thus, the Nasdaq is losing value.
(If the premises are true—agree with the real world—and the form of the syllogism is correct, the conclusion must be *necessarily* true.)

Induction
The Nasdaq has lost value every time *S* has sold off. Thus when *S* is selling off, the Nasdaq is losing value.
(With induction, the conclusion is a hypothesis—an inferential jump. It is one explanation, but there are others that explain a loss of value equally well: the Federal Reserve warned of a tech bubble, the media are hyping rate hikes, other sections in the Nasdaq are experiencing severe selling, or the characteristics of the subset may have changed.)

Abduction
When *S* sells off, the Nasdaq loses value. The Nasdaq has lost value; it must be that *S* is selling off.
(According to abduction, this is the best explanation. But some other reasons could have caused the Nasdaq to lose value, e.g., the beginning of a bear market or releases of earning reports for *S* showing poor performance. Abduction can lead to false conclusions but is often a path to a good explanation, if not a good preliminary hypothesis.)

As a business major, you may have noticed that successful entrepreneurs are risk-takers. They take measured risks in launching a business that could result in the loss of money and possible failure; you have not, however, observed entrepreneurs that are risk averse. You infer, abductively, that *all* entrepreneurs are risk-takers because that is the "best explanation" for your observations. This explanation is contrary to one of the principles of general semantics, the problem with "allness" statements. Despite its seemingly viable trail toward a good explanation, if you intend to claim the correctness of an abductive inference that includes the word "all," you would be wise to test it empirically.

Exhibit 2.4 compares three characteristics (purpose, procedures, and outcomes) to differentiate the reasoning approaches used in problem-solving.

The Toulmin Model

The late Stephen Toulmin was an influential British philosopher known for his interests in ethics, science, and moral reasoning. He was best known for his 1958 book, *The Uses of Argument*, in which a new approach to analyzing arguments became known as the Toulmin

EXHIBIT 2.4 ■ Different Logical Approaches to Problem-Solving		
Deduction	**Induction**	**Abduction**
Purpose		
Test theories and hypotheses through observations that fit general rules.	Start with specific, dependable observations to find patterns, generate hypotheses, or create theory.	Develop theory starting with an incomplete set of facts (observations) to find those most likely for reasoning to the best explanation (theory).
Tests of causal relationships are paramount.	Identify, diagnose, and explore for discovery and clarification.	Reasoning is like using imperfect but available evidence in a creative or intuitive way.
Procedures		
Designs are selected for theory testing, and the protocol is followed rigorously.		Facts, literature, and observations are the starting point for the most obvious and simple hypothesis.
Data collection and analysis are sequential, and their relationship is separate.	Data collection and recollection are iterative in looking for patterns.	Data shape the meaning of categories and themes in "thematic" qualitative research and grounded theory.
Correct and true premises guarantee the conclusions.	Conclusions are likely or probable.	Conclusions are a "best guess," i.e., they are "possibly," not probably, correct.
Outcomes		
Testing or confirming hypotheses. Accurate predictions are assumed to be one confirmation of the theory in question.	Developing and justifying generalizations or theory simultaneously; thereby reducing the need for subsequent empirical testing.	Explaining surprising facts or puzzles using numerical and cognitive reasoning. It "informs" the process of the scientific method by developing the construction of explanatory theory.

Source: Inspired by Morgan, David L., *Integrating Qualitative and Quantitative Methods: A Pragmatic Approach*, Kindle ed. (Thousand Oaks: SAGE, 2013), 47–49; and, Haig, Brian D., "An Abductive Theory of Scientific Method," *Psychological Methods* 10, no. 4 (2005): 371–388.

Model. "He proposed, instead of formal logic's three-part syllogism, a model of persuasive argument consisting of six components. Some, he maintained, apply universally but others did not. 'Arguments, in other words, do not unfold in a Platonic ether, but in particular contexts.'"[25]

When students think about argumentation and debate, Harvard, Georgetown, or the University of California, Berkeley's prestigious intercollegiate debate teams or the Oxford-Cambridge competition come to mind. But Toulmin's application extends to the interpretation of literature, computer science, and artificial intelligence. As Toulmin says, it has universal application to *practical* or *substantial* arguments spoken in plain language. If you do a search for the Toulmin Model in business, you will find it in advertising (including the analysis of negative advertising), business writing, public relations, marketing, consumer studies, accounting reports, management communication, business law, and training for corporate attorneys.

Professor Stephen Toulmin, the late influential British philosopher, proposed a new model for reasoning and analyzing arguments. Its main components are data—warrant—claim. Three additional modules strengthen its utility.

For students of research methods, this model of reasoning has particular importance in structuring the arguments in your paper. In fact, it may be one of the most important reasons for obtaining this book because it may enlarge your understanding of how to support arguments.

In your term project, the research problem is the objective around which everything revolves. It must be stated precisely, unambiguously, and authoritatively. Its rationale for selection, importance to the field, and the benefits to be derived are all arguments. Collectively, they convince the reader that your work is a worthwhile endeavor. Your review of the literature assembles the argument that leads the reader from broadly related studies to those that are directly related to your problem and pertinently bear on its resolution. The connection of the literature to the problem also requires an argument (i.e., building a case that links them). Your selection of design, method, procedures, and sample demand arguments that lead the reader to conclude that your decisions were the most appropriate and sensible for the research purpose. Again, arguments that writers must make convincingly include the interpretation of the findings, the degree to which they answer the research question, and the implications suggested by the findings. It is hard to do this smoothly with a deductive syllogism or clearly with the inductive process, although both are theoretical bases. Like the other two forms of reasoning, abduction presents literary challenges because of its openness to expedient conclusions. However, when you see how Toulmin's model works, you will immediately recognize applications for your work now and in the future.

The **Toulmin Model** is a structure for constructing decisive arguments containing six components that evaluate the pros and cons and the effectiveness of rebuttals and "is more reliable, credible, and in general more efficient and effective . . ." as a modern reasoning structure.[26] The structure is based on the legal system, in which the litigant (1) makes a **claim**, (2) gives **data** to support that claim, and (3) backs the data or evidence with a **warrant** (i.e., shows *why* the evidence supports the claim).[27] These three elements — claim, data, and warrant— are present in every argument. Three additional elements of Toulmin's model may be added as necessary: a **backing** (for the warrant), **rebuttals**, and **qualifier(s)**.

To explain this process, I will first define the elements represented (Exhibit 2.5) and then provide a diagram of the process (Exhibit 2.6) and subsequently connect it to an example from the scandal at Wells Fargo. This should reveal the utility of this reasoning process.

A case study using the Toulmin Model entitled "Women Make Superior Managers" is provided at the end of this chapter.

EXHIBIT 2.5 ■ Definitions of the Elements in the Toulmin Model

Primary Components			Secondary Components		
Data	**Warrant**	**Claim**	**Qualifier**	**Backing**	**Rebuttal**
The data are the grounds, facts, or evidence on which the claim is based. They are used to prove or support the claim.	The warrant demonstrates the connection between data and claim by creating a bridge that shows *why* the evidence supports the claim and makes it true.	The statement, thesis, or assertion being argued. May be fact-based, value-based, or policy-based.	Adds limits, nuances, or specificity to the claim, providing a context under which the argument is true. Helps to counter rebuttals.	(For warrants) Additional support to bring credibility to the warrant's reliability or relevance. Also, explains the connections between the data, warrant, and claim.	Mitigates likely objections and counter-arguments to the claim by suggesting reasons why a counter-claim is flawed, lacks credibility, or is not reasonable or realistic.

Sources: Please refer to the citations at the end of the case "Women Make Superior Managers" later in this chapter for definitions of the Toulmin Model's components. The "Definitions of Components in the Toulmin Model" section of the case presents a more elaborate version of the definitions with citations for their sources. The definitions shown in this chapter's Exhibit 2.6 are summaries. Primary definitional references include the following: Toulmin, Stephen E., *The Uses of Argument*, updated ed. (Cambridge, UK: Cambridge University Press, 2003), 89–100; Wheeler, L. Kip., "Toulmin Model of Argument," Carson-Newman University English Department, https://web.cn.edu/kwheeler/documents/Toulmin.pdf; Karback, Joan, "Using Toulmin's Model of Argumentation," *Journal of Teaching Writing* 6, no. 1 (1987): 81–91; and Wilson, G. Peter, and Carolyn R. Wilson, "The Toulmin Model of Argumentation," NavigatingAccounting.com, November 2016, Creative Commons BY-NC-SA.

EXHIBIT 2.6 ■ **The Toulmin Model of Argumentation and Reasoning**

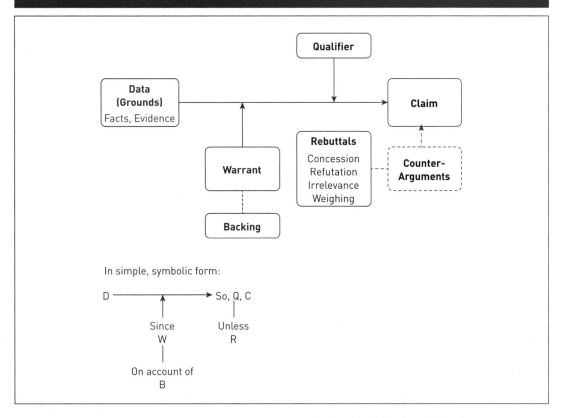

CASE EXAMPLE:

WELLS FARGO—"LIONS HUNTING ZEBRAS"

Refer to the diagram in Exhibit 2.6 to follow the flow of the argument and come back to Exhibit 2.5 for definitions.

Claim: Congress should submit a bill creating a stringent law to criminally prosecute executives at financial institutions like Wells Fargo for fraudulent business practices.

Qualifier: Although the means (tools necessary to commit the crime), motive (the actionable idea), and the opportunity (or unrestrained chance to follow through) must be proven, those executives who aid and abet (i.e., enable managers) should be charged even when they are not the principal initiators of the fraud.

Warrant: "The failure to punish big corporations or their executives when they break the law undermines the foundations of the country: If justice means a prison sentence for a teenager who steals a car, but it means nothing to a CEO who quietly

(Continued)

(Continued)

engineers the theft of billions of dollars, then the promise of equal justice under the law has turned into a lie. The failure to prosecute big, visible crimes has a corrosive effect on the fabric of democracy and our shared belief that we are all equal in the eyes of the law."[a]

Backing: In cases of flagrant corporate lawbreaking, "federal law enforcement agencies—and particularly the Department of Justice (DOJ)—rarely seek prosecution of individuals." Not only does the Securities and Exchange Commission (SEC) "fail to demand accountability, the SEC frequently uses its prosecutorial discretion to grant waivers to big companies so that those companies can continue to enjoy special privileges despite often-repeated misconduct that legally disqualifies them from receiving such benefits."[b] Congress must override inappropriate or illegal application of agency discretion.

Data: Documentation of the Data Timeline—September 8, 2016, to December 13, 2016[c]

- From May 2011 to July 2015, Wells Fargo (WF) employees opened 1.5 million fraudulent bank accounts and 565,000 credit cards not authorized by customers. These accounts were complete with forged signatures, phony email addresses, and fake personal identification numbers (PINs).

- WF CEO John Stumpf blamed, and WF fired, 5,300 "rogue" employees when the scandal broke. To meet daily sales quotas, supervisors hounded the employees, most of them low-ranking staff. Only later did Stumpf recant his blame under pressure from House and Senate investigating committees. According to Stumpf's U.S. Senate testimony, the bank fired only one executive, an area president, for improper sales over a decade.

- WF employees, trying to meet intolerable sales goals and avoid being terminated,

targeted Mexican immigrants who spoke little English, older adults with memory problems, college students opening their first accounts, and small business owners. A former WF employee said, "It was like lions hunting zebras." His colleagues would "look for the weakest, the ones that would put up the least resistance."

- At the same time as the scandal, WF repossessed more than 400 cars of military members without first obtaining a court order as required by the Servicemembers Civil Relief Act (SCRA).

- WF lost Better Business Bureau (BBB) accreditation in many jurisdictions and will not be eligible for reinstatement for 3 years.

- California, Ohio, Illinois, and Massachusetts banned state business with WF as large municipalities across the country followed.

- The Financial Industry Regulatory Authority (FINRA) received U5 forms (a report card) for 600 of the 5,300 fired WF employees, with only 207 detailing the reason for firing as practices that led to bogus accounts.

- WF used U5s to threaten employees to meet quotas. When WF followed through with threats, it amounted to a "scarlet letter" that damaged employees' careers and prohibited another financial firm from rehiring them without WF's retraction.

- WF issued 15,000 low-cost MyTerm life insurance policies through Prudential without customers' knowledge or permission. Often, employees arranged for monthly premium fees to be withdrawn from their customers' accounts. Credit records were tarnished when payments were not made because the customers did not realize they owned the policy. Michael Barborek, a former WF banker in Orange, Texas said, "We were like insurance salespeople without the license. They wanted us to offer it to everybody who came in."

- The life insurance scam bolstered WF's overall sales figures, eventually presented to investors to boost the stock price.

- Under the Dodd–Frank financial-overhaul law, Federal Deposit Insurance Corporation (FDIC) regulators concluded that WF had failed to devise an adequate blueprint for avoiding a taxpayer bailout if it were on the brink of bankruptcy. The rebuke over the bank's so-called "living will" (or too-big-to-fail) submission surprised executives. But they had already failed the initial test in April 2016.

- WF put "rip-off" clauses into its account agreements. Such clauses "deny customers their day in court should their bank wrong them." The legalese requires forced arbitration, which removes customers' disputes from courts, judges, and juries and puts them into an arbitration process. A private firm selected and paid for by the corporation decides claims. "When Wells charged them for accounts they never opened, multiple customers sued. But the bank claimed—successfully— that because customers had these clauses in their *real* accounts, they could thwart customers bringing lawsuits against them for the *fake accounts* [that] Wells Fargo opened up."[d]

- New rules articulated in a memo to federal prosecutors were the first major policy announcement by then–Attorney General Loretta E. Lynch since taking office. "The memo is a tacit acknowledgment of criticism that despite securing record fines from major corporations, the Justice Department under President Obama punished few executives involved in the housing crisis, the financial meltdown, and corporate scandals."[e]

- To date, no financial institution executive has faced prosecution for the widespread mortgage fraud that fueled the crisis

leading to the Great Recession, which still lingers over the economy and has cost the country over $30 trillion and climbing. In that crisis, "The Office of Thrift Supervision, which was supposed to regulate, among others, Countrywide, Washington Mutual, and IndyMac—all of which collectively made hundreds of thousands of fraudulent mortgage loans—made zero criminal referrals. The Office of the Comptroller of the Currency, which is supposed to regulate the largest national banks, made zero criminal referrals. The Federal Reserve appears to have made zero criminal referrals; it made three about discrimination. And the FDIC was smart enough to refuse to answer the question, but nobody thinks they made any material number of criminal referrals [either]."[f]

Counter-Arguments

Opposition to the claim suggests that WF and its executives have suffered enough considering:

1. WF paid $185 million in fines, including a $100 million penalty from the Consumer Financial Protection Bureau. WF paid $35 million to the Office of the Comptroller of the Currency and $50 million to the City and County of Los Angeles. WF agreed to refund about $2.6 million in fees that may have been inappropriately charged.

2. WF agreed to pay $4.1 million to resolve allegations of improperly repossessing more than 400 military members' cars. The Office of the Comptroller of the Currency assessed a $20 million civil penalty and consumer restitution for allegedly violating the SCRA.

3. The FDIC imposed penalties on WF under the too-big-to-fail testing process that prevents WF from creating new international banking units or acquiring any nonbank subsidiaries. If the March 2017 submission

(Continued)

(Continued)

to the FDIC is not acceptable, WF could have its growth capped and, in 2 years, be forced to divest itself of certain assets under the Dodd–Frank Act.

4. CEO Stumpf forfeited unvested equity awards worth about $41 million and did not get a salary while the company's board investigated the bank's sales practices. He received no 2016 bonuses. He subsequently retired.

5. Carrie Tolstedt, former senior executive vice president of community banking and the presumed instigator of the scheme, left the bank before her planned retirement date. She got no severance, forfeited unvested equity awards of $19 million, and did not get a 2016 bonus.

Rebuttal (to the Counter-Argument)

- "Corporate criminals routinely escape meaningful prosecution for their misconduct. The law is unambiguous: if a corporation has violated the law, individuals within the corporation must also have violated the law. If the corporation is subject to charges of wrongdoing, so are those in the corporation who planned, authorized or took the actions."[9]

- Carrie Tolstedt left WF with a $125 million retirement package.

- John Stumpf took a retirement of $133 million. He would be eligible for administrative perks if he stayed on as a consultant to WF for the next 2 years.

- The so-called record-breaking fines are a rounding error and serve only as a minor deterrent to criminal wrongdoing compared to WF's second-quarter profits of $5.6 billon. The financial community was apathetic to the corruption and fines as investors traded the stock up, which moved in a stable range throughout the crisis.

- Managers who were enablers of the sales quota system and encouraged criminally fraudulent activities were unaffected (months later) by penalties or sanctions. Yet 5,300 employees paid the price for their bosses; whistleblowers on ethics violations were evicted from the firm. Despite ample signs of the scandal, executives failed to stop misconduct for years as their personal careers advanced. For executives, the organization's fines were inconsequential because there were no penalties for them personally.

Notes:

[a]Office of Senator Elizabeth Warren, "Rigged Justice: 2016—How Weak Enforcement Lets Corporate Offenders Off Easy," Executive Summary, U.S. Senate, January 20, 2016, https://www.warren.senate.gov/files/documents/Rigged_Justice_2016.pdf.

[b]Ibid.

[c]References for data/evidence in the Toulmin Model example are from the following sources, approximating the timeline shown in the text: Corkery, Michael, "Wells Fargo Fined $185 Million for Fraudulently Opening Accounts," *New York Times*, September 8, 2016, http://www.nytimes.com/2016/09/09/business/dealbook/wells-fargo-fined-for-years-of-harm-to-customers.html; Smith, Yves, "Wells Fargo Fined $185 Million for Opening Phony Customer Accounts, Charging Fees Without Consent; Executives Go Scot Free," *Naked Capitalism* (blog), September 9, 2016, http://www.nakedcapitalism.com/2016/09/wells-fargo-fined-185-million-for-opening-phony-customer-accounts-charging-fees-without-consent-executives-go-scot-free.html;Reuters, "Wells Fargo CEO to Forfeit $41 Million Amid Independent Investigation," *Fortune*, September 28, 2016, http://fortune.com/2016/09/28/wells-fargo-ceo-forfeit-investigation/; Shen, Lucinda, "How Wells Fargo's Scandal Could Change the Way We Bank," *Fortune*, September 30, 2016, http://fortune.com/2016/09/30/wells-fargo-banking/; Shen, Lucinda, "Here's How Much Wells Fargo CEO John Stumpf Is Getting to Leave the Bank," *Fortune*, October 13, 2016, http://fortune.com/2016/10/13/wells-fargo-ceo-john-stumpfs-career-ends-with-133-million-payday/; Cowley, Stacy, "'Lions Hunting Zebras': Ex-Wells Fargo Bankers Describe Abuses," *New York Times*, October 20, 2016, http://www.nytimes.com/2016/10/21/business/dealbook/lions-hunting-zebras-ex-wells-fargo-bankers-describe-abuses.html; Henry, Jim, "Wells Fargo Troubles Go Beyond Fake Account

Scandal," *Forbes*, October 30, 2016, http://www.forbes.com/sites/jimhenry/2016/10/30/wells-fargo-troubles-go-beyond-fake-account-scandal/#15e9e6b72f16; Brown, Rachel, "Wells Fargo Loses BBB Accreditation," *WCNC*, October 20, 2016, http://www.wcnc.com/money/business/wells-fargo-loses-bbb-accreditation/337609202; Reuters, "U5s: Wells Fargo's Sales Scandal Just Got Bigger," *Fortune*, November 3, 2016, http://fortune.com/2016/11/03/wells-fargo-sales-scandal-employees/; Keller, Laura J., Dakin Campbell, and Kartikay Mehrotra, "Wells Fargo's Stars Thrived While 5,000 Workers Got Fired," *Bloomberg*, November 3, 2016, https://www.bloomberg.com/news/articles/2016-11-03/wells-fargo-s-stars-climbed-while-abuses-flourished-beneath-them; Arnold, Chris, "Senators Investigate Reports Wells Fargo Punished Workers," *NPR* (All Things Considered), November 4, 2016, http://www.npr.org/2016/11/04/500728907/senators-investigate-reports-wells-fargo-punished-workers; Cowley, Stacy, and Mathew Goldstein, "Accusations of Fraud at Wells Fargo Spread to Sham Insurance Policies," *New York Times*, December 9, 2016, http://www.nytimes.com/2016/12/09/business/dealbook/wells-fargo-accusations-sham-insurance-policies.html?_r=0; Reuters, "Wells Fargo Scandal: Prudential Investigating Reports of Fraudulent Life Insurance Sales," *Newsweek*, December 10, 2016, http://www.newsweek.com/prudential-life-insurance-wells-fargo-customer-accounts-scandal-530604; Dayen, David, "Another Wells Fargo Scandal Proves Our Financial System Is Still Broken," *The Fiscal Times*, December 12, 2016, http://www.thefiscaltimes.com/Columns/2016/12/12/Another-Wells-Fargo-Scam-Proves-Our-Financial-System-Still-Broken; and Tracy, Ryan, and Emily Glazer, "Wells Fargo Sanctioned by U.S. Regulators for 'Living Will' Deficiencies," *Wall Street Journal*, December 13, 2016, http://www.wsj.com/articles/u-s-regulators-sanction-wells-fargo-declaring-living-will-deficiencies-1481664744.

[d]Lardner, Jim, "What Should Be Done to Stop Banks Like Wells Fargo from Scamming US?," *Americans for Financial Reform* (blog), September 26, 2016, *http://blog.ourfinancialsecurity.org/2016/09/1069/*.

[e]Apuzzo, Matt, and Ben Protess, "Justice Department Sets Sights on Wall Street Executives," *The New York Times*, September 9, 2015, http://www.nytimes.com/2015/09/10/us/politics/new-justice-dept-rules-aimed-at-prosecuting-corporate-executives.html.

[f]Holland, Joshua, "Hundreds of Wall Street Execs Went to Prison During the Last Fraud-Fueled Bank Crisis," *Moyers & Company*, September 17, 2013, http://billmoyers.com/2013/09/17/hundreds-of-wall-street-execs-went-to-prison-during-the-last-fraud-fueled-bank-crisis/.

[g]Warren, Ibid.

DECIPHERING THE RESEARCH LINGO

When we do research, we seek principally to describe, explain, or predict phenomena. Our research question might be "How accurate are various models of sales forecasting in the electronics industry?" Definitions are crucial to answering this question, and we must agree on their meaning. Which forecasting models? What is meant by "accurate?" Do we mean consumer electronics or commercial instruments? What is the range of products included? These questions require the use of concepts, constructs, definitions, variables, hypotheses, and a theory about forecasting.

Concepts

A **concept** is a generalized meaning associated with particular events, objects, conditions, and situations. A concept aggregates objects or events that have common characteristics beyond a single observation. When you think of a laptop or mobile phone, you do not think of a single one but rather collected memories of all laptops or phones abstracted to a set of distinct and definable characteristics. We can all agree on the meanings of concepts such as cat, table, lamp, coin, and employee.

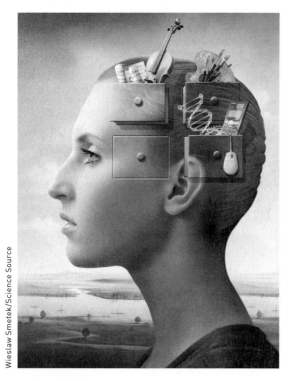

Wieslaw Smetek/Science Source

A concept is a generalized meaning associated with particular events, objects, conditions, and situations. A concept aggregates objects or events that have common characteristics beyond a single observation. A table, for example, has agreed-on properties such as support devices (i.e., legs) and a horizontal surface. It is relatively concrete. "Safety" is more abstract with many characteristics and applications; it is much harder to define and visualize with a uniform meaning.

It is much harder to pinpoint concepts such as household, retail transaction, dwelling unit, and regular customer. Even more challenging are familiar but not well-understood concepts such as personality, leadership, social class, and fiscal policy. For example, the research literature defines personality in more than 400 ways.[28]

The concepts described above represent progressive levels of abstraction. As the concept becomes more abstract, it loses the concrete aspects of the person or thing to which the linguistic expression refers. While the actual properties of a table include support devices (i.e., legs) and a horizontal surface, a high-level abstraction like personality is much harder to visualize. Such abstract concepts are often called constructs. They are not directly observable and may contain multiple parts.

Constructs

A **construct** is an image or idea invented explicitly for a given research or theory-building purpose. We build constructs by combining simpler concepts when the meaning we want to communicate is not directly subject to observation. Doing so provides a shared meaning allowing us to communicate precisely with the research audience. We frequently describe constructs as mental abstractions because seldom are constructs directly observable. For example, we cannot directly observe organizational culture, even though we may associate it with (1) stories and legends about the legacy of early leaders, (2) informal/formal communications or symbols that reveal the visual importance of people and objects, (3) rewards and recognition that signal what matters to the organization, (4) spoken and unspoken rule-oriented behaviors, (5) skills demonstrated by senior leaders, and (6) traits and characteristics of senior leaders.[29] In other words, organizational culture is composed of multiple underlying concepts. Confusion about the meaning of constructs can destroy a research study without the awareness of the researcher, manager, or client. If words have different meanings to individuals, then the intended message communicated about the problem differs markedly from what is perceived.

Definitions

Definitions reduce the danger of miscommunication. There are various kinds of definitions, the most familiar being dictionary definitions. Dictionary definitions define a concept with an explanatory phrase or synonyms. Although dictionary definitions are adequate for general communication, they are often not precise enough for research. Let's take the example of a co-worker who is always happy. What does this mean?

Andrew Ostrovsky/Alamy Stock Photo

More abstract concepts are called constructs. Constructs are built by combining simpler concepts when the meaning we want to communicate is not observable and may contain multiple parts. Although constructs are not directly observable, they can be tested and measured using a number of instruments.

Dictionary definition: Dictionary definitions for happiness are as follows: (a) a state of well-being and contentment or (b) a pleasurable or satisfying experience. The associated synonyms are pleasure, contentment, satisfaction, cheerfulness, merriment, gaiety, joy, joyfulness, joviality, jollity, glee, delight, good spirits, lightheartedness, well-being, enjoyment, exuberance, exhilaration, elation, ecstasy, jubilation, rapture, bliss, blissfulness, euphoria, or transports of delight. The number of connotations associated with "happiness" show that it has many nuances of meaning. Would you use this definition in your research?

Quasi-research definition: As we try to narrow our definition and to become more specific, we look for ways of measuring "happiness." This is the first step toward creating an *operational definition* but "happiness" is a fuzzy concept. An easy technique might be to *count smiles*. By counting the number of smiles a person reveals during a timed observation, we have a more specific definition. But it is not yet an *operational definition*. In fact, it is a bad one. Researchers analyzed video recordings of bowlers and fans at a hockey game and discovered that when people were happy (their team scored), they seldom smiled but did smile for social reasons like accidentally bumping into someone.[30]

Operational definition: In the previous study, the components of happiness were not considered, only a facial gesture. Happiness, or subjective well-being, consists of three parts: positive affect, negative affect, and life satisfaction. Widely used and respected questionnaires approach happiness differently. For example, the Positive and Negative Affect Schedule (PANAS by Watson, Clark,

Definitions in research are tricky. Dictionary definitions define a concept with an explanatory phrase or synonyms. Operational definitions state specific operational, measurement, and testing criteria. Operational definitions use terms that have empirical referents—that is, we must be able to count, measure, or in another way gather information through our senses.

and Tellegen) and the OECD Subjective Well-Being scale both measure positive and negative affect. The Satisfaction With Life Scale (Deiner, Emmons, Larsen, and Griffin) measures life satisfaction. Then there is the Oxford Happiness Questionnaire (Argyle and Hills) and the Subjective Happiness Scale (a.k.a., the General Happiness Scale) created by Lyubomirsky and Lepper. An entirely different measurement deals with neural receptors in the brain. The "rapid progress of neurobiology also enables neurobiologists to analyse the neural underpinning of happiness and might well offer new technologies to achieve 'artificial happiness' in the future."[31] This brings us to a more formal explanation of operational definitions.

Operational definitions state specific operational, measurement, and testing criteria. These terms must have empirical referents—that is, we must be able to count, measure, or in another way gather information through our senses. Whether the construct to be defined is physical (e.g., a tool) or highly abstract (e.g., self-esteem), the definition must specify the characteristics to be studied and how to observe them.

A researcher might be studying self-esteem and define high self-esteem as a high score on Rosenberg's Self-Esteem Scale.[32] Rosenberg's scale is a 10-item scale that claims to measure global self-worth by capturing both positive and negative feelings about the self. The measurement uses 4-point Likert scales ranging from strongly agree to strongly disagree. It contains items such as "I feel that I have a number of good qualities" and "All-in-all, I am inclined to feel that I am a failure." Similarly, a researcher might define the price multiple or price-to-earnings (P/E) ratio as the ratio for valuing a company that measures current share price relative to its per-share earnings. If a company is trading at $50 a share and its earnings over the last 12 months were $1.75 per share, the P/E ratio for the stock would be 50/1.75, or 28. A P/E ratio of 28 can be compared with the historical P/E ratio average of 16.7. Thus, operational definitions transform definitions of concepts and constructs into measurement. **Measurement** occurs when a number is assigned to a characteristic of a person, object, or event, in a reliable and valid way.

Measurement attempts to quantify *properties*, or characteristics. Some properties can be measured directly such as a person's height or weight. Other properties may refer to context-specific characteristics such as rank in an organization. A vice president in a local bank is not the same as a vice president at Google, thereby making comparisons difficult. Still other properties, such as attitudes toward brand image, can only be ascertained by measuring *indicants*. In most situations, the precise relationship between the indicant and the property is unknown and all that is known is that the indicant is an effect or correlate of the property. Thus, the consumer price index and the gross national product are indicants of the state of the nation's economy. The most important point is that the property being studied must be clearly and accurately defined. Indeed, the definition of the property is the first step, and the property must be defined specifically as it relates to the research at hand. It is only after the property has been defined operationally that the appropriate indicants can be determined.

Variables Defined

A **variable** is anything that can vary (i.e., that can assume multiple values and can change or be changed). Variables can be counted or scaled. In manufacturing, a variable might be the time to perform an assembly task or the maximum number of dust particles per cubic meter in the paint department. In demographics, a variable could be age, education, income, family size, participants' characteristics, and so forth. Students observe distance between classes, exam scores, number of students in a class, or the instructor's level of educational attainment as variables. Researchers refer to the property being studied as "varying" when the property takes on different values or numerals. One finds the variability or dispersion in a variable through numerical differences in a *continuous* variable or a symbol classifying membership in a category (*discrete* variable). Once the research process has started, you operationalize concepts and constructs used in the study with a measuring instrument or testing criteria. At this point, concepts/constructs and variables are the same, and the term *variable* commonly prevails.

Variables in Measurement

Variables have different quantitative characteristics depending on the scale they are measured on as shown in Exhibit 2.7.[33] The variable's properties determine the numerical value assigned to the variable.

For example, some variables are **dichotomous**, meaning they have only two values reflecting the presence or absence of a property. Variables such as employment status (employed or unemployed) or political affiliation (Republican or Democrat) have two values measured as 0 and 1 or 1 and 2. When variables take on additional values representing added categories of group membership (e.g., the demographic variables of race or religion), they are called **polytomous (multicategory) variables**. Both dichotomous and polytomous variables are **discrete** because only certain finite values (categories) are possible. A race-ethnicity variable in which "American Indian" is assigned a 5 and "other" is assigned a 6 provides no option for a 5.5. **Categorical or classificatory variables** are discrete variables. There is no inherent ranking, and analysts make measurements on a **nominal scale** (see Exhibit 2.7). A nominal scale does not imply order, distance, or origin; its measurement power is limited to naming. The prime characteristic is that the observations assigned to one category are equivalent within that category and using an assignment criterion, those observations can be said to differ from those assigned to all other categories.

When a variable takes on any value in an ordered set of values within a range, it is called a **continuous variable**. Theoretically, a continuous variable can take on an infinite set of values, but in practice, they are finite. It is arguable that the values of a continuous

EXHIBIT 2.7 ■ Operationalizing Variables by Measurement Level			
Scale	Characteristics	Allowed Operations	Descriptive Statistics
Nominal	Used to name, categorize, or classify	$=, \neq$	Category frequency, category percentage, mode
Ordinal	Used to order (rank) objects or individuals	$=, \neq, <, >$	Median, range, percentile ranking
Interval	Used to order, and has equal distance (intervals) between adjacent points but an arbitrary zero point	$=, \neq, <, >, +, -$	Mean, standard deviation, variance
Ratio	Fully quantitative (all arithmetic operations), ordering, equal intervals, and an absolute zero point	$=, \neq, <, >, +, -, *, /$	Geometric/harmonic mean, coefficient of variation

variable possess at least some intrinsic ranking, but the larger point is that continuous variables are treated as inherently interval or ratio.

An **ordinal (ranking) variable** is a variable that is rank ordered. For instance, you may rank levels of service satisfaction from highly satisfied to highly dissatisfied with an ordinal scale, but there is no way to discern the distance between points (or satisfaction levels). Many preference and opinion scales are ordinal. Recall judgments you make every day that involve relational comparisons. Take the sugar content of a serving size of cereal as an example. In sugar per serving, Kellogg's Raisin Bran is greater than Kellogg's Frosted Flakes, which is greater than regular Cheerios. Similarly, in the hybrid luxury car segment, the Lexus ES 300h gets greater combined (city/highway) miles per gallon than the Infiniti Q70, which in turn has better mileage than the Lexus 500h AWD. These examples satisfy the transitivity postulate, which states that a > b and b > c; therefore, a > c. In data analysis, nominal and ordinal (ranking) variables are treated with nonparametric statistics. Parenthetically, if we knew that the grams per serving of the compared cereals was 18, 12, 1, respectively, and the miles per gallon of the hybrid cars was 40, 30, 26, respectively, the ordinal variable would be ratio because there is equal distance between points and, in measuring grams and miles per gallon, both variables have a 0 in the set. Zero in weight means it does not exist. Therefore, as shown in Exhibit 2.7, all mathematic operations are allowed with ratio data.

When continuous variables are measured as **interval variables**, they have both order and equal distance between points (the distance between 12 and 1 PM is the same as the distance between 3 and 4 AM). Fahrenheit temperature scales have an *arbitrary* zero point but not a unique origin; they are also an example. A zero on a Fahrenheit temperature scale does not indicate the absence of temperature. In addition, IQ, GRE, and SAT scores are interval because they are standardized test scores rescaled to an arbitrary scale. Rating scales that can be empirically demonstrated to have equal distance between points are interval scales.

Finally, continuous variables that meet the requirements for **ratio** scales have all of the powers previously mentioned plus an absolute zero or point of origin. The zero in ratio data (0, 1, 2, 3, . . . n) permits the formation of ratios, whereas its absence in interval data obviates the formation of ratios. Both interval and ratio scales are quantitative and use parametric statistics. In business research, we find currency, sales figures, return rates, income earned per year, and population counts as examples.

Variables in Causal and Correlational Relationships

One finds independent and dependent variables in causal (explanatory) studies. Business researchers are typically interested in discovering relationships between these variables. Informally the relationship is sometimes referred to as stimulus-response or antecedent-measured. However, researchers more precisely describe an **independent variable** (IV) as the presumed cause or treatment variable in an experimental study. The IV is the variable that the researcher manipulates to explain variance in the dependent variable. A **dependent variable** (DV) is the presumed effect in an experimental study. In correlational nonexperimental studies (including statistical modeling, multiple regression, and canonical correlation), the X variable is called the **predictor variable**, and the Y variable is known as the **criterion variable**. In relational and predictive studies, this helps to avoid the assumption of a direct cause-effect relationship. This question shows the relationship between the IV and DV with regard to employees who perform their jobs remotely:

> Will telecommuting (IV) lead to increased job satisfaction (DV)?

The next two questions illustrate correlational relationships and those analyzed with multiple regression:

> What is the relationship between supervisors' modeling of ethical behavior (predictor) and the ethical behaviors of subordinates (criterion)? (correlation or bivariate regression)

> What is the relationship between supervisors' modeling of ethical behavior (predictor$_1$), strong supervisory working alliance (predictor$_2$), and the ethical behaviors of subordinates (criterion)? (multiple regression)

The variables used in the following examples are part of a current controversy in workplace practices stated in the IV-DV example above. This scenario may prompt you to apply the Toulmin Model to evaluate the arguments.

After several decades of allowing their employees to perform their jobs remotely, companies such as Yahoo, Bank of America, Aetna, Honeywell, Best Buy, Hewlett-Packard, and IBM have called their remote workers back into the office, thereby reducing or eliminating their work-from-home or telecommuting programs. At IBM, for example, 5,000 people in marketing, IT, procurement, and Watson-related departments were told to co-locate in one of six U.S. cities or find a new job. Telework is still an option for some IBM workers. Honeywell's decision affected 129,000 workers. The debate centers on the claim that face-to-face teams are more creative and synergistic; they make decisions faster and are more nimble, leading to greater productivity. Ironically, IBM saved 5 million gallons of staff fuel and avoided 450,000 tons of CO_2 emissions in the United States alone in 2007. Teleworking also allowed the company to reduce millions of square feet of office space and increase income by $1 billion from subleasing.[34] Findings from a Global Workplace Analytics report, which looked at the results of more than 4,000 telecommuting studies, revealed twice the number of advantages than disadvantages in telecommuting.[35]

When companies scale back on telecommuting, it may indicate problems in the market and revenues (recall Yahoo and Hewlett-Packard, and consider IBM's 21 consecutive quarters of declining revenues). Eventually, companies will be compelled to get the telecommuting problem right, particularly as the percentage of millennials continues to increase in "flexible location" positions. Millennials, who are projected to change jobs up to 15 times in their careers, won't have a problem moving to a company where flexibility is valued.[36]

A **moderating variable** (MV) influences the strength of the relationship between the IV and DV variables and is characterized statistically as an interaction. Sometimes an MV is included because it is thought to have a significant contributory or contingent effect on the primary IV-DV relationship.

After several decades of allowing employees to perform their jobs remotely, companies such as Yahoo, Bank of America, Aetna, Honeywell, Best Buy, Hewlett-Packard, and IBM have called their remote workers back into the office, thereby reducing or eliminating their work-from-home or telecommuting programs.

Shutterstock/Jade ThaiCatwalk

> Will telecommuting (IV) lead to increased job satisfaction (DV), especially among employees whose childcare needs conflict with traditional work hours (MV)?

Extraneous variables are among a countless number of peripheral variables that could affect a given relationship. **Extraneous variables** are variables not intentionally being studied or are unknown to an experimenter that may affect the outcome or introduce error. For example, environmental cues may influence participant behavior or researcher cues prompt participants to interpret how they should behave. The participants themselves may have individual characteristics unknown to the researcher such as prior knowledge, health issues, fatigue, or other disorders. The setting is also a source of influence: lighting, temperature, or noise. When known, these variables may be controlled so as not to become a *confounding variable* and provide an alternative explanation of the study's intended results. The nature of the work, for example, could affect any work schedule's impact on job satisfaction. The researcher might now introduce a *control variable* (CV). A **control variable** is a variable that is held constant (unchanging) throughout an experiment or observation designed to test the impact of the IV. In the IV-DV relationship, if certain variables are not held constant, they become extraneous factors that can invalidate the study's findings.

> Among financial analysts (CV), will telecommuting (IV) lead to increased job satisfaction (DV), especially among employees whose childcare needs conflict with traditional work hours (MV)?

Intervening variables (IVVs) are a conceptual mechanism through which the IV and MV might affect the DV. They are also known as mediating variables because they help explain how or why the IV affects the DV. Even if a remote-work policy results in higher job satisfaction, this may not be the full explanation. Perhaps telecommuting affects an intervening variable, which, in turn, results in higher job satisfaction. Now, we might hypothesize that the IVV is the amount of worker autonomy.

> Among financial analysts (CV), will telecommuting (IV) increase employee autonomy (IVV), thereby leading to higher job satisfaction (DV), especially among employees whose child care needs conflict with traditional work hours (MV)?

Hypotheses

Hypotheses and propositions have overlapping meanings. A **proposition** makes a statement about concepts that is judged true or false if it refers to observable phenomena. When the proposition is constructed for empirical testing, it is called a **hypothesis**. Thus, a hypothesis is a verifiable counterpart of a proposition. The hypothesis states what is expected to happen in the study's predicted relationship between two or more variables.

You will note that the *interrogative sentences* in the telecommuting examples could be converted to *declarative sentences* as hypotheses. For example, "Telecommuting (IV) leads to increased job satisfaction (DV), especially among employees whose childcare needs conflict with traditional work hours (MV)." I distinguish between a **research hypothesis** and a **statistical null hypothesis** at this reference.[37] Hypotheses guide the investigation of the problem or provide possible explanations for observations. Some might say a hypothesis is also tentative and conjectural, or an insightful guess about how one might answer the "research question" or support the hypothesis. (Research questions are explained in the next chapter.) Note that one supports a hypothesis; it is not "proven." Recall the discussion of induction: the conclusion is a hypothesis. It represents one explanation, but other explanations may explain the fact equally well. "Formulating hypotheses and operationalizing variables" is also illustrated in Chapter 3.

Descriptive hypotheses typically state the existence, size, form, or distribution of some variable. As univariate hypotheses, they contain only one variable; but they may also refer to several variables or groups. The descriptive hypothesis is a testable prediction revealing what you expect in your study. Examples include the following: "The current unemployment rate in Detroit exceeds 10% of the labor force" or "The professional networking site LinkedIn provides fewer employment opportunities in Europe than Xing." Researchers sometimes use a research question in place of a descriptive hypothesis such as "What is the unemployment rate in Detroit?"

Relational hypotheses are statements that describe the relationship between two or more variables. Among relational hypotheses are correlational and explanatory/causal hypotheses. **Correlational hypotheses** state that variables occur together in some specified way that establishes an association or trend. Examples of correlational hypotheses are as follows: "Isolation of clerical workers increases with the amount of Internet use" and "There is a positive relationship between learning course objectives and the number of hours accessing electronic course materials." There is no cause-effect claim in a correlational hypothesis. The phrase "correlation does not imply causation" applies here but could be expanded to "empirically observed covariation is a necessary but not sufficient condition for causality."[38]

An **explanatory or causal hypothesis** suggests that the presence of or a change in one variable (IV) causes an effect to occur in the other variable (DV). Because "cause" translates to "helps to make happen," the IV is not the only possible explanation for changes in the DV, as you saw in the telecommuting example. A causal example might be "Executives of charitable organizations who communicate the vision for their organization (IV) outperform noncommunicative executives from similar charities who do not communicate the vision for their organization on outcomes of revenue (DV_1) and reputation (DV_2)." Another example is "Increased amounts of assignment-related stress lead to diagnoses of fatigue, headaches, and depression among undergraduate students."

When researchers craft research hypotheses, they must also consider both the direction of the relationship (positive, negative, more than, or less than) and which variable influences the outcome. Especially with causal hypotheses, it may be necessary to identify other causes and control their effects. Hypotheses serve significant roles in research: (1) They guide and limit the scope of the study, (2) they identify relevant information, (3) they suggest which research design is most useful, and (4) they create a framework for arranging conclusions.

Theory

A simple definition of theory contains the components we have just discussed. That is, a **theory** systematically *interrelate*s concepts, constructs, definitions, and propositions to explain and predict phenomena (facts). Others expand this definition by including "interrelated constructs (concepts), definitions, and propositions that present a systematic view of phenomena by specifying relations among variables with the purpose of explaining and predicting the phenomena."[39] We have many theories and use them continually to explain or predict what goes on around us. To the extent that our theories are sound and fit the situation, we are successful with our explanations and predictions. Thus, theories are practical not just theoretical. The situation, domain, or setting where the theory applies is equally important because it specifies factors that limit the occurrences of when and where a theory can be used effectively.[40] Thus, the components of the

EXHIBIT 2.8 ■ A Synopsis of the Theory of Disruptive Innovation

"Disruption" describes the process whereby a smaller company with fewer resources can challenge established incumbent businesses successfully. Specifically, as incumbents focus on improving their products and services for their most demanding (and usually most profitable) customers, they exceed the needs of some segments and ignore the needs of others. Entrants that prove disruptive begin by successfully targeting those overlooked segments, gaining a foothold by delivering more suitable functionality, often at a lower price. The incumbents, chasing higher profitability in more demanding segments, tend not to respond vigorously. Entrants then move upmarket, delivering the performance that incumbents' mainstream customers require, while preserving the advantages that drove their early success. When mainstream customers start adopting the entrants' offerings in volume, disruption has occurred.

theory I mentioned satisfy the natural language questions of who, what, when, where, how, and why and the predictive claims of whether a specific event could, should, or would occur.[41]

Let's look at the "theory of disruptive innovation" by Clayton Christensen, a Harvard business professor.[42] Exhibit 2.8 shows an example of a theory that improves predictions about which businesses will succeed (think about Apple under Steve Jobs, Netflix, Google Apps, and Skype, to name a few).

Theory serves us in many useful ways. One of the most famous sayings about theories comes from Kurt Lewin's classic article in 1952 about field theory (yes, that is just after World War II, but it is still incredibly relevant). He said, "There is nothing so practical as a good theory."[43] Lewin's colleagues expanded this notion and further clarified it by saying "theorists should try to provide new ideas for understanding or conceptualizing a (problematic) situation, ideas which may suggest potentially fruitful new avenues of dealing with that situation. Conversely, applied researchers should provide theorists with key information and facts relevant to solving a practical problem, facts that need to be conceptualized in a detailed and coherent manner."[44]

What about practicality? Einstein's theory of relativity is known universally. But did you know that its application to your car's GPS system embodies relativistic effects? Since a satellite moves at about 6,000 miles/hour at over 12,000 miles above the earth while sending signals to earth stations, your GPS experiences higher acceleration due to gravity than the orbiting satellite. Without the benefit of a clock calibrated to nanoseconds to account for gravitational

©iStockphoto.com/koto_feja

Theories of GPS accuracy. How accurate are they? It depends. GPS satellites broadcast their signals in space with a certain accuracy, based on distance or range from multiple GPS satellites. But user accuracy refers to the device's calculated position from a true point, expressed as a radius. You are where you expect to be based on several factors, including satellite geometry, signal blockage, atmospheric conditions, and receiver design features/quality.

creep, your GPS would tell you that a half-mile to your destination would become a 5-mile discrepancy after 1 day.[45]

Theory is also useful in narrowing the range of facts we need to study. Since one can explore any problem from different perspectives, a theory can suggest ways most likely to be fruitful. It may likewise help the researcher define a scheme to impose on data for classification. Finally, theory summarizes and catalogs known phenomena and alludes to facts that lie beyond the immediate scope of observation, thereby predicting further facts.

CASE STUDY:

THE TOULMIN MODEL OF ARGUMENTATION AND REASONING— "WOMEN MAKE SUPERIOR MANAGERS"

For students of research methods, this model of reasoning has particular importance in structuring the arguments for your term project. The research problem must be stated precisely, unambiguously, and authoritatively. Its rationale for selection, importance to the field, and the benefits to be derived are all *arguments*. Collectively, they convince the reader that your work is a worthwhile endeavor. Your review of the literature assembles the argument that leads the reader from broadly related studies to those that are directly related your problem and pertinently bear on its resolution. The connection of the literature to the problem also requires an argument (i.e., building a case that links them). Your selection of design, method, procedures, and sample demand arguments that lead the reader to conclude that your decisions were the most appropriate and sensible for the research purpose. The interpretation of your findings,

THE TOULMIN MODEL OF ARGUMENTATION AND REASONING

(Continued)

(Continued)

the degree to which they answer the research question, and the implications suggested by the findings are, again, arguments that writers must make convincingly.

Toulmin's model is a structure for constructing decisive arguments containing six components that evaluate the pros and cons and the effectiveness of rebuttals. The structure has three primary components: a claim, the data (evidence, grounds) to support that claim, and a warrant that backs the data or evidence. These three elements—

claim, data, and warrant—are present in every argument. Three secondary components of the model may be added as necessary: a backing (for the warrant), rebuttals, and qualifier(s).

To explain this process, I will first provide a diagram, then define the elements represented in that diagram, and subsequently provide an example entitled "Women Make Superior Managers," which reveals the usefulness of this reasoning process. Discussion questions follow the case to test your understanding of the Toulmin Model.

DEFINITIONS OF COMPONENTS IN THE TOULMIN MODEL

Claim: The claim is the ". . . conclusion whose merits we are seeking to establish."[a] It is the statement, thesis, or assertion being argued. It is constructed in such a way that there is no doubt what side of the issue the arguer is on. Claims are often stated in the form of a proposition. The 2017 debate proposition for the 600 colleges and universities in team competition is, Resolved: The United States Federal Government should substantially increase its economic and diplomatic engagement with the People's Republic of China.[b]

Claims fall into three categories:

1. **Fact-Based Claim**: A claim that focuses on empirically verifiable phenomena (through direct observation, experimentation, or other data-supported research). Example: *There are more billionaires in New York State than in the rest of North America.*

2. **Judgment and Value Claim:** Claims involving opinions, attitudes, and subjective evaluations. Example: *Mozart is the best composer of all time.*

3. **Policy-Based Claim:** This claim is advocating courses of action that should be taken. Example: *The United States Treasury should quit producing and distributing pennies.*[c]

Data: The data are the grounds, facts, or evidence on which the claim is based. They are used to prove or support the claim being argued. Data represent the arguer's rationale or perspective for supporting the issue. The data are the foundation of the argument and answer the question, "What is the proof?" The evidence used is often statistics, scientific or company reports, media reports, documented historical or existing events, physical evidence, and authoritative quotes. If testimony is not from a respected authority, it is most certainly attacked.

Warrant: Just as the data provide the answer to the question of what is your proof, the next question is, "How do you get there?"[d] Since the data have committed you to a step toward proof, the challenge of "getting there" is not to bring in new and more data, "but propositions of a rather different kind: rules, principles, inferences-licenses . . . that taking these data as a starting point, the step to the original claim or conclusion is an appropriate and legitimate one."[e] The warrant clearly demonstrates the connection between data and claim by creating a bridge—a link in the form of a logical statement—that shows why the evidence supports the claim and makes it true. There are several classes of warrants that act as widely accepted truths and are acknowledged to have universal application:

- *Generalization:* Connects what is true for a representative sample to what is likely true for the population.[f]
- *Sign:* Connects the evidence as a sign, clue, or symptom of the claim.
- *Authority:* In supporting the claim, it connects the evidence to authoritative sources.
- *Analogy:* Connects the evidence to the claim using analogies of similar relevant situations, events, or precedents.
- *Causality:* Connects the evidence as being caused by or the result of the claim.
- *Principle:* Connects the evidence to the claim as an application of a broader, important principle.

The difference between the questions of "what do you have to go on" and "how do you get there" is not a trivial step. In some cases, it may be possible to distinguish between the two logical functions ". . . if one contrasts the two sentences, 'Whenever A, one *has found* that B' and 'Whenever A, one *may take it* that B.'"[g]

Some warrants allow one to accept a claim unequivocally, whereas others require us to take the step conditionally, or what Toulmin calls a "Qualifier." These phrases include "probably" or "presumably" that "make the step from data to the conclusion either tentatively; or else subject to conditions, exceptions, or qualifications."[h]

Backing: Sometimes, the warrant does not convince the reader or listener. Then, additional support is required to explain the connections between the data, warrant, and claim, support the warrants, or bring credibility to the warrant's reliability or relevance. These "backing" arguments don't prove the claim but support the truth of the warrant. "It is similar to evidence supporting a claim: It can include statistics, quotations, reports, findings, physical evidence, or other data or reasoning. However, there is a big difference: evidence supporting a claim is a necessary component of a logical argument; but, while backing strengthens an argument, it is not an essential component. That said, when the backing is included, it must be explicitly stated rather than implied."[i]

Qualifiers: Qualifiers typically revolve around concerns about the soundness of evidence, the strength of the warrant(s), or counter-arguments. They limit the strength of the argument or statements by proposing the conditions or a context under which the argument is true. Thus, qualifiers add limits, nuances, or specificity to the claim, helping to counter rebuttals. They are frequently stated in words that reflect the likelihood of the claim's correctness: absolute uncertainty, unlikely, possibly, likely, probably, and absolute certainty.[j] The model shows the qualifier beside the claim that it qualifies and above the arguments that could defeat or rebut the warranted conclusion.[k]

Rebuttals: Rebuttals mitigate possible objections and counter-arguments to an author's claim by suggesting reasons why a counter-argument is flawed, why it lacks credible evidence, significance, or is not reasonable or realistic. The writer or speaker anticipates the opposing point of view and considers the best evidence of the opposition so it may be discredited handily. "Dealing with counterarguments and objections is thus a key part of the process of building arguments, refining them, interpreting and analyzing them."[l]

Four Types of Rebuttals

There are four types of rebuttals: concession, refutation, demonstration of irrelevance, and weighing.[m]

Concession: The author "concedes" there are some valid aspects of the opposition's perspective, but admits this only to appear even-handed in acknowledging of merits of a different view. When restating

(Continued)

(Continued)

the value of the claim, you may include minor parts of the opposition's argument as a concession while rejecting others. This strategy is similar to "comparative advantage" case where you stress the superiority of your claim over the status quo or another aspect of the opponent's case.

Refutation: When using refutation, the best defense is a good offense. The writer/speaker undermines the opponents' position revealing important weaknesses and shortcomings, rebuilds arguments supporting her claim, and clarifies her arguments, which may have been weakened by the opposition. This process supports the validity of the original claim and shows that the position is still more widespread, demonstrably true, just, or preferable; and thus, the opposing argument ought to be rejected.

Demonstration of Irrelevance: Irrelevant arguments are exposed by explaining the logical fallacies in the opposition's position, that they have introduced evidence that is unrelated to the thesis, or that their position does not meet the criteria of relevance that defines the issue.

Weighing: *This* is one of the most underused yet significant parts of refutation.[n] Weighing is comparing your arguments with your opponent's. The ways to weigh an argument include the following:

- *Scope:* How broadly is the impact felt?
- *Magnitude:* How severe is the impact?
- *Probability:* How likely is the event, situation, or circumstance?
- *Reversibility:* Can the harms be undone?
- *Time Frame:* Is the harm short term or long term? Will it come about now or later?

"Women Make Superior Managers"

Refer to the diagram ("The Toulmin Model of Argumentation and Reasoning") to follow the flow of the argument and to the box ("Definitions of Components in the Toulmin Model") as a reminder of definitions.

Claim: Women make superior managers.

Data: According to the recent Gallup "State of the American Manager: Analytics and Advice for Leaders" report, employees who work for a female manager rather than a male boss are:

- 1.26 times more likely to agree strongly "there is someone at work who encourages my development and cultivates my potential."

- 1.29 times more likely to agree strongly "in the last six months, someone at work has talked with me about my progress."

- 1.17 times more likely to agree strongly "in the last seven days, I have received recognition or praise for doing good work."

- 41% of female managers (versus 35% of males) are engaged at work (i.e., emotionally committed to the firm, motivated, and productive).[o]

In a study on women's leadership effectiveness including 16,000 leaders (two-thirds male and one-third female), the Zenger Folkman consultancy[p] found that leadership effectiveness is contingent on age. Early career: there is little-perceived difference between men and women; soon, men are more effective; as women mature, they are perceived as more effective than their male counterparts. This advantage was attributed to women working twice as hard for the same rewards and recognition. From a self-development standpoint (managers ask for feedback and make changes), men and women are similar up to age 40, where women continue to improve and men decline by 12% because they assume they are doing well and don't need feedback.

In the same Zenger Folkman study, on a 360-degree instrument measuring 16 competencies, women scored higher on 12 of 16 (with statistically significant differences on 11 competencies). In examining differences in function, "in the traditional male bastions of sales, legal, engineering, IT and the R&D function, women actually received higher effectiveness ratings than males."[q] Finally, in three levels of management (executive manager, senior manager, and middle manager), women were perceived more positively by 4–6%.

Warrants:

- Women have a tight right-left brain connection creating excellent multi-tasking, listening ability, memory, higher concentration, and intuition. (Established by neurological research.)

- Women are better at assessing risk, especially in determining the probability of adverse outcomes. (Established by insurance studies.)

- Most women's communication ability makes them more diplomatic in the workplace. (Established by organizational communication studies.)

Backing: The Bureau of Labor Statistics reports that women hold 51.5% of managerial, professional, and related positions in organizations.[r] Because of the scientific research on women's intrinsic capacities, a substantially increased level of work experience since 1970, and current educational opportunities (women earn almost 60% of undergraduate degrees and 60% of all master's degrees), women have demonstrated the capacity to excel in leadership roles.[s]

Qualifier: The claim is qualified with the caveat that gender is not a precondition for managerial

success. However, and almost certainly, college-educated women with organizational experience have unique attributes including greater work-life balance, superior communication and listening skills, a strong ethical code, excellent consensus building and collaboration skills, and patience. These attributes, according to research, give women an advantage as managers.

Counter-Arguments: The first counter-claim of the opposition is that inexperienced women managers are inclined to imitate tough and authoritative male bosses, which reduces their effectiveness, alienates workers, and constrains future promotions. This practice, in turn, slows the upward movement of all women. Also, when placed in responsible positions, women managers may create an entitlement culture to overcompensate for former male bosses who did not care about balancing work, children, and a working husband. This climate leads to inequities that favor female over male employees. Moreover, many women managers show more interest in their personal success than the development of their subordinates; this is often accurate of women managers with female subordinates.

Dr. Akbari, a sociologist and entrepreneur, quotes a successful female business owner as saying: "'Men may not like each other, but they'll still promote each other. A woman will write off another woman because she doesn't like her shoes.' An oversimplification, yes, but I get her point."[t]

Second, 4 decades after the women's movement, women have not achieved significantly. They have not moved into positions of influence and prominence at a rate necessary to reach parity with men. Despite earning more than 44% of master's degrees in business and management, including 37% of MBAs, women are only 14.6% of executive officers, 8.1% of top earners, and 4.6% of Fortune 500 CEOs.[u]

Third, women should take responsibility for the reduction of their numbers in leadership positions. "Roughly a third of high-achieving women—those with graduate degrees or bachelor's degrees with honors—currently leave their jobs

(Continued)

(Continued)

to spend extended time at home, and 66 percent of high-achieving women at some point switch to career-derailing part-time, reduced-time, or flex-time work schedules."[v]

General Rebuttal: Historically, women have been denied opportunities in business, which has diminished their numbers in managerial and professional positions. "For women, the issue of having more female leaders goes far beyond equality in the workplace. Four-in-ten of them (38%) say having more women in top leadership positions in business and government would do a lot to improve the quality of life for all women. An additional 40% of women say this would have at least some positive impact on all women's lives."[w]

Counter-claims need to be conscious of gender bias, disqualifying stereotypes that would only place women in management positions comparable to "homemakers/caregivers," as well as cultural barriers (e.g., the conflict between leadership stature and female likability). Multi-role needs (affordable child care and access to paid sick days and paid pregnancy leave) are additional burdens faced by female candidates for managerial positions. The unrealistic "anytime, anywhere" criterion (working long hours) for recognized managerial performance cannot be reconciled with the burden of a working manager/working mother.

Male-dominated organizations by definition lack appropriate female role models, mentors, and sponsors (that normally lead to promotions). The lack of role models is perceived as a barrier by 64% of women in the United States.[x] Similarly, the managerial skills nurtured by mentoring, sadly lacking in these organizations, creates the perception that women are not adequately prepared for managerial responsibility.[y]

Issue-Specific Rebuttals:

- **Concession:** For the first argument, the limited merit of a different point of view is conceded. Gender is not a prerequisite for superior managerial skills but is

under-rated, ignored, or disparaged by those unfamiliar with the research in neurobiology and business. Also, exceptions to the claim that "women make superior managers" are known to occur in the workplace. However, the counter-claim was not stated regarding how many women managers (%) behave in this fashion, how often dysfunctional behaviors occur (%), or to what extent the different characterizations are demonstrably true. Furthermore, there is no compelling evidence that women engage in counterproductive managerial behavior with greater frequency than male managers. Without evidence for those assertions, the opposition based its case on simplistic generalizations. An inadequate number of cases or the lack of objective observation or systematic investigation undoubtedly drives such generalizations. Thus, their contentions are equivalent to hearsay.

- **Refutation:** The opposition's second counter-argument addresses the disparity between education and the opportunity to reach the highest levels of executive leadership and pay. It does not address the claim that women do not possess characteristics that make "superior managers." Furthermore, being a superior manager (at several levels) is not synonymous with rising to the level of a Fortune 500 CEO or board member.

- **Relevance:** The third counter-argument has no connection to the claim. There are many statistics about women from entry level to executive positions but those mentioned in the counter-argument are restricted to a class of affluent, high-achieving women who (1) may or may not be in managerial positions, (2) who may or may not possess the characteristics of superior managers (e.g., they might be technically trained professionals in law, medicine, education, or government), and (3) they may or may not return to work at a later time, create a start-up, or change career aspirations. In short, the counter-argument is irrelevant.

Weighing: Two of five criteria can be applied to this case.

- (*Problem Scope*) Problems for women in the workforce, notwithstanding their slow rise in management, are global. The participation rate fell from 52% in 1995 to 49% in 2015.[z] The odds of women's participation remain 30% less than a man's.[aa] The claim is inherently interwoven with past discrimination and does not end with the argument about gender superiority in management. Its tentacles reach into equal pay, working mothers, lack of advocates (not just role models), and the fact that despite leadership training helping women, it helps men more.[bb]

- (*Time Frame*) When we consider women managers, "at the current rate of change, it will take until 2085 for women to reach parity with men in *leadership roles* in our country."[cc]

Discussion Questions

1. What assumptions have been made in this argument?[dd] What do those assumptions tell you about the intended audience? (Consider: What are the sources of information? Who would read or discuss it? Does the argument identify important data or does it assume you are familiar with them? Does the argument use credible sources? If so, does it name them or assume you recognize them?)

2. What is the argument asserting? Can you identify explicit and implicit claims? (Consider: What does the argument want

you to do? Feel a strong emotion? Change your opinions or attitudes? Strengthen a pre-existing belief?)

3. On what grounds? If the data (evidence, grounds) are not explicitly presented, can you think of any data that might make the argument more persuasive? (Consider: Are the data concrete and credible? Or does the argument simply ask you to make assumptions?)

4. Is there a qualifier? (Consider: Does the argument limit the strength of the argument or statements by proposing the conditions or a context under which the argument is true? Will the argument only hold in certain situations, for certain individuals? Do the argument's qualifiers add limits, nuances, or specificity to the claim, helping to counter rebuttals?)

5. What is the warrant? (Consider: Does it demonstrate the connection between data and claim by creating a bridge that shows *why* the evidence supports the claim and makes it true? Of the several classes of warrants, which type is this: generalization, sign, authority, analogy, causality, or principle?)

6. What rebuttals could you make? (Consider: Do you have questions that the evidence or warrant has not answered? What issues might lead you to question the claim? Can you produce counter-arguments to the claim by suggesting reasons why it lacks credible evidence, significance, or is not reasonable or realistic? If you are convinced by the claim, can you refute counter-arguments to the claim with an issue-specific rebuttal? Select any of the following to demonstrate how you would do so: concession, refutation, relevance, or weighing.)

7. What backing is required to justify the claim and convince the reader or listener?

(Continued)

(Continued)

(Consider: Does the claim provide any evidence that it is true? Does the backing support the truth of the warrant? Does the backing contain statistics, quotations, reports, findings, physical evidence, or other data? What support would the argument need to include to counter your rebuttals?)

---

[a]Toulmin, Stephen E., *The Uses of Argument*, updated ed. (Cambridge, UK: Cambridge University Press, 2003), 90.

[b]National Speech and Debate Association, "2016–2017 Policy Debate Topic Announced," SpeechandDebate.org, retrieved March 8, 2016.

[c]Wilson, G. Peter, and Carolyn R. Wilson, "The Toulmin Model of Argumentation" [Original authors; modified by D. Cooper], NavigatingAccounting.com, November 2016, Creative Commons BY-NC-SA: 1, http://www .navigatingaccounting.com/sites/default/files/Posted/ Common/Resources_web_book/Toulmin_Model_of_ Argumentation.pdf.

[d]Toulmin, 90.

[e]Ibid., 91.

[f]Wilson, 2.

[g]Toulmin, 92.

[h]Ibid., 93.

[i]Wilson, 3.

[j]Ibid., 4.

[k]Toulmin, 94.

[l]Wilson, 3.

[m]Quinn, Simon, *Debating in the World Schools Style: A Guide* (New York: International Debate Education Association, 2009), http://archive.idebate.org/content/debating- worlds-school-style-guide.

[n]Bhargava, Nikhil, "The Art of Debate- An Intro to LD" (Lincoln-Douglas style debating), last edited June 1, 2011, https://sites.google.com/site/anintroductiontodebate/home.

[o] Gallup Inc., "State of the American Manager: Analytics and Advice for Leaders," *Gallup*, April 2, 2015, http://www.gallup .com/services/182216/state-american-manager-report.aspx.

[p]Sherwin, Bob, "Why Women are More Effective Leaders Than Men," *Business Insider*, January 24, 2014, http://www .businessinsider.com/study-women-are-better-leaders-2014-1.

[q]Ibid.

[r]Bureau of Labor Statistics, Current Population Survey, "Table 11: Employed Persons by Detailed Occupation, Sex, Race, and Hispanic or Latino Ethnicity," *Household Data Annual Averages 2015*, last modified January 19, 2018, https://www.bls.gov/cps/cpsaat11.htm.

[s]Warner, Judith, "Fact Sheet: The Women's Leadership Gap," Center for American Progress, March 7, 2014, https://www.americanprogress.org/issues/women/ reports/2014/03/07/85457/fact-sheet-the-womens- leadership-gap/.

[t]Akbari, Anna, "Why Women Don't Want a Female Boss," *Dailyworth*, January 20, 2015, https://www.dailyworth. com/posts/3253-why-women-don-t-want-a-female-boss.

[u]Warner, Judith, "Women's Leadership: What's True, What's False, and Why It Matters," *Center for American Progress*, March 7, 2014, https://www.americanprogress. org/issues/women/reports/2014/03/07/85467/womens- leadership/.

[v]Ibid.

[w]Pew Research Center, "Women and Leadership: Public Says Women are Equally Qualified, but Barriers Persist," *Pew Research Center Social & Demographic Trends*, January 14, 2015, http://www.pewsocialtrends. org/2015/01/14/women-and-leadership/.

[x]Catalyst and The Conference Board, "Women in Leadership: A European Business Imperative," Catalyst, June 15, 2002, http://www.catalyst.org/knowledge/ women-leadership-european-business-imperative.

[y]Warner, "Fact Sheet."

[z]International Labour Office, *Women at Work: Trends 2016* (Geneva: International Labour Organization, 2016), http:// www.ilo.org/wcmsp5/groups/public/---dgreports/--- dcomm/---publ/documents/publication/wcms_457317.pdf.

[aa]World Economic Forum, "Ten Years of the Global Gender Gap," published 2016, http://reports.weforum.org/global- gender-gap-report-2015/report-highlights/.

[bb]Frank, Lydia, "How the Gender Pay Gap Widens as Women Get Promoted," *Harvard Business Review*, November 5, 2015, https://hbr.org/2015/11/how-the- gender-pay-gap-widens-as-women-get-promoted.

[cc]Warner, "Fact Sheet."

[dd]Some questions are adapted from this suggested reading: Ramage, John, D., John C. Bean, and June Johnson. *Writing Arguments: A Rhetoric with Readings*, 10th ed. (Boston: Pearson, 2015).

Chapter Summary

- The researcher's essential tools were explained to include the scientific method and its "influence" on the conduct of research. The scientific method is a system for originating and developing knowledge and makes a practical and valuable contribution to science. The theme was that the "doing" of scientific research is not a series of steps; it is a way of thinking about the study of phenomena from diverse perspectives. The method of science is a process of inquiry.

- The scientific method is more than a recipe—it is a mindset. Whereas method implies an algorithm for answering questions, a trained mind possesses a talent for asking them. Curiosity and suspicion characterize this scientific mindset.

- Four types of argument for reasoning to sound conclusions are deduction, induction, abduction, and Toulmin's Model of Argumentation.

  - Deduction is a form of reasoning that purports to be conclusive—the conclusions must necessarily follow from the reasons (premises) given. The conclusion is contained in the truth of the premises and represents a proof if the premises are true and the form of reasoning is valid (i.e., premises must be arranged in a proper form).

  - Induction draws a conclusion from one or more particulars (particular facts or pieces of evidence). The premises are intended to be strong enough that if they were true, it would be *improbable* that you would produce a false conclusion. The conclusion explains the facts and the facts support the conclusion.

  - Abduction is a form of logical inference in which one chooses the hypothesis that would best explain the relevant evidence if that evidence were true. Abductive reasoning begins with a set of accepted facts and infers the simplest, most probable, or best explanation. Whereas true premises and a valid form guarantee a true conclusion in deduction, inductive and abductive premises do not.

  - The Toulmin Model of Argumentation and reasoning was proposed as being especially useful *to students of research methods because it is highly versatile in structuring the arguments in a study's report.* It involves six components that evaluate the pros and cons of an argument and the effectiveness of rebuttals. The first three follow the practice of making a claim, supporting that claim with data, and backing the data or evidence with a warrant—all are present in every argument. Three additional elements of Toulmin's model include a backing (for the warrant), rebuttals, and qualifier(s) that may be added as necessary.

- I defined, explained, and provided examples of the terms (and their variations) that researchers use every day: concepts, constructs, definitions, variables, hypotheses, and theory.

Key Terms

abduction	empirical testing	premise
backing (Toulmin)	explanatory or causal	proposition
categorical or classificatory	hypothesis	qualifier (Toulmin)
variable	extraneous variable	ratio variable
claim (Toulmin)	hypothesis	rebuttal (Toulmin)
concept	independent variable (IV)	relational hypothesis
construct	induction	research hypothesis
continuous variable	interval variable	scientific method
control variable	intervening variable (IVV)	statistical null hypothesis
correlational hypothesis	measurement	theory
criterion variable	moderating variable (MV)	Toulmin Model (reasoning/
data (Toulmin)	nominal scale	argumentation)
deduction	operational definition	variable
dependent variable (DV)	ordinal (ranking) variable	warrant (Toulmin)
descriptive hypothesis	polytomous (multicategory)	
dichotomous variable	variable	
discrete variable	predictor variable	

Discussion Questions

1. What are the characteristics (tenets) of the scientific method?

    a. Is the scientific method synonymous with empiricism?

    b. Does the notion of scientific inquiry being "a series of steps or a recipe" seem like a wrong-headed assumption?

    c. Apply the Reflective Inquiry diagram (Exhibit 2.1) to a business problem from one of your courses in finance, accounting, management, or marketing.

2. Describe the reasoning process using a simple research inquiry of how you would apply deduction, induction, and abduction.

    a. Differentiate the role of premises and conclusions in deduction versus those in induction and abduction.

    b. How are induction and abduction different?

3. How does the Toulmin Model of reasoning help you prepare written and oral arguments to support a case?

    a. Define the three main components of the Toulmin Model. How do the three additional components work and what are they for?

    b. Assume you read four journal articles in organizational behavior on motivation. Develop a brief Toulmin Model to use the information you obtained as evidence (data) to support a conclusion (claim) that you want to make on the motivation of employees. Add the warrant, which shows *why* the evidence supports the claim and makes it true. Go to the example following Exhibit 2.6 if you need a template.

4. The language of research is unique just like medical terms or those in physics. Use any

of your courses to provide an example of the following:

a. concept

b. construct

c. dictionary definition

d. operational definition

e. variable

f. hypothesis

g. proposition

h. theory

5. Differentiate between the four levels of measurement and explain whether as you move from nominal to ratio variables, you accumulate more or less powerful measurement characteristics.

a. On what scale would you measure your age, level of progress in the university (e.g., junior), level of satisfaction with the business curriculum, or the price-to-earnings ratio?

b. What is the difference between a discrete and continuous variable?

c. What are the various types of discrete variables?

6. Construct an example of a hypothesis or research question containing an independent variable, dependent variable, intervening variable, control variable, and moderating variable.

7. Explain the difference between a descriptive, relational, and explanatory hypothesis.

8. Find an article that provides an example of a practical *theory* that most executives would want to read.

©iStockphoto.com/DNY59

3

THE PROCESS
ROAD MAP

Exploring and Planning

LEARNING OBJECTIVES

Performance Objective

Chart a course to *explore* a topic for a term project with emphasis on the problem's origin, selection, and articulation—as a managerial/academic research question(s)—through exploration, and refinement. Continue *planning* by constructing a literature review, stating hypotheses, identifying variables, and exploring viable designs.

Enabling Objectives

1. Provide examples of how the exploring phase of the research process helps you choose a topic, state the research question, formulate narrower investigative questions, and adjust the scope.

2. Itemize the benefits of various exploratory tools to refine your research question and help you determine what you need to secure answers.

3. Explain the procedures for completing an extensive review of the literature in preparation for establishing the argument for your study's viability.

4. State a hypothesis that reflects the aims of your proposed study.

5. Describe the different circumstances where nonexperimental (quantitative or qualitative), experimental, or mixed designs would be optimal.

The business research process is an essential tool that managers use to make decisions and formulate strategies. Students of management and other business disciplines discover that the research process is a critical component in their skill set because it is the primary approach by which they conduct research and complete a project or research paper. It is also a framework for brainstorming, creating, and conducting studies that keep organizations from being outmaneuvered by their competitors.

PHASES OF THE RESEARCH PROCESS

Business research is a process involving several defined phases. Most writers are content to introduce a few activities and let you figure out the transitions and details. The **research process** presented here consists of seven phases: exploring, planning, creating, conducting, collecting, analyzing, and writing. There are *17 activities* or specific elements associated with assembling the various aspects of your research. The **elements of the research process** reflect tasks and decisions that all researchers must make in "doing" research from start to finish. The specificity is practical; it means you can develop a diary or notebook and check off activities you have completed or use your notes to seek more in-depth answers to questions that require greater detail. I refer you to Exhibit 1.3 in Chapter 1, which contains the "Road Map" for this guide.

This chapter covers the departure phase of your journey: *exploring* and *planning*. Chapter 4 describes *creating* and *conducting*. Chapter 5 explains the trek through the numbers, *collecting, analyzing and interpreting*, and then *writing* on what you have found. An overview of the structure of academic, Institutional Review Board (IRB), and business *proposals* sets you up for Chapter 9. Chapter 9 is extremely practical and the culmination of the topics covered up to that point. It examines each section of the research paper and provides examples of how to write each one. Chapter 9 is longer than the other chapters, but that is because it includes over 26 illustrations and even more textual examples.

At the beginning of Chapters 3, 4, and 5, a process diagram orients you to your location on the Road Map and highlights the activities to be covered (see Exhibits 3.1 and 3.2 for examples). When you look at the details, you may feel overwhelmed because you think there are too many elements. Allow me to remind you of something I said in the Preface. So-called baby steps, as they are called in popular psychology, are used with legitimate exposure therapy to reduce stress and anxiety. The scientific research on anxiety reduction is authentic. In studies of how humans evaluate risks, we frequently fail to assess the level of a threat accurately. "We tend to over-personalize risk and to experience an unrealistic sense of peril when we hear or read of a bad event occurring to someone else."[1] This will not happen to you if you remember one piece of advice: allow one step to build upon another. Just take them one at a time and soon it becomes intuitive. Before you know it, you will have mastered 17 activities that give you a comprehensive learning experience in doing research.

Don't assume you must follow the steps in exactly the order presented. It is not necessary to finish each step before going to the next. Recycling and skipping occur. Some researchers begin activities out of sequence, some are carried out simultaneously, and some may be omitted. According to Turabian, "Researchers regularly think ahead to future steps as they work through earlier ones and revisit earlier steps as they deal with a later one."[2] Variations are normal for different research purposes, audiences, and *your sty*le but as stated by Booth et al., "[No] matter how carefully you plan, research follows a crooked path, taking unexpected turns, sometimes up blind alleys, even looping back on itself. . . . When you can manage its parts, you can manage the often intimidating whole and look forward to doing more research with greater confidence."[3]

In this text, I view the predominant activity of the research process as problem oriented. This mirrors a statement by Albert Einstein:

EXHIBIT 3.1 ■ The Research Process: Exploring and Planning

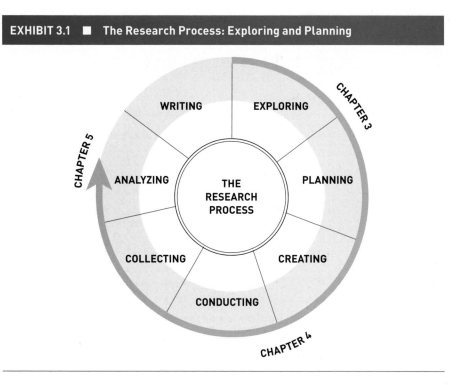

The formulation of a problem is far more often essential than its solution, which may be merely a matter of mathematical or experimental skill. To raise new questions, new possibilities, to regard old problems from a new angle requires creative imagination and marks real advance in science.[4]

That includes the problem's origin, selection, statement, exploration, and refinement. It is important to note that without an explicitly stated, relevant problem, there are not enough corrective strategies that design, method, sampling, data collection, or any other component can use to save you. Thus, problem-oriented elements in the process model get expanded coverage with the added benefit of getting you started confidently. The problem and its literature are emphasized in this chapter and in the final chapter on report writing because they often require extra explanation. Whether your focus is managerial or academic, a thorough understanding of the problem is central to a successful study.

The *exploring* phase is first in Chapter 3. Other phases of the research process follow the arrow and represent the direction for Chapters 4 and 5. Each of the three chapters has a similar graphic. All of the phases of the research process with their elements or activities are shown in Exhibit 3.2.

EXHIBIT 3.2 ■ Research Process Elements		
Chapter	**Phase**	**Elements/Activities**
3	Exploring	1. Choose a business research topic.
		2. State the management or academic research question.
		3. Formulate the investigative questions.
		4. Explore data sources to refine your question and adjust its scope.
	Planning	5. Prepare to solve ethical dilemmas.
		6. Complete an extensive literature review.
		7. Formulate hypotheses and operationalize variables.
		8. Select a research design.
4	Creating	9. Match an efficient method/technique with the design.
		10. Identify or create the measuring instruments.
		11. Implement a sampling plan.
	Conducting	12. Recruit research participants ethically.
		13. Prepare a proposal (academic, IRB protocol, or business).
		14. Conduct a pilot study.
5	Collecting	15. Collect and process the data.
	Analyzing	16. Analyze and interpret the data.
	Writing	17. Write the research report.

PROCESS PHASE 1: EXPLORING

The *exploring* phase of the research process model (Exhibit 3.2) encompasses four elements:

- Choose a business research topic.

- State the management or academic research question.

- Formulate the investigative questions.

- Explore data sources to refine your question and adjust its scope.

Choose a Business Research Topic

The research process begins with exploring a topic. When you start from the beginning without the advantage of an idea or a suggestion from your professor or a requirement from your manager, the first step is to find a topic worth exploring. Here are seven actions to take:

1. Search for topics until you find one of great interest to you and others.

2. Find a limited, focused, and precise topic that allows you to assemble a reasonable amount of information within the prescribed time.

3. Select an achievable topic, one that has a level of difficulty appropriate for your skills.

4. Find topics that are relevant to your functional area of business, such as marketing, management, finance, human resources, strategy, international, and others.

5. Compare possible topics with the course guidelines for your term project or manager's requirements.

6. Determine the evidence your readers will expect. Will they want facts from secondary sources, primary sources, or both? Will they expect quantitative or qualitative data?

7. Determine whether you can find those data.[5]

Topic identification is challenging. First, there are vast ranges of topics to be scanned, and many do not reflect management dilemmas in companies or industries. Second, you must choose from among academic research (basic), practical-managerial research (action-oriented), and research on immediate real-world problems (applied). Students should identify several topics initially so that some may be screened out by preliminary elimination and narrowed to one problem after those remaining have been evaluated using the above criteria. Several online sources are useful for this purpose:

*   Harvard Business School's "Working Knowledge" website identifies over 60 topics, each with numerous titles based on the research of their faculty (http://hbswk.hbs.edu/Pages/browse.aspx?HBSTopic=Communication).

*   EBSCO, a leading provider of online research databases and reference services, provides topics used as research "starters." They represent a review of course materials at 25 universities. Eighteen major subject areas list as many as 76 subtopics in each section (http://support.ebsco.com/knowledge_base/detail .php?id=4220).

- The Stanford Graduate School of Business Library website has online journals, e-books, working papers, and case studies. Their eight topic–based research guide offers a wealth of information (https://www.gsb.stanford.edu/library/conduct-research/topic-guides).

- UCLA's Anderson School of Management allows you to browse research topics alphabetically (http://www.anderson.ucla.edu/rosenfeld-library/business-topics).

- The Oxford University Press Online Resource Centre offers ideas for research topics in 15 categories, each with sample problem statements (http://global.oup.com/uk/orc/busecon/business/harrison2e/student/research_updates/ch06/).

Topics to Avoid

Specific topics to avoid are so numerous as to defy an inventory. However, there are characteristics of problems that should raise red flags for student researchers. Some problem descriptions are complex, value laden, and bound by constraints making them intractable to traditional forms of analysis. This class of problems, so-called **ill-defined problems**, ill-structured problems, or messy problems, are those in which "rules may or may not exist, and nobody tells you whether they do, or what they are. You have to figure all that out for yourself."[6] They contrast with well-defined problems, which have specific goals, clearly defined solution paths, and clear expected solutions.[7] One responds to a well-structured problem with a right answer but to an ill-structured problem with a claim and a justifying argument.[8]

> A notable example of this class of problems is entrepreneurship. An entrepreneur can enter any market she wishes with any product she can develop. Her competitors may respond in an infinite number of ways, and she can only guess how her customers will react. If the entrepreneur doesn't understand her market, she may build a solution to a problem that her market doesn't have. So, for every unit of effort that the entrepreneur puts into moving the company forward, she must also dedicate a unit of time into understanding the rules of the market, and deciding which way forward is. This extra work is a sort of overhead, which is intrinsic in ill-defined problems, but not in well-defined problems.[9]

Thus, you must consider a research topic's feasibility given your resources. Examine the amount of time, cost, method complexity, institutional review hurdles, participant cooperation, data analysis, your statistical sophistication, and your instructor's advice before you leave well-defined problems behind.

State the Management or Academic Research Question

Visualize a pyramid with the research question on the top followed by investigative questions and measurement questions at the bottom. This "pyramid of questions" has three levels moving from general to specific. **Measurement questions** are those we ask the participants in the study using various instruments or devices. For example, in a survey, the measurement questions appear as items in the questionnaire or interview guide. In an observational study, they may take the form of a checklist that observers answer about each participant studied. Measurement questions come up later when I discuss planning and conducting the study (specifically, measuring instruments and the pilot study).

©iStockphoto.com/SergeyNivens

Does the managerial question represent a problem, opportunity, or evaluation? A poorly defined managerial question will move the research off target and result in you becoming lost in the maze.

Managerial Questions

A **managerial question** represents a type of research question associated with business decisions that managers must make. Since the definition of a management problem determines the research task, you must decide if the dilemma facing management is a problem, opportunity, or evaluation of an existing program. A poorly defined management problem will be improperly translated into a question that misdirects the research effort.

The business environment has required organizations to adapt to dramatic changes in the social and political requirements of public policy, technology growth, and innovations in global communications, particularly the Internet and social media. Each change has created new research issues for managers. The complexity of the environment has increased the risks associated with bad decisions, making sound information more valuable.

There are at least four decision categories into which business decisions fall:

- Choice of purposes or objectives

- Generation and evaluation of solutions

- Troubleshooting and control

- The organizational environment

EXHIBIT 3.3   ■   Managerial Decision-Making Categories

Decision Issue	General Question	Managerial Question
Choice of purposes or objectives	What do we want to achieve?	What goals do we want to achieve in the next labor negotiation?
Generation and evaluation of solutions	How can we achieve the ends we seek?	How can we achieve our 5-year goal of doubled sales?
Troubleshooting and control	Why does that unit have lower sales volumes?	Why are the most profitable products or services declining in units sold?
Organizational environment	Who are prospective acquisition targets?	What is the market share held by the acquisition target compared to the size of the market?

Exhibit 3.3 summarizes the categories with examples of general questions and specific management questions.

When a research consultant was asked to help the new management of a bank, the executives were concerned with the bank's stagnating profits. The discussion led to a consensus on the problem as improving the profit picture or "How can we enhance our profit picture?" This implies that management faces the task of developing a strategy for increasing deposits and therefore profits. Although this was a broad but useful starting point, a further discussion led to two issues to solve. While weak deposit growth directly affected profits (competitive concerns), another profit weakness was the harmful organizational culture within the bank. Clarification of management's problem provided clarity for a subsequent statement of the research and investigative questions.

Academic Questions

Academic research is the primary activity of institutional researchers, professors, and graduate students. It aims to test an aspect of a theory or to expand the domain of a theory. Academic research typically results in convention papers, journal articles, grant proposals, reports, or books designed to advance scientific knowledge in the field. The researcher's work product can take months or years to complete before peer review and publishing. However, applied academic questions have a different focus. When directed toward an applied business problem, it is not intended to advance scientific knowledge (although it may), the process is not as lengthy, and the objective falls closer to understanding the problem before taking action.

Your research project will often begin from a class assignment, whereas much of academic research develops within the bounds of a theoretical framework. For scholars of organizational theory, the question might be, "Of the primary characteristics of workforce diversity (age, gender, race, national origin, disability, and sexual orientation), which constitute reasons for the organizational success of diversity initiatives?" The student's research question may address an issue in an educational setting: "How do undergraduate and graduate business students differ on the ethical research concerns of informed consent, confidentiality, and privacy of participants?" Both academic and managerial questions attempt to answer a question or solve a problem. Exhibit 3.4 demonstrates a sample student formulation of a research problem.

EXHIBIT 3.4 ■ A Student's Formulation of a Research Problem

Problem Setting

When the top management team of Matrix Inc. formulated the company's strategic planning objectives 2 years ago, they expressed concerns that their sales forecasting model was not working efficiently. Management realized that there was a gap between applications and what is desirable and attainable to select the most efficient methodology to meet its sales forecasting objectives.

During this time, inefficient inventory levels and inaccurate production schedules resulted from short- and long-term sales forecasts. In addition, workforce forecasting for manufacturing and sales and the allocation of resources to marketing programs suffered. Therefore, top management asked the marketing group to investigate this problem. It allocated funds to the marketing budget to cover the cost of research for selecting the most practical solution for the company. Recommendations from marketing management to improve existing sales forecasting methodology are forthcoming.

Research Questions

1. Are the characteristics of the sales forecasting model at Matrix directly responsible for the observed dysfunctions in short- and long-term forecasts during the past 2 years? If so, is the system salvageable?

2. What are the industry's "best practices" in forecasting sales?

Investigative Question 1

a. How accurate is Matrix's present sales forecasting model?

b. What are the costs and benefits of reconfiguring the existing forecasting system at Matrix?

Investigative Question 2

a. What is the best framework for classifying the range of alternative forecasting models and their characteristics?

b. How accurate and effective are various models of sales forecasting in the electronics industry?

c. What are the most important factors to consider when selecting a sales forecasting model for Matrix's particular situation?

Research Problems Versus Research Questions

A **research problem** is a fact-oriented, information gathering statement of what you would like to investigate or study quantitatively or qualitatively. The problem represents "those tantalizing, enigmatical, unresolved roadblocks to knowledge and human progress for which no answer has yet been found."[10]

The **research question** is the single question that best states the objective of the research study in a clear and focused way. A well-written research question not only guides the project with clarity and precision but also alludes to measurable outcomes and helps construct a logical argument for the study. Many researchers use the terms problem and question interchangeably, but it is helpful to be precise.

The research *question* is not the same as the **research topic**, which is broader. One author uses an example of the topic "the internationalization of German engineering companies." Unlike the topic, the research problem may be translated into a specific question: "What causes German engineering companies to internationalize?"[11] Problems and questions in research are virtually identical in purpose except for the interrogative form. Leedy and Ormrod stated that a *research problem* is ". . . carefully phrased and represents the single goal of the total research effort."[12] They also said that *subproblems* (investigative questions) "can break down the problem into smaller units. . . . Sometimes in the form of specific questions—that are easier to address and resolve."[13] This is consistent with our discussion in Chapter 1 on how investigative questions reflect the critical parts or *facets* of the original problem that will be the basis for hypotheses and are used to identify key variables in the study.

Framing the Research Question

Research questions begin with interrogative words. Exhibit 3.5 illustrates common question words used in research and how they direct the inquiry.[14]

These questions serve to orient the research but should be paired with topic-related content. Yeager[15] uses Norris and Moon's article on government adoption of IT innovations[16] to provide an excellent demonstration of how questions evolve. Yeager *speculates* on the types of questions the authors might have asked.

1. *How rapidly do governments adopt IT applications?*

Comment: This question is too broad to be useful. Replace vague words, such as government and IT, with specific terms such as type of government and type of IT. (At this point, they discover that the International City/County Management Association collects longitudinal data on IT and e-government from cities with populations greater than 20,000.)

EXHIBIT 3.5 ■ The Question and Its Focus	
Question	**Focus of the Research**
Who	Participants, audience
What	Classification, specification
Where	Setting, location, environment
When	Time, context, sequence, trend
How	Action, process, method, operation
Why	Reason, cause, stimulus, temporal order, covariance, explanation
Can	Possibility, likelihood, probability
Do	Performance, action
Which	Comparison

2. *How rapidly do local governments adopt e-government applications that have demonstrated payoffs?*

Comment: The second question remains vague without specifics on "rapidly" and the types of payoffs.

3. *Why are local government adoption rates for e-government applications that have proven to work successfully in other cities faster than adoption rates of other e-government applications?*

Comment: This question is wordy but does narrow the focus with a comparison: adoption rates of e-government applications associated with degrees of success in other cities.

4. *Why does city size impact the adoption of e-government portal capability?*

Comment: Now, the importance of operationalization of definitions becomes apparent (see Chapter 2 and the section in this chapter entitled "Formulate Hypotheses and Operationalize Variables"). For example, how do you measure city size, impact, and e-government portal capability? The definitions prove crucial to refining the question.

5. *Does city size impact the adoption of the following e-government transactions?*

Comment: Which transactions? Here the researchers have reached a junction. They can either develop investigative questions (as described in the next section) or further refine the research question. To use investigative questions, they would need a series of questions to cover various transactional services (e.g., "Does city size impact the adoption of permit applications and renewal transactions through a web portal?"). With a single measure that operationalizes "transaction portal capabilities" using a scale, another research question could be asked.

6.   *Does city size (percent of budget spent on IT) impact the adoption of e-government transaction portal capabilities (TPC scale)?*

In the next section, I will help you specify the criteria for testing the quality of your subproblems/investigative questions.

Formulate the Investigative Questions

Investigative question(s) are those that the research must answer satisfactorily in order to respond to the general research question. In breaking down the research question into specific parts for gathering data, we continue to narrow progressively to more precise questions. Consider the following suggestions when developing your investigative questions:

1.   Each investigative question should be a separate subproject within the larger research question.

2.   Each investigative question should be stated to imply collection and interpretation of the data.

3.   The investigative questions should address all facets of the research question but not exceed its boundaries.

4.   The number of investigative questions should be manageable and fall between two and six.[17]

Do you recall the bank example in which a research consultant was asked to help the new management? The consultant developed two research questions about how weak deposit growth directly affected profits (competitive concerns) and how negative factors within the bank (organizational culture) weakened profits. The first research question on competitive issues produced two investigative questions targeting profitability. Several subquestions under these two investigative questions would provide additional insights into the direction of the research:

1.   *What are the potential customers' perceptions of financial services and their use?*

    a.   What financial services do customers use?

    b.   What financial services do customers desire?

c. What factors influence a customer's choice of a particular service?

d. How appealing are our bank's services compared to the services of the competition?

2. *What is the bank's competitive position?*

a. What is the geographic location of our customers and competitors' customers?

b. What demographic differences do our customers reveal in comparison to our competitors?

c. What differences in services do we provide versus our competitors?

d. What is the awareness of our bank's promotional efforts?

e. How does service growth compare among competing banks?

f. What impressions do potential customers hold of our bank compared to the competition?

Explore Data Sources to Refine Your Question and Adjust Its Scope

Exploration is an influential element in the research process because it has an unrecognized but enormous impact on the success of the study. Refining your research question is crucial. Searching *secondary data sources* (existing data originally collected by others) is a purposeful activity in your quest to collect background information on your topic; it also creates a useful source of quality control. The sources you find will influence the selection of design, instruments, and data analysis for the project.

At the outset, it is a good idea to consider the scope of your research question. A broad question makes topic coverage challenging within the time available for your project; a narrow topic puts pressure on you to find enough sources to produce the depth you need for your literature review. Here are some criteria for judging both issues.

A question is too broad when:

- Its scope exceeds the coverage of your project's guidelines and required detail.

- You find yourself writing too many general statements about general subjects.

- The volume of sources is so great that it is hard to screen for relevance.

A question is too narrow when:

- It can be covered briefly in precise detail in less than the required length of your paper or the customary length of a management report for your organization.

An unstructured exploration of the literature allows you to refine the research question using books, journal articles, government documents, annual reviews, e-books, web pages, blogs, and other sources. This refines your statement of the question and helps you determine if sources contain the answers to the proposed research. Evaluate each source carefully for accuracy, authority, objectivity, currency, and coverage. See Exhibit 3.6.

- It's hard to research because there is little information from scholarly peer-reviewed sources.

- You find mostly familiar sources (general news, business, and entertainment publications). And Wikipedia seems to have more content than anything you have found (Wikipedia's quality control is suspect).[18]

An **unstructured or exploratory literature review** allows you to refine the research question and determine what you need to secure answers to the proposed research. Typically, the process begins with an exploratory literature review (as opposed to a refined literature review)[19] that reveals terminology and contribution areas (books, journal articles, white papers, government documents, annual reviews, statistical databases, and annotated bibliographic sources). Screen these and other references for relevance to your research question, whether managerial or academic. As Exhibit 3.6 shows, screening evaluates sources with the following criteria: accuracy, authority, objectivity, currency, and coverage for books, journal articles, e-books, web pages, blogs, and video and audio recordings. Your review also serves a dual purpose: it helps to refine the question and compile resources for your paper's literature review.

An exploratory analysis takes advantage of different search approaches. For example, the "citation pearl searching" approach starts with a stimulus article like a class reading, author citation or ideas for further study in a textbook, or perhaps your business librarian's suggestions. Using the references, start to assemble a literature base. "Using citation tracking tools like the 'Web of Science' or 'Scopus' you should be able to amass many writings related to the original work including articles cited by the original author and articles that cite the original author."[20]

Another approach for exploratory literature searches is an article that serves as a "stand-alone literature review." These reviews provide state-of-knowledge synopses of your chosen topic with sources that are current and historically significant. In addition, they create powerful insights for writing your formal literature review by revealing gaps in scientific knowledge, methodological weaknesses, and disagreements. Reviews allow you to position your research objective in the context of what is known about the topic. An example of a stand-alone review article in human resources covering a 40-year period is entitled "Diversity in Organizations: Where Are We Now and Where Are We Going?"[21] The journal series *Annual Reviews* is another resource dedicated to literature review articles.[22]

	Print	Web
EXHIBIT 3.6 ■ Evaluating Information Resources		
Accuracy	• Accuracy is the highest priority for research on any research topic. • Data and information must be based on specific observations, measurements, analyses, interpretations, and conclusions. • Are the research methods explained so that results could be reproduced? • Are conclusions based on research that can be verifiable in other sources? • Are sources listed in foot/endnotes, bibliographies, or reference lists? Are they reliable? • Does the article appear in a scholarly journal that is peer reviewed?	• A website that appears "professional" is not sufficient evidence to conclude that the information provided is accurate. • Are the sources for factual information clearly referenced so they can be verified in another source? A page without references may illustrate the ideas of an individual, organization, or business but may not be a source of factual information. • Has the content been edited or peer reviewed? Is it generally well written? High-quality writing, format, grammar, spelling, and punctuation enhance the appearance of accuracy and give the reader confidence in the web document.
Authority	• Who is the author? • What are his or her credentials (education, other publications, professional affiliations, or experience)? • Does the author represent a particular point of view? • Does the author represent specific gender, sexual, racial, political, social, and/or cultural orientations? • Has the author been cited in other bibliographies? • Can you contact the author?	• Who is responsible for the contents of the page (author or webmaster)? • What are the author's qualifications on this topic? Can you find references to the author elsewhere? • In the case of web material from committees, organizations, businesses, or government agencies (rather than individuals), can you verify the legitimacy of the organization, group, or company? • Are the sources known to be reliable, objective, and carefully researched or are they biased toward a particular cause, movement, or agenda? • Is the publication referenced elsewhere?
Objectivity	• Is the information sufficiently objective for your purpose or does it appear to contain bias? • Are other points of view explored? • When a biased presentation appears in scholarly research, is that bias described and weighed against alternative views or interpretations? • Is the source an educational resource? Does it strive to be objective?	• Check the domain name to help determine a possible slant or bias. A government website (.gov), such as the Food and Drug Administration, should describe the benefits of a drug more objectively than the manufacturer (.com). Does the site have economic value for the author or publisher? • Is it a personal website? Does it express personal opinions with objective sources and a reasoned tone? Does it present balanced information?

(Continued)

EXHIBIT 3.6 ■ (Continued)

	Print	Web
	• Does it fill any other personal, professional, or societal needs? • Is there advertising or are there requests for donations associated with the source?	• Is there a link to a page describing the goals of the sponsoring organization or company? A suspect article may reflect an extreme position of the sponsor. • Is advertising separated from informational content?
Currency	• Currency is important where new developments occur frequently. • When was the source first published? What version or edition of the source are you consulting? • Consider whether or not the timeliness of the information will affect its usefulness. Are there differences in editions, such as new introductions or footnotes? • When research results are given, consider not only the date of the publication but also when the research was conducted. • What has changed in your field of study since the publication date?	• Is the information you found up to date? Its appearance on the web is not a guarantee. • Look for the date of the material, (the "last updated" statement at the end of many documents). The "last updated" date given may differ from the currency of the content. • Be cautious of material from the site's archives. While they may be classic sources, the field may have advanced beyond them. • Are there any published reviews, responses, or rebuttals?
Coverage	• Does the information source adequately cover the topic? Documents may cover only part of the topic, and you may need more sources to have a thorough understanding. • Consider how coverage from one source compares with coverage from other sources. • Look for a statement describing the purpose or coverage of the source and consider if the information has depth and breadth sufficient for your needs. • Does the information source leave questions unanswered (ask the "five W's and H" to check: who, what, when, where, why, and how)?	• Consider the target audience for whom a page is written because it has a direct bearing on the site's coverage. Is the target audience identified and appropriate for your needs? • Are the topics addressed successfully with clearly presented arguments and adequate support and evidence? • Does the work you have found update other sources, substantiate materials you have read, or add new information? • Is the web page presenting a new perspective on the topic or just summarizing old sources? If it is the latter, find the originals.

Source: Adapted from "Evaluating Resources," University of California, Berkeley Library, last updated February 20, 2018, http://guides.lib.berkeley.edu/evaluating-resources; "How to Evaluate Website Content," University of Edinburgh Information Services, published July 4, 2017, https://www.ed.ac.uk/information-services/library-museum-gallery/finding-resources/library-databases/databases-overview/evaluating-websites; "Evaluating Information Resources," University of Alaska Fairbanks Elmer E. Rasmuson Library, last modified April 24, 2015, https://library.uaf.edu/ls101-evaluation; and "Evaluating Internet Sources: A Library Resource Guide," Northern Michigan University Lydia M. Olson Library, last updated August 29, 2017, https://library.nmu.edu/guides/userguides/webeval.htm#COVERAGE.

Although published data are a valuable resource for refining your question, they represent only a portion of the existing knowledge in a field. Another form of data is often useful to get a broad perspective on the topic. For example, when you interview people who are experienced or are experts on the topic to seek their ideas about important topical aspects or to discover what exists across the topic's range, this is called an **experience survey**.

Focus groups are unstructured interviews with six to twelve participants and are used in exploratory research and as a follow-up diagnostic tool. Focus groups are helpful in unstructured exploration to refine a problem

Focus groups are composed of a small number of people, led by a moderator in guided or open discussions, to examine a new product or topic. Members are asked about their opinions, attitudes, or beliefs about a concept, product, service, advertisement, or packaging. The results produce qualitative data that may or may not be representative of the general population.

and adjust its scope. However, they are less available to budget-conscious students and should not be used without group process experience or moderator training. Focus groups have been around since World War II, with applications in marketing, advertising, ergonomics, urban planning, and other areas. The technique collects information about opinions, attitudes, and beliefs toward products, services, advertising, and packaging.

Participants are selected using a nonprobability sample but usually not without consideration of demographic and psychographic characteristics of the group. Many experts believe that the participants in focus groups should be homogeneous:

> Homogeneous groups minimize the likelihood of intragroup disagreements and conflicts that may issue from gender, age, social status, and ethnic differences. But focus group samples that incorporate . . . market segment heterogeneity are likely to get to the heart of the matter more quickly.[23]

When ambiguity of the research question is low (e.g., concept testing), group member similarity is effective. However, as the research objective becomes more ambiguous and the topic moves farther out on the exploratory continuum, adding diversity to the group or even selecting a heterogeneous sample expands the array of suggestions or solutions.[24]

Focus groups have flexible design options. For example, the researcher can adjust the normality and comfort of the setting, the moderator's role in keeping the group on topic and interpreting nonverbal cues, and the media used for recording and data collection. These features allow focus groups to be tailored for different exploratory purposes.

The maverick business view on the value of focus groups disputes marketing research textbooks and the opinions of organizations that promote focus groups as a research

Steve Jobs talked to his biographer about focus groups and why they were not used at Apple: "People don't know what they want until you show it to them. . . . Our task is to read things that are not yet on the page." This coincides with a similar view of focus group output. People are very good at answering questions, even when they don't actually know the answer.

mainstay. Apple's chief design officer, (Sir) Jonathan "Jony" Ive, stated, "We don't do focus groups. They just ensure that you don't offend anyone, and produce bland inoffensive products."[25] On another occasion, Ive dismissed the idea, saying that what focus groups accomplish for Apple was the job of the designer: "It's unfair to ask people who don't have a sense of the opportunities of tomorrow from the context of today, to design."[26]

Of course, this was his late boss' philosophy. Steve Jobs is quoted in his biography in a characteristic retort:

> Some people say, "Give customers what they want." But that's not my approach. Our job is to figure out what they're going to want before they do. I think Henry Ford once said, "If I'd asked customers what they wanted, they would have told me, 'A faster horse!'" People don't know what they want until you show it to them. . . . Our task is to read things that are not yet on the page.[27]

You should investigate focus groups for yourself if you think they would be helpful to you. Although they have exploratory advantages, there are disadvantages (beyond cost) that affect their use: influence of the setting, participants echoing other members' ideas versus expanding on them, social desirability bias, preseeded ideas from sponsors to self-fulfill desired outcomes, groupthink, moderator experience and influence, group size, loudest voice domination, external validity, and the reactive effects of testing (see Chapter 8).

When you conclude your exploration using whatever tactic helps you get there, there are questions you can ask yourself that contribute to your success in writing the statement of your problem:

1. Are your concepts and constructs defined satisfactorily to reflect the literature? Have operational definitions been found? (See Chapter 2.)

2. Is it possible to break down the investigative questions with finer granularity?

3. If you plan to use hypotheses in place of research questions, do they meet the requirements mentioned in Chapter 2?

4. Have you outlined the evidence that must be collected to answer your questions? Does the content parallel your investigative questions?

5. Have you used your exploratory literature search to help draft the sections on importance and benefits of the study, delimitations that state what the research does not include, and limitations that predict expected flaws?

After you conduct an exploratory literature review and a brief study using experience surveys or other qualitative methods, the question begins to crystallize. With some questions, you move closer to an answer. In other situations, a different question emerges from the original one. Although the new question may not be materially different, it has evolved in some fashion with better focus to move the project forward.

PROCESS PHASE 2: PLANNING

The *planning* phase of the research process model (refer to Exhibit 3.2) contains four elements:

- Prepare to solve ethical dilemmas.

- Complete an extensive literature review.

- Formulate hypotheses and operationalize variables.

- Select a research design.

Prepare to Solve Ethical Dilemmas

The planning phase is a perfect time to discuss and reflect on your project with fellow students and your professor. You will discover that there are potential ethical dilemmas to resolve and one good way to sort them out is to listen to dissenting and supportive views, which go to the issues of compliance and integrity.

The regulatory aspects of ethics are considered in Chapter 4 (Phase 4, *conducting*), in which requirements of IRBs are described as a prelude to the ethical recruitment of participants. That section provides background on the National Research Act (Public Law 93-348), which was the legislation that created the National Commission for the Protection of Human Subjects of Biomedical and Behavioral Research. It, in turn, produced the *Belmont Report* and the establishment of IRBs at the local level.

In Chapter 4, I will discuss applications of the ethical principles of informed consent, assessment of risks and benefits, and selection of subjects. The latter is apropos to the topic of *ethical recruitment of participants*. For now, let us review ethical standards stated in the *Belmont Report*, Part B, Basic Ethical Principles:

1. **Respect for Persons**. First, individuals should be treated as autonomous agents, and second, persons with diminished autonomy are entitled to protection. Respect for the immature and the incapacitated may require protecting them as they mature or while they are incapacitated. Some persons are in need of extensive protection, even to the point of excluding them from activities that

may harm them; other persons require little protection beyond making sure they undertake activities freely and with awareness of possible adverse consequence.

2. **Beneficence**. Beyond respecting participants' decisions and protecting them, researchers must also make efforts to secure their well-being. Beneficence is understood as an obligation. Two general rules reflect beneficent actions: (1) do not harm, and (2) maximize possible benefits and minimize possible harms. Research also avoids the harm that may have previously been accepted as routine practices, but on closer investigation turn out to be dangerous.

3. **Justice**. An injustice occurs when a benefit to which a person is entitled is denied without good reason or when some burden is imposed unduly. Distinctions based on experience, age, deprivation, competence, merit, and position sometimes constitute criteria justifying differential treatment. There are several widely accepted formulations of just ways to distribute burdens and benefits. For example, the selection of research participants needs to be scrutinized in order to determine whether some classes (e.g., welfare patients, particular racial and ethnic minorities, or persons confined to institutions) are being systematically selected simply because of their easy availability, their compromised position, or their manipulability, rather than for reasons directly related to the problem being studied.[28]

Ethical compliance, however, is not only understanding and adhering to bureaucratic rules to obtain approval of a research project. Ethics is an integral part of each aspect of your study. In fact, ethics is central to a researcher's value system. There are five reasons why researchers should be attentive to ethics: (a) protecting others, (b) assuring trust so research can continue, (c) enhancing research integrity, (d) complying with professional expectations, and (e) providing researchers with a way to respond to new ethical challenges (e.g., Internet research).[29] These reasons, particularly (c), are not so much directed at compliance with regulatory codes but with what is good and bad research behavior. This viewpoint is best described as *aspirational ethics* or a "strong desire to achieve something high or great" and "an aspirational code would be intended to reach a higher ethics standard that supersedes being in compliance."[30] **Research ethics** is defined as follows:

[Research ethics] is explicitly interested in the analysis of ethical issues raised when people are involved as research participants. The first and broadest objective is to protect human participants. The second is to ensure that research is conducted to serve the interests of individuals, groups, and society. The third is to examine research activities and projects for their ethical soundness, particularly the management of risk, protection of confidentiality, and the process of informed consent.[31]

EXHIBIT 3.7 ■ The Ethical Grid

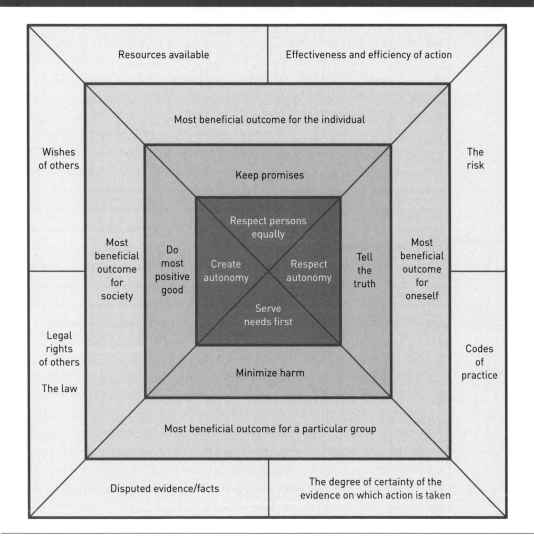

The explication of issues such as ethics as philosophy, rights and obligations (clients, sponsors, researchers, and participants), harm, informed consent, privacy, deception, debriefing, and codes of professional associations are all found in research books. But how does one make ethical decisions more instinctively—almost as a matter of course? Various authors recommend cases, narratives, or vignettes to give student researchers practice in learning to make good decisions and gain confidence in different research contexts.

In a study on teaching ethics in a lively and entertaining way, researchers performed an experiment with 145 students. The study was divided into five parts: (1) an introductory explanation of the "Ethical Grid" by one of its authors[32]; (2) an introduction to a "dilemma" game, in which each player holds four or five scenario question cards (each card describes a brief vignette describing a real-life situation where ethical decisions are made with limited facts and under time pressure); (3) completion of task forms followed by group discussion; (4) a case presentation by one student followed by another discussion; and (5) feedback questionnaires.[33] The Ethical Grid, critical to this section, is shown in Exhibit 3.7.[34]

The Ethical Grid was a stimulus for the experiment and is a tool designed to teach ethical decisions, enhance deliberation, and improve moral reasoning. The user, not the grid, does the analyzing and conflicting answers may result from the same dilemma. The grid consists of four layers or boxes, which are self-contained and detachable—in this illustration, the layers are in grayscale. The outer layer (light gray) of the grid represents "external considerations," which are the more legalistic concerns in ethical decision-making. This layer applies to practice or how practitioners negotiate obstacles, the law, resource use, and institutional issues. A decision may be unlawful, in that a researcher knows that a study will show that passing legislative benefits to an industry donor (and a congressperson) ignores benefits for the congressperson's constituency (which moves us into the next layer: social good). This layer is the "consequential layer," prompting one to consider utilitarian choices for oneself through the good of society ("greatest good for the greatest number"). Suppose an industry is using toxins in manufacturing that pose health risks to workers and consumers (see the third layer: minimize harm, tell the truth, and do the most positive good or "beneficence," which is item 2 from the Ethical Principles) but a staff member conveniently overlooks that finding of their research to expedite passage of the bill. In moral philosophy, this third layer outlines ethical intentions or one's "duties and motives."

Lastly, the center box focuses on the "individual," where respect, autonomy, and trust are major considerations.[35] Here, a researcher may fail to eliminate homeless people even though they are not all competent. But because the sample is small and vulnerable participants have been induced to receive excessive financial or social rewards for joining the recruitment pool, they are left in the sample. Lovett and Seedhouse state that "Grid users can select as many boxes as they wish, though three or fewer will normally be adequate to diagnose the situation. There is no obligation to select one of each colour [the grid's gray scale layers]."[36]

The grid can be approached in various ways, such as working from the center outward or working from the outside in. The latter is most frequently used but you should begin with the layer that feels most appropriate to the narrative you are considering. There is no suggestion that the grid is a replica of moral reasoning but rather that the four layers are aspects of comprehensive ethical analysis.[37] As Seedhouse states:

> Ethics is not only a matter of deciding on principles, considering duties and
> reflecting on likely outcomes in the abstract. Ethical intervention takes place in a
> perpetually uncertain world of limitations. Although it has been shown that law
> and morality do not necessarily correspond, existing laws will have a clear part

to play in some deliberations. Professional codes of practice, although sometimes vague and imprecise, may have a bearing on certain interventions, and it is for the . . . [researcher] to decide when, if ever, these codes provide sufficient advice.[38]

Ethics training has the primary objective of raising the consciousness of the participants and stimulating a discussion of research ethics with fellow researchers. To move from abstract exposition to practice, consider applying the Ethical Grid in a class group discussion with the following scenarios.

1. *Science*, with the concurrence of author Donald P. Green, retracted the December 2014 report "When Contact Changes Minds: An Experiment on Transmission of Support for Gay Equality" by LaCour and Green.[39] The reasons for retracting the paper are as follows: (i) Survey incentives were misrepresented. To encourage participation in the survey, respondents were claimed to have been given cash payments to enroll, to refer family and friends, and to complete multiple surveys. In correspondence received from Michael J. LaCour's attorney, he confirmed that no such payments were made. (ii) The statement on sponsorship was false. In the report, LaCour acknowledged funding from the Williams Institute, the Ford Foundation, and the Evelyn and Walter Haas Jr. Fund. Per correspondence from LaCour's attorney, this statement was not true.[40]

2. In 2010, social psychologist Daryl Bem[41] attracted huge attention when he claimed to have shown that many established psychological phenomena work backward in time. For instance, in one of his experiments, he found that people performed better at a memory task for words they revised in the future. Bem interpreted this as evidence for precognition, or psi—that is, effects that can't be explained by current scientific understanding. Superficially at least, Bem's methodology appeared robust, and he took the laudable step of making his procedures readily available to other researchers. However, many experts have since criticized Bem's methods and statistical analyses, and many replication attempts have failed to support the original findings.[42]

3. In the case of the "Data Sleuth," Professor Data has been a very productive scholar; he has been publishing in major journals for many years. Because of his productivity, he is now known as one of the thought leaders in your field of study. You have recently begun to work with Professor Data and discovered that he has an interesting approach to research. He typically begins by gathering and analyzing data (which may include using a student data set) to "see if the data have anything to say." You have found that Professor Data often manipulates the data and changes the dependent variable to ensure a statistically significant result and increase the probability of a major publication. [43]

"Research ethics is just one part of the whole research enterprise. We must not succumb either institutionally or individually to ethical hypersensitivity, but remain alert to ethical issues as they arise throughout the research process."[44]

Complete an Extensive Literature Review

In Phase 1, I described an unstructured or exploratory literature review (as opposed to a refined or formal one). During the planning phase of the research process, a more extensive review of secondary sources should be started. A **literature review** is "a written document that presents a logically argued case founded on a comprehensive understanding of the current state of knowledge about a topic of study. The case establishes a convincing thesis to answer the study's question."[45] The literature review involves the following:

1. Searching the literature: preview, select, and organize the strongest evidence to support the research question.

2. Developing the argument: arrange your findings to build a body of evidence that explains the salient aspects of the research.

3. Surveying the literature: assemble, organize, and analyze the findings to produce a set of defensible conclusions about what is known.

4. Critiquing the literature: assess how adequately current knowledge answers the research question.

5. Defending the purpose: provide a rationale, importance of the study, and benefits.

6. Writing the review: compose the document, which will become a module in your final report, or you may distill it as a summary for your research proposal.[46]

Properly done, the results of your review should provide concrete outcomes. The results should analyze and synthesize the literature directly related to the problem, provide a foundation for the research question to build upon, and help with the selection of a research method based on what others have used successfully. In addition, the results should "demonstrate that the proposed research contributes something new to the overall body of knowledge or advances the research field's knowledge-base."[47]

Construction of the literature review offers unique choices of materials. **Secondary data** are represented by two source categories: internal and external. An enterprise collects **internal information** for its purposes. Normally, it is proprietary, and competing firms will not have access to it. Internal information's greatest benefit is for researchers within the organization conducting a decision-making study for management. Numerous business functions collect and store data on accounting, customer demographics, finance, marketing, sales, production, inventory, and transportation. Regardless of reasons for collecting data, they can be called upon to solve other problems facing the organization. Through information retrieval, they are retrieved in their stored form. But rather than merely extracting the data, *data mining* is also used to assist the analyst in understanding patterns in various large databases through artificial intelligence and machine learning. While the resource expense is high, the results are impressive. Finally, your company may subscribe to indices, abstracts, bibliographic listings, and studies by private research organizations, trade associations, and governmental sources.

External information, mentioned previously, is published data collected by others for their purposes. Academic researchers use such data, but external secondary sources also help researchers solve managerial questions. The San Jose State University Library "Business Research Guide" outlines examples of sources within each of the following categories:

- Business magazines and financial newspapers

- Trade journals

- Scholarly or professional journals

- Government information and data

- Case studies

- Market research reports

- Professional associations and organizations

- Polls and surveys

- White papers

- Conference papers and proceedings

- Nongovernmental organizations

- Specialized encyclopedias

- Historical data

- Books[48]

The *Harvard Guide to Using Sources* is also recommended.[49]

You will find information in databases on business and management, such as Business Source Complete, Factiva, IBISWorld, LexisNexis Academic, ABI/INFORM

Global, ProQuest, Mergent Online, or public affairs, such as PAIS International, ProQuest Congressional, and Academic Search Complete. These sources provide information unlike that found on the Internet. The scholarly data obtained are possible because significant resources were invested to collect and purchase them. However, a free and open web with little policing to assure quality has less reliable information. Some faculties disqualify the Internet altogether as a viable source of secondary data for papers and projects.

In Chapter 9, I will help you organize the sources for your literature with a "Synthesis Matrix" that consolidates your findings; I will then demonstrate how to write a synopsis from that matrix that can be "plugged in" to your review. I will also provide examples from actual literature reviews.

Formulate Hypotheses and Operationalize Variables

As noted in Chapter 2, the research hypothesis is a declarative statement of what is expected to happen in the study's predicted relationship between two or more variables. The research hypothesis guides the investigation of the problem or provides possible explanations for observations. The following example illustrates the connection between the problem statement and the formulated hypotheses.

Few studies have examined the link between top managers' leadership styles and innovation at the organizational level. After Jung et al. conducted an insightful review of the literature, they proposed that transformational leaders' styles directly and indirectly (through empowerment and organizational climate) influence companies' innovation.[50]

EXHIBIT 3.8 ■ Sample Hypotheses: Managerial Styles and Innovation

I will use H 1, 2, 3 . . . to symbolize the research hypotheses and lower case "a" and "b" as pathways or linkages. Let's look at some of the hypotheses used in their study and then see how they operationalized the variables for those hypotheses.

H1: Transformational leadership is positively related to organizational innovation.

H2: Transformational leadership is positively related to employees' perceptions of (a) empowerment and (b) support for innovation.

H3: Employees perceptions for (a) empowerment and (b) support for innovation have a positive relationship with organizational innovation.

H4: Employees perceptions of (a) empowerment and (b) support for innovation moderate the relationship between transformational leadership and organizational innovation such that the relationship will be stronger when perceived empowerment/support for innovation is high rather than low. (Please note the use of the term "moderate" in H4 to designate moderating variables, described in Chapter 2.)

Scales that appear in the literature were used to operationalize the variables in the study's hypotheses. In most cases, these scales came from separate validation studies. For example, they measured *transformational leadership* with a 20-item, 5-point rating scale from the Multifactor Leadership Questionnaire. *Empowerment* used a 12-item, 7-point scale. A 22-item, 7-point scale measured *support for innovation*. *Organizational innovation* had three proxy measures: total spent on research and development (R&D) in 3 years, annual R&D expenditures as a percentage of gross revenues in 3 years, and an average number of patents obtained annually over 3 years.[51] In Chapter 9, I make suggestions for placement of the hypotheses in your paper.

©iStockphoto.com/DNY59

Choosing a research design is one of the toughest tasks for the researcher. The research question will guide you toward selecting an experimental, quantitative nonexperimental, qualitative, or mixed design. Here are five questions you should ask: (1) What method of data collection works best with the design? (2) What kind of data will you encounter? (3) How will the data be gathered? (4) What kind of participants will you recruit? (5) How will the data be analyzed?

Select a Research Design

The **design** is a logical plan for selecting and arranging the evidence that answers the research question(s); it is the framework for identifying relationships among variables and is the blueprint or overall strategy for the logical structure of the inquiry. In Chapter 6, I address the design-research question connection and answer "what is a design?" On nonexperimental quantitative designs, I make the case that logical problems and the supporting logistics to solve them are very different. The latter is supplemental to the former and should be treated as such; design is *not* method. There is also a classification of designs for business and related fields. Chapter 7 describes the use of qualitative designs in business and how their synergistic relationship with quantitative design produces advantages for the researcher. Chapter 8 is devoted to explaining the nature of experimental designs.

At a conceptual level, designs can be classified as experimental, nonexperimental, and mixed. *Experimental designs* are planned strategies to reveal cause-and-effect relationships among variables through manipulation of the independent variables(s) (IVs), control of factors influencing the outcome (except those being manipulated), and the random assignment of participants to groups or conditions. There are several different types of experiments with varying capacities to meet the standards described in Chapter 8. *Nonexperimental quantitative designs* do not control IVs because their outcomes have already occurred or because the IV is an attribute variable that cannot be manipulated (i.e., you cannot be assigned to the female group when you are a male or to the low verbal GRE score group if you scored 170 on verbal reasoning). In such designs, the researcher makes inferences about relationships among variables from the variations of independent and dependent variables that accompany or follow each other, not through direct intervention or group assignment.

Nonexperimental designs may be quantitative or qualitative. *Nonexperimental quantitative designs*, as described in Chapter 6, consist of three main research objectives and three time dimensions. A quantitative design that is numerical follows the scientific method and is a systematic, objective, and empirical approach to stating and testing hypotheses. *Nonexperimental qualitative designs* and *mixed designs* are explained in Chapter 7. According to Antwi et al., "Qualitative research is used when little is known about a topic or phenomenon and when one wants to discover or learn more about it. It is commonly used to understand people's experiences and to express their perspectives."[52] Qualitative design is used for many research problems to reveal much more depth than is possible with quantitative designs. It is primarily non-numerical and frequently derived from recorded textual data from naturalistic observations in the field. Those data report individuals' experiences, perceptions, and interactions. A mixed design integrates quantitative and qualitative designs, the methods they employ, and a "pragmatic relativist paradigm" into a single study (in contrast to a pro-empirical or pro-qualitative set of assumptions). The study's emphasis may treat the quantitative or qualitative component equally or unequally and the time order of data collection may be concurrent or sequential, depending on the best approach to answering the research question.

The choice of an appropriate design allows researchers to fulfill their objectives and respond to the questions driving the study. A large number of methods, techniques, procedures, protocols, and sampling plans complement the selection of design. Various design categories and disciplinary preferences may make that choice more challenging.

To expand on choosing an appropriate design, suppose you select a nonexperiment with a quantitative emphasis. If a nonexperiment seems like a good fit for your research question, should it be descriptive, explanatory, or predictive? If descriptive, will you use the survey method and collect the data on the Internet or by telephone, mail, or personal interview? Will you collect the data at one time or in intervals? What structure will you use for the questionnaire or interview guide? What level of question wording is appropriate? Should your measurements come from scales or open-ended questions? How will the interviewer influence participants' responses? What training should data collectors receive? How will the data be treated? These questions represent just a few of the decisions that a quantitative design choice and its accompanying method impose on the researcher.

Perhaps you decide on qualitative research and make a selection from a list of possible options like narrative, phenomenology, grounded theory, ethnography, or case studies. You would still answer a different set of questions like those posed above but pertinent to the particular qualitative design. Qualitative research, unlike an online survey, has a lengthier data collection process—at times requiring several months. The time frame typically does not fit a one-semester course but it can be adapted to do so. Here are some other questions to consider if you are contemplating a qualitative design:

- Are you comfortable with the assumptions and worldview of the qualitative tradition?

- Is the audience for your study supportive of qualitative research?

- Is your research question compatible with a qualitative design?

- Have you considered the flexibility provided by qualitative designs in exploring a problem when the literature is weak or missing?

- Are you interested in depth with a small number of participants or breadth with a large number of people in the sample?

- How much time do you have to complete a qualitative study?

- How great is your willingness to interact with participants on a relatively personal level?

- What is your comfort level with ambiguity versus structure and the need to work with fewer procedures?

- What is your experience in working with a large body of information that is not organized at the beginning of your study?

- How well do you meet the requirement for excellent written communication skills, which qualitative researchers must have?[53]

The creative researcher may thrive in this decision environment. The numerous combinations from the abundance of quantitative and qualitative designs may be used to visualize alternate perspectives of the same problem. Imagine holding a three-dimensional replica of a pyramid and rotating it to see a different inscription on each plane. With a design that is optimized by an accompanying method, researchers potentially have more flexibility than if they had only followed the consensus clues in the literature or a single, tool-driven method favored by their discipline. Realistically, I acknowledge that students rarely have the time or resources for mixed methods research or mixed design study, but it is helpful to know that you have options.

Chapter Summary

- The *research process* is composed of seven phases: exploring, planning, creating, conducting, collecting, analyzing, and writing. There are 17 activities or elements associated with the various phases of research (Exhibit 3.2). Understood thoroughly, the process likely has the greatest influence on your knowledge and skill in research. The model is separated into three chapters that follow the standard process of preparing for research and conducting it (Chapters 3, 4, and 5). This chapter covered the first two phases: *exploring* and *planning*. The activities of the research process reflect tasks and decisions that all researchers must make in "doing" research from start to finish.

- The *exploring* phase of the research process model encompasses four elements: (1) choose a business research topic, (2) state the management or academic research question, (3) formulate the investigative questions, and (4) explore data sources to refine your question and adjust its scope. The research process begins with exploring a topic, avoiding ill-defined problems, understanding how research questions differ from investigative and measurement questions, and understanding how to frame or formulate those questions. Then one refines the problem regarding its scope and uses an unstructured literature search, experience survey, focus group, or some combination of exploratory techniques to crystallize the question.

- The *planning* phase of the model contains four elements: (1) prepare to solve ethical dilemmas, (2) complete an extensive literature review, (3) formulate hypotheses and operationalize variables, and (4) select a research design. Ethics training has the primary objective of raising the consciousness of the participants and stimulating a discussion of research ethics with fellow researchers. A formal literature review is assembled to argue the case you are making for your study and to create a comprehensive understanding of the current state of knowledge. This review uses secondary data (internally and externally sourced) to build a convincing thesis that assists you in answering the research question. Studies that use hypotheses require the formulation of those hypotheses and the operationalization of their variables. Selecting an effective design allows researchers to fulfill their objectives and answer the logical (not logistical) questions driving the study. That involves choosing from experimental and nonexperimental (quantitative, qualitative, and mixed) designs. The numerous combinations from the richness of quantitative and qualitative designs help the researcher visualize alternate perspectives of the same problem and make a decision of "best-fit" for their purposes, time, and resources.

- The description of each activity directs the reader on actions to take, references to review (including URLs), and activities that will assist in the exploring and planning phases of the research process.

Key Terms

design	investigative question(s)	research question(s)
element (research process)	literature review (formal)	research topic
experience survey	managerial question	secondary data
external information	measurement questions	unstructured or exploratory
focus groups	research ethics	literature review
ill-defined problems	research problem	
internal information	research process	

Discussion Questions

1. What are the seven phases of the research process described here and why are they organized sequentially to help you make decisions about "doing" research from start to finish?

   a. What are the four elements in the *exploring* phase of the research process?

   b. The choice of a research topic starts with finding a topic that interests you. There were seven other tasks to help you select a topic; what are they and which one is the most important to you?

2. What are ill-defined problems and how would you recognize one?

3. When stating your research question:

   a. What are the four decision categories into which managerial decisions fall?

   b. How do you differentiate between a managerial question, research question, and investigative question?

4. What are the four requirements for formulating investigative questions? Provide an example of how you would apply them.

5. When you do an unstructured exploration, you attempt to refine the research question and determine what you need to secure answers to the proposed research. Typically, the process begins with an exploratory literature review. List and describe the five characteristics that allow you to thoroughly evaluate your information sources.

6. What other mechanisms can be used for exploration? Choose and explain how you would conduct a topic exploration using one.

7. Explain how you would fulfill the three elements in the *planning* phase of the model.

   a. What is the difference between an exploratory and extensive literature review?

   b. What differentiates secondary from primary data?

8. Provide an example from accounting or finance of a testable hypothesis. How would you operationalize the variables in that hypothesis?

9. Provide an example of an experimental, a nonexperimental, and a mixed-design study.

    a. Are nonexperimental studies quantitative or qualitative?

    b. How do worldviews influence a researcher mindset in selecting one?

    c. From what perspective does a researcher who chooses a mixed design operate? Why is that different from the perspective of a quantitative or qualitative researcher?

    d. If you consider doing a qualitative design, what questions should you ask yourself to be certain that your motivation and ability are sufficient to complete it?

THE PROCESS ROAD MAP

Creating and Conducting

LEARNING OBJECTIVES

Performance Objective

Pair a method with your design, select a measuring instrument, and prepare a sampling plan to answer your research question/test a hypothesis. The chosen method, quantitative or qualitative, will determine how the data are collected and analyzed to achieve your goal. Produce a proposal (academic, IRB protocol, or business) incorporating the previous tasks to secure approval for your study; then recruit participants and conduct a pilot study.

Enabling Objectives

1. Illustrate methods and techniques frequently used in business studies.

2. Evaluate the sources and procedures for selecting/creating measuring instruments.

3. Differentiate between a probability versus nonprobability sample. Explain their strengths, limitations, and applications in light of your proposed research.

4. Attend to the ethical treatment of participants. Summarize the role of an IRB and the researcher in this process.

5. Contrast the differences between an exempt, expedited, and full IRB review and how each affects the preparation and timing of a research project.

6. Produce a proposal using course guidelines to achieve acceptance for an academic study, business study, or IRB protocol.

7. Outline the components of a participant recruitment plan.

8. Evaluate the benefits of a pilot study and prepare to implement a small-scale version to detect weaknesses in your plan.

We covered activities under the *exploring* and *planning* phases in Chapter 3. The next step is to study the tasks of *creating* and *conducting*.

PROCESS PHASE 3: CREATING

The *creating* phase of the process model takes its theme from a quote by Zora Neale Hurston: "Research is formalized curiosity. It is poking and prying with a purpose. It is a seeking that he who wishes, may know. . . ."[1] This "formalized" curiosity consists of three elements:

- Match an efficient method/technique with the design.

- Identify or create the measuring instruments.

- Implement a sampling plan.

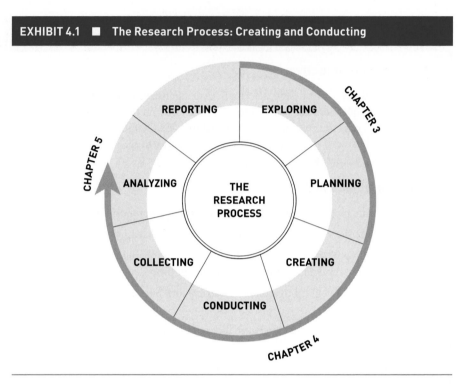

EXHIBIT 4.1 ■ The Research Process: Creating and Conducting

Match an Efficient Method/ Technique With the Design

In Chapter 3, selecting a research design was discussed as one of the planning activities of the research process. I made the point that design is not the same as a method because the design is a logical plan, framework, blueprint, or overall strategy for answering the research question or testing a hypothesis. Its choice is, therefore, a logical decision. A research method, then, represents the different ways that the evidence or data are collected and analyzed to facilitate achieving that goal. Quantitative methods frequently used in business include surveys, observation, and quantitative and qualitative case studies, among others. These methods are associated with descriptive designs. Here, I will focus on surveys and observation.

A **survey**, often referred to as a sample survey because the sample of respondents should be representative of the larger population to which the findings are applied, is a method by which the researcher communicates with participants to secure information. Survey instruments collect cognitive (knowledge) and affective (emotional or feeling) information. They also collect data on past behaviors, intentions, plans, and commitments (i.e., goal-oriented behavior). In addition, data on lifestyle characteristics, demographics, and respondent psychographics are secured.[2]

Thus, questionnaires may tap knowledge or awareness of a product, brand, or issue. They also attempt to discern consumer knowledge or attitudes about new or existing products (e.g., customer satisfaction), brand image, the credibility of promotional spokespersons or the advertisement itself, and respondents' intentions to purchase, repurchase, or switch brands. The latter, as self-reports, require follow-up research to determine if intentions became actions. In management, job satisfaction surveys (leadership, commitment, loyalty, coworkers, and other aspects of the work environment), as well as surveys of management practices and management systems, are common.

The *modes* of survey research are interactive (two-way communication), noninteractive (one-way communication), and mixed. The *techniques*

Per-Anders Pettersson/Contributor/Getty Images

Survey research is a method of descriptive research used to collect primary data from people. The research question, which drives the survey, focuses on specific aspects of participants' opinions, attitudes, beliefs, motivations, and behavior. A researcher often seeks to discover relationships among variables, not merely describe them; and a representative sample from the population is used to generalize findings back to the target population.

used for interactive surveys involve personal or electronic facilitation, including face-to-face (personal) interviews, door-to-door interviews, and shopping mall intercepts—all of which provide linguistic and nonverbal cues from the respondent—and telephone interviews (mobile, landline, computer-assisted, and voice-activated). Telephone and media-driven surveys do not create personal rapport like the in-person interview. Noninteractive surveys include self-administered questionnaires distributed by various means: mail, email, product registration, website, kiosk, text message, social media site, or the researcher. A comparison of the advantages and disadvantages of these techniques can be found at this reference.[3]

A recent study suggests that the wide range of respondents who express dissatisfaction with their research experience may imperil future survey research. According to the "2017 Global Respondent Engagement Study" conducted by GreenBook, three-quarters of all respondents globally were dissatisfied with their participation experience. The *GreenBook Research Industry Trends (GRIT) for Customer Participation in Research* report is carefully followed across industries and geographies. Using online, mobile-only, and telephone surveys of 6,208 consumers in 15 countries and eight languages, the research showed that survey designers have pretty much made the respondent experience a disaster.[4]

As a student or manager preparing a survey for your term project, there are several valuable lessons that should be learned and incorporated in your planning and survey execution. Exhibit 4.2 presents some suggestions.

Let's look at the reasons for the current emphasis on mobile and online research. The Internet grew from 16 million users (.4% of the world population) in 1995 to 4.2 billion users (54.4% of the world population in early 2018. In North America, with an

EXHIBIT 4.2 ■ Trouble Ahead for a Research Favorite: Surveys	
Problem	**Solutions**
55% say that survey design affects willingness to complete it.	It must work on a mobile screen, be short, and contain visuals rather than just text.
55% mobile-first participants say bad design turns them off; 51% believe it impacts willingness to participate.	Make the process simple, intuitive, and fun. Learn from app developers, gamers, and social media.
46% of telephone respondents say time commitment affects attention and complain of "honesty fatigue" with longer surveys.	Telephone landline research is declining but still intrusive, and respondents lack control of the interaction. With 39% completing this survey on a mobile phone and 48% on a desktop/laptop, there are other delivery mechanisms to consider.
81% say the ideal length is 15 minutes or less; with 50% preferring less than 10 minutes.	"Less is more" considering the growing number of mobile-first respondents.
Need for change varies with the medium: surveys, focus groups, communities, product tests, media diaries, consumption diaries, and others.	Issues: duration, clarity of language, rewards, and screening frequently emerge as reasons for dissatisfaction.
36% participate to earn rewards or prizes.	In return for their time, respondents want something of financial value. Also considered was a nonfinancial motivator in qualitative research (e.g., a sense of pride in participating in decision-making).
40% prefer cash as a reward to participate.	Cash is number 1, but cash virtual cards are a strong second choice.
63% prefer to be invited to participate by email.	Become better email marketers to show respondents why their participation will be worth it to them.
33% say that knowing the sponsor impacts participation.	Leverage relationships with known and respected sponsors.

Source: Data are from AYTM Team, "2017 Global Respondent Engagement Study," *GRIT CPR Report: Consumer Participation in Research Report* (New York: GreenBook, March 2017), 3–4, https://www.greenbook.org/grit/cpr.

estimated population of 364 million in early 2018, Internet use was 345 million or a 95% penetration rate.[5]

On the mobile front, U.S. users are up to 5 hours per day on mobile devices. This is a 20% increase from the fourth quarter data of 2016. Social, messaging, media, and entertainment applications occupy 50% of that time.[6]

According to Pew Research Center statistics, U.S. smartphone owners are younger, more affluent, and highly educated. In mid-2011, 35% of adults had smartphones; now,

68% do. In the 18–29 age group, 86% own an iPhone, Android, Blackberry, or Windows phone and there is 83% ownership in the 30–49 age group. In addition, close to half of all Americans own a tablet computer, while desktop or laptop computers remain at their penetration level of 10 years ago. In the smartphone subset, college educational attainment is 81%, while 87% have $75,000 or more in household income.[7]

As these statistics and Exhibit 4.2 reveal, the Internet and mobile devices will have a lasting effect on the research landscape. Despite the design problems described in Exhibit 4.2, online surveys have advantages for academic research and business decision-makers in need of real-time information[8]:

- *Rapid distribution and real-time reporting.* Online surveys can reach thousands of respondents quickly and simultaneously. With results automatically tabulated as returns arrive, trending information is available before the report's final feedback. GPS locations help to confirm known population characteristics. Online surveys provide results in half the time of traditional telephone surveys.

- *Cost savings.* The use of electronic survey methods can cut costs upward of 40%. Electronic surveys eliminate or substantially reduce costs associated with data collection, training, telecommunication, and management. Expenses related to adding respondents are significantly lower than traditional survey techniques.

- *Design personalization.* In the next section ("Identify or Create the Measuring Instruments"), you will discover that there are over 40 websites that help you create online surveys, with tools including question wording, scaling, design, and layout and services like web hosting, data analysis, and reporting. You are also directed to Appendix A to follow the construction of a Google Forms online questionnaire. But personalization goes beyond graphic images and video to allow respondents to pause, resume, see previous answers, and correct inconsistencies—all at their convenience.

- *Online surveys take less time to complete than traditional methods.* They are respondent scheduled for their convenience and, if properly designed, use graphics to stimulate and engage respondents. With links to incentive sites and summary reports, the experience is more enjoyable, resulting in higher response rates.

- *Ability to contact hard-to-reach or "rare or hidden" populations.* Busy professionals, (e.g., physicians, attorneys, and high-level executives) can be reached online more readily than through gatekeepers as well as nonroutine participants.[9]

Drawbacks should not be ignored, however. One long-standing concern is that the Internet does not represent the U.S. population. As previously noted, this criticism is disappearing, with 89% of U.S. adults accessing the Internet in 2018. Second, if the sample

Bloomberg/Contributor/Getty Images

In business research, not all observation involves human participants. In manufacturing, product variations are monitored through the statistical process control, a process attributed to Walter Shewhart, father of statistical quality control, and later advocated by W. Edwards Deming, widely credited with launching Total Quality Management. Observations of production line performance help reduce deviations that result in rejected products and increase consumer confidence in quality.

is self-selecting, the respondents may not look anything like the characteristics of your target population; moreover, if they have repeated and unwanted access to your questionnaire without passwords, a subset will skew the results.

Observational methods involve the researcher's observation of behavioral patterns of people through the detailed and systematic recording of what the research subjects say and do. These methods are used with high amounts of structure (e.g., laboratory settings), in which the researcher creates a situation to see what happens. Less structure occurs in the field. In a field setting, researchers observe behaviors more or less as they would occur routinely.

Observational studies gather a wide variety of information about behavior . . . and observable phenomena: *physical actions*, such as shopping patterns (in-store or via a web interface) or television viewing; *verbal behavior*, such as sales conversations; *expressive behavior*, such as tone of voice or facial expressions; *spatial relations and locations*, such as traffic patterns; *temporal patterns*, such as amount of time spent shopping or driving; *physical objects*, such as the amount of newspapers recycled; *verbal and pictorial records*, such as content of advertisements; and *neurological activity* such as brain activity in response to marketing stimuli.[10]

The main *techniques* for observation are systematic (controlled), naturalistic, and participant. Furthermore, the researcher's role is either covert, in that participants do not notice they are being studied, or overt, in that participants perceive researcher involvement. **Systematic observation** is an alternative to self-reporting (i.e., asking the participants what they do) or other forms of reporting such as behavioral ratings or reports completed by asking others who draw from cumulative experience with the participant's behavior.[11] Error reduction in systematic observation is accomplished through the use of preplanning, decision rules, operationalizing variables, precision and control in data collection, and often by using mechanical/electronic devices for standardization or follow-up validation. With systematic observation, the means of quantification is frequency counts (count coding systems) of target behaviors.

Count coding systems are designed to lead the observer to count the number of instances and/or duration of instances of the key behaviors. All variable metrics (e.g., rates, proportions, indices of sequential associations, latencies) are derivatives of number or duration of key behaviors or time between key behaviors.[12]

Other observational techniques use checklists or rating scales to capture the occurrence and nature of behaviors.

Systematic or controlled observation may occur more often in a laboratory setting to enhance control and facilitate random assignment of participants to groups. The researchers have an overt role because the participants are aware they are being observed, but the researchers are nonparticipants in that they avoid contact.

Naturalistic observation is not created, controlled, or manipulated by the researcher but occurs within an ecology that is natural for those being studied. The variable(s) of interest cannot be manipulated but may be observed passively as spontaneous behaviors of the research subjects. "Compared with controlled/structured methods it is like the difference between studying wild animals in a zoo and studying them in their natural habitat."[13] The advantage of naturalistic observation is the ecological and external validity of the research findings. Data can be collected by quantitative or qualitative techniques, such as narrative, audio, image capture, and video recording.

With **participant observation**, similar to naturalistic observation, researchers are present in a setting that is typical for the participants. They interact with participants or may join or share in the group's activities as a member. Their involvement may be covert (disguised) or overt (undisguised). From an empirical standpoint, the lack of standardized recording, the inability to transcribe direct quotations quickly, and the loss of objectivity in underreporting behaviors pose validity problems. Refer to Chapter 7 on ethnography and the participant observer example.

Observational data recording occurs with *event sampling* (all occurrences of the behavior of interest are recorded), *time sampling* at specified periods (e.g., when workers take breaks, upon completion of a task, when supervision is not present, or at other intervals), and *instantaneous (target time) sampling*. The latter ignores what happens before and after and the researcher preselects the instant of interest and records it.[14]

The matching of methods and techniques to a design requires creativity and invention. Despite traditions, methods are logically unrelated to design. As de Vaus states:

> There is nothing intrinsic about any research design that requires a particular method of data collection. Although cross-sectional surveys are frequently equated with questionnaires and case studies are often equated with participant observation, . . . data for any design can be collected with any data collection method.[15]

de Vaus goes on to show how data for experiments, case studies, longitudinal designs, and cross-sectional designs can all be collected interchangeably with questionnaires, interviews (structured or unstructured), observation, analysis of documents, and unobtrusive measures. The efficient matching of a method or technique to your design rests on how the method-to-design combination optimizes your resources. Efficiency seems more important to students because efficiency suggests the least waste of time, resources, and effort. Your professor will advocate effectiveness; thus, you need to compare the strength and weakness of different methods for answering your research question in light of the scope and complexity of your project. In addition, the timing imposed on your assignment and the guidance you have received affect whether you lean toward efficiency, effectiveness, or aspects of both. At this point, practicality does rule.

In writing this section, you may wonder why I highlighted methods and techniques of data collection that are traditionally associated with nonexperimental research methods. The techniques of data collection often used with survey methods, such as personal interviews and self-administered questionnaires, can also be used with experiments. Ask researchers who have worked in both the laboratory and the field if you are not convinced.

There is not sufficient space to cover many interesting methods and techniques (see the list of over 40 methods in the "research onion," Exhibit 1.2); otherwise, this guide would be neither brief nor have a report-oriented emphasis. On the topics I am about to mention, specialized textbooks are an invaluable source and are why certain research topics here are reduced to a level of detail that is manageable. For example, I do not have space to explain the steps to administer an experiment. Creating and administering a questionnaire or interview guide or planning and conducting an observational study requires a thorough review of numerous topics. Developing a measuring instrument and calculating sample size would add more material that takes away from the final chapter on report writing.

Identify or Create the Measuring Instruments

Measurement in research consists of assigning numbers to empirical events in compliance with a set of rules. Perhaps you want to measure the screen dimensions of a flat-screen television. You place your tape measure diagonally from the bottom right of the screen to the top left and get a measurement used by the manufacturer. The result in inches represents a number to compare the variable "diagonal screen size" to other products you are considering. **Scaling** is a "procedure for the assignment of numbers (or other symbols) to a property of objects in order to impart some of the characteristics of numbers to the properties in question."[16] Scaling involves constructing an instrument that connects qualitative constructs with quantitative metric units. The tape measure is a scale. In Chapter 2, the section on "Variables in Measurement" showed how the different levels of measurement (NOIR: nominal, ordinal, interval, and ratio) require different mathematical operations; this fact, in turn, determines the type of scale used.

Business research concepts and constructs are frequently complex and abstract, while the available measuring instruments can be imprecise. We seek a valid measure to avoid error but usually get something between the true score and the score the measurement provides. When the object is concrete and the measurement tool is standard-ized, we have a better chance of reducing that error. When a concept is abstract (e.g., attitudes toward the Federal Reserve) and the measurement tool is not standardized, we cannot be confident that the instrument reflects true scores. This situation argues for securing measuring instru-ments that have undergone testing to demonstrate their validity and reliability. Parenthetically, **validity** is said to be the extent to which the tool measures what it claims to measure—or accuracy. **Reliability** is the extent to which the tool produces consistent results. Reliable instruments are dependable; they work well at different times under different conditions.

Shutterstock/Bill Fehr

A tape measure is a scale for measuring physical objects. It is flexible and used to determine linear distance. Similarly, but with less precision, an attitude scale measures a participant's attitude about purchase satisfaction. A single-item scale might ask, "How satisfied are you with your last purchase of Allbirds wool runners?" The alternatives are (1) very satisfied, (2) quite satisfied, (3) somewhat satisfied, and (4) not at all satisfied. Notice that unlike the tape measure's equal intervals, the attitude scale is skewed toward positive levels of satisfaction and equal intervals are not apparent.

Selecting the right measuring instrument can be complicated, particularly for student research projects. Instruments are often difficult to find. Previously, I suggested the use of the "citation pearl searching" approach, "stand-alone literature review articles," and special series journals dedicated to literature reviews. While they are useful in the explor-atory phase of problem formulation, many articles do not have sufficient space to publish the author's instruments. You may be fortunate to find an article that is a good match for your project with the exact text of the measures used. Otherwise, an instrument may be copyrighted and may require you to write the author for permission to use it, which may also require payment for use.

These roadblocks prompt new researchers to create their instruments. Chapters on measurement, scaling, or questionnaires and instruments in some research methods text-books contain information on building an instrument. Online resources can also help you create an instrument. Google Forms is an excellent full-featured service that is free. Appendix A takes you step by step through the creation of a questionnaire with Google Forms. This survey instrument was used in a Master's thesis described in Chapter 9 ("Writing the Report"). Other options are also available. For example, Typeform offers custom design themes for a professional look; Survey Monkey is very popular and always worth comparing to other offerings; Client Heartbeat is a paid service with superior analytics; and Zoho Survey, SurveyGizmo, Zoomerang, and SurveyPlanet all offer free versions and paid variations containing more features. Over 40 websites provide tailored question wording, scaling, and full questionnaire services including web hosting, data analysis, and reporting.

EXHIBIT 4.3 ■ Resources for Traditional and Online Surveys

Author	Title	Publisher, URL
Levenson, Alec	*Employee Surveys That Work*	San Francisco, CA: Berrett-Koehler Publishers, 2014. http://www.bkconnection.com
Fowler, Jr., Floyd J.	*Survey Research Methods*, 5th ed.	Thousand Oaks, CA: SAGE, 2014. https://us.sagepub.com/en-us/nam/survey-research-methods/book239405
Dillman, Don A., Jolene D. Smyth, and Leah Melani Christian	*Internet, Phone, Mail, and Mixed-Mode Surveys: The Tailored Design Method*, 4th ed.	New York: Wiley & Sons, 2014. http://www.wiley.com/WileyCDA/WileyTitle/productCd-1118456149.html
Fink, Arlene	*How to Conduct Surveys: A Step-by-Step Guide*, 6th ed.	Thousand Oaks, CA: SAGE, 2017. https://us.sagepub.com/en-us/nam/home
Fowler, Jr., Floyd J., and Carol Cosenza	"Writing Effective Questions," in *International Handbook of Survey Methodology*. Edited by Edith D. de Leeuw, Joop J. Hox, and Don A. Dillman.	Mahwah, NJ: Lawrence Erlbaum, 2008. https://www.routledge.com/products
DeVellis, Robert F.	*Scale Development: Theory and Applications*, 4th ed.	Thousand Oaks, CA: SAGE, 2017. https://us.sagepub.com/en-us/nam/author/robert-f-devellis
Hubbard, Douglas W.	*How to Measure Anything*, 3rd ed.	Hoboken, NJ: John Wiley & Sons, 2014. http://www.wiley.com/WileyCDA/
(Journal)	*Survey Research Methods*	http://www.psc.isr.umich.edu/dis/infoserv/journal/detail/1336
Mavletova, Aigul, and Mick P. Couper	"Sensitive Topics in PC Web and Mobile Web Surveys: Is There a Difference?" *Survey Research Methods* 7, no. 3 (2013): 191–205.	http://www.psc.isr.umich.edu/pubs/abs/8721
Sue, Valerie M., and Lois A. Ritter	*Conducting Online Surveys*	Thousand Oaks, CA: SAGE, 2012. https://us.sagepub.com/en-us/nam/conducting-online-surveys/book235512
Multiple contributors	*The SAGE Handbook of Online Research Methods*, 2nd ed. Edited by Nigel G. Fielding, Raymond M. Lee, and Grant Blank	London: SAGE Publications Ltd., 2017. https://us.sagepub.com/en-us/nam/the-Sage-handbook-of-online-research-methods/book245027

Some current print books, e-books, and journals are also helpful for crafting your instruments. Examples are provided in Exhibit 4.3.[17]

As a new researcher, be careful with self-design. Arbitrary measures designed with your choice of items may appear simple and quick. They are inexpensive to construct and connect nicely to data collection—particularly online. However, it is impossible to judge their validity *in any meaningful way*. Instrument self-creation contributes to measurement error and ultimately affects hypothesis-testing accuracy.

Finally, there are handbooks, bibliographies, and compendiums frequently sought by researchers. *Tests in Print* contains descriptions of over 3,000 testing instruments and is useful for researchers in management, career planning, and psychology.[18] For marketing projects, there is the *Marketing Scales Handbook: Multi-Item Measures for Consumer Insight Research*, which contains over 350 instruments.[19] Organizational researchers will find a valuable resource in *Taking the Measure of Work: A Guide to Validated Scales for Organizational Research and Diagnosis*.[20]

Implement a Sampling Plan

The final planning step in Phase 3 of the research process model is selecting a sampling plan. The basic idea of **sampling** is that by selecting some of the elements of a population (a **sample**), you may draw conclusions about the entire population (Exhibit 4.4). The **population** is the total collection of elements about which we want to make inferences. An **element** is a participant, subject, or object being observed or measured. In the Chapter 2 example of a company's telecommuting policy, the unit of study or element is each telecommuting worker questioned. When we receive a list of all eligible individuals in this population, it is called a **sampling frame**. If we want to *subsample*, the employees (elements) would be financial analysts or those whose childcare needs conflict with traditional work hours. These are called **sampling units** in a multistage sampling plan. If population is small enough, you may prefer to do a **census**, which includes all the elements in the population. For example, an article published in *CIO* lists the top 20 female entrepreneurs to watch in 2018.[21] If these 20 individuals define your target population, there is little point in sampling. Moreover, if the variability is abnormally high among sampling elements, there is virtually no advantage in sampling.

The topic of sampling can be problematic for researchers because of claims of superiority for *probability* versus *nonprobability* samples. A **probability sample** is based on random selection—a controlled procedure that assures each population element is given a known nonzero chance of selection (i.e., the probability that an element will be selected from the population for inclusion). If a coin toss is used, the probability is 1 out of 2, or .5. This type of sample reduces *sampling error* and generally improves representative samples. **Sampling error** is a statistical error that occurs when the results obtained do not represent the true characteristics, attributes, traits, behaviors, or other variables of

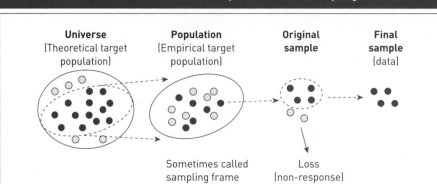

EXHIBIT 4.4   ■   From the Theoretical Population to the Sampling Element

| Universe (Theoretical target population) | Population (Empirical target population) | Original sample | Final sample (data) |

Sometimes called sampling frame

Loss (non-response)

In business, sampling is widely used to gather information about a population of interest. The population is the total collection of elements about which we want to make inferences. The basic idea of sampling is that by selecting some of the elements of a population (a representative sample), you may draw conclusions about the entire population. The list of all eligible individuals in the population is called a sampling frame. An element is a participant, subject, or object being observed or measured.

interest in the population. Statistically, it is the absolute value of the difference between the sample mean, $\bar{x}$, and the true population mean, μ. Regardless of the sampling technique selected, decreasing sampling error is a primary objective. Probability samples are described in Exhibits 4.6 and 4.7.

A **nonprobability sample** is not random and provides no information about the likelihood of an element being included—that is, the probability of selecting an element in the population is unknown. Rather than random selection, the researcher's subjective judgment plays a significant role in selecting a technique to produce recruits that represent the population for the research question. With a *convenience sample*, it is solely the researcher's prerogative to find the most convenient or economical elements; often, the process resembles researchers conducting "person-on-the-street" interviews or approaching whoever walks by first.

When you look at Exhibit 4.5 and the boxes on the right side, you will see that there are a number of nonprobability plans. Note that *purposive sampling* is connected to many variants. In Exhibit 4.6, the definition of *purposive sampling* is as follows: the researcher consciously selects participants for inclusion who have specific characteristics relevant to the study. It does not produce a diverse cross-section. Following the line downward, you will find several purposive techniques, each with advantages for the objective of the research being conducted: extreme case/deviant, homogeneous, typical case, maximum variation, and critical case. The purposes of each are defined in Exhibit 4.6. *Expert sampling*, like *critical case sampling*, is sometimes included in this list because of its utility in exploratory studies in which the focus is on experts with unique experience. Experience surveys using knowledgeable people were mentioned as an exploratory technique in Chapter 3.

EXHIBIT 4.5 ■ Types of Sampling Plans

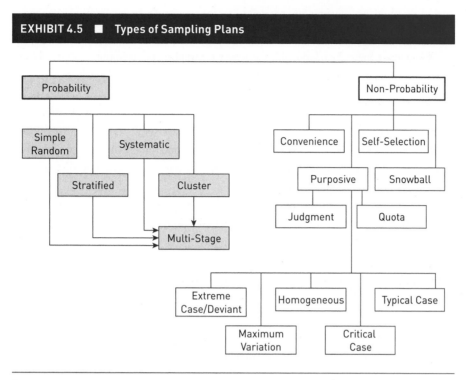

Source: Adapted from Saunders, Mark, Philip Lewis, and Adrian Thornhill, *Research Methods for Business Students*, 7th ed. (Essex, UK: Pearson Education, 2016), Figure 7.2; and Cohen, Deborah, and Benjamin Crabtree, "Qualitative Research Guidelines Project: Sampling," Robert Wood Johnson Foundation, published July 2006, http://www.qualres.org/HomeSamp-3702.html.

Another nonprobability sampling technique used with qualitative (and quantitative) research is *quota sampling*. As defined in Exhibit 4.6, this is another form of purposive sampling used to improve representativeness. If the sample is selected on variables to have the same proportions in the population, the participants should be representative of other variables in the population of which the researcher has no control. This is a nonprobability version of stratified sampling. This implies that the sample is divided to represent the strata in a population. For example, male-female represents two strata. If 40% of employees in a population are female, the researcher would ensure that 40% of the sample was composed of females. Similarly, undergraduate class rank represents four strata, and managerial levels in an organization produce strata equal to the levels being studied.

Snowball sampling is often used to locate subgroups of the population that may be difficult to reach or involve in a research study. Snowball sampling uses a referral approach when already-selected participants reach out to other particularly hard-to-reach participants who, in turn, identify others. It gathers participants like a snowball as it rolls along until the sample size is achieved. In qualitative research, the investigator draws "on theory (i.e., the academic literature) and practice (i.e., the experience of the researcher and the evolutionary nature of the research process)"[22] to make a decision about which sample is the best fit for the research question.

When you review the relationships among the sampling plans in the Exhibit 4.5 flowchart and compare them to their descriptions in Exhibit 4.6, this will be clearer. To learn more about implementing these techniques, consider the book by Steven K. Thompson, *Sampling*,[23] do an Internet search, and review the Chapter 4 discussion questions as a stimulus for class discussion.

In Exhibit 4.5, members of the sample are selected on a probability or nonprobability basis. *Probability sampling* uses **random selection**, which is a controlled procedure assuring that each population element is given a known nonzero chance of selection. *Nonprobability sampling* is subjective and not random. Each element does not have a known nonzero chance of inclusion. You select a sampling plan based on the goals of your research.

The left branch of Exhibit 4.5 reflects sampling plans based on probability, and the right branch shows sampling plans that are nonprobability based. Probability sampling plans are superior to generalize to a population. But even for researchers who believe that the only purpose of research is scientific explanation and prediction, that statement is not entirely accurate. For example, a random sample will give us a cross-section of the population, but not every research question may require it. Often, elements of the total population are not locatable or available. In some studies, the objective is not to generalize to a population parameter (e.g., the researcher might be looking for dramatic variations where individual participants are atypical). Finally, there is time and cost. The time to plan a probability sample and the costs associated with callbacks, re-interviewing, and securing participants who meet the sampling requirements are expensive.

In Exhibit 4.7, you can see the advantages and disadvantages of various probability samples.

Similarly, Curtis et al. have distilled some key features of nonprobability samples for qualitative designs:

- The method of drawing samples is not based on theories of the statistical probability of selection but on other, purposive or theoretical sampling criteria.

- Samples are small, are studied intensively, and each one typically generates a large amount of information.

- Samples are not usually wholly prespecified and, instead, selection is sequential (by a rolling process, interleafed with coding and analysis).

- Sample selection is conceptually driven, either by the theoretical framework, which underpins the research question from the outset, or by an evolving theory that is derived inductively from the data as the research proceeds.

- Qualitative research should be reflexive and explicit about the rationale for case selection because there are ethical and theoretical implications arising from the choices, which are made to include particular cases and exclude others.

- Qualitative samples are designed to make possible analytic generalizations (applied to wider theory on the basis of how selected cases "fit" with general constructs) but not statistical generalizations (applied to wider populations on the basis of representative statistical samples).[24]

EXHIBIT 4.6 ■ Descriptions of Sampling Plans	
Probability Samples	
Simple Random	Each population element has an equal chance of being selected into the sample. All the elements of the population must be available. A sample is drawn using a random number generator/table/computer program once the optimum sample size is calculated.
Systematic	Elements of the population are identified and listed. Selection begins with a random start and follows a sampling fraction. Every kth element is then selected (e.g., random start = 7; interval is 5 = 5th element. The sample then consists of element 7, 12, 17, 22, 27, etc. until the maximum precalculated sample size is reached).
Stratified	A population is divided into subpopulations or strata (e.g., class rank, gender, management level). A random sample is used to select elements from each stratum. The stratum may be proportionate or disproportionate to the population's strata percentages. Results may be weighted and combined.
Cluster	The population is divided into many subgroups of equal or unequal size. Subgroups are selected according to some criterion (e.g., families in the same block). Heterogeneity within subgroups and homogeneity between subgroups is preferred. You then choose some subgroups randomly to be studied in total.
Multistage	Multistage sampling is a form of sampling (e.g., cluster) in which larger clusters are subdivided into subsets, usually for survey research. First-stage clusters (often geographic regions) are created by selecting them for analysis. The selected units are divided into second-stage clusters (neighborhoods). If a third stage is used, within each neighborhood, dwellings are selected. Multistage designs also use combinations of other sampling methods (see arrows in Exhibit 4.5) to create the sample. The first stage might be chosen using a cluster approach and the second stage might be selected with a random sample. Other permutations are possible.
Nonprobability Samples	
Convenience	There are no controls to ensure precision. This type of sampling is the least reliable. Researchers choose whomever they find based on their convenience, participant availability, and those who are readily accessible.
Self-selecting	Participants themselves determine their inclusion. They may respond to invitations or advertisements, as with Internet or campus surveys. Not all self-selectors will have appropriate characteristics for the study.
Snowball	Snowball sampling is a referral approach in which already-selected participants reach out to other particularly hard-to-find participants who, in turn, identify others. It gathers participants like a snowball as it rolls along.

(Continued)

EXHIBIT 4.6 ■ (Continued)	
Nonprobability Samples	
Purposive	The researcher consciously selects participants for inclusion who have specific characteristics relevant to the study. This type of sampling does not produce a diverse cross-section.
Judgment	Judgment is a form of purposive sampling in which the researcher selects participants to conform to some criterion (e.g., prediction of election results from key precincts with a past predictive record).
Quota	Quota sampling is another form of purposive sampling used to improve representativeness. If the sample is selected on variables to have the same proportion of those variables in the population, the participants should be representative on other variables in the population on which the researcher has no control. This is a nonprobability version of stratified sampling.
Extreme/Deviant Case	Extreme sampling involves the selection or discovery of unusual or atypical participants, often outliers that are special in highlighting the goals of the research (e.g., innovative businesses in a stagnant industry). This sometimes occurs after a portion of the data collection and analysis is complete so that maximum variation in participants' characteristics can be determined.
Maximum Variation	Maximum variation is a purposive sampling plan to achieve heterogeneity. The selected participants maximize diversity and difference pertinent to the research question.
Homogeneous	Homogeneous sampling is used when an in-depth description is central to the research question. In addition, homogeneous participants are selected when the research strategy tries to reduce variation, streamline analysis, and expedite group interviewing.
Critical Case	This is the process of selecting a small number of important cases that are expected to "yield the most information and have the greatest impact on the development of knowledge."[a] This form of sampling uses the logic that if the theory works under the conditions of the critical case, it will work anywhere. Researchers discern the features that make a case crucial.
Typical Case	The sample is composed of participants whose characteristics are not unusual, extreme, deviant, or atypical but rather ordinary or average. This is used in research where it is important to describe what is characteristic of the setting.

Source: Details on "nonprobability samples" are adapted from Palinkas, Lawrence A., Sarah M. Horwitz, Carla A. Green, Jennifer P. Wisdom, Naihua Duan, and Kimberly Hoagwood, "Purposeful Sampling for Qualitative Data Collection and Analysis in Mixed Method Implementation Research," *Administration and Policy in Mental Health and Mental Health Services Research* 42, no. 5 (2013), 3; and Cohen, Deborah and Benjamin Crabtree, "Qualitative Research Guidelines Project," Robert Wood Johnson Foundation, published July 2006, http://www.qualres.org/HomeSamp-3702.html.

Note: [a]Patton, M. Q., *Qualitative Research and Evaluation Methods*, 2nd ed. (Thousand Oaks: SAGE, 2001), 236.

EXHIBIT 4.7 ■ Characteristics of Probability Sampling Plans			
Type	**Use**	**Advantages**	**Disadvantages**
Simple Random	Unbiased element selection; equal chance of selection. Requires sampling frame (often computerized).	High representativeness. Uncomplicated computation of sampling error.	High cost; time-consuming. List of population elements required. Does not use natural element grouping.
Systematic	Use when population elements are similar on key variables. Selection based on known interval: select every kth element from a random start.	Moderate cost. High representativeness. No sampling frame required; no requirement for table of random numbers or random number generator. Easy to use.	Less random than simple random sampling. If population is ordered in a periodic way, the sample may be skewed.
Stratified	Use with a heterogeneous population containing different groups (strata); random selection of subgroups from each group. Subgroups may be proportional or disproportional as per the research objective.	Researcher controls representation and size/proportion of strata. Comparisons across strata, which has lower variability for same sample size. When the variable for stratification is related to the dependent variable, sampling error is reduced below that of a simple random sample.	High cost; time-consuming. Requires information about stratum (sampling frame) or incurs added cost if that information must be created. Does not use natural element grouping.
Cluster	Use to divide the total population into separate groups (clusters) when a sampling frame of elements is unavailable. Uses natural element groupings (e.g., neighborhoods) that are internally heterogeneous. There should be homogeneity between clusters. Then a random sample of elements within each cluster is taken.	Lower cost. Higher use than other methods especially for large or geographically dispersed populations. Can be single-stage (as described) or multistage (a complex form) where sampling units become smaller at each stage.	Measurably efficient estimates possible for clusters and population but increased sampling error as clusters decrease and homogeneity within clusters increases.
Multistage	Used with different combinations of sampling techniques to select progressively smaller samples —often starting with clusters. Often starts with the construction of clusters then uses another technique (e.g., random sampling to create a subset of elements for a final sample).	Reduced cost and increased speed, particularly in large-scale survey research. Easier to implement and often more representative of the population than a single sampling plan (e.g., cluster or stratified).	Not as accurate as a simple random for *same size samples*. Requires more testing depending on the combination of sampling techniques used.

PROCESS PHASE 4: CONDUCTING

In the *conducting* phase of the process model, there are three elements:

- Recruit research participants ethically.

- Prepare a proposal (academic, IRB protocol, or business).

- Conduct a pilot study.

These are intensive "hands-on" activities in the research process. The first is an essential step in compliance with your IRB, the second prepares for the acceptance or modification of your proposed research, and the third helps you to anticipate and correct the weaknesses in your actual study before it goes "live." Without the latter, you may discover too late that you cannot remedy deficiencies or, worse, avoid disaster.

Recruit Research Participants Ethically

You must receive written approval from an ethics review board, called an **Institutional Review Board (IRB)**, *before* you start recruiting participants, collecting data, or analyzing data. Research involving human participants, directly or indirectly, must be reviewed and approved by an IRB. There are some exceptions for students who have a class assignment as part of a research course.

Background

Federal law implemented safeguards to help protect the rights and welfare of human participants in research through the National Research Act (Public Law 93-348) in 1974. This legislation created the National Commission for the Protection of Human Subjects of Biomedical and Behavioral Research, which produced the *Belmont Report*, and established IRBs at the local level. Often seen as a response to major scandals in biomedical research, such as the experiments of Nazi physicians (Nuremberg Code of 1948) and the U.S. Public Health Service Tuskegee Syphilis Study (1932–1972), IRBs are identified with their efforts regarding informed, voluntary consent in biomedical research. However, IRBs are also required to approve studies in which social scientists use interviews, respondent surveys, or conduct fieldwork—"even though such work doesn't pose any of the dangers of, say, a drug whose side effects could be deadly."[25]

The boards are governed by Title 45 Code of Federal Regulations Part 46 (45 CFR 46), also known as the "Common Rule," and regulated by the U.S. Department of

Health and Human Services Office for Human Research Protections. IRBs exist at the federal, state, institutional, and accredited commercial levels. According to the American Association of University Professors, "Clinical and biomedical research currently account for approximately 75 percent of all the research that is reviewed by IRBs."[26] The composition of many review boards reflects the nature of the research that comes before them, which explains the criticism for overlaying a "medical model" on the evaluation of social and behavioral research.

In the United States, there are over 5,000 IRBs in operation, mainly at universities, hospitals, and private research facilities.[27] It is not unusual for large research universities to have several IRBs. The foundation of the IRB system is the 1976 *Belmont Report*. That report's section on "Basic Ethical Principles and Their Applications" includes three points that IRBs use as charter principles:

National Archives at Atlanta

The Tuskegee experiment was a medical research project notoriously conducted by doctors from the U.S. Public Health Service (PHS) from 1932 to 1972. The study took place in Macon County, Alabama, and involved hundreds of poor African-American men, mostly sharecroppers. The men had syphilis, a sexually transmitted infection, but didn't know it. Doctors told them they had "bad blood" and gave them placebos, even though penicillin was available in the 1940s, which would have made them treatable. There were originally 399 men with latent syphilis and a control group of 201 others, free of the disease. By 1972, the study was publicized and public outrage led to termination of the project. Twenty-eight participants had died from syphilis, and 100 more passed away from related complications. About 40 spouses had been diagnosed, and the disease had been passed to 19 children at birth. What makes this truly tragic is the sheer lack of ethics shown by PHS.

Source: Nix, Elizabeth, "Tuskegee Experiment: The Infamous Syphilis Study," *History*, published May 16, 2017, https://www.history.com/news/the-infamous-40-year-tuskegee-study.

1. ***Informed consent*** means that the participant in the research must be competent to consent and must have information about what will happen so that they can consent voluntarily. That information includes "the research procedure, their purposes, risks and anticipated benefits, alternative procedures (where therapy is involved), and a statement offering the subject the opportunity to ask questions and to withdraw at any time from the research."

2. ***Systematic assessment*** *of risks and benefits* (by the IRB) evaluates the probabilities and magnitudes of possible harm and anticipated benefits.

3. ***Equitable recruitment*** *and selection of participants* by procedures that justly distribute burdens and benefits of the research. For example, criteria should include gender, race, national origin, religion, creed, education, and socioeconomic diversity appropriate to the population of study. A justification for exclusion of distinct groups is required in the study's protocol.[28]

A complete description of the planned research (i.e., protocol) must be submitted with initial applications for IRB or exempt review. The research protocol should provide the information needed for reviewers to determine that the regulatory and Human Research Protection Program (HRPP) policy requirements have been met. There is no required format or template; different sections and formatting may be used, provided the necessary information is included.

Process

Before researchers begin a study, whether funded or unfunded, they submit a **research protocol**, a detailed application describing the planned research, which IRB reviewers use to determine if regulatory requirements have been achieved. The research protocol has similar components to a proposal that explains the purpose, design, methods, procedures, sampling, and so forth of a research study. The IRB will review, approve, modify, or disapprove the initiation of research and may monitor it for compliance. A very useful reference is "The Application for Human Subjects Research Projects," shown in the American Psychological Association's *The Institutional Review Board (IRB): A College Planning Guide.*[29] Studies are classified into one of three categories: exempt, expedited, or full review.

Your professor may require you to prepare a traditional proposal for your course project whether your research has an academic orientation or you are working with a corporation. Usually, you would seek your professor's approval through a written proposal before constructing a research protocol for the university IRB if one is needed at your institution. IRB protocols for graduate students are often not more than 10 pages. Traditional academic proposals, IRB protocols, and business proposals are compared in the next section of this chapter.

Exempt proposals pose no risk to human subjects and are completed by the IRB chair; ordinarily, this is a 2-week process, although the time frame differs among institutions. Many business research projects are exempt from IRB review because they pose little or no risk to human participants, but an exemption application (a one- to two-page checklist) is submitted and certified nonetheless. *Expedited proposals* involve minimal risk to participants, and a few members of the committee review them. Research considered of minimal risk commonly involves interviews, focus groups, and surveys. A *full review* usually requires a researcher to make a presentation to the full committee, since the research involves more than minimal risk. In all cases, the wait time depends on required revisions. A National Institutes of Health (NIH) study showed that while research proposals had a low rejection rate, more than 80% of proposals required modification because they were not approved as submitted.[30]

If you are not exempt, as is frequently the case with honors students or graduate students doing thesis or dissertation research, you should factor in the time necessary to complete the process. Students will need the involvement of a faculty advisor to comply with appropriate university policies or know that they are exempt. Research not under the control of an IRB includes research conducted for classroom assignments under the professor's supervision, the analysis of publicly available data without participant identification, and oral histories. The regulatory definition of research is "a systematic investigation designed to develop or contribute to generalizable knowledge" and a human subject is defined as "a living individual about whom an investigator . . . conducting research obtains (1) data through intervention or interaction with the individual or (2) identifiable private information."[31] This definition helps to determine an exemption.

Universities do not allow student investigators to self-exempt their projects. It is best to consult with your professor if you think your project may be exempt and submit an exemption request, if required. Instructors of research methods courses are encouraged to coordinate with their IRB, receive NIH or Collaborative Institutional Training Initiative (CITI) human subjects training certification, coordinate student projects "as classroom assignments," and use an IRB contact to expedite procedures and approvals when necessary. Other exemptions are found in 45 CFR 46, §46.101.[32]

Challenges

Perhaps you have developed an opinion about IRBs even if you are agnostic to the role of government regulation. For *graduate students*, "working with IRBs will be one of their most significant challenges—both while earning their doctorates, and during their careers if they enter the academic world."[33] The reason is "mission creep" or a tendency of IRBs to add "requirements driven not by regulations or ethics, but concerns over the possibility of lawsuits and bad publicity."[34] Compounding the problem is that there is no mechanism in the regulations for appeal of their decisions. IRB decisions may not be reversed by any administrator, official, or state or federal agency, including another IRB (21 CFR 56.109, 5 CFR 46.109). Technically, investigators can apply to another IRB in the hope of getting a different result. IRB shopping is possible but rare because it usually does not end well.[35] Another way to see this process is through the lens of IRB process reform. In the resources I cite, you can view the problem through the eyes of researchers and their colleagues whose personal experiences with IRBs paint a more obstructionist picture of the process.[36]

Advice

Is there a way for students to assure a positive result in an IRB application? A *gradPSYCH* article suggests some ways to navigate the system:

- Write clearly. Avoid jargon when explaining your study. Describe the research's purpose and methodology succinctly.

- Cover the main points in the protocol. Describe all the potential benefits of your research, how you will recruit participants, who are in the study population, obtain consent, and protect confidentiality.

- Use successful protocols on topics similar to yours to increase chances for success (these are frequently on the university's IRB website).

- Get feedback. Ask classmates and professors to look for gaps in your proposal.

- Learn how IRBs work. Read the IRB regulations at the federal Office for Human Research Protections website and your local IRB's website.

- Understand IRB timelines. Since many IRBs meet monthly, build extra time into your application process so that any changes don't eat into the time you need to recruit your subjects and gather your data.[37]

Recruiting

According to authorities, "Recruiting subjects is often one of the most challenging aspects of research. Nonrandom subject selection can bias [population] parameter estimates, and an insufficient number of subjects inflates Type II error."[38] The development and implementation of a **recruitment plan** is a vital operational aspect of your research. In trying to help you with a plan, I looked for commonality and consistency across a sample of 20 large research universities and their IRBs. The guidelines found in my sample varied so widely that it was impossible to make a list of what to do and avoid. If you are not exempt from IRB evaluation and are somewhat inexperienced, ask your professor to guide you through the process.

Your recruitment plan follows IRB/professor approval and should consider several activities: (a) identifying the eligible population, (b) targeting and enlisting volunteers, (c) creating an unbiased presentation of the research purpose, (d) recruiting for your sampling plan to account for an anticipated dropout rate and meeting sample size and power requirements, (e) obtaining verifiable informed consent, and (f) retaining participants.[39] The National Institute of Mental Health (NIMH) has prepared a helpful resource in the form of a detailed table of issues in the recruitment process (e.g., benefits and barriers to participation, informational materials, and participant recruitment and retention strategies) with associated examples and suggestions for dealing with each item.[40]

Exhibit 4.8 shows a comprehensive set of methods and media to recruit participants. Not all methods are accepted by IRBs. Nevertheless, the method(s) you select must be described in your IRB submission along with recruiting "materials," which are reviewed and approved before use. Northwestern and Stanford University IRB rules provide examples of the level of information for recruiting materials.[41]

Prepare a Proposal (Academic, IRB Protocol, or Business)

There are few opportune places in the research process to introduce the research proposal. If described too early, the reader has a limited perspective to understand the components.

EXHIBIT 4.8 ■ Recruitment Methods and Media

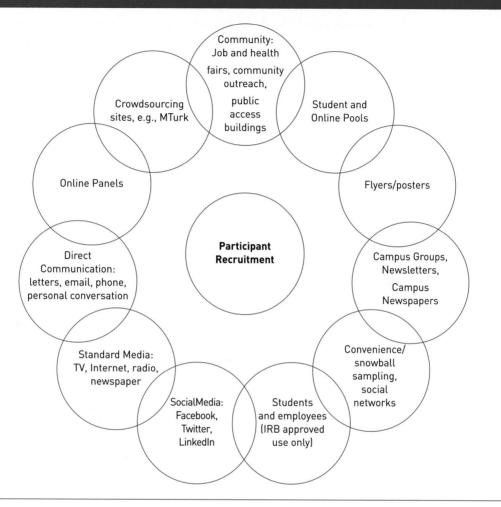

If presented too late, it appears as an afterthought. Consequently, I am linking this section to the previous explanation of IRBs and the role of *research protocols* in making decisions about protecting the rights and welfare of human participants.

Academic proposals are required by one's professor, corporate sponsor, or granting institution to be certain the research meets standards established by the discipline and conventional scientific practices. The **IRB protocol** is a reorganized extension of that submission because while it covers similar components of the research process, its goal goes further: it determines if what is proposed constitutes "research" and protects the rights and welfare of human subjects by minimizing harm or injury. The IRB protocol assesses the information on risks and benefits of participation, informed consent, privacy and data confidentiality, and ongoing safety during the study. In business, when management considers spending funds and other resources on a project, it desires to see a description, a business research proposal, of what will be done and what outcomes might be expected. This description offers management an opportunity to evaluate single or multiple projects regarding costs and benefits.

A proposal is more than an outline you present your professor for approval to begin your term project. According to Krathwohl and Smith, a **proposal**

> . . . describes a plan of work to learn something of real or potential significance about an area of interest. It is a logical presentation. Its opening problem statement draws the reader into the plan: showing its significance, describing how it builds upon previous work (both substantively and methodologically), and outlining the investigation. The overall plans flow from the problem statement: specific steps are described in the methods section, their sequence is illuminated graphically in the work plan (and if one is included, by the schedule), and their feasibility is shown by the availability of resources. The enthusiasm of the proposal carries the reader along; the reader is impressed with the proposal's perspective on the problem, is reassured by the technical and scholarly competence shown, and is provided with a model of the clarity of thought and writing that can be expected in the final write-up.[42]

With over 780 AACSB business schools in more than 50 countries, *proposal requirements differ by institution*. There are also differences among IRBs and required corporate formats. The research proposal will be described in three versions: a traditional academic proposal, an IRB protocol, and a business proposal. Many of the parts are similar but are found in different locations of the respective documents or modified for special purposes. The components are compared in Exhibit 4.8. Although research in business is frequently classified as "exempt" by an IRB, there is still an IRB process to secure the exemption. A sample application for an exemption request is provided in Appendix B. If you are confused as to whether your research requires an IRB review, your professor or IRB will offer guidance. As a second step, a "review determination tree" is offered at this reference.[43] Similarly, a **business proposal** is a written document sent to a prospective client (solicited or unsolicited) to obtain their business. It consists, at a minimum, of an introduction, a statement of the client's problem, value of the project to the client, proposed methods and procedures to approach the problem, schedule and budget, and conclusion. It is designed to gain organizational access, acquire resources, and convince decision-makers that what is proposed will result in useful information or practical solutions to their problems. An example business proposal is found in Appendix C.

Academic Proposals

Academic proposals generally include the following components: cover page/title, abstract, introduction/theoretical framework, statement of the problem, synopsis of the literature, methods and procedures, ethical considerations, timeline, budget and facilities, references, and appendices.[44]

Cover Page/Title. The title page typically consists of the purpose (A Research Proposal for . . .), the study's title, your name, where submitted, and the date. The beginning of Chapter 9 discusses titles, including style manual requirements, length, the importance of wording, use of humor, and how the title can become a one-sentence abstract of your project.

Abstract. The abstract is also described in more detail in Chapter 9. An abstract may or may not be required by your professor for an academic research proposal, but it is usually part of the structure in an IRB protocol. The abstract concisely summarizes the proposal's contents in one paragraph consisting of 150 to 300 words and is placed on a separate page. For example, the abstract would contain two or three sentences on the theoretical framework, rationale and potential impact of the work, research question, literature, hypotheses, research design, method, population and sample, instrumentation, procedures, data collection and analysis, ethical considerations, time frame, and often, expected outcomes. Your professor will guide you in determining which aspects should receive prominence. If your abstract were the only part of the term project that your professor, an IRB, or corporate entity could read, would your overview persuade them to "green light" your research?

Introduction and Theoretical Framework. "The introduction is the part of the paper that provides readers with the background information for the research reported in the paper. Its purpose is to establish a framework for the research so that readers can understand how it is related to other research," says Wilkinson.[45] The purpose is to:

1. Stimulate topical interest and demonstrate foresight in what you plan to accomplish.

2. Create the groundwork for the problem or question that prompts the study.

3. Establish the problem's niche within the broader scholarly literature.

4. Identify an interest(s) for the study's audience: adding to the field's literature, solving or contributing to the solution of a practical problem, or improving decision-making for policy formation.

Statement of the Problem. "The problem statement describes the context for the study and it also identifies the general analysis approach."[46] State concisely the problem's background with a clear problem statement that makes the focus recognizable and shows its significance. Is it feasible given the time available for a term project? In addition, answer the "why" or "so what" questions to establish its relevance.

1. A brief overview of the literature outlines the problem's scope. (See below for alternate placement.)

2. Express the problem as a research question (or questions) and investigative questions.

3. Identify and define variables central to the study.

4. Operationalize the variables for assessment and testing (if necessary).

5. Convert the research question to a hypothesis (hypotheses), if appropriate for the design/method.

6. Establish the assumptions that underpin the research and justify the degree of accuracy each is likely to possess. Some possible examples are as follows: respondents will answer the questionnaire truthfully, the environment will be minimally intrusive, the chosen sample will yield sufficient size to account for attrition, participants represent the population or group being studied, or ethical considerations meet IRB criteria. There may be other assumptions that help the reader compare their assumptions with yours.

7. State the limitations of the research. As a trustworthy researcher, acknowledge weaknesses in the design, method, sampling, procedures, data collection, analysis, resources, and time that may limit your results and the integrity of the findings.

8. Define the boundaries of your study, the delimitations. Be explicit so there is no expectation that you will wander into territory that may be related or interesting but goes beyond the scope and focus of the problem. Do not be timid about saying what you are *not* going to do.

9. Explain the importance and benefits of the research. What is the impetus for studying the problem, what motivated your interest, how does it contribute to the literature of the field, and what practical use is it? According to the World Health Organization, "It should answer the question of why and what: why the research needs to be done and what will be its relevance. The magnitude, frequency, affected geographical areas, ethnic and gender considerations of the problem should be followed by a brief description of the most relevant studies published on the subject."[47]

Synopsis of the Literature. In a proposal, this section assumes an exploratory search of the literature was completed but may not yet be exhaustive. You will have found sufficient material that relates to and clarifies the problem so that you can create a synopsis of what you have found. Consider the following in writing the proposal's literature section even though it will not likely be the completed version of your literature review for the final report.

1. Suggest an organization plan for the literature review in an overview statement.

2. Focus, for now, on literature directly bearing on the problem and how it brackets the issues you are attempting to establish. Are deficiencies or disagreements in past literature revealed? How will your study remedy these?

3. Propose the problem's context and rationale in light of how each work you cite contributes to an understanding of your proposed research.

4. Provide a critical analysis of the literature.

5. Describe how the literature you selected is connected.

6. Explain how your study fits within the boundaries of the chosen literature.

7. Justify your research questions and hypotheses in conjunctions with the literature.

8. State your hypotheses after reporting pertinent sections of the literature or after the literature is completed; connect your hypotheses to the known literature. Your professor may have a preference regarding placement of hypotheses.

9. Take care when citing references, so that paraphrasing and synthesizing authors' words are not confused with making small changes in wording. Credit all the authors you source in the text according to the style manual prescribed by your professor or graduate school.

10. If you have completed a comprehensive review of research, seek ways to synthesize (see the "Literature Synthesis Matrix" in Chapter 9), organize, and connect the parts with transitions, internal summaries, and a general summary. This section will become a "virtually completed" module to drop into your report once your proposal is approved.

11. Compare this proposal section with the literature review instructions in Chapter 3 and the write-up in Chapter 9.

Methods and Procedures. "The methods or procedures section is really the heart of the research proposal. The activities should be described with as much detail as possible, and the continuity between them should be apparent."[48] In the Methods section, the reader's takeaway is the answer to why you selected this design and why it is the most appropriate to answer your question.

1. *Design.* This section should contain information on study type/paradigm (quantitative, qualitative, or mixed) and the objective of the research: descriptive, explanatory, or predictive. The design type should be mentioned with a brief rationale for its selection and principal assumptions (e.g., experimental [pretest-posttest control group design, quasi-experiment], nonexperimental design, or qualitative design). Although most student term projects are cross-sectional, why is a cross-sectional study superior to a retrospective or longitudinal design in your case?

2. *Method.* When you write this paragraph, you will characterize the different ways that the evidence or data are collected and analyzed for attaining the study's goal. Perhaps you have chosen a survey, observational method, or specific experimental design. Your use of a particular method requires further delineation to support the decision that *this* method is appropriate for answering the research question. For example, which modes of survey research and *techniques* will you use? Does your survey involve interaction as in personal or electronic facilitation, face-to-face (personal) interviews, door-to-door interviews, shopping mall intercepts, or telephone interviews (mobile, landline)? Alternatively, will you take a noninteractive approach with a self-administered questionnaire distributed by mail, email, website, text message, or the researcher?

3. *Role of the researcher.* Will the researcher's presence cause the participants to behave in ways out of the ordinary? Will participants detect divergences from their everyday routine or be influenced by the researcher or another event thereby inducing atypical changes in behavior?

4. *Environment or setting.* According to Bhattacharya, "The research setting can be seen as the physical, social, and cultural site in which the researcher conducts the study. In qualitative research, the focus is mainly on meaning making, and the researcher studies the participants in their natural setting. The contrast with postpositivist, experimental, and quantitative research settings lies in the fact that here the investigator does not attempt to completely control the conditions of the study in a laboratory setting, instead focusing on situated activities that locate her or him in the context."[49]

    In quantitative research, you should cover whether the setting offers a controlled environment that facilitates precision and standardization. Can the variables be controlled or do events occur in an everyday setting (field) where respondents/participants are in their normal environment with less researcher control? Does the trade-off between a more contrived versus naturalistic setting impact recruitment success, attrition, and collection and interpretation of the findings? How does this connect to the role of the researcher? Do you have permission to use the site? What rules or regulations of the site affect participants and data collection?

5. *Sampling procedures and participants.* What is the population involved? How will the sample be drawn—that is, by which sampling technique and what is the justification and statistical power used in sample size determination? What characteristics, demographics, or psychographics describe the sample participants? How will the participant volunteers be recruited, screened (included and excluded), and followed up? What are the procedures by which participants withdraw from the study?

6. *Instruments, measuring devices, and materials.* Have you selected a standardized "recognized" measuring instrument from the literature (i.e., previously used in earlier studies with findings on reliability and validity, or from a compendium of measurement scales, or is your instrument self-designed)? If the latter, how do you intend to test it (pilot study?) to demonstrate its reliability? How, when, and where will it be administered, by whom, and how much time is required for completion? Are there any variations (e.g., reverse scoring, different forms of the same instrument, special instructions) that could affect the collected data? Is an apparatus (equipment or media) used to present a stimulus?

7. *Procedures.* Establish and review the overall plan for data collection, including how risks to participants will be avoided, anonymity and confidentiality maintained, informed consent secured, and personal information handled, stored, and subsequently destroyed.

8. *Data analysis.* If you are using a pilot study, it is advantageous to summarize its results and the analytic tools that were used, how effective they were, and if you might use a different approach for the full study. Employ your initial statistical findings to estimate sample size, power, and precision. In addition, describe the collection and recording protocols as well as the software intended for qualitative analysis. If a pilot was not used, specify the statistical analysis techniques you propose to describe and test your data. By stating your intentions clearly, you generate greater confidence for the readers who approve your proposal, thereby enabling them to evaluate/advise you on alternatives.

Ethical Considerations. Read and incorporate the principals of ethics in David B. Resnik's article, "What Is Ethics in Research and Why Is It Important?" Here, ethics is discussed as "norms for conduct that distinguish between acceptable and unacceptable behavior" and as "a method, procedure, or perspective for deciding how to act and for analyzing complex problems and issues." This article lists and provides links to research ethics for different professional associations and disciplines.[50]

Timeline. Create a timeline for the study (topic selection and refinement, exploratory research and preliminary literature review, required organizations, facilities, participants, alternative designs, implementation strategies for methods, identification and permissions for instruments, data collection procedures, data analysis, ethical compliance, professor approval, and implementation of the final the study). Start with your finishing date and conservatively estimate the amount of time needed for each activity. Consider the complexity of the study, IRB permissions, and data collection for the project. Also, include an estimate of the amount of time for drafting and editing the completed report.

Budget and Facilities. Graduate students will need to describe any financial incentives for participants, facility arrangements, and the cost of permissions, photocopying, equipment, travel, training, and gratuities for assistants, minus offsets from sponsors or grants.

References. Referencing is important to proposals and final reports because it allows you to credit the words, ideas, and research of writers you have used in your study. It shows you are a responsible scholar and that you avoid plagiarism, and it helps your reader find sources in your bibliography or reference list for further reading.

1. Follow guidelines in the *Publication Manual of* the *American Psychological Association* or *Chicago Manual of Style* (see Chapter 9) regarding the citation of references in the text and References section.

2. Continually update your reference notebook, literature synthesis matrix, or diary so that no citation or quotation is missed while you assemble your research.

3. The reference list contains references cited in the text. Distinguish between a References list and a *bibliography* based on your professor or advisory committee's requirements.

Appendices. Although your professor may have different requirements, the following items are among those typically found in a proposal's appendix:

1. Rating scales, measures (with permissions), questionnaires or interview guides, and observational checklists.

2. Instructions to participants, scripts, and recruiting materials.

3. Exempt application, sample informed consent form, and other required IRB documents.

Exhibit 4.9 compares the components of an academic proposal, IRB protocol, and business proposal.

EXHIBIT 4.9 ■ A Comparison of Proposal Components		
Academic Proposal (Details of each section are described in the text)	**IRB Protocol: A Regulatory Document**	**Business Proposal**
Cover Page/Title	Cover Page: Principal Investigator (PI), Project Title, Date, Start-End Dates	Cover Page/Title Prepared for; Principal Investigator(s), Date
	Table of Contents (if longer than 10 pages)	Table of Contents
Abstract	Abstract	Preliminary Executive Summary (optional)
Introduction and Theoretical Framework	Scholarly Background; Rationale From Existing Literature	Problem: client and researcher perspectives
Statement of the Problem	Purpose of the Investigation/ Objectives/Problem Statement Research Question/Hypothesis	Project Chronology: (graphic) Project Strategy Explanation
Synopsis of the Literature		Brief Discussion of Available Literature
Methods, Procedures, and Analysis	Study Design: study type, sample, measurement, recruitment, screening, inclusion/exclusion; study procedures	Methodology Sample Design (detailed)
	Setting, regulations, and customs affecting the research setting	Fieldwork Highlights
Ethical Considerations	Resources: required number of subjects, time, facilities, budget, sponsor support, Internet research permissions, staff qualifications	Ethical Considerations: voluntary participation by employees, end-users, account managers, vendors, competitors

(Continued)

EXHIBIT 4.9 ■ (Continued)		
Academic Proposal (Details of each section are described in the text)	**IRB Protocol: A Regulatory Document**	**Business Proposal**
	Participants: incentives, withdraw options, deception, risks (harm), benefits	Instrument (Questionnaire) Design: translation, back-translation (for international)
	Anonymity and confidentiality of data, privacy; destruction of data	Data Collection by principals and vendors
	Voluntary participation and documented informed consent	Data Analysis with expected outcomes
	Safety monitoring and evaluation of vulnerable populations: minorities, prisoners, pregnant women, elderly individuals, economically disadvantaged persons, children, and students. Debriefing statement	Data Analysis Specifics (e.g., market segmentation, competitor comparisons, key driver analysis)
Timeline	Data Management and Statistical Analysis	Project Deliverables/Action Plans/Recommendations
	Assurance Statement (Statement of Compliance) and Signature	Client Team—Consulting Team Responsibilities
Budget and Facilities (optional)	Proper IRB forms for submission	Consulting Team and Strategic Partner Credentials/Prior Work
		Project Costs and Terms
References	References/Bibliography	References
Appendices	Appendices	Appendices
	Disseminating Results	Notes and Copyright

Conduct a Pilot Study

The "conducting" phase of the research process includes a pilot study. A **pilot study** is a small-scale version of the larger study performed to detect weaknesses in the research design, instructions to participants, measuring instruments, nonresponse and attrition rates, missing data percentages, and proxy data for the final decision about a sampling plan and its size. Therefore, the pilot draws participants from the target population and uses data collection methods and collection sites including designated organizations. The pilot study may reveal unanticipated political issues in an organizational study that were unknown when the management question was formulated. These findings may impact the feasibility of conducting the study. Numerous benefits make pilot studies valuable to researchers:

- Fine-tuning a research question or investigative questions

- Refining a hypothesis or set of hypotheses

- Evaluating the target population and research field site

- Estimating the success of the proposed recruitment strategy

- Testing research instruments such as survey questionnaires, interview or discussion guides, and standardized versus researcher-devised instruments

- Securing variability estimates from the data to help determine sample size in probability sampling plans

- Collecting preliminary data for use in revealing problems with data analysis procedures and statistics

- Determining the resources (time, costs, staff) needed for the full-scale study

- Training the research staff to execute the study

- Producing preliminary results to convince funding sources that a full-scale study is feasible and worth funding

- Securing other forms of institutional support and investment from stakeholders[51]

The pilot study simulates the chosen procedures and protocols for data collection. If the study is a survey to be conducted by mail, the pilot questionnaire should also be mailed. Simulation is required as well for online, telephone, and personal interviews and mixed-model survey methods just as for experiments and qualitative studies. If the design calls for observation from an unobtrusive researcher, this behavior should be rehearsed.

The optimal size of the pilot group ranges from 10 to 40 participants depending on the design and statistical sample size requirement of the data analysis techniques planned for the full-scale study. A percentage range of 10% to 20% of the actual sample has also been suggested.[52] In practice, suggestions for sizes at the upper end of the range are often too large to be realistic, which presents a dilemma for assessing measuring instruments that require a larger sample for statistical reliability estimates. Also, in small populations or in some qualitative studies that require fewer participants, large pilot samples run the risk of exhausting the recruiting pool or sensitizing participants to the study's purpose.

Variations on pilot testing include pretesting and feasibility studies. **Pretesting** may rely on a small subsample of actual participants to refine a measuring instrument, including its instructions, questions, or scales. Pretesting attempts to discover ambiguities in wording, difficult to understand questions, and time for completion and collection. Items that produce a large nonresponse percentage can be identified. When a researcher has assistance in administering the questionnaire or another instrument, pretesting also helps to evaluate staff capabilities and the need for further training. With self-administered questionnaires, it is more difficult to do advance evaluations. Researchers may use the "think aloud" approach and ask "pretest respondents to verbalize their thoughts as they complete the questionnaire," which reveals participant interpretations and understanding of response alternatives.[53] **Feasibility studies** are used when there are concerns that the obstacles of time, cost, and resources may cancel the full-scale project.

Chapter Summary

- The *research process* consists of exploring, planning, creating, conducting, collecting, analyzing, and writing (the written report). It is the road map or instructional start-up manual that explains the orderly progression of your research project. I separated the model into shorter, more digestible chapters that follow the flow of preparing for research and conducting it. In this chapter, the phases of *creating* and *conducting* research were covered. Exhibit 4.1 illustrates some of the most labor-intensive activities of the research process.

- The *creating* phase involves three elements: matching an efficient method/technique with the design, identifying or devising the measuring instruments, and implementing a sampling plan.

- The *conducting* phase of the process contains three elements: recruiting research participants ethically, preparing a proposal (academic, IRB protocol, or business), and conducting a pilot study.

These are "hands-on" activities in the research process. The former involves obtaining IRB approval for the use of human participants in research. The proposal is the logical presentation of your work plan, in which you describe the significance of your research topic and its relationship to previous work and outline the methods and sequence of steps to collect and process the data. Its importance lies in the approval or disapproval of your project based on the scholarly and technical competence you show. The pilot study prepares you to anticipate and correct weaknesses in the actual study through a trial run. It gives you critical information on participants' reactions to your instruments, numerical estimates for sampling, and a preliminary evaluation of statistical techniques. Pretesting collects information to make modifications to the instruments prior to administration. It relies on a small group of participants to refine a measuring instrument, including its instructions, questions, or scales.

Key Terms

academic proposal	observational methods	research protocol
business proposal	participant observation	sample
element	pilot study	sampling
equitable recruitment	population	sampling frame
feasibility studies	pretesting	scaling
informed consent	probability sample	survey
Institutional Review Board (IRB)	proposal	systematic assessment (IRB)
IRB protocol	random selection	systematic observation
naturalistic observation	recruitment plan	validity
nonprobability sample	reliability	

Discussion Questions

1. What are the three elements of the *creating* phase of the research process model?

2. Name three *methods* frequently used in business research.

3. In survey research, there are three modes or conventional ways of implementation: interactive, noninteractive, and mixed. Explain the advantages and disadvantages of each.

   a. Which *techniques* are associated with each mode?

   b. What kinds of problems do survey designers encounter?

   c. Why is there greater emphasis on mobile and online surveys? How will that affect more traditional forms of data collection in the future?

4. What are the main techniques used in observation?

   a. Describe a business study in which you use a specific observational technique.

   Devise an observational study using human and nonhuman participants. What business processes are likely to involve nonhuman participants?

   b. Apply the discussion of ethical dilemmas from Chapters 3 and 4 to observational methods. What are the implications of informed consent, privacy, and deception in observational studies?

5. Define measurement. How would you explain to a new student the difference and/or relationship between measurement and scaling?

   a. What issues of reliability and validity are created when you create the measuring instrument?

   b. What are some dependable sources for selecting a measuring instrument?

   c. Illustrate with one or two questions using an online service's instrument creation software.

6. Describe the concept of sampling. How do populations, sampling frames, and sampling elements differ?

   a. What are the major types of probability samples?

   b. Why would you choose a probability sample over a nonprobability sample?

   c. What are the key benefits of nonprobability samples for qualitative designs?

   d. List and explain four or five nonprobability samples you would consider.

   e. What is random selection and why is it not necessary for nonprobability samples?

   f. Which probability sample is the most efficient?

   g. When would you choose to do a census rather than a sample?

7. Describe the three elements of the *conducting* phase of the research process.

8. What are Institutional Review Boards (IRBs) and what is their purpose from a historical and contemporary standpoint?

   a. What are the three sacred ethical principles derived from the *Belmont Report* and enforced by IRBs?

   b. What is the difference between exempt, expedited, and full review classifications for IRB protocols?

   c. How can you increase your chances of getting a positive result from an IRB, especially if your research is not classified as a class project?

   d. What is the relationship between your recruitment plan for acquiring participants and acceptable IRB practices/requirements?

9. Compare the elements required for an academic proposal, an IRB protocol, and a business proposal.

10. List the benefits of a pilot study.

    a. Is time the only reason that many novice researchers avoid something so essential?

    b. Distinguish between pilot, pretesting, and feasibility studies.

THE PROCESS ROAD MAP

Collecting, Analyzing, and Writing

LEARNING OBJECTIVES

Performance Objective

Collect quantitative data through numerical instruments and qualitative data through the techniques discussed in this chapter and Chapter 7. Edit the data to detect errors and omissions, consistency across participants, and unclear, incomplete, or inappropriate responses. *Analyze* your data initially by describing, searching for patterns, and looking for relationships that answer your questions through exploratory graphical analysis, descriptive summary statistics, and inferential testing and evaluation of hypotheses.

Enabling Objectives

1. Edit your data to detect errors and omissions and certify them to obtain quality standards.

2. Prepare for data irregularities such as out-of-range responses and various types of missing data.

3. Find specialized sources for handling open and closed question coding, textual coding, missing data diagnostics, and the treatment of "don't know" responses.

4. Become familiar with the use of exploratory data analysis to discover patterns in your data that guide your selection of inferential statistics.

5. Prepare for reporting your findings by reviewing the structure of business and academic reports.

6. Discover how IMRAD (Introduction, Methods, Results, and Discussion) can be adapted to the needs of your target audience.

This chapter completes the phases and activities of the research process. Thus, upon concluding this chapter, you will have an understanding of 17 individual activities in the process model. Those phases that remain involve collecting, analyzing, and writing.

Exhibit 5.1 reminds you that Phases 1 through 4 are complete. It also highlights collecting, analyzing, and writing.

PROCESS PHASE 5: COLLECTING AND ANALYZING

This phase of the process model consists of two elements:

- Collect and Process the Data

- Analyze and Interpret the Data

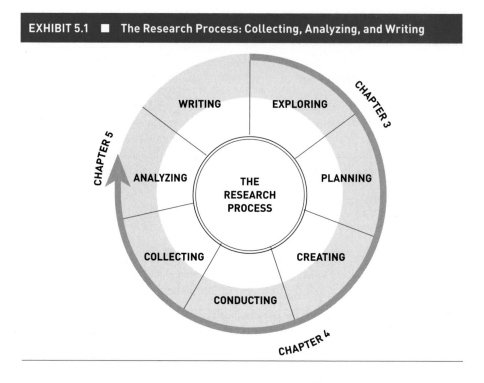

EXHIBIT 5.1 ■ The Research Process: Collecting, Analyzing, and Writing

○   Exploratory, Descriptive, and Inferential Statistics

○   Assumptions for Use and Steps for Statistical Testing

Collect and Process the Data

Data collection, the systematic process of gathering information on variables of interest related to the research question or hypothesis, occurs in various settings ranging from small focus groups to multinational organizations. Your choice of research method determines how the data are collected. **Research data** are "data that [are] collected, observed, or created, for purposes of analysis to produce original research results."[1] Researchers and their staff members collect and record research data with questionnaires, standardized tests, observational forms or checklists, laboratory notes, field notes, audio/video recordings, social media monitoring, instrument calibration logs, and many other devices.

What kinds of data are collected? Quantitative data are used to explain phenomena through a numerical approach that uses mathematically based methods, especially statistics.[2] "Qualitative data are not necessarily or usually numerical, and therefore cannot be analysed by using statistics."[3] Exceptions occur when the method selected can use computer software for qualitative or mixed-methods projects. Mainly, qualitative data are textual (interview transcripts, field notes, or documents such as e-mails, reports, or meeting minutes) or video, audio, and photos. Schutt compares qualitative with quantitative data this way[4]:

- Emphasis on context rather than universal generalizations

- Attention to meanings and rich descriptions of the world rather than quantifiable measures of specific variables

- The expectation that the researchers' and others' values may influence the course of collection and analysis rather than presume the process is value free

- The collection of more data on a few cases rather than minimal data on numerous cases

- Responses in detail, without predetermined categories, rather than an emphasis on programmed categories

- The researcher as "instrument" rather than the designer of a device to measure variables

Qualitative data are produced by a wide array of methods: ethnography, netnography (cyberethnography and virtual ethnography), ethnomethodology, qualitative comparative analysis, narrative analysis, conversation analysis, case-oriented understanding, and grounded theory. A thorough description of the procedures for collecting and processing the data from these methods is beyond the scope of this chapter. However, Lewins and colleagues[5] provide a summary of the data preparation process, including the commonalities across methods such as writing about the data in summary form and coding text segments into thematic ideas. Like quantitative data, you organize qualitative data manually or with computer programs. Computer-assisted qualitative, textual, and pictorial data analysis might use QSR NVivo, ATLAS.ti, MAXQDA, or HyperResearch.

Coding and Editing

Editing detects errors and omissions, corrects them when possible, and certifies the achievement of minimum data quality standards. Data are edited to ensure consistency across participants (with quantitative data). For qualitative data, the researcher wants to discover why the data are not consistent and consistency should not be forced. With survey methods, for example, editing reduces errors in recording and clarifies unclear, incomplete, and inappropriate responses. Although most data are in digital form, mainly from web-based data collection, paper-and-pencil measures require careful editing.

After the data are edited, they are prepared for analysis. Since the report does not present raw data, codes reduce the responses into a flexible system for processing and storage.

Coding (mapping for manipulating geographic data sets) involves assigning numbers or other symbols to answers so the responses can be grouped into a limited number of categories that streamline the analysis. For example, the gender variable has categories of male and female, which are coded M and F, 1 and 2, or 0 and 1. Coding should use all available attributes (and their codes) to preserve detail, as shown in the example in Exhibit 5.2. Variables may always be reduced (also known as condensing, collapsing, or bracketing) to a smaller number of alternative codes later. For example, the nine-code education variable in Exhibit 5.2 could become four codes: grade school, high school, college, and graduate school. A recode function in statistical software accomplishes this by creating a new and parallel variable with fewer categories.

A **codebook** or coding sheet contains each variable in the study and specifies the application of coding rules to the variables (see Exhibit 5.2). The codes follow researcher-devised decision rules for sorting, tabulating, and analyzing.

One advantage of a codebook is you can locate a variable's position and specify its numerical range in the data file. (The data file looks like a spreadsheet or matrix with rows of cells called cases or participants and columns of cells called variables.) If you are doing your data entry, a codebook facilitates the construction of your data set.

The final step in processing the data is creating the electronic data file. **Data entry** transforms the coded data you gathered to a medium for viewing and statistical analysis. Optical scanning, voice recognition, barcode readers, web-based survey databases, CATI/CAPI, and keyboard entry facilitate the researcher's data entry needs. The data editor in SPSS, SAS, MINITAB, or R software facilitates the creation of a data file.

EXHIBIT 5.2 ■ Excerpt From a Codebook		
Variable	**Format**	**Description, Variable Label, Coded Value, Value Label**
EDUC	Numeric	The highest level of education completed?
	Width = 1	Label: Education level
	Decimals = 0	1 No formal education
		2 Some grade school
		3 Completed grade school
		4 Some high school
		5 Completed high school
		6 Some college
		7 Completed college
		8 Some graduate school
		9 Completed graduate school

Microsoft Excel, if you are using their statistics or importing a spreadsheet, may also be used to examine the data file for both respondent and data entry errors as well as out-of-range responses and missing data.

Data Irregularities

Out-of-range responses are those that are above or below predetermined ranges (i.e., values that are not plausible). Let's say that you are studying Millennials, whom the Pew Research Center defined as being age 18–34 years in 2015.[6] When you apply your software's out-of-range application (or procedures such as Frequencies, Descriptive Statistics, or Histograms) to the age variable, you find values below the range at 16 and above the range at up to 38. Some writers advocate eliminating raw data that are obviously defective, but that recommendation poses a problem when the analyst understands that advice to mean removing an entire row. Removing a row reduces the sample size and deletes otherwise useable responses of that participant on all other variables. The typical guideline is to replace the **out-of-range response** with an 8, 88, or 888 and adjust the column width as necessary. This assumes that the existing range does not include an 8 or 88, and so forth.

Missing data pose additional problems especially when they show a systematic rather than random pattern. **Missing data** in a study occur "when there are no data whatsoever for a respondent (nonresponse) or when some variables for a respondent are unknown (item nonresponse) because of refusal to provide or failure to collect the response."[7]

The primary ways to handle missing data are as follows:

- Analyze only the available data (i.e., ignore the missing data).

- Use statistical models that allow for missing data.

- Impute the missing data with replacement values, and treat these as if they were observed (e.g., impute or fill in a missing value using a statistical process such as substituting the mean or median of the variable or using predicted values from regression analysis).

- Impute the missing data and report that they were imputed with uncertainty.[8]

If you have coded (or recoded) for alternatives such as don't know, refused to answer, or invalid response, you have the option of reading and classifying the variable with software like SAS as "special" missing data versus "ordinary" missing data. If a nonresponse on education (Exhibit 5.2) is found to be a genuine missing value, it may be coded (and documented on your coding sheet) as 10 or left blank. Once you evaluate, replace, or remove unusable data, you can move forward with the analysis by giving the software special instructions.

See the data analysis guide that accompanies your statistical software for more details on open and closed question coding, coding of text, missing data diagnostics, and the handling of "don't know" responses. For a tutorial on how to use the SPSS Data Editor, see the website link at this reference.[9] Statistical programs like those mentioned in this section have modules to accomplish data diagnostic tasks and improve data integrity.

Analyze and Interpret the Data

In his article on problems with the way that statistics are conducted and reported, Daniel Wright humorously but accurately noted: "Conducting data analysis is like drinking a fine wine. It is important to swirl and sniff the wine, to unpack the complex bouquet and to appreciate the experience. Gulping the wine doesn't work."[10] At this point in the process, you will start a preliminary analysis by describing, searching for patterns, and looking for relationships that answer your questions. In this section, please note the citations, as many will add immeasurably to your knowledge and confidence to proceed with data analysis. **Data analysis** is the process of systematically using statistics or modeling techniques to explore the data through graphical illustration, descriptive summary statistics, and the analysis, testing, and evaluation of hypotheses. These activities roughly correspond to *exploratory data analysis*, *descriptive statistics*, and *confirmatory data analysis* (or *inferential statistics*). I will address each type of analysis in the following sections, and Chapter 9 includes an expanded example of the reporting of statistical results.

©iStockphoto.com/tadamichi

Data analysis is the process of systematically using statistics or modeling techniques to explore the data through graphical illustration, descriptive summary statistics, and the analysis, testing, and evaluation of hypotheses. But let's not fool ourselves; data analysis can be easy to get wrong. If you retrieve some data from the Internet, you will receive all kinds of error messages when you do something wrong. Possibly, the host doesn't exist or you may have arranged the search words in the wrong order. The same is not true for most data analysis methods because these are numerical algorithms that will produce some output even if the input data do not make sense. So you always need to be aware of what you are doing and mentally trace the steps to have a well-informed expectation of the results.

Source: Braun, Mikio L., "Data Analysis: The Hard Parts," *Marginally Interesting* (blog), February 17, 2014, http://blog.mikiobraun.de/2014/02/data-analysis-hard-parts.html.

Exploratory Data Analysis

Exploratory data analysis (EDA) is a data analysis perspective or way of thinking about the data in which the data direct subsequent analyses—and may revise your planned analysis through insights revealed using graphical displays that show what the data are saying. The role of graphics is essential to EDA, as John Tukey, its developer, concluded: "The greatest value of a picture is when it forces us to notice what we never expected to see."[11] EDA is different from techniques that produce numerical summaries or nongraphical displays; the EDA

EXHIBIT 5.3 ■ Histogram

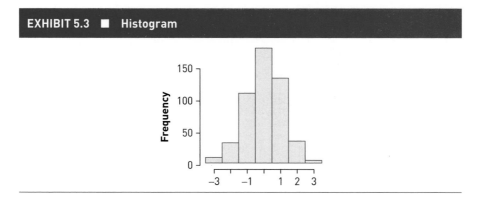

analyst is skeptical of summary techniques because they often conceal characteristics of distributions. EDA encompasses numerous techniques that you may find useful for displaying and examining distributions. A **distribution** arrays data from the lowest to the highest scores on their scales and together with the frequency of occurrence, the observations produce a distribution of values, observed or theoretical. In addition to "frequencies," which are found in every statistical software package, here are some EDA examples.

When it is possible to group the variable's values into intervals, **histograms** display interval-ratio data. They look like a bar plot in which each bar runs vertically. The histogram displays all of the distribution's intervals, even those without observed values. Histograms can be helpful for examining the shape of and gaps in the distribution. You may decide to superimpose a normal curve over the data, which reveals how your data depart from normality.

Stem-and-leaf displays are closely related to histograms (turn the histogram display on its side) but present actual data values that can be inspected directly without the use of enclosed bars (see Exhibit 5.4). This visual shows the distribution of values within the interval and preserves their rank order for finding the median, quartiles, and other summary statistics. Although some business researchers do not use the stem-and-leaf display, it has excellent diagnostic qualities. For example, this display is useful for linking a particular

EXHIBIT 5.4 ■ Stem-and-Leaf Display of CEO Ages

3 | 9
4 | 2 3 4 6 7 9
5 | 1 2 3 3 5 7 7 8 9
6 | 1 3 3 4
key 5 | 3 = 53

observation back to the data file and the participant who produced it. With stem-and-leaf displays, the range of values can be seen at a glance, revealing the shape and variability of the distribution, gaps where no values exist, areas where values cluster, and outliers.

Boxplots, or *box-and-whisker plots*, reduce the detail of the stem-and-leaf display to provide a different image of the distribution's location (median), spread, shape, tail length, and outliers. Their construction is based on data points, which are annotated on the right side in Exhibit 5.5. The plots look like a rectangle with whiskers extending to

EXHIBIT 5.5 ■ Annotated Box-and-Whisker Plot

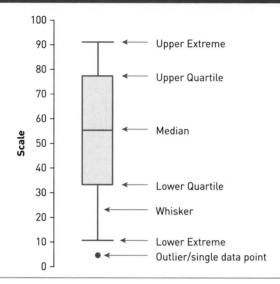

Source: Ribecca, Severino, "Box and Whisker Plot," *The Data Visualisation Catalogue*, http://www.datavizcata logue.com/methods/box_plot.html.

the top and bottom. Boxplots are usually vertical, but horizontal formats can be used. Multiple boxplots compare subsets of your data on the same scale. For example, industry sectors can be compared with each other regarding a variable of interest, such as an economic measure.

EDA visualization plots also include Q-Q (quantile-quantile) plots, normal plots (that show if your data depart from a theoretical normal distribution), and plots for means, standard deviations, normal probability, scatterplots, and a dozen more. These, in turn, provide insight into the structure of your variables and distributional characteristics and accelerate the checking of assumptions (because inferential statistics have requirements for their use). EDA also detects errors for deletion or imputation (replacing missing data with substitute values) and gives you a preliminary look at the relationships between explanatory and outcome variables.

Descriptive Statistics

The characteristics of location, spread, and shape are summary statistics that describe the distributions that you visualized with EDA. More frequently, they are called measures of central tendency, variability, and shape of the distribution. Their definitions, use, and formulas fall under the heading of **descriptive statistics**. Descriptive statistics focus on the characteristics of the collected observations and do not assume that the data came from a larger population. A description or enumeration is the first step for researchers to take their data analysis from a data set to an understanding of a sample or (small) population under study.

Descriptive statistics are not very informative for describing asymmetrical (non-normal) distributions. Some researchers calculate numeric summaries and pronounce the data fit for use with inferential statistics. They do not consider the nature of **nonresistant statistics**, like the mean and standard deviation. Moreover, they are not heeding the requirements for the use of inferential statistics. Many inferential statistics are sensitive to the effects of extreme values in the tails of the distribution; thus, normally distributed variables are specified as a requirement for the use of many statistics.

Let's describe an example.[12] Suppose a researcher has a data set {5, 6, 6, 7, 7, 7, 8, 8, 9}. The mean is 7, and the standard deviation is 1.23. If only one value is replaced with an extreme score (90 replaces 9), the new mean becomes over two times larger at 16 and the standard deviation increases to 27.78. The mean is greater than most of the numbers in the distribution, and the standard deviation is more than 22 times its original size. In short, by replacing only one score of this distribution, the central tendency and variability summaries are disturbed to the point that *they no longer represent the other eight values.*

Had researchers been able to "see" the data rather than produce an index number, they would have known that the median and quartiles would have been the better choice. Why? Because when I made the change above, the median remained at 7 and the quartiles remained at 6 and 8, respectively. The median and quartiles are **resistant statistics** because they are unaffected by outliers and change only slightly with small replacements of the data set. I propose a different set of assumptions based on the evidence from the example:

1. A distribution's shape is just as consequential as its central tendency or variability.

2. Visual representations are superior to numerical ones.

3. The choice of summary statistics to describe a variable is contingent on the suitability of those statistics for the shape of the distribution.

Central Tendency. To complete a review of descriptive statistics, let's start with the measures of **central tendency** or location. They include the mean, median, and mode (please refer to Chapter 2, Exhibit 2.8, for the table on measurement levels and their descriptive statistics counterparts). The **mean** is the arithmetic average and the measure of central tendency most often used for interval-ratio data. It can be misleading when the distribution contains extreme scores, large or small, as I previously demonstrated. The **median** is the midpoint of the distribution. Half of the observations fall above and below the median. The median is best with ordinal data and, as a resistant statistic, it is the preferred measure for interval-ratio data when the distribution is asymmetric. The **mode** is the most frequently occurring value. A bimodal distribution has two different modes appearing as peaks in a probability density function or a histogram. If they are unequal, there is a major and minor mode. If more modes exist, the distribution is said to be multimodal. The mode is used for nominal data analysis.

Variability. Measures of **variability** (alternatively referred to as dispersion or spread) are the variance, standard deviation, range, interquartile range, and quartile deviation. Collectively they describe how scores cluster or scatter in a distribution. The **variance** is the average of the squared deviation scores from the mean. If all values are identical, the variance is 0. It is used with interval-ratio data along with the more frequently reported standard deviation. The **standard deviation** is the positive square root of the variance. It improves (and should replace for reporting purposes) the variance's interpretability because it removes the variance's square and expresses deviations in their original units (e.g., net profits in dollars, not dollars squared). The **range** is the difference between the largest and smallest value in the distribution and is computed from the minimum and maximum scores. The range, best used with ordinal data, is useful in that it serves as a comparison for homogeneity. For homogeneous distributions, the ratio of the range to the standard deviation should be between 2 and 6. A value above 6 signals heterogeneity.

Continuing with variability, we find the **interquartile range** (IQR). The IQR is the difference between the first and third quartiles of the distribution and is also referred to as the midspread. The IQR is associated with ordinal data and used in conjunction with the median. It also is the proper descriptive value for interval-ratio data that are asymmetrical. The **quartile deviation (Q)** or semi-interquartile range is also used with the median for ordinal data. In a normal distribution, the median plus one-quartile deviation on either side encompasses 50% of the observations. (Exhibit 5.5 illustrates this.) With a normal distribution, Q's relationship with the standard deviation is constant ($Q = .6745$ standard deviations). Q is helpful for understanding interval-ratio data of a skewed nature. There is no measure of variability for nominal data.

Shape. The **measures of shape** are skewness and kurtosis, which describe departures from the symmetry of a distribution and its relative flatness (or peakedness), respectively. **Skewness** is a measure of a distribution's deviation from symmetry.

In a symmetrical distribution, the mean, median, and mode are in the same location. When cases stretch toward one tail or the other, the distribution is called skewed. With a skewed distribution, the mean moves toward the direction of the skewed tail—that is, the outliers or extreme scores pull the mean in their direction. A right skew is a positive value, and a left skew is a negative value (Exhibit 5.6). When the distribution approaches

EXHIBIT 5.6 ■ Positive and Negative Skews

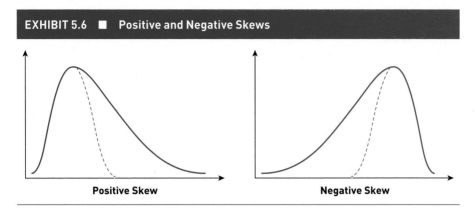

Positive Skew   Negative Skew

symmetry, the value for skewness (*sk*) is approximately 0. Check this detail with your software program.

Kurtosis, as illustrated in Exhibit 5.7, is a measure of a distribution's peakedness or flatness. Distributions, where scores cluster densely or pile up in the center along with more observations than normal in the extreme tails, are peaked and kurtosis (*ku*) will have a positive value. Flatter distributions will have minimal tails and a *ku* that is negative. Normal distributions approach 0. As with skewness, the larger the absolute value of the index, the more extreme the characteristic.

EXHIBIT 5.7 ■ Kurtosis

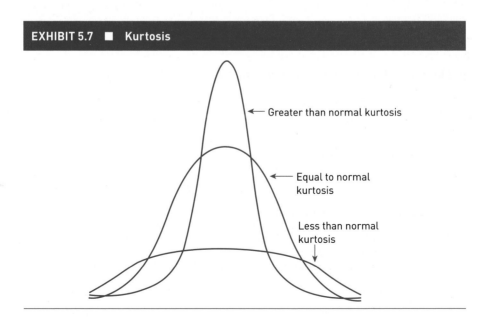

← Greater than normal kurtosis

← Equal to normal kurtosis

Less than normal kurtosis

Inferential Statistics

Inferential statistics use data from a sample to make inferences, or estimates, about a population in contrast to the numerical summaries of descriptive statistics. Inferential statistics test hypotheses and derive estimates for decisions based on an analysis of available sampling data. A hypothesis is established, and it is rejected or fails to be rejected on these data alone.

There are two *classes* of significance tests: parametric and nonparametric. And, in general, there are two *types* of tests: tests of group differences and tests of association. **Parametric tests** rely on assumptions about the population from which the sample was drawn. For example, parametric tests assume a normal distribution, among other requirements. Some tests are quite robust and hold up well despite violations. With others, a departure from linearity or equality of variance may threaten the validity of the results. **Nonparametric tests** have fewer and less stringent assumptions about the shape or parameters of the underlying population distribution. They do not specify a normally distributed population—that is, they are *distribution free*, or equality of variance is not relevant. The data are non-normal, they come from an unknown distribution, they cannot be transformed, the central limit theorem cannot be applied, and the data are nominal or ordinal. Some statistics may require independence of cases, while others are designed for situations with related cases.

Nonparametric tests are the only ones appropriate for nominal data; they are the only technically correct tests to use with ordinal data. Nonparametric tests also may be utilized with data originally collected as interval ratio, but this decision wastes information (because the interval-ratio measurements have to be reduced from equal intervals to categories or ordered comparisons).

Assumptions for Using Parametric Statistics

The researcher is responsible for reviewing the **statistical assumptions** or requirements for the chosen test and performing diagnostic checks on the data to assure the test's fitness. There are common assumptions and more advanced assumptions. Let's look first at general requirements for parametric statistics. Keep in mind that some tests place a stronger emphasis on one or more of these than do others:

- The variables must be continuous (interval-ratio measures); this is a necessity.

- The observations come from random samples from their respective populations.

- Cases have values on both the dependent and independent variables.

- For multiple regression, homoscedasticity must be met (meaning that the variance of errors is the same across all levels of the independent variable).

- Outliers should signal caution.

- The sample size should be large enough so that the distribution of the sample mean differences is approximately normal.

- When using a matched-pairs (related) statistic, the pairing should relate to the variable being measured (i.e., if you are studying the performance of sales executives, it makes no sense to match them on their height).

- In multiple group comparisons, you should have equality of variance—that is, the population variances of the groups being compared are equal (unless the number of cases in each group is similar). You can check this using the Brown-Forsythe or Welch robust F test, found within the statistics program menu for analysis of variance (ANOVA).

When in doubt about a statistic, consult your statistics text or a data analysis guide such as Marija Norusis's *SPSS Guide to Data Analysis*.[13]

Selecting a Test

Consider three questions when choosing a test:

1. Does the testing situation involve one, two, or *k* samples?

2. With two or more (*k*) samples, are the individual observations independent or related?

3. What level of data (NOIR) did the measurement scale collect?

These three criteria are used to develop a classification of the major tests: parametric, nonparametric, and measures of association. Exhibit 5.8 illustrates this classification.

For example, your testing situation involves two samples; the samples are related (dependent), and the data are interval. The table recommends the one-sample (paired) t-test as the appropriate choice. Additional criteria refine your decision: Are the samples of equal or unequal size? Have the data been weighted? Have the data been transformed? Based on answers to such questions, you can reach a final decision.

Decision trees are a systematic method to select tests. They start with questions about the number and nature of the variables (continuous, discrete, dichotomous, independent, dependent, and so forth). They progress to questions about the nature of the relationship being compared or tested. One long-lived reference (from the 1970s) by the University of Michigan Institute for Social Research was revised by the SAS

EXHIBIT 5.8 ■ Recommended Statistical Techniques

Measurement Level	One-Sample	Two-Samples		k-Samples		Measures of Association
		Related Samples	Independent Samples	Related Samples	Independent Samples	
Parametric						
Interval-Ratio	• t-test • Z-test	• Paired sample t-test	• t-test • Z-test	• ANOVA-repeated measures	• ANOVA***	• Pearson's r • Eta* • Biserial Corr. • Partial Corr. • Multiple Corr. • Bivariate Regression
Nonparametric						
Ordinal	• Kolmogorov-Smirnov one-sample • Runs test	• Sign test • Wilcoxon matched-pairs	• Median test • Mann-Whitney U • KS • Wald-Wolfowitz	• Friedman two-way ANOVA	• Median extension • Kruskal-Wallis one-way ANOVA	• Gamma • Kendall's tau** • Somers's d • Spearman's rho
Nominal	• Binomial Chi-Square one-sample	• McNemar	• Fisher's Exact • Chi-square	• Cochran Q	• Chi-square k-samples	• Phi • Cramer's V • Contingen. C • Lambda • G & K tau • Uncertainty Coeff. • Kappa

Source: Adapted from Emory, C. William. *Business Research Methods*, 3rd ed. (Homewood, IL: Richard D. Irwin, 1985), 360.

Notes: * Nonlinear

** Kendall tau variations: *b* and *c*, partial rank and *W*

*** One, two-way, N-way ANOVA have *post hoc* tests for (multiple) comparisons of group mean scores and the tests have different assumptions (e.g., pairwise comparison, complex comparison, equal *n*, unequal *n*, equal variances assumed, unequal variances not assumed): Fisher's LSD, Bonferroni, Tukey HSD or WSD, Tukey-Kramer, Holm-Bonferroni, Newman-Keuls, Duncan's (MRT), Rodger's, Scheffe'S, Dunnett T3 & C, Sidak, Benjamini-Hochberg, Games-Howell, Tamhane T2.

Institute.[14] Current examples of statistical decision trees are found in this book's Appendix D.

Steps for Statistical Testing

To preface this section on testing procedures, I should recount recent developments. In the era when p-values were accessed through reference tables in book appendices, before easy access to computers and statistical software, an arbitrary conventional threshold was used in much of the research community to establish guidelines for p-values: ≥.05 (not significant), <.05 (significant), and <.01 (highly significant). (A **p-value** is the probability of obtaining a value of the test statistics as extreme as, or more extreme than, the actual value obtained when the null hypothesis is true.) This practice is no longer advised because the precise p-value obtained is shown in the software's output and may be compared to the level of significance you set for the study.[15]

During the last few years, there were discussions in the literature about how p-values and statistical significance were misused and misunderstood. In 2016, the American Statistical Association (ASA) took its first official position on a statistical practice—how to use p-values. ASA's pronouncement consisted of six principles and was intended for researchers, practitioners, and science writers who were not statisticians.[16] The third principle states: "Scientific conclusions and business or policy decisions should not be based only on whether a *p*-value passes a specific threshold." Commenting on this principle, Frost notes:

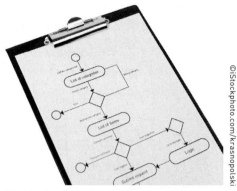

A decision tree is like a map of the outcome of your choices. A statistical decision tree starts with a single node, which may ask a question like "Summarize an entire distribution?," and then branches into possible outcomes (e.g., "Central tendency" or "Variability?"). Each outcome leads to additional nodes, which lead to other possibilities. This expansion of possibilities gives it a tree-like shape. Decision trees can be used for project planning or mapping a plan of action as well as predicting the best statistical technique to choose. See Appendix D for decision trees that help you choose descriptive, parametric, nonparametric, and correlation statistics.

> Using P values in conjunction with a significance level to decide when to reject the null hypothesis *increases* your chance of making the correct decision. However, there is no magical threshold that distinguishes between the studies that have a true effect and those that don't with 100% accuracy.[17]

Recent developments in statistics have been incorporated into this section on testing procedures. The sequence of steps for statistical testing includes the following[18]:

1. State the null hypothesis.

2. Choose the statistical test.

©iStockphoto.com/krasnopolski

3. Select, beforehand, the desired level of significance, which corresponds with the study's importance to practice or theory (e.g., <.05, <.01, <.001).

4. Satisfy the data requirements (assumptions) by using diagnostics for the chosen test.

5. Enter the test variables and testing options into the dialogue box or boxes of your program.

6. Interpret the output, such as the calculated value of the test statistic, degrees of freedom, significance (p-value), mean difference, and confidence interval for the mean difference.

7. Use the p-value in conjunction with the significance level to "risk assess" the null.

8. Use the "effect size" to distinguish between statistical significance and practical significance (i.e., the strength of the IV); assess "statistical power" to determine the test's power to reject a hypothesis ($\geq$.80 for a given effect and sample size).

9. Make a decision based on test results and contextual factors; state your conclusions.

Commentary on Statistical Testing Steps. *Step 1.* The **null hypothesis** is a statement of no difference between the population parameter and the sampling statistic being compared to it. The **alternative hypothesis** (or research hypothesis discussed in Chapter 2) is the logical opposite of the null and states that there *is* a difference. That difference may be represented as greater than, less than, or not the same. Alternative hypotheses correspond to two-tailed and one-tailed tests. A **two-tailed test** is nondirectional and splits the probability of an unlikely outcome into two regions of rejection (i.e., the two tails of the distribution). A **one-tailed test** places the entire probability into the tail of the distribution specified by the direction of the alternative hypothesis.

Step 2. Test selections were discussed and illustrated in Exhibit 5.8. Decision trees make your choice even easier (see Appendix D).

Step 3. Good scientific practices require that you state the significance level for testing *a priori*, at least before data collection. **Statistical significance** in hypothesis testing is the probability associated with determining if a result is unlikely to have occurred by chance alone. Statistical significance is achieved by a p-value that is less than the significance level (designated as α, alpha). Consider this: if you were doing HIV research for the CDC or testing for the efficacy of different pilot training programs for commercial aviation, you would likely want a very low probability of rejecting a true null hypothesis. Using a smaller alpha lowers the risk of making a wrong decision.

Step 4. Review the "Assumptions for Using Parametric Statistics," and conduct the necessary diagnostics before proceeding.

Step 5. The software programs I have mentioned are SPSS, SAS, MINITAB, and R. There are many other programs that use pull-down menus and dialogue boxes for selecting the test and identifying the test variables from the variables list.

Step 6. Interpreting the output involves familiarity with the different indices used for each procedure you choose. Tutorials are available[19] and software guides are quite helpful in this regard. The statistic determines the amount of tabled output. A one-sample t-test procedure produces two tables. In contrast, a multiple regression analysis in SPSS would have five tables with many indices. The "Results" section in Chapter 9 provides examples of p-values, degrees of freedom, mean differences, and confidence intervals.

Step 7. To make this determination, use the tables containing numeric output generated by your statistical test to find the p-value and then compare it to the significance level that you set in advance. The p-value shown in the output is a computed significance level that coincides with the **calculated value** of the test statistic (just as if you calculated the formula by hand). By comparing it to the significance level (if $p < \alpha$, reject the null), you are prepared to decide to reject or not reject the null hypothesis. But before you do, consider the mean difference and the confidence interval.

Let's look at an example of "risk-assessing" the null. Two pilot training programs for commercial aviation are being compared to reduce flight takeoff accidents. In the first study, Training A is less effective than Training B. A p-value of <.05 is cited for the decision. The carrier abandons Training A and puts its resources into Training B. Subsequently, a second study replicated the first one. This time, there is no difference between the two training programs ($p \geq .05$). The carrier switches back to its initial Training A program because of its shorter duration and lower expense. The first study's p-value was .048 and the second was .052. These results are so close to the arbitrary significance level (.05) that the researchers should (1) determine the *effect size*[20] or magnitude of the difference between the training programs' mean scores, (2) establish the *power* of the test,[21] (3) be sure that the sample size was calculated using power and effect size, and (4) look for other explanations for flight takeoff accidents. The causes of accidents vary widely for this type of incident (e.g., blowing a tire, smoke in the cockpit, bird strike, icy runway, engine fire, and so forth). Are the researchers focusing on training as an indicator of pilot error when they should study mechanical and environmental factors?

Step 8. The "Results" section in Chapter 9 shows the relationships between effect size, power, and sample size. It also provides reasons why establishing your sample size in advance gives you preliminary estimates for the statistic's power and allows you to determine if the effect size is sufficient.

Step 9. Recalling the previous discussions about the significance level, arbitrary thresholds, p-values, and other indices you have seen with the test results, you now make a decision about the null hypothesis. Contextual factors play a role in this decision and require introspection. For example: How sound is the choice of the study's design for the research question? Have your measurements been validated in settings similar to yours or did you create them without testing for reliability and validity? How confident are you that your sample is a good representation of the population? Is there any external evidence for the effect you have observed?

PROCESS PHASE 6: WRITING

The *writing* phase of the research process model contains one element: write the research report. It is the "arrival" point on the process road map. The coverage of this phase here serves as a *preview* of Chapter 9. This section is limited to the *structure* of business versus academic reports, whereas Chapter 9 covers the details in sequence.

Write the Research Report

The culmination of the research process is writing the report. The **research report** represents your communication to your research audience of the nature and importance of your problem, what sources you have discovered to enlighten its background, the methods you chose to collect primary data, the analysis, the interpretation, and the conclusions or solutions found. In the first chapter, I said that by the time you have reached this point, you would have enough background to start your term project early with sufficient confidence to invent the term project and write the paper.

When you start writing your report, work on cultivating a growth mindset. A growth mindset affects creativity. A fixed perspective shuts down exploration and discovery. Writing to explore need not conflict with writing to report. When you engage with the subject before you have all the answers, you may find unsuspected connections, uncover different facets of the topic, and even change the direction or structure of the piece. Although these diversions may consume more time, the resulting work is often better, and the process of writing more fulfilling.

©iStockphoto.com/triloks

Source: Janzer, Anne, "How to Create an Internal Mindset Conducive to Writing," Jane Friedman (blog), June 20, 2016, https://www.janefriedman.com/mindset/.

Chapter 9 is devoted to a thorough discussion of strategies for report writing. As such, I will only provide a synopsis of organizing principles here. A quality presentation of research findings can have a profound effect on a reader's perceptions of a study's value. Thus, although this is the last element in the research process, it is one of the most important. Its style and organization will differ according to the audience, occasion, and purpose of the research.

If the research is conducted to solve a management problem of an applied nature, the communication of results may cover a range of communication options. Although most business organizations have their format for written reports, there are some commonalities:

- *Title Page*: the report's name reflecting its purpose; recipient's name, title, and organization; author(s) of the report; and submission date.

- *Executive Summary*: a one-page stand-alone document written as a condensed version of the report under the assumption that some readers will only read this page. It includes the study's purpose, methodology, principal findings, conclusions, and recommendations.

- *Table of Contents*: numbered location and overview of the report's contents.

- *Introduction*: background/impetus for the study; problem statement and its significance; scope; organization of the report; and available secondary sources bearing on the problem and methods for collecting primary data.

- *Body of the Report*: a focused analysis that describes the interpretation and evaluation of principal (relevant) findings, as well as the meaning of these findings in the form of conclusions with or without recommendations. The decision maker (client or sponsor) may have requested supportable courses of action.

- *Appendices* (optional): supporting materials, required statistical information not presented in the body, and credentials of the individual or firm presenting the report.

- *Works Cited/Bibliography/References*: a list of references used *in* rather than *for* the report and explanatory notes when footnotes are not used.[22]

Academic reports regularly follow a scientific report format. **IMRAD** is an acronym for a structure emphasizing the Introduction, Methods, Results, and Discussion. IMRAD originated in the physical sciences but is now used as an organizing template by many disciplines in business and the social and behavioral sciences. It is used for dissertations, theses, and student research reports as well as research articles in journals—excluding field and case studies. The IMRAD structure is similar to the American Psychological Association (APA) style manual format, which many business schools require for reference citations. Adaptations to expand the main sections are common mainly to accommodate the title, abstract, acknowledgments, and references. There are other variations for class research papers, theses, and dissertations. For example, the Introduction might contain some of these sections:

- Background

- Statement of the Problem (Research and Investigative Questions)

- Literature Review (optional placement)

- Hypotheses

- Assumptions

- Delimitations

- Definition of Terms

- Importance and Benefits of the Research

The "review of related literature" may be part of the Introduction, or *it could stand alone as a separate heading*. IMRAD is also used to organize conference and poster presentations. The student's professor or thesis advisor or the university's graduate school ensures that reports meet the requirements of their respective colleges and disciplines. Chapter 9 contains information on style guides often used in business schools.

Four questions guide the writer: (1) What is the aim of the report? (2) Who is the audience and what do they expect? (3) What are the reporting circumstances and limitations? (4) How will the report be used? Reports should be well organized, physically inviting, and readable. These goals are achievable when writers are careful with details, style, and comprehensibility.

Disseminating your findings is an integral part of reporting, as mentioned in Chapter 1 ("Outcomes"). Specialty sources and other books describe formats for sharing your work through conference and poster presentations (often at undergraduate conferences) and for business reports with oral presentations or circulation of reports to executives, sponsors, or clients. See the following references for getting the word out.[23]

Chapter Summary

- The *research process,* composed of seven phases and 17 elements or activities, was separated into shorter, more digestible chapters that follow the flow of preparing for research and conducting it. In this chapter, I covered *collecting, analyzing,* and *interpreting the data and writing* the report. Chapter 9 deals exclusively with writing your report.

- *Collecting and processing* the data includes editing, coding, building a data file, and performing data cleaning tasks. The systematic process of data collection, or gathering information on variables of interest, occurs in various settings ranging from small focus groups with a single facilitator to multinational organizations where many data collectors may be required. The scale of the project and resources determine your choice of the research method, and in turn, determine how the data are collected.

- The *analyzing* phase of the research process model contains one element: analyzing and interpreting the data. This activity involves testing quantitative or qualitative data. Data analysis is the process of systematically using statistics or modeling techniques to explore the data through graphical illustration (EDA), descriptive summary statistics, and the analysis, testing, and evaluation of hypotheses. EDA is a way of thinking about the data where visualization of the data directs subsequent analysis. The measures of central tendency, variability, and shape of the distribution fall under the heading of descriptive statistics. Descriptive statistics focus on the characteristics of the collected observations. A description or enumeration is the first step for researchers to take their data analysis from a data set to an understanding of a sample or (small) population under study.

- Inferential statistics use data from a sample to make inferences, or estimates, about a population. They test hypotheses and derive inputs for decisions based on an analysis of available sampling data. A hypothesis is established, and it is rejected or fails to be rejected on these data alone. The researcher is responsible for reviewing the statistical assumptions or requirements for the chosen hypothesis test and performing diagnostic checks on the data to assure the test's appropriateness. Selecting a test is the result of guidance from statistics textbooks, decision tables, or decision trees. The sequence for statistical testing was presented with a commentary on each step.

- The section "Selecting a Test" introduces Appendix D, which contains decision trees to help you find proper statistics for your study.

- The *writing* phase of the model is the final phase and contains one activity: a brief overview of writing the written report. It is the culmination of the research process, and it addresses both business and academic report "outlines." Your report represents your communication with a business or academic audience about the nature and importance of the problem, the sources you have discovered to enlighten its background through secondary data, its design, methods, and approach to collect primary data. It also includes the analysis, interpretation, and the conclusions or solutions found. Its completion is a creative contribution to academic knowledge or solving an applied business problem.

- The *writing* phase of the research process introduces Chapter 9, which both illustrates and explains the write-up of your report in a step-by-step fashion.

Key Terms

alternative hypothesis	IMRAD	p-value
boxplots	inferential statistics	quartile deviation (Q)
calculated value	interquartile range	range
central tendency	kurtosis	research data
codebook	mean	research report
coding	measures of shape	resistant statistics
data analysis	median	skewness
data collection	missing data	standard deviation
data entry	mode	statistical assumptions
decision trees	nonparametric tests	statistical significance
descriptive statistics	nonresistant statistics	stem-and-leaf displays
distributions	null hypothesis	two-tailed test
editing	one-tailed test	variability
exploratory data analysis (EDA)	out-of-range response	variance
histograms	parametric tests	

Discussion Questions

1. What are the three elements of the *collecting* phase of the research process?

2. Distinguish between quantitative data and qualitative data using a comparison of their different features.

3. Describe the process of data editing, data cleaning, coding (mapping), and devising a codebook for data entry with an editor of a statistical software package.

   a. Why are out-of-range responses problematic and what are the best ways to ensure that they do not invalidate the interpretation of statistical summary and inferential tests?

   b. What kinds of issues arise from missing data?

   c. How would you "impute" a value in a missing data situation?

4. Define data analysis with an example of each aspect of the definition.

   a. Explain the primary techniques used in exploratory data analysis and discuss why visualization of data distributions is superior to summary statistics (indices).

   b. If you had to select among histograms, stem-and-leaf displays, and box-and-whisker plots to describe a variable in a report, which would you choose and why? Would it be the same choice if you were "data snooping" for yourself?

   c. Why are statistical measures that concentrate on "shape" more consequential than typical summary statistics?

5. What are the measures of central tendency and variability?

   a. Referring to Exhibit 2.8, describe why the measurement level determines which descriptive statistic you chose to summarize a variable.

   b. With interval-level data, why is the standard deviation superior to the variance for the explanation of findings, especially for a nonstatistical reader?

   c. What is the importance of a distribution's shape and how does kurtosis tell you how much a variable's distribution has departed from normality?

   d. Where are the extreme values in a skewed distribution? What do they do to the mean? Thus, would you use the mean or median as an index of central tendency?

6. What is the purpose of inferential statistics and why is it customary (and practical) to distinguish between parametric and nonparametric data?

   a. What are the major assumptions of parametric statistics?

   b. If nonparametric statistics are *distribution free*, does that mean that they rely on or do not rely on assumptions that the data are from a probability distribution? What other differences have you discovered?

   c. What are the three critical questions you would ask in choosing a statistical test?

   d. How do "one-tailed tests" differ from "two-tailed tests?" If you select a one-tailed test, where in a graphic visualization of the variable's distribution would you find the region(s) of rejection for the null hypothesis?

   e. Decision trees (Appendix D) are used as a guide, not a definitive remedy, for choosing a statistical test. How might they augment tables and statistic textbooks to help you find the most appropriate statistic for your purpose (data description, hypothesis test, correlation, etc.)?

f. What is the connection between a p-value and the null hypothesis?

g. How is a p-value different from the level of significance?

7. State the nine steps in statistical testing and discuss the meaning of and operations involved in each.

8. Research reports are organized differently based on whether the audience is primarily composed of managers or academics. Describe the common components of a research report for management.

9. Explain how IMRAD is used to organize academic reports and what variations or additions you might consider beneficial for the reader.

10. A research writer is guided by four strategic questions. Discuss the implications of each for the audience and the writer's credibility.

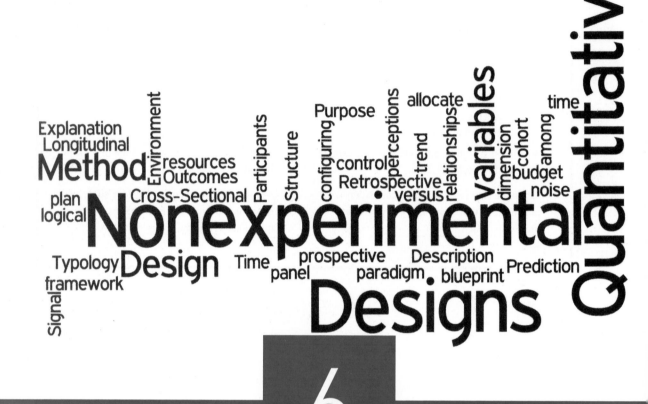

6

NONEXPERIMENTAL QUANTITATIVE DESIGNS

68

LEARNING OBJECTIVES

Performance Objective

Apply your knowledge of research design and its classifications (purpose/objective by time dimension) to understand nonexperimental quantitative designs in a business context. Use the design criteria, the 3×3 matrix, and examples of business studies to select a design for your project.

Enabling Objectives

1. Discuss how the research question affects the choice of design.

2. Define the essential components of research design.

3. Assess the role of manipulation of variables in nonexperimental quantitative design.

4. Justify why design should not be confused with a method.

5. Advocate why a coherent classification of design assists students and practitioners.

6. Discuss the criteria used to evaluate business designs.

7. Describe the 3×3 matrix created to classify business studies using the study's purpose/objective and the time dimension.

This chapter is the first of three on research design. In this chapter, I emphasize design definitions and characteristics, distinguish design from method, and cover nonexperimental *quantitative* design. Qualitative and mixed design and experimental design will be discussed in Chapters 7 and 8, respectively.

DESIGN AND THE RESEARCH QUESTION

Chapter 1 illustrated some of the different "purposes" for business research: reporting, exploring, describing, explaining, predicting, and changing (or action research). These were studies that address the purposes of business research, but *not all purposes* are designs. In Chapter 2, I said that theories respond to the natural language questions of who, what, when, where, how, and why and the predictive claims of could, should, or would a specific event occur.

A particular type of design may answer many of these questions (e.g., description helps us to understand questions of what, who, when, and where). Causal research, which is experimental and nonexperimental, seeks to explain, deal with cause-and-effect relationships, and attempt to answer the questions of how and why. Prediction deals with the questions of could, should, or would an event occur. Research questions primarily address three fundamental problems:

1. What is (or was) going on? (Description)

2. Why (or how) is it going on? (Explanation)

3. What will or might occur in the future? (Prediction)

Design is profoundly affected by the research question. "Good description provokes the 'why' questions of explanatory research."[1] For example, if we want to know what changes in running a business have occurred over the last 20 years, we might list several trends, one of which is how effortlessly human resources are connected all over the globe. This question prompts us to ask another: "Why is this taking place? But before asking 'why?' we must be sure about the fact and dimensions of the phenomenon" that *describe* changes in the business environment.[2] Alternatively, one may seek to answer a predictive question about the occurrence of an event.

WHAT IS RESEARCH DESIGN?

Research design has two functions: (a) to answer research questions and (b) in experiments, to control variance. Chapter 8 addresses the second function, control. Definitions from respected authors suggest:

> The function of a research design is to ensure that the evidence obtained enables us to answer the initial question as unambiguously as possible. Obtaining relevant evidence entails specifying the type of evidence needed to answer the research question, to test a theory, to evaluate a programme or to accurately describe some phenomenon . . . in a convincing way.[3]

> Design describes the art of arranging for the evidence gathered, or planning of evidence so that a convincing chain of reasoning is constructed.[4]

> Research design is the plan and structure of investigation so conceived as to obtain answers to research questions. The plan is the overall scheme or program of the research. It includes an outline of what the investigator will do from writing hypotheses and their operational implications to the final analysis of data. A structure is the framework, organization, or configuration of . . . the relations among variables of a study.[5]

> The research design constitutes the blueprint for the collection, measurement, and analysis of data. It aids the scientist in the allocation of his limited resources

by imposing crucial choices [on the selection of methods, data collection, sample size, the degree of structure and] . . . should the analysis be primarily quantitative or qualitative?[6]

Victor Margolin once said, "Design does not signify a class of objects that can be pinned down like butterflies."[7] Thus, these definitions differ in perspective but they have a similar preoccupation with finding answers to the research question or evaluating the truth-value of a hypothesis. My definition synthesizes five components. **Research design** is:

1. A logical plan to select and arrange the evidence that answers the research question(s)

2. A framework to specify the relationships among a study's variables

3. A blueprint to outline each procedure from the hypotheses to the analysis of data

4. A means of configuring the study to its paradigm (e.g., achieving findings that are numeric, systematic, generalizable, and replicable; or obtaining non-numerical observations that reveal and detail the experience and constructed meanings of individuals, groups, situations, or contexts)

5. A means to determine how to allocate limited resources of time and budget

NONEXPERIMENTAL DESIGN

Researchers in business, education, and the social-behavioral sciences differentiate between experimental and nonexperimental designs because experimental designs produce reliable evidence of causality, whereas nonexperimental designs cannot manipulate the independent variable, exert sufficient control, or randomly assign participants to the study's groups or conditions. They can, however, use probability sampling, incorporate powerful multivariate models, and are adaptable to many settings in business where experiments are unusable. **Nonexperimental design** is a

. . . systematic empirical inquiry in which the scientist does not have direct control of independent variables because their manifestations have already occurred or because they are inherently not manipulable. Inferences about relations among variables are made without direct intervention, from concomitant variations of independent and dependent variables.[8]

Nonexperimental research is unmistakably vital to research design:

It can even be said that nonexperimental research is more important than experimental research. This is, of course, not a methodological observation.

It means, rather, that most social scientific and educational research problems do not lend themselves to experimentation, although many of them do lend themselves to controlled inquiry of the nonexperimental kind.[9]

There are also circumstances where a nonexperimental approach may be superior from a design perspective due to the researcher's skill: "An experiment may use random assignment and involve manipulation of the treatment variable and still be essentially worthless as a basis for drawing conclusions. It is essential that rigorous controls, careful execution, planning, thoughtfulness, etc., accompany a valid design."[10]

NONEXPERIMENTAL DESIGNS IN BUSINESS

Business problems pose perplexing academic questions and managerial dilemmas, but because many are not amenable to experimentation, nonexperimental designs are good alternatives. The research question, given preferential coverage in the research process chapters and now influencing our discussion of design, can test the need for a nonexperimental design under different conditions. For example, the research question or hypothesis may be framed in such a way that the researcher:

- Only observes a single variable rather than a statistical relationship between two variables.

- Investigates a noncausal statistical relationship between two variables and their effects.

- Analyzes a causal relationship, but the independent variable cannot be manipulated, or participants cannot be randomly assigned to treatments or conditions.

- Cannot use an experimental design because manipulating the independent variable could cause harm to the participants (ethical responsibility).

- Cannot use an experimental design because it is impractical (lack of opportunity, financial cost, or the presence of attribute variables that cannot be used in random assignment).

- Needs to identify, describe, or measure relationships among variables for use in a future experimental study.[11]

Again, the choice between the experimental and nonexperimental approaches is dictated by the nature of the research question. But the two approaches can also be used *to address the same research question in complementary ways.*[12]

DESIGN IS *NOT* METHOD

It should be clear that design is not about second-level data concerns or the mechanics of research. Design should never be confused with a research method or a technique for gathering data. Many research methods textbooks obscure this fact. Why?

When no unified typology exists for research design, there is no direction for researchers and writers and a vacuum prevails.

Many sources, for example, frequently label exploratory studies as a design but their research "purpose" has the explicit goal of discovery (see Chapter 1). They aim to identify, diagnose, explore, or define a problem. Typically, this type of study occurs *before* the research question is formulated and ends *before* a formalized design begins. If your study is exploratory and you intend to operate a fluid discovery mode, you must still clearly delineate your objectives. Even then, calling it "exploratory" is not an excuse for lack of definition nor is it a rationale for elevating it to design status.

The research vernacular also camouflages what design is by making the term interchangeable with method and technique. Many researchers conducting policy studies refer to their approach as a design. However, the creators of Interactive Management techniques (Delphi, Nominal Group Technique, Interpretative Structural Modeling, and others)[13] call them techniques, processes, or tools for achieving consensus in group judgment, dealing with complex systems, and performing strategic planning.

Confusion also arises from defining a design as a data collection technique rather than as the logical structure of the study. Habitually, researchers pair designs with procedures, such as experiments with objective tests and scales, surveys with questionnaires, or case studies with observation. Data can be collected for any design through numerous means. Experimental data result not only from tests and instruments but also interviews, self-administered questionnaires, projective techniques, observation, and physiological measures. While a discipline's conventional wisdom may advocate one collection strategy as more compatible with their traditions, it may not be the most *logical choice* for the research question. According to de Vaus, "How the data are collected is irrelevant to the logic of the design."[14] Gorard adds that design "will be independent of, and logically prior to, the methods of data collection and analysis employed."[15]

Why is this important? This is important because "designs are often evaluated against the strengths and weaknesses of the method rather than their ability to draw relatively unambiguous conclusions or to select between rival plausible hypotheses."[16] As Yin's convincing argument concludes, research design "deals with a *logical* problem and not a *logistical* problem."[17]

The difference between logical problems and the supporting logistics to solve them is not insignificant. Elaborating on de Vaus's analogy of designers and builders, before architects develop a work plan, they first envision the nature of the structure, its use, and the inhabitants' needs. Like the structure of a research inquiry, these kinds of

Shutterstock/Rido

Research design is a logical plan to select and arrange the evidence that answers the research question(s). Design is not method. It is not about second-level data concerns or the mechanics of research. As the logical structure of the study, the research design should not be confused with a technique for data collection. This is important because designs are often evaluated against the strengths and weaknesses of the method used rather than their ability to draw relatively unambiguous conclusions or select between rival plausible hypotheses.

issues precede the blueprint, its work plan, and the materials.

Next, architects envision the form, spatial relationships, and ambiance to facilitate a structure's functional, social, environmental, and aesthetic requirements. Like research questions, their designs reflect structures with often-contradictory client requirements for shape, space, size, and safety. This is similar to the requirements that managers and consulting clients place on researchers. Finally, for the architect, available materials, weather, and site conditions are further complications. For students, time, skill, experience, and IRBs confound and delay the completion of their task. Researchers understand (or should understand) this analogy and that methods and tradecraft are not a substitute for good design.[18]

DESIGN TYPOLOGIES

There is little agreement in business, education, or the social and behavioral sciences as to an acceptable classification, or typology, of nonexperimental research designs. Even if it is flawed, a design classification would have pedagogical advantages and help students make choices that integrate their study's framework with the process of executing it. In addition, selecting functional designs for business solutions better assists practitioners. "Classification can bring about multiple advantages. . . . It can augment the research process, including hypothesis formation, testing, interpretation, and reporting."[19]

A **typology** is a form of classification that conceptually separates a set of items on multiple characteristics and distills them into fewer generalizable dimensions, which are intended to be nonoverlapping (mutually exclusive) and exhaustive categories. It is easy to forget the importance of typologies in business. Here are a few typologies to jog your memory: Porter's classification of market elements, Rogers's adoption of innovations, Mintzberg's organizational configurations, Schein's three levels of organizational culture, Kotter's organizational culture and performance, Merchant and Simons's managerial control, Denison's personalities and organizational performance, and Borgatti and Foster's network paradigm of organizational research. More contemporary examples include crowdsourcing metrics, e-business models, and emerging market characteristics. In the physical sciences, taxonomies are commonplace in astronomy, anatomy, chemistry, biology, botany, and other fields.

Reynolds reminds us that naming, organizing, and categorizing the "things" of a study are the first tasks of science and are basic to building scientific knowledge. Without this foundation, science cannot move to higher-level tasks of explaining and predicting.[20] Reynolds's test for the usefulness of typologies includes:

- Exhaustiveness

- Mutual exclusivity

- Theoretical relevance
  - Parsimony
  - A common level of abstraction
  - Explanatory and predictive power
  - A language with descriptive relevance for theory building

Tiryakian added that the dimension or dimensions that are "differentiated into types must be explicitly stated."[21]

In creating a design typology, specific standards gauge the degree to which proposed designs meet benchmarks for inclusion. I have approached these standards in four ways:

1. A comparison of existing designs using the five-point design definition introduced in this chapter. Respected scholars are the sources of the definition's provenance.

2. Practical descriptive criteria, which cover the scope of the research purpose and objective.

3. The comparison of typological standards (primarily, exhaustiveness and mutual exclusivity) in their application across the range of designs found. This application of typology "may support lecturers, students, supervisors, researchers, peer-reviewers, practitioners, etc., to have a more articulate, reflexive and critical orientation with regard to research design in order to maximize the validity of findings and advance theory, methodology and practice."[22]

4. An informal survey on the status of nonexperimental quantitative designs derived from 30 contemporary research textbooks in business and fields with similar research approaches.

Criteria

The nine classification criteria presented in Exhibit 6.1 represent an input for the design typology shown in Exhibit 6.3. When you are writing the "Design" section for your report, many of these criteria may help you clarify the characteristics of your study and familiarize readers with your approach. Before we examine Exhibit 6.3, a qualifier is in order. Although this chapter's focus is nonexperimental quantitative design, the research paradigm should include the research orientation. In business, a quantitative point of view emphasizes numbers, measurement, control, breadth, generalization, large samples, standardized procedures, and researcher detachment from the process. A qualitative

	Criterion	Description
EXHIBIT 6.1 ■ Design Classification Criteria		
1	Structure	A structured design features a research question with specificity that guides the study; the study contains well-formulated investigative questions, hypotheses, a review of the related literature, precise procedures, and specifications for collecting the evidence needed to solve the logical problem posed by the study's question.
2	Researcher control of variables	Control refers to the difference between experimental and nonexperimental design with their degrees of manipulation, control, and random assignment[a] and, when applicable, the use of probability sampling or group equivalence producing techniques.
3	Signal versus noise	Designs can be signal enhancers or noise reducers. A powerful treatment with high internal validity (a strong signal) and a precise, reliable, and valid measurement (low noise) provides a greater likelihood of observing the hypothesized effect.[b] Apart from experimentation, error and bias contribute to noise, and the selected design should reduce them (e.g., errors related to measurement, researcher, response, sampling, selection, effect size, etc.).
4	Purpose	Designs are characterized by purpose. Research purposes include reporting, exploring, describing, explaining, predicting, interpreting, evaluating, contextualizing, or participating to facilitate change (action).
5	Time dimension	Studies may be categorized as cross-sectional, longitudinal/prospective, and retrospective. In the first case, data collection occurs at one point in time. In the second, data collection starts in the present and extends into the future with (multiple) comparisons across time. In the third, the data exist from the past concerning an existing occurrence.[c]
6	Environment	The setting for a study is often dichotomized as laboratory versus field, contrived versus noncontrived, conspicuous versus unobtrusive. Dichotomies as opposed to continuums lead to pejorative labeling of environments as artificial or "not normal" for the events of study. The question is "normal for whom?" The study of boards of directors, teams, and managers can occur in either a field or laboratory setting. In a laboratory, researchers sometimes create the phenomenon as it occurs in nature, called **experimental realism**. Combined with the control offered by a laboratory, this substantially increases internal validity of a study. In a less controlled or uncontrolled environment (often characterized as the "field," e.g., an organization, public area, or a private residence), research lends itself to the observation of natural behavior. Field studies have the potential to improve external validity of the findings.[d]

	Criterion	Description
7	Participants' perceptions	Related to the environmental criterion is the way in which participants perceive the intervention of the researcher. Usually, when participants behave or respond differently, it is because they believe that something out of the ordinary is happening in their lives. There are three conditions that affect this criterion. Participants perceive: a. No deviations from everyday routines b. Deviations, but unrelated to the researcher c. Deviations as researcher induced[e] These conditions affect perceptions from the extremes of realism to artificiality. We aim for studies that obtain participants who are unaware of any intervention, but that is not always possible in research of organizations, marketing, or finance.
8	Outcomes	The degree to which the design's attributes are perfected to produce results involves questions of efficacy, effectiveness, and efficiency. The first (efficacy) asks, "Can it work?" or to what extent does the researcher's intervention accomplish the task under ideal circumstances? The second (effectiveness) asks, "Does it work in practice?" The third (efficiency) asks, "Is it worth it?," or under normal circumstances, "Is there a favorable cost-benefit ratio for the resources consumed by the design?"[f]

Notes:

[a]De Vaus, David A. *Research Design in Social Research* (Thousand Oaks: SAGE, 2001), 43–84; Bryman, A., and James J. Teevan, *Social Research Methods*, 3rd ed. (Toronto: Oxford University Press, 2005), 27–35.

[b]Trochim, William M., "Experimental Design: Classifying Experimental Designs," *The Research Methods Knowledge Base*, 2nd ed., version current as of October 20, 2006, http://www.socialresearchmethods.net/kb/expclass.php.

[c]Johnson, Burke, "Toward a New Classification of Nonexperimental Quantitative Research," *Educational Researcher* 30, no. 2 (2001): 9; and Belli, Gabriella, "Nonexperimental Quantitative Research," in *Research Essentials: An Introduction to Designs and Practices*, eds. Stephen D. Lapan and MaryLynn T. Quartaroli (San Francisco: Jossey-Bass, 2009), 66.

[d]Wand, Y., and R. Weber, "On the Ontological Expressiveness of Information Systems Analysis and Design Grammars," *Journal of Information Systems* 3, no. 4 (1993): 220; and Scholten, Annemarie Zand, "Research Designs: 3.05 Lab vs. Field." Lecture notes from Quantitative Methods, University of Amsterdam, https://www.coursera.org/learn/quantitative-methods/lecture/wdLk9/3-05-lab-vs-field.

[e]Redding, W. Charles, "Research Settings: Field Studies," in *Methods of Research in Communication*, eds. Philip Emmert and William D. Brooks (Boston: Houghton Mifflin, 1970), 140–142.18.

[f]Haynes, Brian, "Can it Work? Does it Work? Is it Worth It?" *BMJ* 319 (1999): 652; quoted from A. L. Cochrane, *Effectiveness and Efficiency: Random Reflection of Health Services* (London: Nuffield Provincial Hospitals Trust, 1972): 23, https://www.nuffieldtrust.org.uk/research/effectiveness-and-efficiency-random-reflections-on-health-services.

preference seeks to understand the context of others' meanings and depth and detail with fewer but selectively chosen cases, naturalistic approaches, and researcher emersion into the process. Mixed-method designs integrate the strengths associated with both approaches.[23]

The Status of Design in Business and Allied Disciplines

In 1991, Pedhazur and Schmelkin,[24] writing on nonexperimental design, said "there is no consensus regarding the term used to refer to designs." In 2001, Johnson[25] reviewed 23 research methods books from the social and behavioral sciences. Ten years had changed nothing: "[C]onfusion arises from the practice of treating a technique for data collection as an indispensable definition of design rather than the design as the logical structure of the study. He discovered over two dozen different labels being used, sometimes with slight variations in the wording."[26] In 2009, Belli added new textbooks and her findings were similar.[27]

Exhibit 6.2 shows the current status of nonexperimental quantitative designs derived from 30 contemporary research textbooks in business and comparable fields. Its purpose is to inform you about the status of design classification in research methods, which affects teaching and methodological coherence. Exhibit 6.2 is also used in this chapter as an input for a typology by organizing designs separately from methods and techniques.

EXHIBIT 6.2 ■ Nonexperimental Quantitative Design Classifications by Discipline		
Authors	**Types of Nonexperimental Quantitative Designs**	**Reference**
Business/Marketing		
Sekaran & Bougie (2016)	Descriptive (survey with time dimension), correlational, case study (quantitative), field experiment, *ex post facto*	*Research Methods for Business: A Skill-Building Approach*, 7th ed. (West Sussex, UK: Wiley, 2016)
Saunders, Lewis, & Thornhill (2016)	Descriptive, descripto-explanatory (a precursor to explanation), explanation, evaluative, exploratory	*Research Methods for Business Students*, 7th ed. (Essex, UK: Pearson Education Ltd., 2016)
Babin & Zikmund (2016)	Exploratory (quantitative), descriptive	*Essentials of Marketing Research*, 6th ed. (Boston: Cengage Learning, 2016)
Hair, Celsi, Money, Samouel, & Page (2015)	Exploratory (quantitative), descriptive	*Essentials of Business Research Methods*, 2nd ed. (New York: Routledge, 2015)
Bryman & Bell (2015)	Time dimension: cross-sectional, longitudinal; case, comparative	*Research Methods*, 4th ed. (Oxford: Oxford University Press, 2015)
Cooper & Schindler (2014)	Exploratory, descriptive, *ex post facto*	*Business Research Methods*, 12th ed. (New York: McGraw-Hill, 2014)
Zikmund, Babin, Carr, & Griffin (2013)	Descriptive (survey), exploratory (quantitative)	*Business Research Methods*, 9th ed. (Mason, OH: South-Western/Cengage Learning, 2013)
Maholtra & Birks (2007)	Exploratory (quantitative), descriptive (survey with time dimension)	*Marketing Research: An Applied Orientation*, 3rd European ed. (Essex, UK: Prentice-Hall/Pearson, 2007)

Authors	Types of Nonexperimental Quantitative Designs	Reference
Social-Behavioral		
Privitera (2017)	Correlational, survey	*Research Methods for the Behavioral Sciences*, 2nd ed. (Thousand Oaks, CA: SAGE, 2017)
Gravetter & Forzano (2016)	Correlational, differential (one variable to separate groups), survey, observation	*Research Methods for the Behavioral Sciences*, 5th ed. (Boston: Cengage, 2016)
Crano, Brewer, & Lac (2015)	Correlational, field experiments	*Principles and Methods of Social Research*, 3rd ed. (New York: Routledge, 2015)
Shaughnessy, Zechmeister, & Zechmeister (2015)	Descriptive (survey and observation)	*Research Methods in Psychology*, 10th ed. (New York: McGraw-Hill, 2015)
Stangor (2015)	Descriptive (surveys and naturalistic observation), correlational	*Research Methods for the Behavioral Sciences*, 5th ed. (Stamford, CT: Cengage Learning, 2015)
Cozby & Bates (2015)	Survey, observational	*Methods in Behavioral Research*, 12th ed. (New York: McGraw-Hill, 2015)
Beins (2013)	Correlational, survey, observational	*Research Methods: A Tool for Life*, 3rd ed. (Boston: Pearson, 2013)
Pelham & Blanton (2013)	Survey: single-variable, correlational: multiple-variable	*Conducting Research in Psychology: Measuring the Weight of Smoke*, 4th ed. (Belmont, CA: Wadsworth, 2013)
Bernard (2013)	Naturalistic experiments, comparative field experiments	*Social Research Methods: Qualitative and Quantitative Approaches*, 2nd ed. (Thousand Oaks, CA: SAGE, 2013)
Morling (2012)	Correlational, surveys (subset: observation)	*Research Methods in Psychology: Evaluating a World of Information* (New York: W.W. Norton, 2012)
Price (2012)	Single-variable, correlational, quasi-experimental	*Psychology Research Methods: Core Skills and Concepts* (Washington, DC: Flat World Knowledge, 2012)
Weathington, Cunningham, & Pittenger (2010)	Correlational, surveys	*Research Methods for the Behavioral and Social Sciences*, 1st ed. (New York: Wiley, 2010)
Gliner, Morgan, & Leech (2009)	Descriptive, correlational, comparative	*Research Methods in Applied Settings: An Integrated Approach to Design and Analysis*, 2nd ed. (New York: Routledge, 2009)

(Continued)

Authors	Types of Nonexperimental Quantitative Designs	Reference
EXHIBIT 6.2 ■ (Continued)		
Pedhazur & Schmelkin (1991)	Predictive, explanatory-nonexperimental	*Measurement, Design, and Analysis: An Integrated Approach* (Hillsdale, NJ: Lawrence Erlbaum, 1991)
Education		
Mills & Gay (2016)	Correlational, causal-comparative, survey	*Educational Research: Competencies for Analysis and Applications*, 11th ed. (New York: Pearson Education: 2016)
Fraenkel, Wallen, & Hyun (2015)	Correlational, causal-comparative, survey	*How to Design and Evaluate Research in Education*, 9th ed. (New York: McGraw-Hill, 2015)
Johnson & Christensen (2014)	Descriptive, predictive, explanatory by time dimension: cross-sectional, longitudinal, and retrospective	*Educational Research: Quantitative, Qualitative, and Mixed Approaches*, 5th ed. (Thousand Oaks, SAGE, 2014)
Creswell (2014)	Correlational, causal-comparative, survey	*Research Design: Qualitative, Quantitative, and Mixed Methods Approaches*, 4th ed. (Thousand Oaks: SAGE, 2014)
Ary, Jacobs, Sorensen, & Walker (2013)	Correlational, *ex post facto*/causal-comparative, descriptive (survey)	*Introduction to Research in Education*, 9th ed. (Boston: Cengage Learning, 2013)
McMillan & Schumacher (2010)	Correlational, comparative, simple descriptive, survey	*Research in Education: Evidence-Based Inquiry*, 7th ed., Kindle ed. (Boston: Pearson, 2010)
Krathwohl (2009)	Survey, meta-analysis, causal-comparative, *ex post facto*, after-the-fact natural experiment	*Methods of Educational and Social Science Research: The Logic of Methods*, 3rd ed. (Long Grove, IL: Waveland Press, 2009)
Best & Kahn (2006)	Correlational, causal-comparative, descriptive (survey)	*Research in Education*, 10th ed. (Boston: Pearson, 2006)

Source: Adapted and updated from Johnson, Burke, "Toward a New Classification of Nonexperimental Quantitative Research," *Educational Researcher* 30, no. 2 (2001): 9, and expanded to include business research authors.

The textbook survey found that the terms design, method, technique, strategy, approach, type, study, investigation, and analysis were used interchangeably, making it challenging to distinguish one meaning from another, even in context. If a design designation was incorrectly attributed to an author(s) in Exhibit 6.2, it is likely because idiosyncratic definitions have endured for years and may be an artifact of the methodological culture.

The results of this analysis reveal the divergence in what different disciplines and research methods authors propose. Although similarities exist within fields, the confusion creates obstacles to interdisciplinary communication, cooperation, and understanding. This may be attributed to disciplinary traditions and, to some extent, methodological misinterpretation. In advocating for various designs, authors ignored the requirements for a sound typology as set forth by Reynolds, Tiryakian, and Hempel.[28] Appendix E reports a synopsis of the findings from the design study.

BUSINESS RESEARCH DESIGN

The design typology shown in Exhibit 6.3 resulted from

- The research design definitions,

- Distinguishing between design and method,

- Characteristics of useful typologies, and

- Design criteria from Exhibit 6.1 and textbook authors' inputs in Exhibit 6.2.

The result of this typology is not exhaustive but simplifies classification, reduces confusion, and suggests design opportunities. In the next sections, you will see how answering questions about your *research objective* or *purpose* directs you to a design and how the *time dimension* or *temporal characteristics* of the study can be cross-classified with the research objective to produce a comprehension depiction. The time dimension, on the columns, and the objectives, on the rows, complete a nine-cell 3×3 matrix, shown in Exhibit 6.3.

Research Objectives: Descriptive, Predictive, and Explanatory

A typology of nonexperimental quantitative research design in the form of a 3×3 matrix[29] streamlines Exhibit 6.3 when superimposed on the nonexperimental categories. The different classification inputs mentioned previously augmented the typology.

Two questions bring clarity to the issue and are central to the purpose of design: research objective and time dimension. The first question involves the research objective and has three subissues.

1. **"What is the primary purpose or objective of the research (when there is no manipulation present)?"**

    a. Were the researchers primarily describing the phenomenon?

    b. Were the researchers documenting the characteristics of the phenomenon?

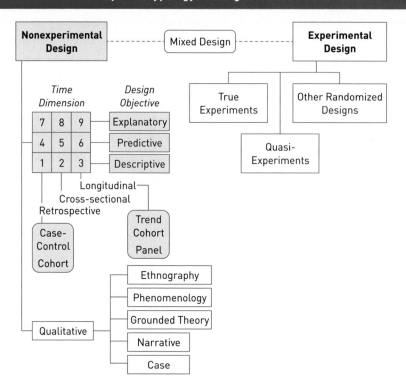

EXHIBIT 6.3 ■ A Simplified Typology of Design for Business Research

Source: Nonexperimental quantitative design components are highlighted. The shaded boxes represent the coverage of this chapter, whereas the white boxes are design topics for Chapters 7 and 8. The 3 × 3 matrix under the nonexperimental heading is adapted and used by permission of R. Burke Johnson. The typology shown in Exhibit 6.3 is a theory-based typology. There are two dimensions under nonexperimental design: (1) a quantitative classification of design [see Johnson, Burke, "Toward a New Classification of Nonexperimental Quantitative Research," *Educational Researcher* 30, no. 2 (2001): 9, regarding the 3 × 3 matrix] and (2) a qualitative classification. Elsewhere in this book, you have read about several more qualitative designs and their derivations. Here, I introduce five qualitative designs, presented in Chapter 7, that support the work of John W. Creswell. Creswell's exposition and comparison of the five dominant qualitative designs is found in Creswell, John W., and Cheryl N. Poth. *Qualitative Inquiry and Research Design: Choosing Among Five Approaches.* 4th ed. (Thousand Oaks, CA: SAGE, 2018), 65–110.

In addition, answer the following[30]:

c. Were the researchers describing what exists about the size, form, frequency, or distribution of a variable with no attempt to analyze the effects of the variable(s) on the phenomenon?

d. Were the researchers investigating associations among variables to describe individuals, groups, situations, events, or populations solely as a precursor to explanation?

If the answer is "yes" to any or all of the above, the design is a **descriptive nonexperimental design.**

2. **The second set of questions is as follows:**

   a. Did the researchers conduct the research so that they could predict or forecast some event or phenomenon in the future (without regard for cause and effect)?

   In addition, answer the following:

   b. Did the researchers conduct the research to predict a definite course of action, evaluate future values, or assess the likelihood of a future behavior, condition, or outcome with one or more DVs?

If the answer is "yes" to either or both, the design is a **predictive nonexperimental design**.

3. **The third set of questions is as follows:**

   a. Were the researchers trying to develop or test a theory about a phenomenon to explain "how" and "why" it operates?

   b. Were the researchers trying to explain how the phenomenon operates by identifying the causal factors that produce a change in it?

Again, if the answer is "yes" to either or both, the design is an **explanatory nonexperimental design**.

The questions on research objectives yield three designs: *descriptive*, *predictive*, and *explanatory*, as shown in Exhibit 6.3.

Time Dimension: Cross-Sectional, Longitudinal, and Retrospective

The following question is the second dimension used to classify designs: "What is the time dimension in which the researchers collected their data?" Accepted **time dimensions** are cross-sectional, longitudinal, and retrospective studies. Business research examples for each cell of the matrix (numbered 1 through 9) are presented in conjunction with the time dimensions. Appendix F expands the discussion of longitudinal designs, showing how trend, cohort, and panel types could be created within the framework of one study.

Studies Illustrating Time Dimension by Research Objective

Cross-Sectional

Cross-sectional studies collect data at one point in time (thereby producing a snapshot) or during a single short interval to make comparisons across different types of participants or variables. A probability or nonprobability sample may be used depending on the researchers' need for representativeness or when an unusual or atypical group is targeted.

The problem of flight delays or cancellations produces headaches for airlines. The aviation industry seeks to reduce these delays by predicting mechanical failures in advance.

In a study of Total Quality Management (TQM), Lai et al. investigated the current status of TQM implementation in quality-oriented companies in Hong Kong.[31] Their structured questionnaire surveyed companies in manufacturing, service, construction, and public utilities with an in-place operational system (ISO 9000 certified). They initially sampled 1,092 respondents by mail questionnaire, which returned an effective n=342 responses (or 28%). Companies in public utilities and service industries had a higher level of TQM implementation, although all industry types surveyed valued the measurement systems in the program implementation process highly.

The Lai et al. study of TQM implementation is a descriptive, cross-sectional study assigned to cell 2 of the Exhibit 6.3 matrix.

A recent *Harvard Business Review* article by LaRiviere et al. reveals the problem of flight delays or cancellations and the headaches they produce for airlines.[32] The aviation industry is exceptionally interested in reducing these delays by predicting mechanical failures in advance. Microsoft data analysts on the team at the Cortana Intelligence Suite predict the probability of these events in the future based on existing data, such as maintenance logs and flight routes. According to LaRiviere et al., "A machine-learning solution based on historical data and *applied in real time* predicts the type of mechanical issue that will result in a delay or cancellation of a flight within the next 24 hours, allowing the airlines to take maintenance actions while aircraft are being serviced."

LaRiviere et al.'s description of predictive analytics reveals a predictive, cross-sectional study assigned to cell 5 of the Exhibit 6.3 matrix. The data that drive the machine-learning algorithm are retrospective (cell 4), but the application to a predictive object (aircraft) is real-time cross-sectional data because the delay or cancellation of that flight had not occurred when the study was begun.

A services marketing study by Cronin et al.[33] took place in a medium-sized southeastern metropolitan area. It addressed two questions: Does adding a direct measure of value to models of consumer decision-making based on service quality and sacrifice (the service's monetary and nonmonetary acquisition costs) enhance the model's explanation of consumers' purchase intentions? Is service value best modeled as a value-added function? Two studies were incorporated into one with two different sets of service organizations. In the first study, three sectors that offered services designed to meet discretionary needs were observed: spectator sports, participation sports, and entertainment.

In the second study, services that satisfy consumers' continual needs were identified: health care, long-distance carriers, and fast food. Interviews using identical instruments were conducted jointly and followed up with calls to confirm demographics. The sampling involved a modified version of snowballing and contained 1,944 respondents across six sectors. Variables were operationalized by the literature. The results of the path analyses (actually, Structural Equation Modeling) in the two models showed that both fit the data and the comparative fit index exceeded .90 in each sector. However, adding a direct measure of service value to models that are defined solely by service quality and sacrifice increases the ability of the model to explain variance in consumers' purchase intentions. The authors' second hypothesis states that service value is best modeled as an additive function (and the additive model performed better in every case) rather than a multiplicative function suggested in the marketing literature. The evidence suggests that "service value" (the cost-benefit difference that consumers ascribe to service acquisition) is a more important determining factor of consumer perceptions than either quality or cost (sacrifice) factors.

> The Cronin et al. study of service-value marketing is an explanatory cross-sectional study assigned to cell 8 of the Exhibit 6.3 matrix.

Longitudinal

Longitudinal (prospective) studies collect data from respondents (or multiple groups) at several points in time starting in the present and going into the future. This approach facilitates observation of response continuity and detects changes that are used for comparisons across time. Often the same variables are examined over many decades, or in the case of the "Genetic Studies of Genius" (the Terman Study of the Gifted), since 1921.[34] There are three types of longitudinal studies: trend, cohort, and panel. See Appendix F.

Longitudinal (Trend, Cohort, and Panel) Studies in the Literature. A **longitudinal trend** study samples different groups of people (but independent samples from the same general population) at various points in time but typically asks the same questions. Several firms use sophisticated, automated telephone surveys to track public opinion on a broad range of issues at designated intervals (with greater frequency during election campaigns). Polling results are watched carefully during U.S. Presidential contests. In fact, current (real-time) polls are a harbinger that something has happened or is about to occur—but may not last long. Questions about the candidates' qualifications on domestic and foreign policy, terrorism, or general trustworthiness produce results that change over time and reflect evolving opinions of the electorate. Trend polling draws a different probability sample (with a stated margin of error) from the same population to show changes in opinions, attitudes, or beliefs on topics of interest to political organizations, unions, consultants, and businesses.

Trend polling draws a different probability sample from the same population at different points in time. The purpose is to show changes in opinions, attitudes, or beliefs on topics of interest to political organizations, unions, consultants, and businesses. For example, when a new product is released, a sample of purchasers is drawn and questioned. A year later, a different sample is drawn from the same population to determine if a change is present.

An example of a longitudinal trend study was conducted during a 10-year period and centered on public attitudes toward higher education.[35] These indicators are relevant for human resource professionals anticipating changes in the composition of the labor force. The researchers studied the importance of higher education in 1993, 1998, 2000, and 2003. Using a random-digit-dialing technology where every adult head of household in the 48 contiguous states had an equal chance of contact, national samples were selected. Some indicators showed that public attitudes toward higher education have become more apprehensive, especially for those groups most affected by rising university costs, including parents of high school students, African Americans, and Hispanics.

A **longitudinal cohort** study is one in which a population or subpopulation includes individuals who have a common characteristic or have experienced a similar event during a fixed period (typically birth). These individuals provide a cross-section to be compared at intervals through time. A cohort might be a study's participants who were born in 1995, graduates of the same age from different colleges with the same degree, or executives at the CIO level in the automobile industry with coronary artery disease. The respondents may not necessarily be the same throughout the rounds of the study, but they must be from the cohort population or one of the cohort's subgroups to document incidence rates, which apply to the original research question.

A **longitudinal panel** study samples and tracks the same respondents (usually individuals or households) by collecting repeated measures on the same set of variables at two or more points in time. An iteration of data collection is referred to as a *wave* or *round*. There is no upper limit on rounds, but studies ordinarily don't exceed 10 rounds or they may become confused with *time-series studies*. Panel studies have the advantage of showing both net and gross changes in the dependent variable, unlike trend studies. This is a benefit when there is interest "in establishing evidence of causality because data on the independent and control variables can be obtained prior to the data on the dependent variable from the people in the panel. This helps to establish the proper time order . . ." for causality.[36] Respondents on panels do not routinely share a similar event like a cohort.

Nielsen's Homescan Shopper Panel, a **continuous panel**, has been operating for over 25 years with more than 100,000 households in the United States and over 250,000 households in 25 countries. It continuously tracks consumers' grocery purchases when the participant scans barcodes after each trip to the grocery. Homescan also includes purchases from retailers that do not cooperate with scanner-collected data. It collects household location and demographic information on the participants as well as business trends by product, category, or market. Other online marketing panels have as many as 1.8 million consumers. Continuous panel size reflects the need to compensate for attrition, especially for lengthy studies.

> The Nielsen Homescan's 25-year-old study is a descriptive, longitudinal study of the continuous panel type assigned to cell 3 of the Exhibit 6.3 matrix.

Lands' End has **discontinuous panels** (sometimes called "omnibus" panels) of approximately 1,500 respondents who complete up to eight online questionnaires per year for gift cards. These panels differ from continuous panels because the recruited participants and the pursued information differ with each project's goals. Synovate's Global Omnibus, in operation since 1986, uses discontinuous panels to collect data by telephone in 55 countries.[37]

A 2000 study by Venkatesh et al.[38] investigated gender differences in individual adoption and sustained use of new technology in the workplace using the theory of planned behavior (TPB). User reactions and technology usage behavior were studied over 5 months among 355 workers who were introduced to a new software application. The sample was reasonably balanced across four sites. Of the 355, 160 were women (45%); all were tested according to TPB at all points of measurement. All participants had prior computer experience, with an average of 6 years. User reactions to the technology were measured at three points in time: immediately after training, after 1 month of experience, and after 3 months of experience. Regression analyses examined the TPB relationships and the role of intention and behavior. A dummy variable tested the moderation of the different relationships by gender. Potential confounding of gender differences by income, organizational level, education, and computer self-efficacy was ruled out with three-stage hierarchical regression. Determinants of technology adoption and usage behavior confirmed that attitudes toward use influenced men's decisions. However, women were strongly influenced by subjective norms and perceived behavioral control.

The longitudinal analysis of the data revealed that intention predicted short-term use, which, in turn, predicted sustained use. The findings showed that men and women use different processes of decision-making in evaluating new technologies. The implication for managers implementing new technology is to understand the factors that lead to user acceptance and sustained usage.

> The Venkatesh et al. study of gender differences in the technology-adoption process is a predictive, longitudinal study assigned to cell 6 of the Exhibit 6.3 matrix.

Benmelech and Frydman's 2015 investigation[39] is illustrated in Appendix F as a way to create three longitudinal studies in one. Here, it is used to represent one cell of the matrix. Their study reveals that CEOs who were former service members pursue lower corporate investment and R&D, do not use excessive leverage, are less likely to be involved in corporate fraud, and perform better during industry downturns. The results of the multiple regression analyses show that military service has significant explanatory power for managerial decisions and firm outcomes. Their sample contained 4,013 managers, 2,402 companies, and 22,044 manager-year observations from which they constructed a "manager-firm matched panel" data set. The sample was based on all executives from the cohorts 1913–1960.

> Benmelech and Frydman's study of "military CEOs" is an explanatory, longitudinal, hybrid panel-cohort study assigned to cell 9 of the Exhibit 6.3 matrix.

Retrospective

A **retrospective study** has a historical emphasis, looking back to more than one period—ideally, to make comparisons or establish a trend. According to Johnson, "The researcher looks backward in time (typically starting with the dependent variable and moving backward to locate information on independent variables that help explain current differences on the dependent variable)."[40] Thus, the outcome has already occurred when the study has begun. Records provide information about past experiences or events. They may involve a database, archival data, or even recorded interviews with participants known to have experienced a condition or event. Unrecorded interviews are problematic for memory or *recall bias*.

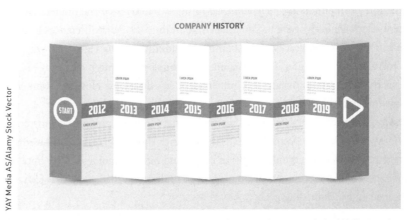

A retrospective study has a historical emphasis, looking back to more than one period— ideally, to make comparisons or establish a trend. This type of study compares groups of individuals who are alike in many ways but differ by a particular characteristic (e.g., male executives who smoke and those who do not) in terms of a predicted outcome (i.e., Is smoking a trigger for chronic obstructive pulmonary disease?).

Goodwin and colleagues[41] studied retrospectively Australian accounting practices. They examined the possible impact of adopting the International Financial Reporting Standards (IFRS) instead of the Australian equivalent. A sample of 1,065 listed firms used retrospective reconciliations from the Australian Generally Accepted Accounting Principles (AGAAP) to the IFRS from the notes of annual accounts. IFRS standards were applicable for reporting periods beginning after December 31, 2004; the comparison occurred for the period immediately before IFRS adoption. IFRS reporting increased total liabilities, decreased equity, and produced a higher leverage ratio. In addition, more firms had earnings decreases than increases. There was no evidence that IFRS earnings and book value were more value relevant than AGAAP earnings and book value. Other findings on changes for share-based payment, intangibles, provisions, and impairment components were considered value relevant but not consistent with market perceptions. The study's statistically significant differences between IFRS and AGAAP led to an explanation of these differences with multivariable price-level regressions. The high R-square values gave credence to the claim that models with specific, statistically significant, high coefficient predictors have explanatory power for determining how different reporting standards in accounting produce divergent results.

> The Goodwin et al. study is an explanatory, retrospective study assigned to cell 7 of the Exhibit 6.3 matrix.

Travel and tourism are one of the world's largest sectors, with a global economic contribution of almost 7.6 trillion U.S. dollars in 2014. Despite travel fears of terrorism and problems in the European Union, the sector was expected to grow by 3.1% currently.[42] During travel, a broad spectrum of travel-related diseases, temporary and otherwise, can make the experience unpleasant. Zimmermann et al.[43] analyzed the clinical and demographic data representing the frequency of a presumed travel-associated condition with 360 travelers presenting symptoms and diseases when returning ill from the tropics. The participants sought medical care at a tertiary hospital between 2003 and 2007. The cases were correlated with the areas visited as well as the duration of the trip and travel purpose.

> The Zimmermann et al. study, correctly identified in the authors' title, is a descriptive, retrospective study assigned to cell 1 of the Exhibit 6.3 matrix.

A predictive retrospective study by Yen et al. was designed to predict employer's economic costs (medical claims and losses from absenteeism) using regression models.[44] The sample contained 1,284 hourly employees of a large manufacturing facility who completed a Health Risk Appraisal (HRA) in 1985 with recorded absenteeism from 1986 through 1987. The sampled subjects were covered by the company's medical plan for the same 2 consecutive years. The sample was divided into three subgroups: men younger than 35, men 35 and older, and women. Two predictors were fixed: medical plan selection and employer-sponsored fitness center status. Fifteen additional HRA variables fell into the categories of demographics, lifestyle, psychological perceptions, biological risks, and medical/absence history.

The retrospective data predicted employer medical and absenteeism costs with six predictors: age, a perception index, self-reported absences, smoking, and use of drugs or medication. The medical plan selection predicted insurance costs but not the cost of absenteeism. Health effects on costs were found to be age and sex specific and provided support for corporate health-promotion efforts and smoking cessation programs, especially for males 35 and older.

> The Yen et al. study predicting an employer's economic cost from medical claims and absenteeism is a predictive retrospective study assigned to cell 4 of the Exhibit 6.3 matrix.

Variations on Retrospective Studies

Retrospective studies also are configured as *case-control* and *cohort*. One example of a **retrospective case-control** study involves a current wellness problem in manufacturing. Advocacy groups have claimed that chemicals used in processor chip factories in South Korea and China cause workers to develop leukemia and non-Hodgkin's lymphoma. These factories supply top-brand manufacturers. The carcinogens, benzene and trichloroethylene, appear to be circulated in dust-free "clean rooms" where semiconductors are assembled. A case-control study was conducted to identify individuals who are already diagnosed (cases) with a control group that is similar but without a cancer diagnosis. Retroactive questions that covered previously equivalent employment, the length of employment in the company's clean room, time spent working in the room, and symptoms provided data for comparing cases with the controls on exposure rates, thus revealing a potential link to the diseases.

> This hypothetical case-control group study uses retrospective data to identify causal linkages between exposure to various chemical carcinogens and two forms of cancer. This study is an explanatory, retrospective study of the case-control type and is assigned to cell 7 of the Exhibit 6.3 matrix.

In the **retrospective cohort** study, researchers go back in time with individuals who are alike in several dimensions but one group differs on a characteristic of interest (i.e., an event, condition, exposure, diagnosis, or outcome).

In 2009, the National Institute for Occupational Safety and Health conducted a multiyear study of former employees at a microelectronics and business machines manufacturing facility in Endicott, New York, in response to concerns from residents, Congressional representatives, and community stakeholders about contamination.[45] Silver et al. developed a cohort consisting of 34,494 people who were employed for more than 90 days between 1969 and 2001. The study assessed overall causes of death among former workers, the incidence of testicular diagnoses, and congenital disabilities among children of former workers. Researchers reconstructed work histories back to 1984 by department, time, and building location at the facility. The researchers evaluated each person's potential job exposure to four specific chemicals and three chemical groups widely used at the site. The investigators collected cancer information and death certificate data on former employees. Regression models evaluated the relationships between the health outcomes of *a priori* interest and (1) cumulative chemical exposure scores or (2) duration worked in seven main manufacturing buildings. In hourly male employees, Standardized Mortality Ratios were significantly elevated for non-Hodgkin's lymphoma and rectal cancer. A positive, statistically significant relation was observed between exposure scores for tetrachloroethylene and nervous system diseases. Location and time worked in three of the manufacturing buildings were positively related to a risk of cause-specific mortality. Although there were several outcomes that exceeded the predicted death figures for diagnoses, the overall cohort showed a very healthy workforce, with mortality from all causes and, to a lesser extent, all cancers showing statistically significant deficits compared to job exposure deaths in the workforce and the general population.

> The Silver et al. study at a microelectronics and business machines manufacturing facility seeks to use a cohort to explain the incidence of cancer deaths among workers exposed to carcinogens and other chemicals. This study is an explanatory, retrospective study of the cohort type, and it is assigned to cell 7 of the Exhibit 6.3 matrix.

Summary of Business Examples in the 3 × 3 Matrix

From a practical standpoint, it is possible to classify almost all business studies that are quantitative and nonexperimental within this framework, as the examples in Exhibit 6.4 show. Although it was not feasible to survey and catalog every variety of study in each business discipline, specific disciplinary cases that clarified the contents of the nine-cell matrix increase the likelihood of usefulness:

- Manufacturing: carcinogen exposure with processor chips, worker chemical exposure, and mortality.

- Management/organizational behavior: TQM, antecedents of CEO performance, adoption and sustained use of innovation in the workplace.

EXHIBIT 6.4 ■ Completing the 3 × 3 Typology for Nonexperimental Quantitative Design

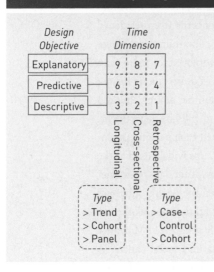

Cell

1. Descriptive retrospective: Zimmermann et al. (2016)

2. Descriptive cross-sectional: Lai et al. (2002)

3. Descriptive longitudinal: Nielsen Homescan, Panel (2015); Public Polling, Trend.

4. Predictive retrospective: Yen et al. (1992)

5. Predictive cross-sectional: LaRiviere et al. (2016)

6. Predictive longitudinal: Venkatesh et al. (2000)

7. Explanatory retrospective: Goodwin et al. (2008); Asian Clean-Room, Case-Control; Silver et al., Cohort (2014)

8. Explanatory cross-sectional: Cronin et al. (1997)

9. Explanatory longitudinal: Benmelech & Frydman, Hybrid Panel-Cohort (2015)

- Logistics and transportation: aircraft on-time departures.

- Marketing: consumer services decision-making, retail goods purchase tracking.

- Human resources: expectations of workforce education, costs of medical claims and absenteeism.

- Accounting: impact of opposing reporting standards.

- Hospitality management: travel and tourism.

What are the advantages of viewing research design this way? Successful identification of nonexperimental quantitative design is simplified because it:

1. Corresponds with scholars' definitions of design characteristics.

2. Defines designs by the objective and purpose of the research and cross-compares them with precise temporal study dimensions, thus improving exhaustiveness.

3. Centers on the structure and the logical, not logistical, purpose of the study—disregarding method, technique, statistics, or ancillary considerations, and thereby supports the contention that data collection techniques are irrelevant to defining designs.

4. Places emphasis on a well-formulated research question/hypothesis instead of whatever *discovery* effort clarifies the goal or transpires before the question is articulated.

5. Calls attention to the control of antecedent or concurrent extraneous variables as well as confounding and intervening variables, especially in explanatory designs.

6. Fosters deliberate efforts to reduce sources of bias and noise.

7. Accepts the need to qualify outcomes by considering the researcher's degree of control in the investigative setting and the participants' perceptions of the researchers in their environment.

8. Meets the tests of mutual exclusivity and theoretical relevance, particularly parsimony and a common level of abstraction.

Chapter Summary

- Research questions primarily address three fundamental problems. Descriptive research addresses questions of what, who, when, and where. Causal research deals with the questions of why and how. Predictive research involves questions of could, should, or would an event occur in the future.

- An argument was presented for how the research question is connected to design.

- Research design is (1) a logical plan for selecting and arranging the evidence that answers the research question(s); (2) a framework for specifying the relationships among a study's variables; (3) a blueprint outlining each procedure from the hypotheses to the analysis of data; (4) a way of configuring the study to its paradigm (e.g., achieving findings that are numeric, systematic, generalizable, and replicable or obtaining non-numerical observations that reveal and detail the experience and constructed meanings of individuals, groups, situations, or contexts); and (5) a means for determining how to allocate limited resources of time and budget.

- The nonexperimental quantitative design was defined as a "systematic empirical inquiry in which the scientist does not have direct control of independent variables because their manifestations have already occurred or because they are inherently not capable of being manipulated. Inferences about relations among variables are made without direct intervention, from concomitant variations of independent and dependent variables."[46]

- A case was made for business problems posing perplexing academic questions and managerial dilemmas where nonexperimental designs appear as good alternatives especially when conditions are not amenable to experimentation.

- The logical structure of the study dominates logistics in organizing evidence to answer the research question. Design should not be confused with a research method or a technique for gathering data.

- There has been little agreement in business, social or behavioral science, or education as to an acceptable design typology, but one is needed because of numerous theoretical and pedagogical advantages for educators, researchers, managers, and students.

- The author reviewed 30 current research methods textbooks in business and other fields and found that confusion has continued to exist for almost 3 decades, resulting from the practice of treating designs, methods, and techniques for data collection alike rather than isolating the design as the logical structure of the study. Only the descriptive design met the theoretical tests for typological usefulness.

- A 3 × 3 classification of nonexperimental quantitative designs was proposed that resulted from answering fundamental

questions about the objectives of the study (producing descriptive, explanatory, and predictive designs) and the time dimension for collecting data (longitudinal, cross-sectional, and retrospective). Definitions and studies to illustrate the resulting nine cells of the matrix followed. The studies were linked to functional areas of business along with how the typology met the criteria for successful identification of design.

Key Terms

continuous panel

cross-sectional

descriptive nonexperimental design

discontinuous panel

experimental realism

explanatory nonexperimental design

longitudinal cohort

longitudinal panel

longitudinal (prospective) study

longitudinal trend

nonexperimental design

predictive nonexperimental design

research design

retrospective case-control

retrospective cohort

retrospective study

time dimensions

typology

Discussion Questions

1. What are the three fundamental questions concerning *design* that the research question triggers?

   a. Define the five functions of research design that serve as its definition.

   b. Argue the case that nonexperimental design is unmistakably vital to design.

   c. What function do research questions or hypotheses play in selecting a design for a business study and how should the researcher structure such questions?

   d. What is the role of manipulation of variables in nonexperimental design?

2. If research design is not about second-level data concerns or the logistics and mechanics of research, why is there confusion about what constitutes a method versus a design? Argue the proposition that knowing the difference is essential for researchers.

3. If naming, organizing, and categorizing the "things" of a study are the first tasks of science and are basic to building scientific knowledge, describe some of the classifications (typologies) used in different fields of business.

4. What are some of the criteria that may help you clarify the characteristics of your study's design and familiarize readers with your approach?

5. Nonexperimental quantitative research can be classified by cross tabulating three research objectives by three time dimensions. What are the objectives? List and explain the classification of time dimensions in which researchers collect their data.

6. Using Appendix E and Exhibit 6.2, distinguish between:

   a. Correlational and causal-comparative studies

   b. Descriptive and predictive studies

   c. Causal and *ex post facto* studies

7. Provide an example of a longitudinal continuous panel study from marketing or management. What type of information is tracked?

8. Define a cohort analysis and differentiate it from a case-control study.

9. Appendix F demonstrated that it is possible to create three types of longitudinal studies in one. Devise a similar example using the literature of any business discipline.

10. Compare a retrospective study with a cross-sectional study and describe their benefits and liabilities. What questions are they intended to answer?

©iStockphoto.com/Brasil2

7

QUALITATIVE DESIGNS AND MIXED DESIGNS

LEARNING OBJECTIVES

Performance Objective

Create a mini-qualitative research study using any of the five major designs in this chapter as a model. Emphasize content, meaning (not quantifiable variables), detail with fewer cases, and yourself as the data collection instrument.

Enabling Objectives

1. Describe the complementary relationship between qualitative and quantitative research.

2. Assess the fit between the worldview of qualitative researchers and their purpose to discover and understand individuals' experiences, perceptions, and interactions and to make sense of derived meanings from participants' thoughts, actions, and events.

3. Debate the legitimacy of the goals more frequently associated with qualitative research.

4. Illustrate the five major qualitative designs with examples from business research.

5. Defend the mixed design as a pragmatic approach to solve complex research questions.

6. Describe how the versatility of mixed designs allows them to be configured by considering the time order of the research and the dominance (priority) given to a quantitative or qualitative approach.

QUALITATIVE AND QUANTITATIVE DESIGN: A SYNERGISTIC RELATIONSHIP

Exhibit 7.1 shows both qualitative and mixed designs highlighted. The high-level classification on the left side of the diagram is "nonexperimental design." It includes qualitative designs and preserves the legitimacy of both design goals to answer a research question. Mixed design, in the middle of the diagram, reminds us that a design synthesis is not only possible but also desirable to answer many research questions. "The fact that both research orientations must deal with similar (albeit at times inverted) problems is not adequately acknowledged."[1]

There is no way for any researcher to opt for the use of either a quantitative or qualitative method without verifying their adequacy for the phenomena under study and theoretical questions raised. Thus, instead of juxtaposing quantitative and qualitative methods, we can consider them as parallel lines of method construction. Which of the two is selected depends upon the nature of the research question, rather than on some socially consensus-based value (or "right" or "wrong" methods, or "hard" or "soft" science).[2]

Upon reading this chapter, you will discover a complementary relationship between qualitative and quantitative research. At least, it will be apparent that qualitative and quantitative approaches are not antithetical to each other. Qualitative methods are useful for recognizing and appreciating the meaning of conclusions that quantitative methods produce. Conversely, quantitative strategies give qualitative findings a different perspective and potential for generalizability, thereby making them empirically testable, if that is the researcher's goal. A statement by Mark Turner illustrates the confluence of qualitative and quantitative designs using narrative as an example: "Narrative imagining—story—is the fundamental instrument of thought. Rational capacities depend upon it. It is our chief means of looking into the future, of predicting, of planning, and of explaining."[3] This sounds very similar to quantitative objectives of describing, explaining, and predicting.

EXHIBIT 7.1   ■   A Simplified Typology of Business Qualitative and Mixed Design

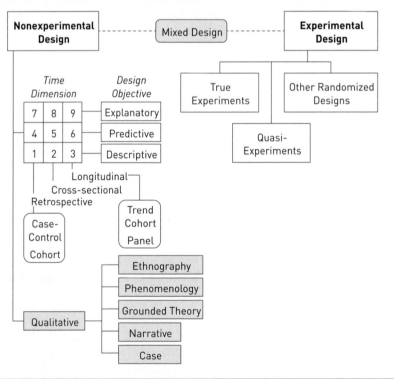

Note: Qualitative and Mixed Design components are highlighted. The shaded boxes represent the coverage of this chapter, whereas the white boxes are design topics for Chapters 6 and 8."

AN INTRODUCTION
TO QUALITATIVE DESIGN

Qualitative researchers hold an interpretivist/naturalistic worldview. The purpose of **qualitative design** is to discover and understand individuals' experiences, perceptions, and interactions and to make sense of and interpret the derived meanings from their thoughts, actions, and events in the wider context of inquiry. These experiences may be everyday occurrences or problematic (even traumatic) instances that give meaning to individuals' lives. The inductive logical approach seeks depth and a detailed understanding of the problem's context, with much less concern about generalizability. In fact, numerical quantitative designs are "not very good at all at communicating what it is actually like to be a member of a particular group in a particular situation." Qualitative designs excel in that regard.[4]

Often, a research methods textbook will quote a passage from literary work to paint a verbal picture that differentiates qualitative and quantitative paradigms. Rarely is the quote complete and powerful aspects of the context are lost. Ironically, imagery and figurative language allow the reader to experience vicariously what qualitative research is all about—a depth of description and detail, or a sense of being there. In the early spring of 1940, John Steinbeck and his friend Edward Ricketts, a marine biologist, took a boat from Monterey Bay down the California coast around Cape San Lucas and into the Gulf of California (Sea of Cortez), venturing north to Puerto Refugio and back. It was a trip composed of leisure and specimen collecting. Steinbeck and Ricketts discovered about 50 new species and recorded 500 species along the shoreline and in the tidal pools of their numerous stops.[5]

A year later, a book was published based on Ricketts's journal and Steinbeck's description of the shared experience. Early in the book, Steinbeck recounts:

> We knew that what we would see and record and construct would be warped, as all knowledge patterns are warped, first, by the collective pressure and stream of our time and race, second, by the thrust of our individual personalities. But knowing this, we might not fall into many holes—we might maintain some balance between our warp and the separate thing, the external reality. The oneness of these two might take its contribution from both. For example: the Mexican sierra has 'XVII-15-IX' spines in the dorsal fin. These can be easily counted. But if the sierra strikes hard on

The Western Flyer, the boat that John Steinbeck and his friend Edward Ricketts, a marine biologist, took from Monterey Bay down the California coast and into the Gulf of California (Sea of Cortez). Steinbeck's literary work on that trip painted a figurative picture that illuminates the qualitative paradigm and differentiates it from the quantitative.

Photo courtesy of Colin Levings with the assistance of Kelly Cabal of the Western Flyer Foundation.

the line so that our hands are burned, if the fish sounds and nearly escapes and finally comes in over the rail, his colors pulsing and his tail beating in the air, a whole new relational externality has come into being—an entity which is more than the sum of the fish plus the fisherman. The only way to count the spines of the sierra unaffected by this second relational reality is to sit in a laboratory, open an evil-smelling jar, remove a stiff colorless fish from formalin solution, count the spines, and write the truth 'D. XVII-15-IX.' There you have recorded a reality which cannot be assailed—probably the least important reality concerning either the fish or yourself.

It is good to know what you are doing. The man with his pickled fish has set down one truth and has recorded in his experience many lies. The fish is not that color, that texture, that dead, nor does he smell that way. . . . The man with his pickled fish has sacrificed a great observation about himself, the fish, and the focal point, which is his thought on both the sierra and himself.[6]

In Chapter 1, I illustrated the *purposes* of business research through various types of studies. That coverage, although introductory, revealed the breadth of the field from reporting an event to changing an organization. Furthermore, the discussion of research orientations leading to qualitative research not only reveals its breadth or scope but also calls attention to the fact that with any worldview, the purpose must be connected to the research question. For example, what is the purpose(s) of investigating the question, "What are the sources used by 'early adopters' to discover that a new technological innovation is being introduced?" You can select several purposes from the following list proposed by Newman et al. Before they design a study, researchers can also compare their intentions against a checklist of objectives. You will note differences in the objectives described in Chapter 6 in criterion 4 of Exhibit 6.1 ("Design Classification Criteria"). Those goals are more frequently associated with quantitative research—yet there is overlap onto the qualitative side. In their article on research purposes, Newman et al. proposed a broad framework. The extensive categories are summarized here:

- Generate new ideas.

- Test new ideas.

- Measure change.

- Predict.

- Examine the past.

- Understand complex phenomena.

- Add to the knowledge base.

- Inform constituencies.

- Have a personal, social, institutional, and organizational impact.[7]

These categories suggest that the purpose at the end of the study could differ from that at the beginning. According to Newman et al.,

> . . . these concerns do not take away from the responsibility of the researcher to articulate up front what the purpose is. Implications of the findings flow from the detours and reconceptualizations through which the original purpose has traversed. That initial purpose does not disappear, but the fact that the results shift the purpose in itself might be *the important* finding or implication.[8]

The designs and design "types" in qualitative research are purpose driven and include ethnography, netnography (cyberethnography and virtual ethnography), phenomenology, ethnomethodology, grounded theory, narrative analysis, case study, historical analysis, conversation analysis, life story, interactional and visual texts, and many more. My coverage of five major designs among this spectrum of qualitative designs may seem too limiting, but it is representative and provides a degree of simplification for the benefit of new researchers. Chapter 6 discussed the importance of these five general types in Creswell's approach, where he also describes groundbreaking and influential studies by authors using these five designs.[9]

Data collection for qualitative studies that use **observation** involves "the selection, provocation, recording, and encoding of that set of behaviors and settings concerning organisms (in situ) which is consistent with empirical aims."[10] It includes categories of participant-outsider, participant, nonparticipant, concealment, and covert. In systematic or structured observation, three types of behavior have been studied extensively: verbal, nonverbal, and overt/spatial. These encompass, respectively, people talking in their natural environment; body movement, facial expression, vocal tone, and speech patterns; and how individuals use personal-social space and territory.[11] In *Marketing Research*, Cooper and Schindler provide a thorough discussion of behavioral and nonbehavioral observation (including physical condition analysis, process analysis, and record analysis).[12]

Many types of interviews are also used in data collection: ethnographic, narrative, guided, biographic, problem-centered, episodic, in-depth, structured, semi-structured open-ended, and group or focus groups.[13] Some studies anticipate **participant reactivity** (an awareness of being observed that may result in negative, positive, or no reaction) to interventions. Qualitative researchers may include unobtrusive measures in their studies to ameliorate this. **Unobtrusive measures** "refer to data gathered by means that do not involve direct elicitation of information from research subjects. Unobtrusive measures are unique and 'non-reactive.'"[14] Unobtrusive measures were described by Eugene Webb, Donald Campbell, Richard Schwartz, and Lee Sechrest in 1966 and updated in 2000.[15] The authors suggested research approaches that do not involve direct contact with the research participants because "eliciting data from research participants is capable of affecting the character of the responses obtained, and that the presence of the researcher within the research situation can introduce potentially distorting factors that need to be taken into consideration."[16]

Unobtrusive measures are unlike interviews or surveys in that they seek indirect ways of making observations to avoid reactions to the researcher's presence or involvement in the data-gathering process. This is a distinct advantage: literally seeing actual behavior versus self-reported behavior.

The unobtrusive approach seeks unusual data sources, including the physical traces such as erosion measures (selective wear and tear, such as tire tread as an index of mileage), accretion measures (accumulation or deposit, such as discarded containers or documents in trash cans to determine brand consumption or private information), the use of documents of various kinds (public archives, corporate records, institutional data, and personal documents), and visual traces found in art, graffiti, and film. Structured observation, although subsumed under observational methods, requires the researcher to observe at a distance and not to intrude into the research setting or have behavioral control over those observed.

Although the technology of the 1960s did not foresee laptops and tablets nor "grounded theory and post-structuralist modifications to content analysis, nor the recent interest and revival of the camera and video,"[17] the authors did not offer adequate guidance in the design of such research. This was likely because unusual creativity was required and that is difficult to explain. Take, for example, the fact that floor tiles around the hatching-chick exhibit at Chicago's Museum of Science and Industry were replaced every 6 weeks. In other parts of the museum, tiles were not replaced for years. The selective erosion of the tiles, measured by their replacement rate, was an indicator of the popularity of the exhibit.[18] A researcher needs to be intimately familiar with the research environment to be so ingenious.

Like other forms of data collection, unobtrusive measures have ethical concerns, especially in terms of privacy and surveillance. The question of when to obtain consent and how realistic it is to require informed consent is asked frequently. "Researchers should protect the confidences and identity of those they research, they should guard the *privacy* of those they study. In this respect, peoples' lives should not be unduly intruded upon. . . [for] any research which involves certain groups or that may have findings which publicly reflect on them in some way, seek the subject's *permission* or *consent*."[19]

For the most part, the qualitative data are **textual**—that is, they are in the form of interview transcripts, field notes from different observer and interviewer roles, diaries, journals, social media textual information, and documents such as e-mails, reports, meeting minutes, memos, and personal letters. More studies are using audio-visual technology (video, audio, and image capture, with the media used separately or combined to augment and on occasion validate other forms of data). Textual data remain a significant part of qualitative research, and Schutt observes their importance:

> The focus on text—on qualitative data rather than on numbers—is the most important feature of qualitative analysis. The "text" that qualitative researchers analyze is most often transcripts of interviews or notes from participant observation sessions, but the text can also refer to pictures or other images that the researcher examines.[20]

Here is a synopsis to refresh your memory of the contrast of qualitative and quantitative data:

- Emphasis on context, not generalizability

- Attention to meanings and rich descriptions, not quantifiable measures on specific variables

- The researcher as an "instrument," rather than the impersonal designer of a measuring tool

- The expectation that values may influence data collection and analysis, not the presumption of a value-free process

- The collection of detailed data on a few cases, not numerous cases with minimal detail

- Responses that coalesce as categories evolve, rather than preprogrammed categories [21]

Since the data are typically textual, in large quantities, and often "unfiltered," their analysis and management are different from quantitative data and the data analytic process that leads to statistical testing. Manual organization of qualitative data is common; however, computer-assisted textual and pictorial analysis may be used to convert data from the collection format to a numeric format. This technology becomes a prerequisite for analysis of large-scale projects. Chapter 5 mentioned specialized computer programs.

Ethnography

Ethnography is "the study of a culture or cultures that some group of people shares, using participant observation over an extended period of time."[22] An entire cultural group or a subgroup that interacts over time may be the study's target. A subgroup or

Ethnography may target an entire cultural group or a subgroup that interacts over time. When interviewing is used, the ethnographer seeks out the people most knowledgeable about the culture, called key informants.

microculture in business might include the culture of departments, cross-functional teams, or an organization. "Thus, ethnography is a qualitative design in which the researcher describes and interprets the shared and learned patterns of values, behaviors, beliefs, and language of a culture-sharing group."[23]

The collection of data through observation may also include nonparticipant observation, interviews, and the analysis of cultural artifacts (photographs, art, music, or books).[24] When interviewing is used, the ethnographer seeks out the people most knowledgeable about the culture, called **key informants**.

An ethnographic study usually involves an investigator who participates in the culture, increasingly creating trust while experiencing the environment in a way similar to the participants. Often this immersion process occurs over a protracted period. To achieve immersion, an ethnographer should have "a measure [of] fluency in the language of the society being studied, spending enough time among the people in order to know how they live, what they say they do, what they actually do, what they believe, and their system of valuation."[25] Myers, who writes on qualitative research in business and management, suggests the following:

Ethnographic research should be the research method of choice if you are planning to study organizational culture. This is because organizational culture includes not just the explicit values and behaviours of the members of an organization, but also taken-for-granted assumptions that are virtually impossible to discover if you are there for only a short time. If you obtain your data primarily from interviews, as in case study research, you will only ever scratch the surface of the culture of an organization. Hence the need for ethnographic research: it is the only method that enables a researcher to spend long enough in the field such that he or she can start to discern the unwritten rules of how things work or how they are supposed to work. These unwritten rules are seldom verbalized but can be discovered by patient ethnographic fieldwork.[26]

Myers provides examples of several ethnographic studies in business, including efficiency in auditing, the use of franchising by retail companies as a means of entering foreign markets, the identification of the "speed trap" pathology in organizations making fast decisions, and the study of entertainment products such as *Star Trek*'s subculture of consumption.[27]

Known for being a prolific researcher in industrial, workplace ethnography, Donald Roy took positions in 21 different occupations in over 20 industries as a **participant observer**. He was interested in small group interaction, social conflict, and union organizing. In a well-known study often used in organizational behavior classes ("Banana Time"), Roy became a punch press operator in an isolated part of a dismal factory where his only outside view was through barred windows of a dingy room at an adjacent warehouse wall. Here he spent 2 months with three fellow operators on a punch press. His experience is an account of

> . . . how one group of machine operators kept from "going nuts" in a situation of monotonous work activity [with] attempts to lay bare . . . interactions which made up the content of their adjustment. The talking, fun, and fooling, which provided a solution to the elemental problem of "psychological survival" describes the rituals that a small workgroup used to make their highly repetitive, 12-hour work day bearable.[28]

The three men were friendly, middle-aged, foreign-born, talkative, and downwardly mobile, having emigrated from Eastern Europe before the Nazis took over. Roy identified "times," named by the machine operators as coffee time, peach time, banana time, fish time, and coke time, which were short breaks from work activities to build relationships, and numerous "themes," from "kidding themes" to serious conversations that stimulated interaction on recurring topics within the group.

According to Gold, there are four roles for the *participant observer*. This typology establishes responsibilities for each function:

- The *complete participant* takes an insider role, is fully part of the setting, and often observes covertly.

- The *participant as observer* gains access to a setting by having natural and nonresearch reasons for being there. As observers, they are part of the group being studied.

- The *observer as participant* has minimal involvement in the social setting under study. There is some connection to the setting but the observer is not normally part of the social setting.

- The *complete observer* does not take any part in the social setting (e.g., members of a human resource department watching an interview from behind a one-way mirror).[29]

In an example of organizational culture, Watson went to work for a year with GEC Plessey Telecommunications, formed earlier between two competitive businesses with a new stakeholder, Siemens.[30] The thinking at the top was to build a culture linked to their new vision and strategy. Watson's goal was to get as close to managers facing the pressures of change management with the simultaneous stresses of the typical managerial experience. While he was working in human resources, which led the organization's change management, he discovered that all the buzz words of "culture change," "empowerment," and "customer focus" were only superficial and daily issues to a large extent had hardly changed. The impact on the managers' personal and private lives, 10 years later, showed the struggle of having to address changing the values and assumptions of employees in mergers and takeovers and balancing their managerial role with their responsibilities as wives, husbands, parents, and children.[31]

A variation of ethnography, **netnography** (related to *cyberethnography* and *virtual ethnography*), uses ethnographic methods to study online communities developed by people with similar interests or backgrounds.[32] Online communities form a culture that becomes a source of identification for them. The cultural characteristics of online groups lead researchers to study their patterns of establishing and sustaining relationships. Other variations include *ethnology* (the comparative study of cultural groups) and *ethnohistory* (the study of the cultural past of a group of people). "An ethnohistory is often done in the early stages of a standard ethnography in order to get a sense of the group's cultural history."[33]

Phenomenology

Phenomenology studies human experiences through the introspective descriptions of the people involved. These occurrences are called **lived experiences**. The goal of phenomenological studies is to extract the essence and meaning of the lived experience through the participant's conscious perception of their feelings and actions surrounding the event.[34] The experience may relate to some traumatic event (divorce, natural disaster, terrorist act, September 11, plant closing, layoff, termination, or the death of a family member or work colleague). Alternatively, it could be a festive event (birth, wedding, or promotion) or anything significant beyond a trivial mention. Through one or more interviews, the researcher attempts to detect an underlying principle, conclusion, or generality.[35] Normally, the data are obtained through in-depth interviews, but participants may also write about their experiences.

To understand the lived experience from the viewpoint of the subject, researchers must account for their beliefs and feelings. The researcher identifies "what she or he expects to discover and

Brendan Smialowski/AFP/Getty Images

Phenomenology studies "lived experiences" through the introspective descriptions of the people involved. Here, people embrace during a vigil for the mass shooting victims at the Pulse nightclub in June 2016 in Orlando, Florida.

then deliberately puts aside these ideas; this process is called **bracketing**."[36] According to Johnson and Christensen, "Phenomenological researchers often search for commonalities across individuals (rather than only focusing on what is unique to a single individual)."[37] For example, what are the essences of employees' experiences in an organization's decision not to recall them for work and make their layoff (reduction in force) permanent? What is the lived experience of employees' outplacement program including their training on resume writing, job-seeking strategies, social networking, and interview preparation?

As a means of interpretation, Thompson's marketing-relevant study of consumer experiences advocates part-to-whole analysis of participants' accounts by proceeding through an iterative process. This involves reading texts (interview transcripts) fully to gain a sense of the whole picture first. His research provides a "framework for interpreting the stories consumers tell about their experiences of products, services, brand images, and shopping."[38] One of Thompson's examples is a 40-year-old financial executive who is transitioning from "supermom" and reveals a life narrative manifesting itself existentially through symbolic meanings she connects with superficial consumer behaviors in a supermarket:

> Jean: Food Lion, it's a little smaller than the superstores. I don't think a grocery should try to be everything, and it is almost a physical challenge to get through Kroger because you have to get cosmetics and pharmacy and film development and video rental. I am organized to the point where I have a set number of things I need to get, and I want to get in there and out. We don't buy cigarettes; we don't buy ice cream or potato chips or cookies. We just buy basics, and Food Lion is the best place for us. They don't have as grandiose a variety of things, but I don't need that. Another family activity we have is cooking together so we make a lot of things from scratch, so you don't need a lot of prepared items for that. So we go in there armed with the *Joy of Cooking*, and we pretty much get the job done at Food Lion (#6).[39]

Phenomenology consists of different orientations that, according to Creswell, should be investigated before commencing a study: hermeneutical, epoche, transcendental, textural descriptive, structural descriptive, and essence.[40]

Grounded Theory

Grounded theory, discovered and developed by Glaser and Strauss in the 1960s, has gained popularity over time.[41] **Grounded theory** (GT) is an approach to analyzing qualitative data in which repeated ideas are identified, summarized, and grouped into conceptual categories or broader themes, and a theory is built systematically from the ground up with "grounded" inductive observations[42] and deductive approaches to theory development.

O'Reilly et al., writing on "Demystifying Grounded Theory for Business Research," contend that GT is elusive and misunderstood even by its advocates. Many studies claim to use it but apply only a la carte features or jargon and do not implement its fundamental principles.[43] Nevertheless, GT has been used in numerous business fields for theory building and testing from the 1970s: management, marketing, organizational behavior, international business, business-to-business (B2B) research, logistics services, MIS, and others.

One of the first studies in organizational behavior conceptualized how the behaviors of academic employees affect the functioning of their departments. Thirty-four members of entirely different academic disciplines in five colleges were interviewed in the sample. The researchers collected additional data to amend the categories found. The procedures followed the core principles of GT: constant comparison and theoretical sampling (discussed later), to allow a model of the departmental organization to emerge. The researchers' theory summarized the manner in which different structures of authority, accountability, and power linked to the tasks and problems confronted by departmental employees.[44]

As a process, GT practitioners start with the data and develop an interpretation that is "grounded in" those data. Repetition observed throughout the data helps identify ideas. A smaller number of broader themes then emerge. Finally, identified themes are written into a theoretical narrative—an interpretation—of the subjective experience of the participants. Evidence in the form of direct quotations from the participants supports the narrative.[45]

For the most part, data are collected in **naturalistic settings** (field settings). The data collection primarily consists of participant observation and interviews, which are recorded through notes and tape recordings.[46] The collection and analysis process occurs simultaneously throughout the project in a **constant comparison**—that is, a comparison of incoming data with those already collected so that the researcher does not wait until the end of the study to accumulate all of the data. Collection and analysis occur simultaneously, guiding subsequent data collection. This process aims to guarantee the accuracy of evidence in the conceptual category, assign codes, and establish the generality of a particular fact.[47]

The second part of GT involves "theoretical sampling" or "recruiting participants with differing experiences of the phenomenon so as to explore multiple dimensions of the social process under study."[48] **Theoretical sampling**, based on concept representativeness and consistency, has four components that build on each other:

1. Data collection from observations, interviews, and visual materials;

2. Open coding using conceptual labeling (often line-by-line evaluations) and categorizing;

3. Axial coding or finding relationships between categories; and

4. Selective coding involving selection of a core category and checking for conceptual "density."

Cycling between selective, axial, and open coding allows constant comparison between incidents, data, and theory and provides for precision and consistency, thereby avoiding bias. Similarly, working simultaneously on data collection and open coding facilitates the acquisition of conceptual details from memos and field notes.[49] The GT process finishes when no new concepts emerge from the data and the theory is well validated (i.e., "theoretical saturation" occurs).[50]

In Myers's work on qualitative research in management, you will find examples of the application of GT. For example, he studied the alignment of management control systems in strategic investment decisions and R&D researchers exchanging informal resources across organizational boundaries (to enhance the informational lifeblood of the firm). Myers also investigated ways of anticipating customer value strategies, conducted a dual study on the interface of work-home balance, and produced an inquiry into the collaboration and interaction between buyers and suppliers in the Chinese automotive industry.[51]

There is some misunderstanding and misuse of GT and *qualitative content analysis*. Quantitative **content analysis** was originally a *quantitative* research technique "for the objective, systematic, and quantitative description of the manifest content of communication."[52] Quantitative content analysis is a flexible tool often used by trend-watching groups like Faith Popcorn's BrainReserve ("17 Trends That Reveal the Future"), the Naisbitt Group's John Naisbitt (*China's Megatrends: The 8 Pillars of a New Society*, 2010), and Inferential Focus (early warning and implications of change). Changes are discerned from written materials (magazines or newspapers) or oral records before they can be confirmed statistically as trends. Content analysis has traditionally been used to analyze open-ended survey questions, interview transcripts, focus group transcripts, and records of observational research. In ethnography, thematic analysis, a form of content analysis, allows you to interpret themes or "let them emerge," unlike counting verbs or nouns.

Recently, the use of content analysis has extended to social media, sentiment analysis, and big data applications. This modernization of use bridges the traditions of qualitative and quantitative paradigms. Management researchers are increasingly analyzing and using text and qualitative data but face the same obstacles as other disciplines: adequate measures, coding schemes, reliability and validity, and conduct of manual versus computer-aided content analysis.

For example, *quantitative content analysis* requires a means of quantification such as measurements of space and time, the number of hashtags or "likes" in social media, analysis of media and advertising effectiveness, counts of people or objects in an image, or the frequency with which words, sentences, or themes appear.

In these applications, content analysis is applied to the "subjective interpretation of the content of text data through the systematic classification process of coding and identifying themes or patterns."[53] The process follows a sequence where, after sampling, the coding scheme is developed. This involves detailed instructions for identifying and subsequently classifying the units of interest. Then data are collected and mapped by assigning numerical symbols to a codebook. Software programs have long processed coded data for extracting trends at the macro level and generating summary statistics and inferential tests of hypotheses or research questions at lower levels. (Refer to the software programs previously mentioned in Chapter 5, "Collect and Process the Data," as well as Stata, SPSS, SAS, Tableau, and R.) Intercoder consistency checks for coder bias are performed through inter-rater reliability statistics such as Cohen's kappa.

By using inductive, deductive, abductive, or a combination of logical approaches, content analysis can extract meaning from manifest (surface content) but it is always more difficult to extract latent, underlying or more hidden content. An example of a *qualitative content analysis* on sexual harassment in the workplace is shown in Exhibit 7.2.

Narrative

Narrative analysis is a form of qualitative design where the researcher focuses on how respondents impose order on the flow of experience in their lives and thus make sense of the events and actions they have experienced.[54] It uses lived and told stories of a few participants to understand these experiences, which are commonly connected chronologically. Moreover, the purpose of narrative inquiry is to reveal the meanings of the individuals' experiences as opposed to objective, decontextualized truths.[55]

AP Photo/Manuel Balce Ceneta Images

Narrative analysis is a form of qualitative design where the researcher focuses on how people make sense of the events and actions they have experienced in their lives. It uses lived and told stories of participants to understand these experiences. Radio documentary producer Dave Isay of StoryCorps in Washington, D.C., is creating an oral history of America through the stories of everyday people.

Riessman states that narrative interviewing has commonalities with traditional social science interviewing, in that both rely on open or closed (fixed-response) questions. However, unlike the mainstream survey practice, the goal of narrative interviews is to create detailed answers rather than brief ones or standard responses. Here is her advice for narrative analysts:

Narratives come in many forms and sizes, ranging from short, tightly bounded stories told to answer a single question to long narratives that build over the course of several interviews and traverse temporal and geographical space—biographical accounts that refer to entire lives or careers.[56]

EXHIBIT 7.2 ■ Qualitative Content Analysis: Sexual Harassment in the Workplace

Text Transcribed From Focus Groups and Written Narrative	Codes	Subcategories	Interpretation
Woman 1: I was surprised, taken aback. Initially, I thought I might have done something wrong. Then, I thought it had to be a mistake. I wasn't seeing it for what it was. Perhaps it was an innocent gesture. But, I still could not believe my eyes.	Surprised I'm at fault A mistake Misreading Denial	Harassment not likely true	
Woman 2: I felt really odd when I heard there had been incidents of sexual harassment in the department. But no one knew much about it. Probably, it was a rumor. Maybe it was retaliation against a manager. But I looked like all the other women. How could I be the only one now getting unwanted sexual advances?	Feeling odd Rumors No good explanation Why me? meme? Only me?	Harassment is happening	
Male colleague: When I first heard, it was like "what?" How is that possible? But when I found out who was involved, I didn't care or maybe I was concerned if it all got out, every male would be suspect. I just didn't handle all this very well.	Surprise Incredulous Didn't care Worried; what if revealed? Didn't understand	Cannot comprehend or accept	Investigation revealed pervasive patterns of harassment based on additional respondents' and litigants' testimony
Woman 3: The male broker I worked with was kind at first. Then he called me his "work wife." I laughed it off. Soon, he asked about my proportions and preferred sexual positions and advised me to perform a sexual act on a new client.	"Grooming" Dismissed offensive behavior. Harassment suit filed. Company terminated complainant. Sued again for sexual harassment/retaliation: won.	Legally established the occurrence of sexual harassment	
More text →	Additional codes →	More subcategories	

Source: Table format modified from Figure 1 ("The Process of Qualitative Content Analysis, Moving From Text to an Interpretation of the Abstract Meaning") in Rosen, Anna, Maria Emmelin, Annelie Carlson, Solveig Hammarroth, Eva Karlsson, and Anneli Ivarsson, "Mass Screening for Celiac Disease From the Perspective of Newly Diagnosed Adolescents and Their Parents: A Mixed-Methods Study," *BMC Public Health* 11 (2011): 822.

Storytelling of this nature requires a conversational climate with typical turn-taking composed of an entrance, openings, transition, and exit communication. Riessman further suggests:

> Generating narrative requires longer turns at talk than are customary in ordinary conversations . . . and one story can lead to another, as narrator and questioner/ listener negotiate openings for extended turns and associative shifts in topic. When shifts occur, it is useful to explore . . . associations and meanings that might connect several stories.[57]

As Somers asserts, "Everything we know, from making families, to coping with illness, to carrying out strikes and revolutions is at least in part a result of numerous cross-cutting relational story-lines in which social actors find or locate themselves."[58]

An understanding of narrative includes considering the types of standard narratives that emerge:

- *Biographical*: when the researcher records and writes the experiences of another's life

- *Autoethnography*: written by the individual subject of the study with overtones of possessing a psychological orientation embodying the idea of multiple layers of consciousness: the self as vulnerable, coherent, critiquing, discursive, and evocative

- *Life History*: containing the entirety of the participant's life found in single or multiple episodes, private circumstances, or communal folklore

- *Oral History*: gathering reflections of the participant or participants regarding causes and effects of the story in context [59]

Beyond standard forms, narratives describe more than textual stories; graphic books showed how the narrative of 9/11 could be depicted successfully through a photography exhibition.[60]

In a study on the causes of conflict between marketers and engineers, Keaveney investigated a persistent problem often found in high-technology companies.[61] Her work extends the marketing literature through narrative analysis and the use of the critical incident technique. Narratives from both marketers and engineers were interpreted using attribution theory in addition to recent management research on interfunctional conflict. The findings emphasize a high proportion of personal attributions, illustrating high levels of relationship conflict. These results contrast with the task conflict findings, which are more typical in the marketing literature.

Another example involves a U.K.-based study in organizational development and learning, which focuses on giving meaning to experiences in the management of change in successful organizations.[62] The study's methodology demonstrates how narrative analysis can serve as a useful learning process. "The key point is that change demands new learning and this expresses itself in changes in the prevailing narratives that in total constitute the culture of the organization."[63]

The U.K. study occurred at ThyssenKrupp Automotive Tallent Chassis, an automotive supplier. The company had evolved over 20 years from a struggling engineering firm to a successful production facility for subframe components of leading automotive brands. Over a period of 3 months, researchers conducted 30 individual, face-to-face, and in-depth interviews with 27 current and three former employees. These people were said to have long service with diverse experience (e.g., those who have moved from the shop floor into management) and could provide a historical perspective through stories.

The interviews lasted up to 2 hours and focused on the individuals' stories and interpretations of their change experiences at the firm. Each participant elaborated on personal experiences in the enterprise. "Nearly all interviews covered similar topics, including changes and milestones of the company's development, working climate, communication policy, leadership, and reasons for Tallent's success."[64]

The study produced a significant number of shared narratives on themes such as customer focus, profitability, flexibility, and commitment. A consensus of how the firm had moved forward was interwoven with common jargon. The employees' understanding of change in the global economy, as well as the vision and strategy for making the company succeed, produced "profound changes in the behavior, perceptions, and identities of managers and workers alike . . . [and were] exemplified in the prevailing patterns of narrative that make up the changed organizational culture of this company."[65]

Case Studies

Case design may be either qualitative or quantitative. For example, Gerring summarized definitions from numerous authors that refer to a case as (1) a method that is qualitative, small-N; (2) research content that is ethnographic, clinical, participant observation, or field; (3) a study characterized by process tracing; (4) an investigation of the properties of a single case; or (5) studies that examine a single phenomenon, instance, or example.[66] All of these definitions have an interest in defining a case by how the researchers use the design.

Let's distill these definitions. A **case study** entails the study of a case within a real-life, contemporary context or setting.[67] Creswell clarifies the design as

> . . . a type of design in qualitative research in which the investigator explores a
> real-life, contemporary bounded system (a *case*) or multiple bounded systems

(cases) over time, through detailed, in-depth collection involving *multiple sources of information*, e.g., observations, interviews, audiovisual material, and documents and reports), and reports *a case description* and *case themes*.[68]

Cases can take the form of investigating a small unit, team, group, program, event, complex functioning unit, or other phenomena in the context of real life. The real-life context is a case's strength compared to other forms of inquiry.[69] However, if researchers have any intention of generalizing from the findings, they should select representative cases.

Cases may be of two types: *single* or *multiple*. A single-case study may involve a review of an illustrative or atypical case, such as the inner working of a product-planning group that consistently brings innovations to the market. Researchers should decide if a single case study best represents the phenomenon or if they could obtain a more comprehensive view through a multiple-case study. In a multiple-case study, "You should decide whether the two (or more) cases are to represent confirmatory cases (i.e., presumed replications of the same phenomenon), contrasting cases (e.g., a success and a failure), or theoretically diverse cases. . . ."[70] The latter might include the mix of characteristics, innate and learned, shared by successful entrepreneurs in different enterprises. When using three or more cases, readers look for variety in size, geography, ethnicity, or variations in demographics, *per se*. These comparisons across several situations clarify similarities and differences.[71]

Case studies are said to be **bounded systems**, or systems (composed of persons, groups, dynamic situations, or processes) bounded in time and place. A case can be any bounded system that is of interest.[72] The boundaries determine what is included and excluded from the case. Boundaries stretch when, in organizational behavior terms, relevant actors in the case are **boundary spanners**, or operate as liaisons with other units.

The case environment produces multiple sources of data. These sources include questionnaires, interviews (open-ended conversations), observations (direct and participant), written accounts through archival records, or documents in the form of newspaper and magazine articles, reports, or participant e-mails. Artifacts and diaries are also useful. The methods or the media themselves may lead to researcher expectancy effects in which the researcher's biases may misrepresent participants' communications.

Myers also provides examples of case studies, including an open-book contingency theory of management accounting, a case and cross-case analysis of mergers and acquisitions from the

A case study facilitates a close examination of a dynamic phenomenon through an in-depth investigation (often using observations and interviews). This depth of detail is not feasible with a large number of participants when the study objective is a quantitative "averaging" of responses. Although a small geographical area or a small number of participants is normally selected, contemporary real-life situations and events are revealed through detailed contextual analysis. This analysis may continue for an extended period. Departments or teams are typical in business studies.

seller's side, multiple case studies in supply chain build-to-order management, and the creation of regional Asian brands such as Tiger Beer from Singapore.[73]

An MIT/Sloan leadership case entitled "Chris Peterson at DSS Consulting" describes a real-life situation of a team single-case study of working in an environment isolated from the larger organization. Some team members span the bounded system, and the case data reveal communications within the team, management, and clients. The boxed synopsis aims to illustrate the case features previously discussed, to develop a depiction of leaders developing teams that have connections to groups, both inside and outside the organization, and to highlight the importance of a leader ensuring that the team's efforts are aligned with the organizational strategy.[74]

CASE EXAMPLE
CHRIS PETERSON AT DSS CONSULTING

The firm, created in 1997, targeted small school districts in need of administrative support. By 2005, the founders reduced their involvement as DSS services started to become less relevant to the evolving complexities in school districts. They needed new types of services to remain viable. Realizing the need for a shift in strategy, Meg Cooke was promoted to COO, with only 4 years in the company and previous promotions that put her on an upward trajectory. Changes were made to transform the structure from a traditional functional one to cross-functional teams. After being with the firm since 2001, Chris was promoted to lead a team and head the Southwestern region. Her consultants had diverse backgrounds, worked well together, and collaborated differently from other teams.

Chris was pleased with the way her team adapted to their work and maintained motivation and satisfaction despite the controversial reorganization at DSS. She had selected the team and built a unified group but received little support from other units at DSS.

Chris's team decided that they could create a niche service for small school districts in need of an integrated planning and budgeting system.

Chris developed good relationships with prospective clients and also met occasionally with Meg to update her. It appeared, however, that Meg spent more time with other leaders and her meetings with Chris were brief. Being ignored was perplexing to Chris, given her team's progress.

Client questions from the districts centered on the new product's price and the comparison with other products on the market. The project was not free standing. Support came from a third-party vendor's database, a program for seeding information to the database by an outside consulting firm, written forms that districts would need to adopt, and a set of instructions for consultants to coach the district personnel. This complexity required going outside their circle to find specialists inside DSS for support. Some units were unhelpful or rebuffed Chris's team.

A meeting with Meg resulted in little direct action to assist Chris with organizational support and feedback. Tepid support implied to Chris and the team that Meg was political and played favorites. Independently the team filled knowledge gaps that were refused by functional specialists in DSS. A beta project came together in 10 days. A district test site agreed to a product demonstration.

(Continued)

(Continued)

Chris looked forward to a meeting with Meg and the Friday morning session started off well. Despite positive compliments from Meg on Chris and her team, Meg pressed her on the marketing of future projects to larger districts. Sizeable districts had indigenous resources to make Chris's project pointless.

When Chris arrived at work the following Monday, she discovered that Meg wanted a meeting at 10:30 a.m. Meg told Chris that the firm would not go forward with her scheduling and budgeting project. Chris was incredulous and asked for an explanation. Meg replied that "the number of new products DSS could support was limited and that teams in the other regions had not reported any interest on the part of the districts they had worked with for this type of product."[75] Chris pushed back on Meg's decision, saying she could not comprehend how other regional teams could negatively evaluate demand when they did not know what the system could do. Meg's decision to cancel the project was final. Silence followed, after which Meg put Chris in an impossible situation: she could either lead the team in a new direction or return to the IT practice as a functional specialist.

In summary, we have reviewed the qualitative designs of ethnography, phenomenology, grounded theory, narrative, and case studies. Examples from the business literature helped to explicate the applications and benefits of each. Exhibit 7.3 is designed to assist you in making design comparisons among the characteristics of purpose, focus (environment or process), data collection, and analysis of these major qualitative designs.

MIXED DESIGN

Mixed designs can be controversial even though they began in Galileo's time. The practice of mixed design has established itself by (1) eclectically selecting and integrating the best qualitative and quantitative designs to answer the question, (2) believing that a plurality of worldviews underlie its use, and (3) an awareness that *divergence* of results (not only *convergence*) often produces greater insights into complex phenomena.[76]

A **mixed design** is defined as a research design that integrates quantitative and qualitative designs, the methods they employ, and a *pragmatic relativist paradigm* into a single study that prioritizes either a quantitative or qualitative strategy as dominant or accepts them as having equal status in answering the research question. When you designate one design as dominant, the supplemental design provides data to add insight, enrich understanding, draw interpretations, supplement findings, or further test the results. Mixed designs may be *concurrent* (simultaneous), which are "projects conducted at the same time, with the results compared or contrasted on completion," or *sequential*, with "projects conducted one after another to further inquiry, with the first project informing the

EXHIBIT 7.3 ■ Characteristics of the Five Major Qualitative Designs

Design	Purpose	Focus	Methods of Data Collection	Methods of Data Analysis
Ethnography	Understand how behavior reflects the culture of a group of people.	A particular field site in which a group of individuals shares a common culture.	Participant observation over time; structured or unstructured interviews with "informants." Artifact-document collection.	Identification of significant phenomena and underlying themes, structures, and beliefs. Organization of data into a logical whole (e.g., chronology, typical day).
Phenomenology	Understand an incident or event's essence from participants' point of view.	A phenomenon as it is typically lived, shared, and perceived by human beings.	In-depth structured interviews. Purposeful sampling of 5–25 individuals.	Search for *meaningful concepts* that reflect various aspects of the experience; integration of concepts into a prototypical experience.
Grounded Theory	Inductive derivation of theory from data. Collected in a natural setting that describes and explains.	A process of human actions and interactions and how they result from and influence one another.	Interviews. Any other relevant data sources, such as observations.	Systematic method of coding the data into categories and identifying relationships; continual interweaving of data collection and data analysis. Theory construction from categories and interrelationships.
Narrative	Exploring participants' life experiences through their stories on which they impose a narrative of events.	Significance of individuals' lived experiences; the what/how of story; spoken or written version with others in events.	Researcher and participant(s) cooperate in a dialog. Data from field notes, letters, transcripts, journals, interviews, records, and autobiography. Audio, video, or photographic narrative.	Coding: breaking down data into constituent parts. Sorting the pieces like a puzzle into groups for fit and to form smaller parts of the picture. Analyzing: data compared for similarities, sequences, and patterns.
Case	Understanding one person or situation (or a very small number) in great depth.	One case, a few cases, event, program or within the natural setting.	Observations. Interviews. Multiple methods: written documents and audiovisual material.	Categorization and interpretation of data concerning common themes. Synthesis into an overall portrait of the case(s). Cross-case comparisons.

Source: Modified to include narrative and exclude content analysis. Adapted from Leedy, Paul D., and Jeanne Ellis Ormrod, *Practical Research: Planning and Design*, 11th ed. (New York: Pearson Education, 2016), 258, Table 9.1. It should be noted that content analysis is a broad family of *techniques* not a qualitative design. Whether you define content analysis by Harold Laswell (1948), Bernard Berelson (1952), Ole Holsti (1969), Klaus Krippendorff (2004), or many contemporary sources, it is a data analytic tool associated with manual and computerized text, image, archival, and sentiment analytics.

nature of the second project."[77] I find Steinbeck's second observation about the fish, the Mexican sierra, apropos to mixed design:

> . . . [W]e could, if we wished, describe the sierra [counting the number of spines] . . . but also we could see the fish alive and swimming, plunge against the lines, drag it threshing over the rail, and even finally eat it. And there is no reason why either approach should be inaccurate. Spine-count description need not suffer because another approach is also used. Perhaps out of the two approaches, we thought, there might emerge a picture more complete and even more accurate than either alone could produce.[78]

Mixed designs represent an option when a single design approach is not sufficient to answer the research question. Johnson formalizes the *scope* of mixed design and addresses what it is and how it operates:

> *Mixed methods research* is formally defined here as *the class of research where the researcher mixes or combines quantitative and qualitative research techniques, methods, approaches, concepts or language into a single study.* Philosophically, it is the "third wave" or third research movement, a movement that moves past the paradigm wars by offering a logical and practical alternative. Philosophically, mixed research makes use of the pragmatic method and system of philosophy. Its logic of inquiry includes the use of induction (or discovery of patterns), deduction (testing of theories and hypotheses), and abduction (uncovering and relying on the best of a set of explanations for understanding one's results).[79]

Sometimes, it is also helpful to describe something by what it is not, especially when the description is humorously accurate[80]:

> Mixed method designs are NOT a *blending* of research methods. We do not collect data in a willy-nilly fashion and then try to think of a way to combine it in the analysis so we can "see what we have got." Mixed method designs are not, as we have heard them described, like a stir fry, a collection of nuts, or a more expensive drink.

Like any other design you might select for your study's question or hypothesis, a mixed design requires the same adherence to protocols, attention to methodological detail, and compliance with procedures. However, a mixed design often requires more effort to accomplish its objectives.

The mixed design needs to accomplish the following:

- Span different audiences

- Balance methodological ontological divides

- Overcome "trained incapacities" through diversified experience and skills on the research team[81]

- Conceptualize so that the study's structure does not overemphasize one orientation's strength to the detriment of the other's weakness but produces a natural synergy *even when one approach is required to be more dominant to answer the research question*

- Coordinate the timelines for completion of the studies, particularly if one depends on data from another for analysis or interpretation

Another requirement to establish the rigor of mixed design, as well as integrate quantitative, qualitative, and mixed designs, is triangulation. **Triangulation** (convergent validation) "is a process of verification that increases validity by incorporating several viewpoints and methods . . . [and] refers to the combination of two or more theories, data sources, methods or investigators in one study of a single phenomenon to converge on a single construct, and can be employed in both quantitative (validation) and qualitative (inquiry) studies."[82] This argues that data integration is the center of mixed designs: "Integration is really the heart of the whole mixed methods exercise because the purpose of mixing methods is to get information from multiple sources and so the issues in bringing together the information are crucial."[83] Do findings from different methods agree? That is the crux of triangulation.

In an agenda projecting the future of mixed design into 2020, Mertens et al. were concerned about a similar apprehension voiced in this book: the relationship between the research question, design, and methods. In the "dictatorship model," the question determines quantitative, qualitative, or mixed methods approach with a bias toward answering the question using the methods in the researcher's "toolbox." This approach works well in cases in which "the methodology is the servant of questions."[84] With an interactive model, the centrality of the research question is seen to interact with purposes, theories and beliefs, methods, and validity considerations. In this model, "the idea is that research questions inform and are informed by methods, that is, there is a reciprocal relationship between questions and methods. Research questions influence the methods we use, but methods may also influence the research questions we ask."[85]

Selecting a Mixed Design

There are numerous ways to select and configure mixed design studies. First, the mixed design can be established at the beginning of the study, and one or another strategy can emerge as the study is underway. Often a pilot study for quantitative or qualitative research will reveal that a supplement is required to achieve the study's purpose. A second approach uses typologies, such as the three-page table in which Creswell and Plano Clark identified 15 authors, their disciplines, and specific designs that the authors identify or advocate.[86] A third practical approach might be labeled a "guiding framework." This strategy matches the design to the research problem, purpose, and question:

> Scholars writing about mixed-methods research uniformly agree that the questions of interest play a central role in the process of designing any mixed methods study. The importance of the research problem and questions is a fundamental principle of mixed methods research design. This perspective stems from the pragmatic foundations for conducting mixed methods research where the notion of "what works" applies well to selecting the methods that "work" best to address a study's problem and questions.[87]

Exhibit 7.4 summarizes the notation system created by Morse,[88] which provides short-hand to understand the design features and their combinations.

EXHIBIT 7.4 ■ Notation for Mixed Designs

Notation	Example	Meaning
Time Order	Concurrent Sequential	Studies conducted at the same time.
		Studies conducted one after another.
Weight, Priority, or Dominance		
Upper Case Letters	QUAN, QUAL	Quantitative or Qualitative has the increased weight or priority.
Lower Case Letters	quan, qual	quantitative or qualitative is supplemental.
Connectivity		
Plus sign: +	QUAN + QUAL	The two designs occur concurrently with a simultaneous collection of data.
Arrow: →	QUAN → qual	The two designs occur in a sequence.
Parentheses: ( )	QUAN → (qual)	A supplemental design is embedded (nested) within a design that has higher priority.
Example: unequal status	qual → QUAN	A sequential design that is primarily quantitative but preceded by a qualitative study.
Example: equal status	QUAN + QUAL	The two concurrent designs have equal status.
	QUAL → QUAL	The two sequential designs have equal status.

You are already familiar with the nomenclature for paradigm weighting. The researcher prioritizes (equalizes, weights, or ascribes dominance) to either qualitative or quantitative designs depending on the importance placed on the "fit" of the paradigm for the research question. By conducting the research concurrently (simultaneously), both qualitative and quantitative data are collected during a single phase of the study. When sequential timing occurs, the researcher "implements 'strands' in two distinct phases, with collection and analysis of one type of data occurring after the collection and analysis of the other type."[89] A **strand** is a study's component that incorporates the major processes of conducting quantitative or qualitative research: posing a research question, collecting data, analyzing data, and interpreting results.[90]

The process of integrating or combining the strands is based on four strategies: (1) merging two datasets, (2) connecting the analysis of one data set to another, (3) **embedding** from one form of data into a dominant design, and (4) using theory to inform the process of binding the data sets together. Creswell and Plano Clark's treatment of this topic explains how to do that and what results to expect.[91] Along with the timing of data collection, the researcher further determines how the data will be used in the analysis and interpretation phases of the study. The crossing of these two design elements ostensibly establishes the matrix in Exhibit 7.5.

In Exhibit 7.5, you see mixed design options that are a consequence of crossing **time order** and **paradigm weighting**. My matrix adds a third row to accommodate embedded designs, which are by definition unequal since a supplementary design is nested in a dominant design. However, embedded designs can be concurrent or sequential and the matrix thus includes a symbolic undivided row. The column to the far right (data options) is *not* intended to align with the rows of the matrix but rather presents standard forms of data handling: merging, embedding, and connecting.

Two studies help clarify Exhibit 7.5. The first is a study of marketing and relationships in software solutions in small and medium-sized enterprises (SMEs). The authors assert they designed a QUAL → quan approach (see the bottom right cell in Exhibit 7.5). The first stage involved researcher immersion for an extended period in two case-study SMEs within the B2B sector while the researchers also observed marketing decisions and development of customer relationships with prospective clients. This included qualitative observation and interviewing of their customers. The interviews helped to seed an online questionnaire (with the use of the multivariate technique, conjoint analysis) to augment the findings quantitatively and with a larger sample. The conjoint analysis determined the importance of customers' decision attributes by asking them to make trade-offs among a list of criteria they found important in deciding about a software supplier. Between two and four levels (or characteristics) of each attribute were used as measurement items. The online survey was targeted to 256 firms as a purposive sample of market companies in their geographical area. "Software quality" was the most important attribute by prospective customers when selecting suppliers. "Professionalism"

EXHIBIT 7.5 ■ Mixed Designs Based on Paradigm Weighting and Time Order

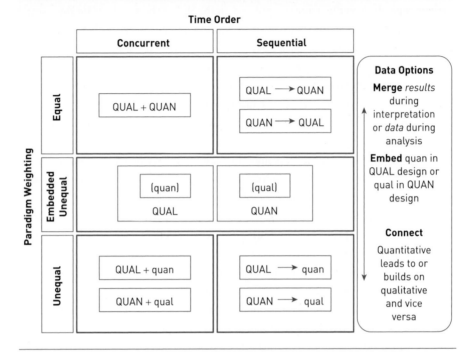

Sources: Adapted from Creswell, John W., and Vicki L. Plano Clark, *Designing and Conducting Mixed Methods Research*, 1st ed. (Thousand Oaks, CA: SAGE, 2007), 85, Table 4.2; Creswell, John W., and Vicki L. Plano Clark, *Designing and Conducting Mixed Methods Research*, 2nd ed. (Thousand Oaks, CA: SAGE Publications, 2011), 109, Table 4.1; Johnson, R. B., and L. B. Christensen. *Educational Research: Quantitative, Qualitative, and Mixed Approaches.* 5th ed. (Thousand Oaks, CA: SAGE, 2014), Chapter 18: Mixed Research: Lecture Notes, 5–6, Figure 18.2; and Johnson, R. B., and A. J. Onwuegbuzie, "Mixed Methods Research: A Research Paradigm Whose Time Has Come," *Educational Researcher* 33, no. 7 (2004): 21–22.

was second, reinforcing previous findings that service quality is as equally important as product quality. "Understanding the customer" was third, supporting communication as an indispensable part of developing a customized solution. The authors stated that mixed methods increased the strength of the results by offsetting the weaknesses of one method with the strengths of the other.[92] Do you think this was a qual → QUAN approach?

The second study investigated whether standardized project management (SPM) increased (product) development management success. The authors characterized their strategy as empirical but involving a sequential three-stage approach with qualitative components. This is best represented by the design in the second row on the right side of Exhibit 7.5. It is predominantly quantitative with qualitative data and analysis embedded by virtue of the first and third stages of the project. The first stage used semi-structured interviews of 12 project managers in six organizations "to develop SPM constructs from a real-life context." Open-ended questions asked the project managers to "tell stories" of SPM initiatives. In addition, observations and document analysis produced a deeper understanding of the issues.

This work became input for the development of seven hypotheses and the creation of a questionnaire that was administered to 55 participants in project management workshops. The questionnaire contained 5-point Likert scales to identify project accomplishment on such variables as schedule, cost, quality, and customer satisfaction goals. The statistics used were t-tests, correlations, and multiple regressions. Follow-up case interviews (qualitative) were conducted and a content analysis enriched the findings. Hypothesis testing revealed that three factors (standardized project management tools, leadership, and process) have a role in SPM efforts and the other four unsupported hypotheses may be of lower interest.[93]

In the Preface, I said that I value and voice the ascendency of qualitative research, mixed designs, and their contribution to research in business and management. Mixed methods are used more frequently and their results are published in numerous business fields. Although authors face obstacles within their fields and from journal editorial boards with strong paradigmatic views, various business fields have demonstrated value-added benefits of mixed design compared with a mono-method. Numerous studies formalize these results for international business, management, human resource development, information systems, strategic management, information technology, marketing, and articles in *Administrative Science Quarterly* and the *Academy of Management Journal*.[94]

EXHIBIT 7.6 ■ Summary of Design Strategies by Business Discipline

Percentage by Business Discipline and Design Strategy

Discipline	Quantitative	Qualitative	Mixed	Total n/row
Marketing	75%	11%	14%	734
International Business	68%	15%	17%	394
Strategic Management	78%	5%	17%	570
Organizational Behavior	85%	7.5%	7.5%	231
Operations Management	78%	12%	10%	187
Entrepreneurship	76%	16%	8%	235
Total n and % per column	1,784 (76%)	240 (10%)	327 (14%)	2,351 (100%)

Source: Cameron, Roslyn, and Jose F. Molina-Azorin, "The Use of Mixed Methods Across Seven Business and Management Fields" (paper presented at 10th International Federation of Scholarly Associations of Management Paris, France, July 8–10, 2010), 11.

Finally, Cameron and Molina-Azorin set out to gauge the level of acceptance of mixed methods in management using a synthesis of large-scale methodological scans across seven management fields: marketing, international business, strategic management, organizational behavior, operations management, entrepreneurship, and human resource management.[95] Their findings are shown in Exhibit 7.6.

Not surprisingly, quantitative designs are first (76%), followed by mixed methods (14%) and qualitative (10%) designs. Mixed methods produced respectable results in international business, strategic management, and marketing: 17%, 17%, and 14%, respectively. These percentages will improve as future research updates the findings, mixed methods achieve greater acceptance, publications feature more mixed methods designs, and research training and collaboration increases. The findings support the need for mixed methods awareness among business students and stress the importance of training and development for researchers.

Chapter Summary

- Nonexperimental design includes qualitative design and preserves the legitimacy of qualitative design goals to answer a research question. The designs in qualitative research include ethnography, netnography (cyberethnography and virtual ethnography), phenomenology, ethnomethodology, grounded theory, historical analysis, narrative analysis, case study, conversation analysis, life story, interactional and visual texts, and more. My choice of five (ethnology, phenomenology, grounded theory, narrative, and case) represents five major approaches to qualitative research recognized by authorities and provides a degree of simplification for the benefit of new researchers.

- Data collection for qualitative studies is performed through observation (participant-outsider, participant, nonparticipant, concealment, and covert), archival data, online, and various types of interviews (ethnographic, narrative, guided, biographic, problem-centered, episodic, in-depth,

structured, semi-structured, open-ended, and group or focus groups).

- Since the data are typically textual, in large quantities, and often "unfiltered," their analysis and management are different from quantitative data. Although qualitative data are usually organized manually, computer-assisted textual and pictorial analysis may be used to convert data from the collection format to a numeric format.

- *Ethnography* studies a culture or cultures that some group of people share, using participant observation over an extended period. An entire cultural group or a subgroup that interacts over time may be the study's target.

- *Phenomenology* investigates human experiences through the introspective descriptions of the people involved. These experiences are called *lived experiences*. The goal of phenomenological design is to extract the essence and meaning of the lived experience through the participants' conscious perception of their feelings and actions surrounding the event.

- *Grounded theory* is a design for analyzing qualitative data in which repeated ideas are identified, summarized, and grouped into conceptual categories or broader themes and a theory is built systematically from the ground up with "grounded" inductive observations.

- *Narrative* design is where the researcher focuses on how respondents impose order on the flow of life experience and thus make sense of the events and actions they have experienced. It uses lived and told stories of a few participants to understand these experiences, which are commonly connected chronologically.

- *Case* design entails the study of a case within a real-life, contemporary context or setting. It is a type of design in which the investigator explores a contemporary bounded system or multiple bounded systems over time, through detailed, in-depth collection involving multiple sources of information.

- *Mixed designs* integrate quantitative and qualitative designs, the methods they employ, and a pragmatic relativist paradigm into a single study that prioritizes a quantitative or qualitative strategy as dominant or accepts them as having equal status in answering the research question. Mixed designs may be concurrent (simultaneous), with projects conducted at the same time, or sequential, with the first project informing the nature of the second.

- Mixed design identification results from crossing *paradigm weighting* and *time order*, as shown in Exhibit 7.4. The researcher prioritizes (equalizes, weights, or ascribes dominance) to either paradigm depending on the importance placed on the "fit" of the paradigm for the research question and optimal timing for data-design synergy. Two examples are illustrated in the matrix.

- The ascendency of qualitative research, mixed designs, and their contribution to research in business and management were discussed. A case was made for disciplinary acceptance of mixed methods research, the need for editorial boards to respond positively to more mixed methods articles, and the need to improve awareness and training.

Key Terms

boundary spanner	key informant	participant reactivity
bounded system	lived experience	phenomenology
bracketing	mixed design	qualitative design
case study	narrative	strand
constant comparison	naturalistic setting	textual data
content analysis	netnography	theoretical sampling
embedding	observation	time order
ethnography	paradigm weighting	triangulation
grounded theory	participant observer	unobtrusive measure

Discussion Questions

1. Devise a good argument to support the contention that there is a complementary relationship between qualitative and quantitative design.

2. Describe how the interpretivist/naturalistic worldview energizes and legitimizes qualitative design.

   a. Define qualitative design.

   b. Describe its purposes and goals.

   c. Provide some examples that illustrate the wide spectrum of qualitative research.

   What are the categories of observational methods and techniques that are used to collect data for qualitative studies? What is the role of the interview in qualitative research and what types are used?

3. How are unobtrusive measures unlike observation and interviewing? How do they anticipate respondent reactivity? How do they affect the privacy of participants under surveillance?

4. Participant observation is used in qualitative research and in disciplines beside business (e.g., communication studies, cultural anthropology, sociology, and social psychology). In the section on ethnography, what form of participant observer role did the researcher in industrial workplace ethnography, Donald Roy, take during his participation/observation of the three friendly, foreign-born, middle-aged men in the dismal factory? What other researcher roles might have been possible in this environment?

5. What are the sources of textual data that are analyzed in qualitative studies?

6. How is content analysis used to code, categorize, and interpret textual data?

7. Provide examples of the following qualitative studies in business settings:

   a. Ethnography

   b. Phenomenology

   c. Grounded theory

   d. Narrative

   e. Case studies

8. Compare the purpose, focus, methods of data collection, and methods of data analysis for the five qualitative studies listed.

9. Define mixed design (what characteristics does it have and not have) and determine if its worldview/paradigm is suited to its purpose.

10. Mixed design identification results from crossing *paradigm weighting* and *time order*, as shown in Exhibit 7.4.

    a. How does the researcher prioritize (equalize, weight, or ascribe dominance) to either paradigm?

    b. How does optimal timing of the studies result in a data-design synergy?

    c. Find a mixed design study in the literature of your field and show where it fits in the classification matrix.

8

EXPERIMENTAL DESIGNS

LEARNING OBJECTIVES

Performance Objective

Prepare an experimental design scenario as an alternative proposal for your term project based on the experimental knowledge you have acquired. Focus on problems most commonly encountered in business.

Enabling Objectives

1. List the major classifications of experimental design.

2. Specify the three conditions and four criteria indispensable for causality.

3. Distinguish between internal and external validity and identify threats to each that endanger the results of a study.

4. Explain why a true experimental design is regarded as the most accurate form of experimental research and describe the role of a control (or comparison) group in relation to the treatment.

5. Support the position that it is unethical to withhold treatment from a control group in instances where the treatment provides substantial benefit.

6. Classify other randomized designs that rely on random assignment to produce group equivalence, to balance treatment and control groups, or to compensate for confounding variables.

7. Explain the advantages of a quasi-experiment and how it promotes increased realism and ecological validity when conditions only vary naturally (not by researcher manipulation).

8. Illustrate how matching and other techniques balance treatment and control groups to reduce the effect of confounding variables.

In this last chapter on design, I introduce many of the features of the *experimental model* and also discuss variations in experimental design. This chapter also covers causality, validity, and the use of matching and other mechanisms to balance treatment and control groups when random assignment is not possible.

OPTIMIZING BUSINESS EXPERIMENTS

In a recent *Harvard Business Review* (*HBR*), Thomke and Manzi discussed business experiments they had conducted or studied during their 40-plus years of collective experience with companies. Those firms included Bank of America, BMW, Hilton, Kraft, Petco, Staples, Subway, and Walmart.[1] Thomke and Manzi's advice was considered so valuable for their readers that *HBR* elevated the article to their "10 Must Reads" and it was also a McKinsey Awards Finalist. The authors suggested five questions that companies should answer before beginning a *business experiment*. Their guidance should entice you to consider experimental design or at least be knowledgeable enough to recommend it as a rigorous test to determine if a new product or program will succeed. Here is a quick summary of their suggestions and a few examples from their article.

1. *Does the experiment have a clear purpose?*

When executives disagree on a proposed action, an experiment may be the most pragmatic way to answer the question, provided that the hypothesis is stated in unequivocal terms. (We addressed the importance of specificity in research questions and hypotheses in Chapters 2 and 3.) In 2013, Kohl's did just that by testing the following hypothesis: "Opening stores an hour later to reduce operating costs will not lead to a significant drop in sales." Results of the experiment involving 100 Kohl's stores supported the hypothesis.

2. *Have stakeholders committed to abide by the results?*

This requirement reduces dissension on the management committee and prevents influential persons from selecting evidence that only supports their point of view. Publix Super Markets, which does business predominantly in the Southeastern United States, has a procedure to ensure commitment. A proposal is submitted for financial analysis and then to a committee, which includes the finance executive. Finance then approves programs that have followed the process and have positive experimental results. Other companies with similar approval protocols carefully evaluate the cost-benefit of testing.

3. *Is the experiment doable?*

The business environment's complexity (from the supply chain to the distribution channels to end users) makes it challenging to sort out the cause-and-effect relationships of the variables under investigation, especially because the environment changes rapidly and confounding variables, not just the IV and DV, thus change as well. Large samples address this problem regarding effect size but are often impractical because of scaling the experiment's size and cost.

4. *How can we ensure reliable results?*

Thomke and Manzi suggest three ways to increase validity and reliability: randomized field trials, blind tests, and big data. With *randomization* in the field, companies may take a large group of individuals with the same characteristics and randomly divide them into test and control groups. Capital One, for example, has a history of demanding field trials even for questions like the color of envelopes for product offers. Petco previously selected its 30 best stores for treatment and the 30 worst as controls. As you might expect, the results were impressive but failed at launch. Now Petco, along with Publix and others, includes customer demographics, competitor proximity, and store size to get more valid and reliable results. *Blind tests* reduce participant perceptions that deviations are occurring, thus causing them to behave differently. Often, a company's employees are not aware of an ongoing experiment. (We define single, double, and triple blinding later in the section on internal validity.) *Big data* are useful in resolving disputed results. Take a company in which different groups produced conflicting results in separate experiments on the same program. According to Thomke and Manzi, "To determine which results to trust, the company employed big data, including transaction-level data (store items, the times of day when the sale occurred, prices), store attributes, and data on the environments around the stores (competition, demographics, weather)."[2]

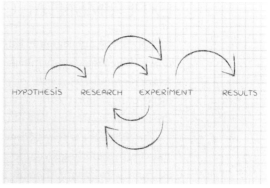

Norwegian economist Trygve Haavelmo, who won the 1989 Nobel Prize, observed that there are two types of experiments: "those we should like to make" and "the stream of experiments that nature is steadily turning out from her own enormous laboratory, and which we merely watch as passive observers." If firms can recognize when natural experiments occur, they can learn from them at little or no additional expense. For example, when an apparel retailer opened its first store in a state, it was required by law to start charging sales tax on online and catalog orders shipped to that state, whereas previously those purchases had been tax free. This provided an opportunity to discover how sales taxes affected online and catalog demand.

Source: Anderson, Eric T., and Duncan Simester, "A Step-by-Step Guide to Smart Business Experiments," *Harvard Business Review*, March 2011, https://hbr.org/2011/03/a-step-by-step-guide-to-smart-business-experiments.

5. Have we gotten the most value out of the experiment?

Because of the diversity of customers, markets, and geographies for many retail companies, the "where" question is critical. For example, Petco's initiatives are used in stores that are the most similar to the test stores that produced the best results. The issue of exploiting the captured data is also important. Previously, Publix had an 80:20 ratio of testing time versus analysis. Their goal is to reverse that ratio, thereby extracting more useful information.

The authors conclude by answering why experiments are valuable for business decision-making:

> The lesson is not merely that business experimentation can lead to better ways of doing things. It can also give companies the confidence to overturn wrongheaded conventional wisdom and the faulty business intuition that even seasoned executives can display. And smarter decision-making ultimately leads to improved performance.[3]

Do not neglect considering an experimental design for a business study. There is a rich history of experimental design in marketing, such as consumer behavior, advertising, retail store environments, sales, and partner satisfaction in marketing alliances. Experiments are also used in many subfields of management as well as in economics/international economics where studies include individual choice, game theory, and the organization and functioning of markets.

EXPERIMENTAL CLASSIFICATIONS

Campbell and Stanley observed, "By experiment we refer to that portion of research in which variables are manipulated and their effects upon other variables observed."[4] *Experimental designs* consist of *true experiments* (sometimes called randomized experiments or randomized controlled trials), *other randomized designs*, and *quasi-experiments*. *Pre-experiments* are discussed only briefly for comparison purposes.

The design of a **true experiment** is a detailed strategy that is planned to reveal cause-and-effect relationships among variables through manipulation, control, and random assignment to groups. Because of its powerful nature in identifying such relationships, this design is often considered the "gold standard" for evaluating other designs. However, hypotheses claiming causal relationships are bold and susceptible to alternative explanations.

The second group of experimental designs, *other randomized designs* (shown in Exhibit 8.1), provide flexibility in handling numerous variables simultaneously and can be applied to a

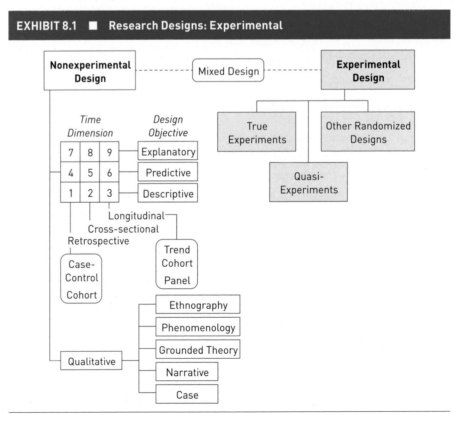

EXHIBIT 8.1   ■   Research Designs: Experimental

Note: Experimental Design components are highlighted. The shaded boxes represent the coverage of this chapter, whereas the white boxes are design topics from Chapters 6 and 7.

wide range of research questions that involve field settings. These designs result from random assignment of participants to treatment groups or are based on randomization.

The third group is *quasi-experiments*, which eliminate the problem with directionality but participants are *not* randomly assigned and confounding variables that affect participant selection are not removed. Researchers use these designs for their convenience and their relatively less conspicuous and disruptive nature to participants.

In this chapter, I isolate the right side of Exhibit 8.1 due to the sheer quantity of information on experimental design. Because the nonexperimental category includes many quantitative and qualitative designs, the left side of the graphic was explained in Chapters 6 and 7. After you read this chapter, you will have an extensive choice of experimental and nonexperimental designs from which to create your study.

CHARACTERISTICS OF EXPERIMENTAL DESIGN

Upon reading this section, one thing should be evident: "Good design is obvious. Great design is transparent."[5] Let's begin the technical discussion of experimental design by defining the necessary conditions for experiments to make claims of causality: (a) manipulation, (b) control, and (c) random assignment.

Conditions for Claims of Causality

With experimental design, a "defining characteristic is active manipulation of an independent variable (i.e., it is only in experimental research that 'manipulation' is present)."[6] This depiction of **manipulation** suggests that a researcher manipulates or systematically varies the levels of an independent variable (IV) and then measures the outcome of interest, the dependent variable (DV). The manipulated condition (IV) is also known as the "treatment" or "intervention." Levels of the condition are often referred to in shorthand by researchers (e.g., in an experiment of training effectiveness, the three levels are Seminar, OJT, and None). Simplicity and common sense determine the levels of an independent variable. If salary is hypothesized to influence employees exercising stock options, the salary variable might be divided into high, medium, and low, representing three levels of the independent variable. Manipulating an independent variable means changing "its level systematically so that different groups of participants are exposed to different levels

Researchers manipulate or systematically vary the levels of an independent variable (IV) and then measure the outcome of interest, the dependent variable (DV). Here engineer-participants are testing hologram-themed augmented reality glasses where wearers interact with screens and full-color virtual objects. Early models show the repair of light switches with the help of virtual assistants, who draw diagrams and arrows within the picture that the Microsoft HoloLens is seeing.

©iStockphoto.com/filadendron

of that variable, or the same group of participants is exposed to different levels at different times."[7] The term systematic, as used in this statement, implies the existence of procedures to minimize error and bias while increasing confidence in the efficacy of the manipulated treatment. Manipulation is the first feature of the experimental design.

Notice that the manipulation of an independent variable must involve the *active* intervention of the researcher. Comparing groups of people who differ on the independent variable before the study begins is not the same as manipulating that variable.[8]

A defining feature of experimental design is random assignment or the assignment of participants to groups (experimental versus control or to different treatment conditions) using a random procedure such as a coin toss with the expectation of getting a 50:50 chance result. Coin tossing is not as useful for randomization as you may think. In a study at the University of British Columbia, 13 participants tossed a coin 300 times trying to achieve a "heads" result. Each participant attained more heads than tails and this difference was statistically significant for seven participants. One of those achieved 68% success with heads.

Note: See Clark, Matthew P.A., and Brian D. Westerberg, "How Random Is the Toss of a Coin?," *Canadian Medical Association Journal* 181, no. 12 (2009): E306–E308.

The second feature is researcher **control** of variables. "In such a design, the researcher considers many possible factors that might cause or influence a particular condition or phenomenon … [and] then attempts to control for all influential factors *except* those whose possible effects are the focus of the investigation."[9] Variables other than the IV and DV are extraneous to the study and presumed to be controlled by randomizing them across participants so that the groups are equal. This effort prevents outside factors from influencing the outcome; however, extraneous variables can creep in at every stage of the process. To be vigilant, researchers can "control extraneous variables through the experimental setting, consent, instructions, sampling techniques, assignment techniques, observation techniques, measurement techniques, interactions with participants, and the use of research designs with control groups."[10]

The third feature of an experimental design is **random assignment** or the assignment of participants to groups (or different treatment conditions) using a random procedure such as a coin toss or random number generator. Random assignment assures that (1) each participant has an equal chance of being assigned to a group and (2) the assignment of one participant is independent of the assignment of another. (*Participant*, in case you missed it in previous references, is the current term referring to an individual taking part in a research study, but I occasionally use the 100-year-old term, "subject," as a time-honored convention.)

Shutterstock/Ronstik

Random assignment should not be confused with random sampling, which is an entirely different procedure.[11] Unlike random assignment to groups, which occurs before the experimental condition, **random sampling** from a population aims to ensure that each element in the sampling frame has an equal chance of being included in the sample. When researchers use random sampling, especially in nonexperimental studies, control is enhanced through improved internal validity (by reduction of systematic and random error) and external validity is expanded. "When random samples are not practically possible (you then have a sample in search of a population)."[12] In the most robust experimental designs, random assignment is intended to produce equivalent groups, which is different from a known chance of selection. Random assignment ensures group similarity as the study begins.

Simple Causal Relationships

How do we recognize a causal relationship? David Hume and John Stuart Mill first proposed the criteria that we still use today. Mill's Method of Agreement states that "When two or more cases of a given phenomenon have one and only one condition in common, then that condition may be regarded as the cause (or effect) of the phenomenon."[13] Building on that statement, we find the following four essential **criteria for causality**[14]:

1. The cause (IV) and effect (DV) are related. The first criterion means there needs to be a way to follow the effect back to the cause. If in a factory study, plant layout was not a factor in the production process, then we can't argue that the production layout caused late deliveries to the customer.

2. The cause precedes the effect. A time order must be observed: changes in the IV must happen before changes in the DV. Causal precedence is the temporal antecedence condition.

3. The cause and effect occur together consistently. That is, cause and effect should go together or *covary*. Let's say we have a list of possible subcauses for late deliveries to the customer. These become hypotheses that we plan to test, and they include lengthy preparation time, poorly optimized plant layout, errors in the production process, poor planning, inadequate assembler training, low-quality raw materials, improper maintenance of equipment, and packaging and shipping.[15] When we test low-quality raw materials, we find that late deliveries occur. And if the raw

A plant's layout and the design of the production process are vital to business operations. An optimized layout boosts production, meets employees' needs, and ensures a smooth workflow. It also optimizes material, machinery, and information flow through a system. On the other hand, a bad layout increases the cost of manufacturing by causing unnecessary handling of materials and movement of equipment and workers.

©iStockphoto.com/vm

materials are optimum, then late deliveries are absent. If the cause is inconsistent in its effectiveness, then we should find stronger or weaker effects accordingly.

4. Alternative explanations can be ruled out. The relationship between the IV and DV must *not* be due to a confounding extraneous "third" variable (i.e., no credible third variable accounts for the relationship between the IV and DV, or can cause both).

Let's tie these criteria together with an illustration. Suppose I hypothesize that poor training of assemblers in manufacturing causes late deliveries to the customer. The treatment is specialized training for assemblers by process engineers. Assemblers are randomly assigned to treatment and **control groups** or **comparison groups**. The control group does not receive specialized training (the cause is absent). However, both groups are on identical assembly lines. A pretest-posttest shows that the experimental group's skills have improved. The comparison group shows no effect. If my hypothesis were correct, I would expect this to lower late deliveries. The cause and effect, training and late deliveries, are in proximity; they happen close together in time, so we suspect that they are connected.

However, there is more to it than that. The cause (assembler training) needs to happen before the effect (the decrease in late deliveries). One can demonstrate this by controlling the presence of the cause (training). The cause and effect should occur together consistently. That is, more intensive training should dependably correspond with fewer late deliveries up to a threshold where other factors are responsible for deliveries. We should also be suspicious of the explanation and test our other subcauses (hypotheses) regarding late deliveries to rule out *third variable effects*, such as material preparation time, plant layout, work culture, process errors, poor planning, low-quality materials, and equipment maintenance.[16] We should also be careful with random assignment to experimental and comparison groups as well as confirm identical processes on the assembly lines.

Validity in Experimentation

You judge experimental designs by how well they meet the tests of validity. A design's validity is evaluated by the extent to which it is jeopardized by hazards—or what the experimental literature calls "threats." Campbell and Stanley[17] initially labeled and explained eight threats to internal validity and four threats to external validity. Over the years, the number of threats proliferated, with Cook and Campbell[18] expanding their list to 33 and Shadish et al. settling on 37.[19]

A thorough elaboration of many items is well beyond the coverage of this guide. Thus, I confine my list to four general types of validity and provide explanations for two.

1. **Statistical Conclusion Validity**: the validity of inferences about the correlation (covariation) between treatment and outcome.

2. **Internal Validity**: the validity of inferences about whether observed covariation between *A* (the presumed treatment) and *B* (the presumed

outcome) reflects a causal relationship from *A* to *B*, as those variables were manipulated or measured.

3. **Construct Validity**: the validity of inferences made from the operations in a study to the theoretical constructs those operations are intended to represent. (See Chapter 2 on the nature of "constructs.")

4. **External Validity**: the validity of inferences about whether the cause-effect relationship generalizes to persons, settings, treatment variables, and measurement variables.[20]

Campbell and Stanley advise us that the importance of threats should not be underestimated:

> . . . [T]he first line of attack toward good causal inference is to design studies that reduce the number of plausible rival hypotheses available to account for the data. The fewer such plausible rival hypotheses remaining, the greater the degree of "confirmation." Assessing remaining threats to validity after a study is completed is the second line of attack, which is harder to do convincingly but is often the only choice when better designs cannot be used or when criticizing completed studies.[21]

Internal Validity

An experiment has high internal validity if you have confidence that the treatment has been the source of change in the dependent variable. Internal validity asks, "Do the conclusions we draw about a demonstrated relationship correctly imply cause?" Variables other than the treatment (IV) that influence internal validity are as follows:

- *Extraneous variables* may compete with the IV in explaining the outcome of a study in a cause-and-effect context.

- A **confounding variable** is an extraneous variable that does indeed influence the dependent variable. It can systematically vary or influence the IV and the DV.[22]

Exhibit 8.2 presents 12 primary vulnerabilities to internal validity; more are shown in this chapter's references.

External Validity

External validity is high when the results of an experiment are believed to apply to some larger population. External validity asks, "Do observed causal relationships generalize across persons, settings, treatment variables, measurement variables, and times?"

EXHIBIT 8.2 ■ Sources and Threats to Internal Validity

Threat	Source	Description	Remedy
Maturation	Participants	An alternative explanation is caused by subjects' state of mind, natural change, or development over time: short-term and long-term scenarios.	Control group
Selection	Participants	Groups lack equivalency. There are systematic differences in participants other than the presumed cause.	Control group Randomization
Maturation by Selection	Participants	The rate of change in specific groups is different over the course of the experiment.	Randomization
Low Construct Validity	Instruments	A measure's construct validity should correspond to an empirically grounded theory and correlate with a known measure possessing *convergent* and *discriminant* validity. You discover a construct's uniqueness through statistical tools like factor analysis.	Reanalyze the instrument
Instrumentation	Instruments	The instrument, data collection, or observer changes over the course of the study due to unforeseen or careless procedures. Instrument decay (e.g., a physical device's calibration over time) may also occur.	Consistent protocols
Score Regression Toward the Mean	Instruments	Participants with an extreme score on one test get a lower score on the other test—there is a tendency for scores to move toward the mean. A participant with a high score on the pretest receives a lower score on the posttest and vice versa. Calculating the extent of regression is possible.[a]	Evaluate participants from the sample likely to have extreme scores on the DV
Testing	Instruments	Participants are sensitized to the IV (e.g., pretesting). Learning effects are not attributable to the IV.	Control group Specialized designs
Experimenter Expectancy	Artifacts	Changes in conscious or unconscious researcher behavior affect participants' response to the IV.	Blind designs[c]
Demand Characteristics	Artifacts	There are differential responses to cues in the experimental and control groups; participants are knowing or expectant about what is happening or is expected to occur.	Cover stories Double-blind designs[c]

Threat	Source	Description	Remedy
Temporal Precedence	Design/Procedure	There is ambiguity as to whether the cause precedes the effect.	Accurate temporal manipulation
History		An unforeseen event occurs before or between pretests and posttests of the study (e.g., a union meeting where participants in the study are present and discuss an educational campaign for employees).	Individual testing to partial out the effect (not always possible or efficient)
Attrition (mortality)		Dropout rates are particularly likely in the experimental group and also in the control.[b]	Randomization Retesting

Source: Compiled with input from Campbell, Donald T., and Julian C. Stanley, *Experimental and Quasi-Experimental Designs for Research*, reprint (New York: Houghton Mifflin, 1963), 8; Leedy, Paul D., and Jeanne E. Ormrod, *Practical Research: Planning and Design*, 11th ed. (Boston: Pearson, 2016), 181, Figure 7.1; and Kirk, Roger E., *Experimental Design*, 4th ed. (Thousand Oaks: SAGE, 2013), 16–21.

Notes:

[a]Prm = 100(1 &– r), where Prm is the percent of regression to the mean and r is the correlation between the two measures. Perfectly correlated variables have no regression effects

[b]See "Attrition" in Exhibit 6.4 from Cook, Thomas D., and Donald T. Campbell, "The Design and Conduct of Quasi-Experiments and True Experiments in Field Settings," Handbook of Industrial and Organizational Psychology, ed. Marvin D. Dunnette (Chicago: Rand McNally, 1976), 223. Experimental attrition occurs because participants are not willing to continue, are not available, have relocated, or are disturbed by the treatment—which sometimes occurs in the experimental group. However, *resentful demoralization* of the disadvantaged occurs when the treatment is desirable, the experiment is obtrusive, and *control group* members become resentful that they are deprived of the treatment and lower their cooperation or leave. Other factors affect equalizing experimental and control groups include the following: (1) *diffusion or imitation of treatment*: if people in the experimental and control groups talk, then those in the control group may learn of the treatment, eliminating the difference between the groups; (2) *compensatory equalization*: where the experimental treatment is much more desirable, there may be an administrative reluctance to deprive the control group members and compensatory actions for the control groups may confound the experiment; and (3) *compensatory rivalry*: this may occur when members of the control group know they are in the control group, which may generate competitive pressures and cause the control group members to try harder.

[c]Blinding occurs when one or more persons are unaware of the intervention. Single blinding refers to blinding of participants *or* investigators. Double blinding refers to blinding of both participants *and* investigators. Triple blinding refers to participants, investigators, *and* data analysts and may also include study writers.

The following are some examples of external validity in checklist form:

- *Population Validity: generalizing* to and across populations

- *Ecological Validity: generalizing* across settings

- *Temporal Validity: generalizing* across time

- *Treatment Variation Validity: generalizing* across variations of the treatment

- *Outcome Validity: generalizing* across related dependent variables[23]

"As a general rule, studies are higher in external validity when the participants and the situation studied are similar to those that the researchers want to generalize to," says Price.[24] There are four potential threats to external validity:

1. *Testing Reactivity*: the interaction effect of testing in which a pretest might increase or decrease participant sensitivity to the IV, making the results unrepresentative for the unpretested population

2. *Interaction Effects*: biases resulting from selection (lack of group equivalency) that interact with the IV (Exhibit 8.2)

3. *Reactive Arrangements*: the effects of people being exposed to the IV in nonexperimental settings

4. *Multiple Interferences*: when participants experience multiple treatments, the effects of prior treatments are not erasable[25]

Researchers strive for a balance between internal and external validity. Too little control reduces their ability to derive causal conclusions; too much control restricts capacity to generalize the results.

PRE-EXPERIMENTS

Although Campbell and Stanley used pre-experiments as a reference point, the pre-experiment does not meet the standards of a bona fide experiment. While it may be useful as an exploratory tool, the pre-experiment is evaluated negatively for threats to internal and external validity. One authoritative source states that "… such studies have such a total absence of control as to be of almost no scientific value."[26]

Accepting this argument, I do not include pre-experiments as designs. They are unique only for comparison with other experimental designs. **Pre-experiments** typically have no control group available for contrast (or an equivalent nontreatment group). The three primitive pre-experiments are as follows:

1. *One-Shot Study:* From this study, it is difficult to draw conclusions because one cannot prove there is a cause-and-effect relationship between the intervention and outcome.

2. *One Group Pretest-Posttest:* This design shows some improvement because a change occurred, but you don't know why because it does not account for an event, maturation, or altered collection method that could occur between data points.

3. *Static Group Comparison:* This is best of the three because it shows that change occurred but is still problematic in the elimination of a control group; groups are *not* equivalent at the beginning (participant selection could result in groups that differ on relevant variables), and it is hard to conclude the reason for observed differences.

TRUE EXPERIMENTS

True experiments (or randomized experiments) are the strongest designs for determining a cause-and-effect relationship. They maximize internal validity. They are also known as *randomized controlled trials* (RCTs) because researchers can control the number and types of intervention. They are a causal study's best defense against counterclaims of alternative causes. During an RCT, the only expected difference between the experimental and control groups is the outcome variable under study. Three essential ingredients of a true experiment were previously described as (a) investigator *manipulation* of the IV; (b) *control* of the study situation, protocol, and setting (including the use of a control group); and (c) *random assignment*. Furthermore, a true experiment should be a study of only one population.

Example: Pretest-Posttest Control Group

To establish a frame of reference, let's look at an example of a true experiment (the pretest-posttest control group design in Exhibit 8.3), as described by Campbell and Stanley.[27] Participants are randomly assigned to experimental and control groups, thereby making the two groups similar. The experimental group is composed of participants receiving the experimental treatment.

EXHIBIT 8.3 ■ Pretest-Posttest Control Group Diagram

Time	t_1	t_2	t_3	Time t_1, t_2, t_3
Randomize	Pretest	Treatment	Posttest	R random assignment of participants
R_E	O_1	X_E	O_2	O the test or observation
R_C	O_3		O_4	E the experimental group
				C the control or comparison group
Ideal Case	E C			

Source: The uniform code and graphic presentation are adapted from Levy, Yair, and Timothy J. Ellis, "A Guide for Novice Researchers on Experimental and Quasi-Experimental Studies in Information Systems Research," *Interdisciplinary Journal of Information, Knowledge, and Management* 6 (2011): 154.

It is possible to have more than one experimental group but that requires using a different design than the one illustrated. True experiments have a control group(s). Control participants are also randomly assigned and created in the same manner as the experimental group, but they do not receive the treatment. The control group provides a reliable baseline for comparison of the treatment's effect on the experimental outcome. How important is this comparison? "Well causality is even more plausible if you can compare [it] to a situation where the cause is absent, showing that the effect does not occur when the cause is absent."[28]

Example: Solomon Four-Group Design

Another notable true experimental design is the Solomon four-group design, shown in Exhibit 8.4. This design has a better reputation because it represents the first overt attempt to address external validity issues.

With E-B and C-2 lacking a pretest, you may determine the effects of testing and the interaction of testing and the treatment (X). Not only is generalizability increased but you may also compare the efficacy of X through four evaluations: $O_2 > O_1$, $O_2 > O_4$, $O_5 > O_6$, and $O_5 > O_3$.[29] The effect of randomization may also be confirmed with an $O_1 - O_3$ comparison.

The other true experimental design is the posttest-only control group design, in which the pretest is said to be nonessential if you subscribe to the notion that the lack of initial bias between groups is a function of randomization.

EXHIBIT 8.4 ■ Solomon Four-Group Diagram

Time	t_1	t_2	t_3
Randomize	Pretest	Treatment	Posttest
R_E	O_1	X_{E-A}	O_2
R_{C1}	O_3		O_4
R_E		X_{E-B}	O_5
R_{C2}			O_6

Time t_1, t_2, t_3
E_A Exp. Gp. A
E_B Exp. Gp. B
C_1 Control 1
C_2 Control 2

Ideal Case	E-A E-B C-1 C-2		

Control Groups

Control groups receive no treatment—the experimental stimulus is withheld, or some standard treatment is used. Control members are selected by random assignment (sometimes matching) to have the same characteristics as the treatment group. Both groups experience identical conditions during the experiment except the control group is not exposed to the treatment condition. Frankfort-Nachmias et al. assert that an advantage of control groups is that they can reduce threats to internal validity (refer to Exhibit 8.2) as follows:

- History does not become a rival hypothesis because the control and experimental groups are both exposed to the same events.

- Maturation is counteracted because both groups undergo the same changes.

- Instrument change can be prevented with a control group; if the instrument's unreliability produces differences between posttest and pretest scores, this will be revealed in both groups. This solution to instrumentation is only effective when both groups are exposed to identical testing conditions.

- Regarding testing, if the reactive effect of measurement is present, it is manifested in both groups.[30]

The authors also contend that control groups do not address the issue of attrition (mortality), since one group may lose more participants than the other. However, a control group can help counteract the factors that interact with selection.[31]

True Experiments and Attribute Variables

A true experiment should *not* be used to answer a research question that is not amenable to its requirements. In a series of ongoing studies about women in management, McKinsey & Company concluded with a caveat:

> Companies with a higher proportion of women in their management committees are also the companies that have the best performance. While these studies do not demonstrate a causal link, they do, however, give us a factual snapshot that can only argue in favour of greater gender diversity ... [based on the performance factors of return on equity, stock price growth, and operating result].[32]

Ikon Images/Alamy Stock Photo

What if we took this conclusion as a hypothesis and tested it using a true experiment? This is not possible. True experiments require random assignment of participants to different groups. Gender, like other personal characteristics (ethnicity, personality, education, intelligence), is a **subject or attribute variable** and is not changeable. Participants recruited for experiments come to the experimental setting with characteristics established by heredity and environment. Someone cannot be randomly assigned to be a male or female—thus, no

An attribute variable is a variable that is a characteristic or trait of a participant, which researchers cannot manipulate but can only measure. It might be a variable that is fixed like gender, race, or psychological condition. Researchers cannot manipulate any characteristic that is inherent or preprogrammed.

random assignment or manipulation by an experimenter can take place.[33] In contrast, an experiment can help researchers investigate "how participants react to people who vary in these characteristics."

OTHER RANDOMIZED DESIGNS

Adjacent to "True Experiments" in Exhibit 8.1 is a category labeled "Other Randomized-Based Designs." Other **randomized-based designs** rely on random assignment to produce group equivalence, to balance treatment and control groups, or to compensate for confounding variables. Randomization is important to understanding these designs. However, I leave extensive diagramming and coverage of each design to books devoted to that purpose. The previously cited work by Montgomery (*Design and Analysis of Experiments*) provides thorough coverage on designs such as *randomized block*, *Latin square*, *factorial/fractional factorial*, *split plot*, *repeated measures*, *hierarchical*, and *covariance*. You will discover a few others there too.

The types of randomization used to empower these designs include simple randomization (discussed in the section "Conditions for Claims of Causality"), block randomization, stratified randomization, and covariate adaptive randomization.[34]

Simple randomization involves the assignment of participants to control and treatment groups through conventional methods (dice, coin toss, odd-even numbers in a card deck, or random number tables and generators). **Block randomization** results in groups of equal size. Researchers determine the optimal block size for the experiment (sometimes because of the group or cell sizes required by a statistic) and then randomly chose blocks to establish participant assignment. Additional steps are taken to control covariates and restore balance.

Stratified randomization focuses on controlling confounding variables (covariates) that influence the study's outcome. Researchers identify specific covariates through the literature, experience, or foreknowledge of the recruitment pool before group assignment. For example, in a study of hiring decisions, a resume will tell us the length of time a person held a position and the time between jobs. Stratified randomization is "achieved by generating a separate block for each combination of covariates, and subjects are assigned to the appropriate block of covariates."[35]

Covariate adaptive randomization is an alternative to stratified randomization. It assigns new participants to treatment groups involving the technique of "minimization." The process of allocation depends on characteristics of previously recruited participants already assigned. For example, assume you had 20 participants already recruited and the 21st is a male with a high score on a covariate (age). After you compare the treatment and control groups by examining totals for each category, the participant is assigned to the group that produces the most balance. This approach is a form of dynamic allocation or, in our case, "covariate adaptive randomization" because "unlike stratified randomization, minimization works toward minimizing the total imbalance for *all factors together* instead of considering mutually exclusive subgroups."[36]

Signal Versus Noise and Randomization-Based Designs

Experimental designs may be **signal enhancers or noise reducers**.[37] The signal is analogous to the study variable—the program or treatment being implemented. Noise introduces variability from all the extraneous variables that confuse the strength of the signal. This includes the following: (1) *demand effects* or clues from the setting of the experiment, the equipment, or distractions from the locality; (2) *researcher effects* or cues like nonverbal behaviors of the investigators or impressions that the participants receive about how they should respond; (3) *participant effects* such as a subject's disposition on a particular day, a health irregularity, or prior knowledge possessed by an individual participant, and so forth; and (4) *situational effects* or environmental factors such as temperature, lighting, or discomfort issues. Using a signal-noise ratio, dividing the signal by the noise, the signal should be high relative to the noise. A strong signal (a potent treatment) and accurate measurement (low noise) provide greater likelihood of observing the effect of the treatment or IV. A strong treatment with weak measurement or a weak treatment with strong measurement reduces the effectiveness of the experiment.

Factorial Designs

Factorial designs are *signal-enhancing experimental designs*. A **factorial design** is a randomized experiment (completely or by blocking) using multiple factors to determine their influence on the study's objective. A **factor** is a controlled IV subdivided into levels that are set by the researcher. Each factor must have two or more **factor levels** or values, otherwise it does not "vary." If the factor is tire wear, three levels of the factor might be regular highway, all-weather, and high-performance tires. The levels can cover the full range of offerings or brands or, as in the tire example, just a subset.

Let's consider an example of personality tests, which are increasingly used by human resource professionals. Approximately 2.5 million people take the Myers-Briggs test every year and it is used by 88% of Fortune 500 companies, despite its reliability.[38] Personality questionnaires evaluate how you like to work, relate to others, deal with emotions, and feel about your self-image. Even senior executive candidates at well-known companies take pre-employment tests.

Continuing with the example we just described, suppose we are studying the effect of room temperature in the testing facility and personality test taking.[39] We compare test scores of two independent groups who took the test in an 85-degree room versus those who took it in a 70-degree room. Our experiment has one IV of temperature (not two), but it does have two levels: 70 and 85 degrees. We are also interested in test difficulty, so we add a second IV that also has two levels: simple and complex test difficulty. We now have a 2×2

EXHIBIT 8.5 ■ Factorial Table

	IV-1 Room Temp	
IV-2 Test Difficulty	70 Degrees	85 Degrees
Complex	Complex-70	Complex-85
Simple	Simple-70	Simple-85

between-subjects factorial design. We then randomly assign subjects to four groups, and our matrix is illustrated in Exhibit 8.5.

From the comparison in Exhibit 8.6, you can conclude that the applicants perform better in higher temperatures regardless of test difficulty and they perform better on the simple test regardless of temperature.

In a different scenario, the *shaded* squares in Exhibit 8.7 show an "interaction effect"—crossing lines. Those taking the more complex test performed better under lower temperatures but did worse in the 85-degree condition than those taking the simple version of the test.

EXHIBIT 8.6 ■ Factorial Plot

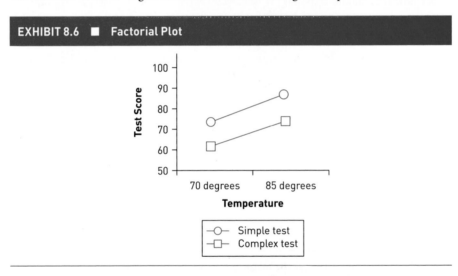

EXHIBIT 8.7 ■ Factorial Plot With Interaction Effects

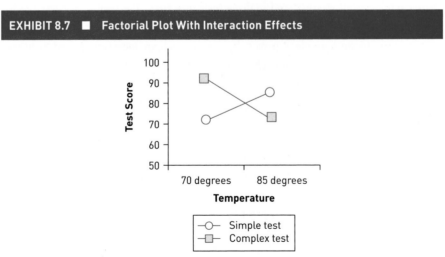

Advantages of factorial designs include the (1) ability to enhance the "signal" or treatment, (2) potential to examine numerous treatment variations without conducting several sequential experiments, (3) capacity to evaluate interaction effects, and (4) design's abundance of variations to fit different research questions. Among available designs are the 2×2 factorial, a two-factor model where there are more than two levels, the three-factor design, and the incomplete factorial design.[40]

Covariance Analysis and Blocking

There are two types of *noise-reducing experimental designs*: **covariance designs** and **blocking designs**.[41] The analysis of covariance design (ANCOVA or ANACOVA) is a pretest-posttest randomized experimental design. The pretest observation is the same as the posttest but is not required to be identical to the pretest; it can be any variable measured before the intervention. It is also possible for this design to have more than one covariate. The pretest covaries with the outcome measure to accomplish the goal of removing noise, thus the design's name. ANCOVA is the statistical analysis tool used. Regarding "covariates," you might read in a literature review for your project that a "posttest of managerial performance was adjusted for income and educational level." That is, the DV effects were adjusted for these two continuous variables identified as covariates.

The randomized block design is equivalent to the random form of probability sampling: stratification. Like stratification, randomized block designs reduce noise or unexpected variance in the data. This design divides the sample into relatively homogeneous subgroups or "blocks"—like strata. (See sampling plans in Chapter 4.) Each block or homogeneous subgroup becomes a focal point for the experiment. Each block having less variability than the whole sample reduces variability or noise. Estimating the treatment effect across the entire sample is less efficient for performing data analysis; therefore, the block estimates are used. Pooling these more efficient estimates across blocks usually provides an overall estimate better than designs without blocking.[42]

QUASI-EXPERIMENTS

"The prefix *quasi* means 'resembling.' Thus, **quasi-experimental** research is research that resembles experimental research but is not true experimental research."[43] The design specifies a baseline (preintervention) comparison group that tries to achieve a composition as similar to the treatment group as possible. By manipulating the independent variable before the dependent variable, quasi-experiments eliminate any problem with directionality. Nevertheless, *without* random assignment of participants to treatment conditions, confounding variables related to participant selection are not removed. The use of existing or intact groups induces researchers and participants to favor this design for its convenience and relatively less conspicuous and disruptive nature. It is researcher friendly.

Quasi-experiments mimic true experiments except for random assignment, which distinguishes them "because the conclusions that may be drawn from the research depend

In field settings, the researcher has limited leverage over selection but might assign each intact group (a department or team) to either an experimental or control condition. The teams in this photo allow the researcher to have two experimental groups and one control if the experiment calls for it.

upon this distinction. The degree of *risk* in inferring causal relationships is much greater with quasi-experiments.[44] The "quasi-" design is frequently conducted in field settings (industrial, educational, or medical intervention) where random assignment is difficult or impossible. Quasi-experiments resolve issues related to setting, methodology, practical concerns, or ethics that often plague true experiments.

Assignment to conditions occurs using **self-selection** (participants choose the treatment for themselves) or the researcher chooses **intact groups** for assignment. In field settings, the researcher has limited leverage over selection but might assign each *intact group* (a department or team) to either an experimental or control condition. (See the section on "Matching" later in this chapter.) However, the investigator does have influence when controlling the implementation of nonrandom assignment, scheduling observations/measures, equalizing the composition of comparison groups, and affecting some of the features of the treatment.

Example: Nonequivalent Groups Design

In a true experiment, participants in a between-subjects design are randomly assigned to conditions resulting in a similarity of the groups. Indeed, they are considered equivalent. Dissimilarity occurs when participants are not randomly assigned. A **nonequivalent groups design** is a frequently used quasi-experimental between-subjects design in which participants are not equivalent (i.e., not randomly assigned to conditions). The two forms of assignment mentioned previously are self-selecting and intact groups. The latter is used more frequently because it allows the researcher to select different classes in a university, members from similar clubs, or customers from similar stores. The self-selecting form is weaker because participants are recruited and consent to participate based on their interest in being an experimental participant for an undisclosed reason.

In this design, there is a pretest, treatment, and then the dependent variable is measured again using a posttest to see if there is a change from pretest to posttest. The experimental group receives the treatment; the control group receives no treatment while serving as the comparison benchmark. Here, the researcher must consider the literature on the type of treatment and confounding variables known to affect both treatment and instruments/measures, given the limits of nonrandomization.[45] This statement is illustrated in the forthcoming example.

The design has four observations. At each measurement, there may be multiple variables assessed. Two observations (pretests) occur in advance of the treatment, one for the treatment group and one for the control group. The remaining two occur after the treatment (posttest) for each group, diagrammed in Exhibit 8.8.

As an example, researchers decide to evaluate teaching SQL to computer science students. SQL is a high-demand programming language that powers many organizations (e.g., businesses, hospitals, banks, universities, etc.) and even Androids and iPhones access SQL databases.[46]

The researchers selected a treatment group composed of one section of a CS400 class and a control group comprising another section of the class. They tried to select groups that were similar; however, in a nonequivalent groups design, student participants self-select into a class of their preference. This self-selection becomes an intact group or class section. The researchers are unaware that some students selected Professor Thompson's class because of his deliberate presentations, whereas high-achieving students selected Professor Collins because she provides practical examples and is more enthusiastic. Neither class section knew that the defining difference in their course curriculum was the presence (or absence) of an SQL programming module.

EXHIBIT 8.8 ■ Nonequivalent Groups Diagram

t_1	t_2	t_3
Pretest	Treatment	Posttest
O_1	X_E	O_2
O_3		O_4

The experimental group (Collin's class) received five learning modules with the addition of SQL. The control group (Thompson's class) received the same five modules without SQL. Presumably, SQL instruction caused the difference in the two group's programming abilities. Or did it? The differences revealed in Exhibit 8.8 (t_3) may not be due to the experimental treatment at all. Other factors have implications for performance improvement scores, including (1) teaching styles, (2) professor gender, (3) student age, (4) GPA, (5) classroom environment, (6) time of day, (7) student motivation, (8) participation in the student programming club, and (9) breadth of programming experience.

Thus, the researcher should be cognizant of these variables to rule out potential interference. Researchers are not always aware of all of the dimensions on which groups differ, which may be unobservable or unknowable. For causal inference to provide good estimation and be efficient, researchers seek to compare treatment and control groups that are highly similar. As Campbell and Stanley noted regarding this design, "The more similar the experimental and the control groups are in their recruitment, and the more this similarity is confirmed by the scores on the pretest, the more effective this control becomes."[47] If the groups are different, the prediction of the outcome for the control group will be made with information from individuals who are not only distinct from the treatment group but are also different from others in the control group.

If the researchers have thoroughly prepared, the design is said to control for the effects of history, maturation, testing, and instrumentation. Eliminating confounding variables increases the internal validity of this design. Nevertheless, the cautions about intersession history should be taken seriously. For example, there is history (the events other than the treatment that occur between the pretest and posttest), maturation (participant changes during the time, such as an SQL brown-bag lecture for the department), and regression to the mean (where extreme scores on one occasion tend to move toward the average score the next time).

Other quasi-designs include time series, equivalent materials samples, proxy pretest design, double pretest design, nonequivalent dependent variables design, pattern matching design, and the regression point displacement design.[48]

Matching

Matching is linked to the validity of quasi-experiments and should not be ignored. This warning includes other designs where randomization cannot occur. Methods to compensate for confounding variables depend on what the researcher knows about the experimental and control participants. Matching tries to accomplish the seemingly impossible: to separate out the causal effect from the effects related to preexisting differences between treatment and control groups that were never randomized.[49] **Matching** in many quasi- and field experiments attempts to obtain comparable groups to recreate the feature of randomization; its intent is equivalent or balanced groups. In practice, this involves selecting control group participants using specific criteria (variables) relevant to a study's targeted variables, particularly the DV.

A **quota matrix**[50] is a technique used on a small scale. The matrix represents participant characteristics (variables) affecting the study, which are initially disproportionate because participants recruited for the study are not randomized or evenly distributed in the treatment and control groups. This matrix typically uses categorical variables (e.g., gender, ethnicity, age group) and is reminiscent of a cross-tabulation table. The process ideally results in an even number of participants in each cell so that an allocated number of matched participants are available for selection from the recruitment pool. Additional approaches include stratification, pair matching, and balanced covariates.

Exhibit 8.9 shows another approach. Here, matching is used "to create a control sample, selected from a large donor pool of potential members [so] that the covariate distribution in the matched control group becomes more similar in its covariate distribution to the treated sample."[51] With the quota matrix, discrete or categorical variables are the basis for matching. A **covariate**, on the other hand, is a continuous variable that acts as a control; it is not manipulated but rather is observed and can affect the outcome of the study. A continuous covariate could be education level or test score. In the earlier computer-programming example, a pretest logic score might be a continuous covariate; however, differences among participants on the variables mentioned might overwhelm the instructional SQL treatment.

Follow the numbered steps in the Exhibit 8.9 diagram: (1) → the recruitment produces a pool of potential recruits who are → (2) screened and either selected for the experimental group or returned to the pool of "potential matches" → (3) because they were unsuitable. The pool of potential matches (minus those not considered/rejected or those already selected for the experimental group) is then → (4) matched using criteria from the experimental group's characteristics and become control group participants. The treatment and measurement of outcomes follow at the "compare" arrow. See the expanded process detail at this reference.[52]

EXHIBIT 8.9 ■ Matching From a Donor Pool of Potential Control Participants

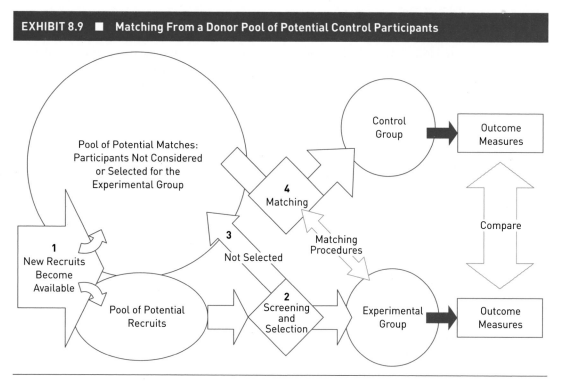

Source: Adapted from Loman, Tony, "Matching Procedures in Field Experiments," *Institute of Applied Research*, 2003, http://capacitybuilding.net/Matching%20Procedures%20in%20Field%20Experiments.pdf.

Other Approaches to Balance Groups

There are several other techniques for balancing treatment and control groups while reducing the effect of and compensating for confounding variables. More advanced methods include regression modeling (of the relationship between the covariates and the outcome measure),[53] nonparametric regression (which has less strict assumptions), distance matching, difference-in-differences, the regression-discontinuity design, and propensity score analysis (modeling the relationship between covariates and treatment assignment). Advanced students will find sources on propensity score analysis at this reference.[54] The **regression-discontinuity design** (RDD) is underused but has internal validity characteristics that produce inferences comparable to randomized experiments/RCTs and is stronger than nonequivalent groups designs.[55] The RDD is like the pretest-posttest comparison group design but assigns participants to a treatment, or what the designers call a *program*, and to the comparison group using a criterion. The criterion is a cut-off score from the preprogram ("pretest") measure. While a pretest is usually the same instrument administered before and after a treatment, the term "preprogram" thus implies more broadly that before and after measures may be the same or different." The preprogram measure is a continuous variable from which a cut-off or threshold is established, allowing comparisons of observations *close* to either side of the line and thereby estimating an average program effect. Because of the closeness of the scores adjacent to the cut-off, the program group and the control are very similar. As a result, RDD designs are superior to *ex post facto* designs in many ways.[56]

Chapter Summary

- This chapter covered true experiments (sometimes called randomized experiments or randomized control trials), other randomized designs, and quasi-experiments. Pre-experiments were mentioned for comparison purposes only.

- Five questions that companies should answer before beginning a business experiment are as follows: (1) Does the experiment have a clear purpose? (2) Have stakeholders committed to abide by the results? (3) Is the experiment doable? (4) How can we ensure reliable results? (5) Have we gotten the most value out of the experiment?

- The necessary requirements for experiments to make claims of causality are (a) manipulation, (b) control, and (c) random assignment.

- Four essential criteria for establishing causality in the experimental context are as follows: (1) the cause (IV) and effect (DV) are related; (2) the cause precedes the effect (i.e., a time order must be observed); (3) the cause and

effect occur together consistently (i.e., cause and effect should *covary*); and (4) alternative explanations can be ruled out: the relationship between the IV and DV must *not* be due to a confounding extraneous "third" variable.

- Threats to validity reduce drawing sound inferences. This chapter reviewed four general categories of validity, provided an internal validity exhibit to help you evaluate your design, and discussed how external validity affects the generalizability of findings.

- True experiments with examples, the need for control groups, and when not to use true experiments were reviewed. Two other categories, other randomized designs (e.g., factorial and covariance analysis/blocking) and quasi-experiments, were also discussed.

- Different matching procedures create equivalent or balanced groups for quasi-experiments. Some of the strategies that attempt to approximate the feature of random assignment were discussed.

Key Terms

block randomization

blocking design

comparison group

confounding variable

construct validity

control

control group

covariance design

covariate

covariate adaptive
  randomization

criteria for causality

factor

factor level

factorial design

intact group

internal validity

manipulation

matching

nonequivalent groups design

pre-experiment

quasi-experimental

quota matrix

random assignment

random sampling

randomized-based design

regression-discontinuity design

self-selection (to groups)

signal enhancer or
  noise reducer

simple randomization

statistical conclusion validity

stratified randomization

subject or attribute variable

true experiment

Discussion Questions

1. What five questions should companies answer before committing to a business experiment or be sufficiently knowledgeable about to consider it as a rigorous test for a new product or program launch?

2. Compare and contrast the three major categories of experimental design. Why do some have stronger claims of detecting causality?

3. Discuss the following as essential characteristics of experiments:

   a. Active manipulation of an independent variable. How does the researcher accomplish this?

   b. Researcher control of variables. Discuss why it is essential to control factors that might cause or influence a particular condition *except* those whose possible effects are the focus of the investigation.

   c. Random assignment of participants to groups (or different conditions). How

does random assignment assure that (i) each participant has an equal chance of being assigned to a group and (ii) that the assignment of one participant is independent of the assignment of others?

4. What is the difference between random assignment and random sampling? Explain how each is implemented.

5. List four essential criteria for determining causality and explain what must occur to provide assurance that the criterion is met.

6. Differentiate between statistical conclusion validity, internal validity, construct validity, and external validity. Provide examples of each.

7. Describe as many threats to internal validity as you recall and then do the following:

   a. Identify their source.

   b. Describe what remedies are available to the researcher to deal with them.

(Continued)

(Continued)

8. External validity includes population, ecology, temporal, treatment variation, and outcome.

    a. What are the implications of these types of external validity for applying the results of an experiment to a larger population?

    b. Describe the threats to external validity and how they can be managed.

9. Provide an example of a true experimental design.

    a. What is a control group and why is it used?

    b. How do attribute variables defeat random assignment of participants to groups?

10. Other randomized-based designs rely on random assignment to produce group equivalence, to balance treatment and control groups, or to compensate for confounding variables. Describe four types of randomization not including simple randomization.

11. How do quasi-experiments differ from factorial and blocking experiments?

    a. What separates quasi- from true experiments?

    b. Why are quasi-experiments favored for field settings?

    c. Why is matching used in many quasi-experiments?

    d. What are the difficulties for researchers in allowing participants to self-select or to use intact groups?

    e. What measurement level of a variable (NOIR) is used for a quota matrix and how do quota matrices help to match participants in an experiment?

    f. What does "covariate" matching mean and why is it superior to quota matching?

12. Suggest an experimental design for each of the following situations:

    a. A test of salesperson compensation plans where the dependent variable is sales volumes ($) per month. The levels of the IV are as follows:

    (i) Straight salary

    (ii) Salary plus bonus

    (iii) Base plus commission

    (iv) Straight commission

    (v) Variable commission

    (vi) Draw against commission

    b. During a national influenza outbreak, certain people are at higher risk of serious flu complications like respiratory issues requiring hospitalization. A large pharmaceutical company is concerned that their primary antibiotic to treat lung infections is generalized and not targeted to treat co-infections of flu virus and bacteria. They are aware that certain patients are at higher risk of developing severe pneumonia. The company has identified the following categories for testing:

    (i) Children younger than 2 years

    (ii) Adults aged 65 years and older

    (iii) Pregnant women and women up to 2 weeks postpartum

    (iv) Nursing home residents

    (v) People with chronic lung disease

    What other medical conditions/group profiles would you include in the experiment and how would you structure the experiment to discover the effectiveness of the company's drug for specific groups and by level of administered dosage? (Hint: compare your decision to factorial or blocking experiments.)

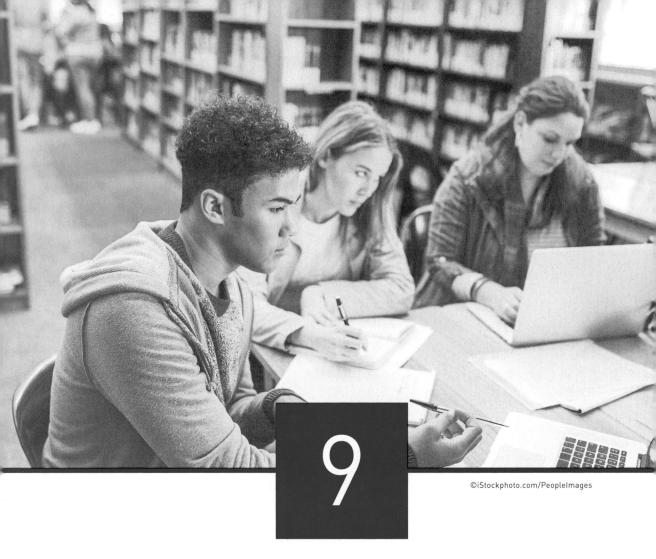

9

WRITING THE REPORT

LEARNING OBJECTIVES

Performance Objective

Prepare the manuscript for your research report by attending to good writing practices, organizing your writing according to the style manual required for your project (business report versus student research), using the tools described to promote organizational flexibility and increased efficiency, and incorporating suggestions for crafting each section of the report.

Enabling Objectives

1. Compare the qualities of good report writing (e.g., APA Chapter 3, Turabian Chapters 5–7, Booth et al. Chapters 13 and 14) with the examples provided by students and professors in each section of the chapter.

2. Describe the organizational elements of an academic report versus a business report.

3. Construct a title that captures the reader's attention in one sentence using the research question, variables, and background.

4. Create a brief summary (Abstract) of the study's contents with at least a sentence each on the background, problem, sample and participants, design, method, procedures, results, and principal conclusions.

5. Produce an Introduction that contains an overview of the problem, explores its importance, discusses the related literature, and states the hypotheses and how they all reflect the literature that your argument developed.

6. Master the tools that simplify constructing your project: the Literature Synthesis Matrix (organizing literature), the CARS model (organization), and modifications to IMRAD (presentation flexibility).

7. Compare APA's Method section with models tailored for business studies; select the approach most consistent with course guidelines.

8. Investigate power analysis and effect size to qualify the findings of your statistical results.

9. Discover the value of sequencing your key results to reflect the order of your research and investigative questions and, ideally, the order of your hypotheses.

10. Discuss why the Results section should not include interpretation of the reported findings.

11. Organize your Discussion section to parallel the sequential organization in the Results section without restating the details of the results; divide it into a summary of findings, theoretical context and implications, practical implications, limitations of the research, and suggestions for future research.

OVERVIEW

This chapter is about preparing the manuscript for your research report. Your audience is likely composed of your professor and student colleagues. Alternatively, you may have a corporate audience if you are a new manager taking a research course or using this book to help you with work-related research and reporting. By definition, this chapter is about good writing, which is writing that is artfully adapted to its unique purpose. In the words of novelist Carl Hiaasen, one thing should stand out from reading this chapter: "You can do the best research and be making the strongest intellectual argument, but if your readers don't get past the third paragraph you've wasted your energy and valuable ink."[1]

Good writing commands attention by demonstrating its thematic importance, presenting a persuasive argument, and anticipating and answering readers' questions before they ask them. Good writing has structure and logic. A well-organized manuscript is not only clear; its logic and aesthetic are evident. It reveals the writer's craft by accepting the burden of molding thoughts into something well defined and user-friendly. As seamlessly as possible, it uses sentence variety, structure, correct grammar and spelling, and skillful paragraphing. Good writing includes precise and economical word choice with well-crafted sentences. It rids itself of the ostentatiousness that characterizes some forms of academic writing. Good writing is simple, but not simplistic; it not only develops ideas that become recognizable and accessible but also deconstructs complexity to make it easily understood.[2]

Since academic writing is specialized, authorities will guide us. Some of those authorities are publication guides and the authors who comment on their requirements. At the end of Chapter 5, you were introduced to the basic outline and content for most business reports. You also discovered that IMRAD (Introduction, Methods, Results, and Discussion) is the structure for organizing academic reports, which is similar to the structure recommended by the *Publication Manual of the American Psychological Association* (APA).[3] Although many business schools use APA style for scholarly writing, some also use *The Chicago Manual of Style* (CMS). Sometimes, Kate Turabian's condensed version of CMS, *A Manual for Writers of Research Papers, Theses, and Dissertations*, is required.[4] It is possible but less likely that you will receive a special style requirement from your professor.

This book was designed for business students and managers. It seeks to help new researchers become more self-reliant not just during the research experience but also in writing the report. Its aim is to move less experienced students from uncertainty to confidence with everything they need to report their results. This guide does not neglect managers. Academic reports and business research reports differ in structure and are compared in exhibits throughout this chapter.

Especially because IMRAD is flexible in accommodating variations for class research papers, the template I will use for describing the organization of your term project will reflect both IMRAD and APA—hopefully the best of both worlds. Modifications for different sections are optional and will only require changes to headings and format to bring you in line with the specifications of your assignment. Consistency is probably more important than a particular style manual—*if you have a choice of manuals*. Remember, mixing style manuals is anathema to professors.

This chapter starts with reasons why writing your paper should have a standard structure. Then, authors who contributed work as examples will be introduced. From there, the discussion will center on the parts of the report: Title, Abstract, Introduction, Method, Results, Discussion, References, and Appendices. Throughout the chapter, you will discover options that you may find valuable, including an approach to organizing your literature (the Synthesis Matrix and Gingko which is more thoroughly explained in Appendix G), two optional ways to organize the Introduction of your paper ("Creating a Research Space—CARS" and "Expanding the Headings: The Problem and Its Setting"), and a modification of the traditional Method section.

Over the years, students have asked, "Why should I follow a style guide?" "Why can't I organize my way?" There is a difference between writing an essay and reporting the results of research. Even an essay for an English class would require the Modern Language Association's *MLA Handbook*.[5] Following guidelines that readers are accustomed to prompts you to adapt to the needs of the audience and gives the audience a familiar path to follow. In no way does following guidelines reduce your creativity. As noted by Booth et al. in *The Craft of Research*, meeting readers' expectations makes sense:

> But the most important reason for learning to report research in ways readers
> expect is that when you write for others, you demand more of yourself than when
> you write for yourself alone. By the time you fix your ideas in writing, they are
> so familiar to you that you need help to see them not for what you want them to
> be but for what they really are. You will understand your own work better when
> you try to anticipate your readers' inevitable and critical questions: How have you
> evaluated your evidence? Why do you think it's relevant? What ideas have you
> considered but rejected?[6]

One of the reasons why this chapter is longer than normal is that it uses examples primarily as the way to explain sections of the report. Instead of giving you a one-sentence example for how to write a section (frustrating!), several examples of moderate length are provided so you can emulate the approach taken. One source is a journal article, and another is a recent MBA thesis; contributions from other authors are also included. Professor Rafik Elias (California State University, Los Angeles) provided the journal article, which considers the ethical implications of business students' love of money and tendencies toward Machiavellianism and opportunism—psychological constructs (referred to as the "Love of Money" study).[7] Anna Fanoberova and Hanna Kuczkowska (Umeå School of Business and Economics, Sweden) offered their recent thesis on the effects of source credibility and information quality on consumer attitudes and purchase intention in online apparel shopping (referred to as the "Apparel Products" study).[8] Unless noted, the commentary on manuscript content follows the current APA style manual and various commentators who interpret APA's requirements.[9]

Some document preparation steps apply to all components of your paper. Starting with the Title page, number each manuscript page consecutively with Arabic numerals and place the page numbers in the top right corner. Double-space the document, including "after every line in the title, headings, footnotes, quotations, references, and figure captions . . . never use single-spacing or one-and-a-half spacing except in tables or figures."[10] Set margins to 1 inch all around, and left justify the text so that it has a ragged right margin. Indent the first line of each paragraph ½ inch or five to seven spaces (see APA 8.03). If you are just starting to write, you will make further progress when you compare your ideas, draft, or nearly completed work with the examples here. The following sections provide specific guidance on each component of your report.

TITLE

The **Title page** is separate and comprises the first page of your manuscript. It summarizes the main idea of your study by identifying variables and theoretical issues. While the proposed length is not more than 12 to 15 words (currently APA recommends no more than 12 words), that number is difficult to meet if every stylistic goal is to be reached. Those goals include describing the relationships between variables, having an independent or stand-alone nature to explain the study, avoiding abbreviations, and choosing words and keywords carefully for indexers, compilers, and retrieval systems. The title should connect the independent and dependent variables in a clear fashion or refer to the theoretical substance of the article. In this section, a 25-word title is used not because that length is desirable but authors sometimes find lengthy descriptions unavoidable. There are cases where elaboration helps to clarify a complex topic, and then a subtitle follows the main title with a colon. Doing this in 12–15 words *is* possible, however.

Practically, a shorter topic captures the readers' interest faster than a complex one that tries to squeeze into one sentence the research question, variables, and background. Succinctness makes it easier to grasp the essence of the study. Titles of articles, reviews, and editorials in recent issues of the *Academy of Management Journal* and their other publications (e.g., *Academy of Management Review*, *Academy of Management Perspectives*, and *Academy of Management Learning & Education*) show that concise wording is very desirable. Note the use of subtitles. They all are 12 words or less.

- "Historic Corporate Social Responsibility"

- "Conceptualizing Historical Organization Studies"

- "An Approach–Avoidance Framework of Workplace Aggression"

- "Whatever It Takes to Win: Rivalry Increases Unethical Behavior"

- "On Writing Up Qualitative Research in Management Learning and Education"

- "Come Aboard! Exploring the Effects of Directorships in the Executive Labor Market"

- "Beginning's End: How Founders Psychologically Disengage From Their Organizations"

- "Better Together? Signaling Interactions in New Venture Pursuit of Initial External Capital"

Some authors suggest that informal, clever, or amusing titles make an impression, especially when the reader gets the message quickly and memorably.[11] "Writers with established reputations sometimes use clever titles containing very little information, but their works are read routinely because of past contributions to the literature."[12] Be careful, though; when a title is too "cute," it can backfire. Authors choose to use clever titles because they

- Want to show that they are not stodgy intellectuals but are a lot of fun.

- Want to show they're no strangers to literature or popular culture.

- Find allusion almost inevitable. When a study compares two things, authors can't seem to avoid starting their title with "A tale of two . . ."

- Are attracted by the perceived inappropriateness of combining science and humor.

- Use the title as a clever response to the title of an earlier study.[13]

Here are a few instances of allusion and proverbial titles:

- "Believe It or Not: On the Possibility of Suspending Belief"

- "Discovering That the Shoe Fits: The Self-Validating Role of Stereotypes"

- "For Whom the Mind Wanders, and When: An Experience-Sampling Study of Working Memory and Executive Control in Daily Life"[14]

Exhibit 9.1 shows a sample title page. The top of the title page includes the running head (a shortened form of the title that is left justified and approximately 50 characters in length, including spacing and punctuation) and a page number (right justified in the top right corner). The running head uses all capital letters. Your word processor will place the running head on each page (Word: View > Header & Footer). The title is composed of uppercase and lowercase letters (i.e., title case), centered in the upper half of the page in 12-point Times New Roman font. The authors' names are centered on the next line with affiliations (institutions) beneath the names. Check your course assignment specifications for an additional requirement of a transmittal letter, Table of Contents, and Lists of Figures and Tables. Usually, class requirements call for your name in the middle to lower half of the page, along with the submittal date, professor's name, and a course designation.

EXHIBIT 9.1 ■ Manuscript Title Page

SOURCE CREDIBILITY AND INFORMATION QUALITY ON ATTITUDES AND PURCHASE INTENTIONS   1

Effects of Source Credibility and Information Quality on Attitudes
and Purchase Intentions of Apparel Products:
A Quantitative Study of Online Shopping Among Consumers in Sweden

Anna Fanoberova and Hanna Kuczkowska

Umeå School of Business and Economics

This space is often used with journal articles:
Acknowledgements: financial support, reviewers, assistance.
Author correspondence information.

This space typically substitutes for Acknowledgements
in student papers:
Your name, assignment, due date,
professor, class designation.

ABSTRACT

Abstracts have a precise focus: they report what you have done and are not a rambling overview of the topic. That said, abstracts are often discipline specific in that different aspects of the content may be expanded or contracted to conform to customs of the field and their readers. Abstracts also differ by purpose. Exhibit 9.2 compares the abstract of an academic report to the **executive summary** of a business report and shows their different emphases.

The APA also recommends adaptations for different types of research: empirical, literature reviews or meta-analyses, theory papers, methodological studies, and case studies.[15] The abstract is important because it determines whether a reader will continue to read the paper or skip it. Ideally, it is a brief summary of the study's contents with at least a sentence each on the background, problem, sample and participants, design, method,

---

EXHIBIT 9.2 ■ A Comparison of an Abstract and Executive Summary	
Academic Report	**Business Report**
Abstract	**Executive Summary**
An abstract is placed on a separate numbered page and is one page in length. It is presented in a single paragraph without indentation and contains approximately 150–250 words. The abstract includes at least one sentence summarizing the study's background, problem, scope, characteristics of the sample and its participants, design, method, procedures, results, and principal conclusions. Recommendations are typically not included because the discussion and possible replication of the findings usually precede various applications.	Business reports customarily contain an "executive summary," originally designed for busy executives who did not have time to read the entire report. The executive summary is a stand-alone page intended for decision-making outside the academic community. It contains no quotations and is one page in length. It is placed at the beginning of the report, either before or after the table of contents, but before the introduction. It is given a Roman numeral rather than an Arabic page number. The executive summary should include one or two sentences about each of the following: • The purpose of the business report • The background of the report from the company's perspective • Sources of information • Methodology • Main findings • Conclusions and recommendations

Source: Kimberley, Nell, and Glenda Crosling, *Q Manual: A Student Guide for Producing Quality Work on Time*, 5th ed. (Victoria, Australia: Faculty of Business and Economics, Monash University, 2012). Figure 7-19 adapted by permission of Nell Kimberley.

procedures, results, and principal conclusions. The abstract is ordinarily written *after* the manuscript is completed so the writer can select and rephrase (not cut and paste) sentences from each part of the manuscript. The prolific American novelist, Joyce Carol Oates, once said, "The first sentence can't be written until the final sentence is written."[16] Although this thought involves revising for an unbroken stream of continuity, it is equally applied to the abstract. To write a convincing abstract, you must know the closing of the report's Discussion section. Compare your manuscript headings with the abstract to ensure that you have complete coverage.

The abstract is placed on a separate page directly after the title page. In addition to the running head and page number, the word "Abstract" is centered in bold uppercase and lowercase letters on the upper part of the page. For most journal articles, abstracts are between 150 and 250 words in length, although theses or student papers have more latitude. Abstracts are not indented and are presented in a single paragraph. The abstract in Exhibit 9.3 appeared in a publication and followed the journal's requirements. It contains 111 words and is not structured with a summary sentence on each section.

The abstract for the student thesis shown in Exhibit 9.4 is 291 words, not including the running head.

INTRODUCTION

Advice for writing the Introduction covers guidance from the APA guidelines, an approach to organizing your literature, "The Synthesis Matrix," and two optional ways to

---

EXHIBIT 9.3 ■ Journal Article Abstract (Love of Money Study)

Abstract

The love of money psychological variable has been linked to unethical behavior in business. The current study examines business students' love of money and relates it to two important psychological determinants: Machiavellianism and opportunism. A total of 474 business students in two universities were surveyed. The majority of business students were money admirers, and many were money worshippers. They scored average on Machiavellianism (i.e. the tendency to manipulate others for their self-interest) and below average on opportunism. The results showed that business students high on Machiavellianism have a higher love of money. Similar results appeared regarding opportunistic behavior and the love of money. The study has important implications for business instructors.

EXHIBIT 9.4 ■ Thesis Abstract (Apparel Products Study)

SOURCE CREDIBILITY AND INFORMATION QUALITY ON ATTITUDES AND PURCHASE INTENTIONS   2

Abstract

Digital media give access to diverse information sources, but their credibility and information quality are difficult to evaluate. Issues of source credibility and information quality are important for online shopping; otherwise, consumers have to rely on information provided by online retailers and other sources to make a good purchase decision. This thesis examines the effects of source credibility and information quality on attitude toward using the information source and purchase intention of consumers who intend to buy apparel products through the Internet. Previous research investigated one information source. This study addresses this gap with three online information sources: retailer source, electronic word-of-mouth source (eWOM), and neutral source. The framework applies to online apparel product purchases where no similar studies have been conducted. The method, a cross-sectional survey, employed a self-administered questionnaire delivered online to a sample of 180 respondents. The research question asks: what kinds of effects do source credibility and information quality have on attitude toward using information source and purchase intention of apparel products? Findings show that aspects of source credibility, such as trustworthiness, expertise, and attractiveness, have positive effects on the attitude toward using eWOM source, while only trustworthiness and expertise positively affect the attitude toward using neutral source. For eWOM and neutral source, relationships between factors of information quality and the attitude toward using the information source were found insignificant. For retailer source, factors of information quality, accuracy, and relevance, show positive effects on the attitude toward using retailer source. For all three sources, attitudes toward using the information source and subjective norms positively affect purchase intentions. Implications of the research pertained to the improvement of perceived credibility and information quality of each information source to increase consumers' willingness to use the source during an information search.

arrange the beginning of your paper ("Creating a Research Space" and "Expanding the Headings: The Problem and Its Setting").

APA Guidelines

The **Introduction** of your report starts on the third page of the manuscript and contains the running head and page number, as does each page that follows in the report. The introduction is not labeled as such because it is the opening of the manuscript. Your professor may make an exception to this rule if all headings and subheadings are desired at the beginning of the paper. The introduction establishes the precedent of a continuous manuscript with no breaks between the sections that follow (i.e., a new heading does not start a new page).

APA recommends that your manuscript begin with an introduction to the problem, an exploration of its importance, a discussion of the related literature, and a statement of the hypotheses and how they reflect the literature that your argument developed. In some research designs, you may have one or more research and investigative questions rather than a hypothesis. These questions would substitute for a formal hypothesis and would be placed after the literature.

The statement of the problem's importance is your *raison d'être* for conducting the study. It represents the argument for explaining why the research question is worth pursuing, that new research is needed, and why the reader's interest is warranted. APA's recommendation on an *exploration of the problem's importance* proposes creating an argument for why the research question is interesting, important, and worthy of new research. "For basic research, the statement about importance might involve the need to resolve any inconsistency in results of past work and/or extend the reach of a theoretical formulation. For applied research, this might involve the need to solve a social problem . . ." as well as determining how your research contributes to the field.[17]

The literature review or contribution of relevant scholarship may occupy several paragraphs to several pages. Typically, this section comprises most of the content in the introduction. The studies cited should be connected to your research question in such a way that there is no doubt that your question is meaningful and deserves more attention. This precludes introducing marginally related works or attempting an exhaustive literature review. The most pertinent studies bearing on your problem are those that establish its relevance. The background studies that you cite should, therefore, have either precedence or show a unique linkage to the present. When you describe a study, your synthesis should avoid nonessential details but emphasize major findings, conclusions, and implications.

It is useful to visualize your literature as a funnel, so you start from a comprehensive perspective and move toward specific studies directly related to your problem. When you find that your literature is best explained by grouping studies in sections, you should summarize the previous argument for that section and connect it with a transition to the next section so the organization flows smoothly. These are "signposts" for your reader in the Toulmin approach; they are warrants that connect your data (studies) to the claim (summaries of arguments or sub-arguments). Summaries also capture important aspects of design, methods, and procedures. The literature's methodological hints and justifications help to establish rationales for your decisions in the Method section. Hypotheses represent the final section of the Introduction. The variables in the hypotheses are defined operationally (i.e., standardized by measures or procedures) and connected to works cited or theory, as shown in Exhibit 9.5.

The placement of hypotheses is not always prioritized in a list at the end of the introduction. Sometimes, the hypotheses show the evolution of a research or investigative question that the literature helps you translate into a statement for empirical testing. Then, a hypothesis is linked to the summary of a literature section (as Exhibit 9.5 shows), in which another section of literature follows and one or more hypotheses are derived.

In the Swedish study of source credibility and information quality on attitudes and purchase intentions, the authors conducted a comprehensive literature review. Its complexity required categorizing the literature and then organizing it by subtopics spanning several pages. After the authors summarized one section, they included a transition that moved the reader to the next. Ultimately, a series of literature synopses lead to multiple hypotheses. In other words, each summary section of the literature produced a corresponding hypothesis. This structure is shown in Exhibit 9.6. Hypotheses not shown in Exhibit 9.6 are listed at the bottom of Exhibit 9.7, the initial conceptual model that clarifies the relationships among hypotheses.

Organizing the Literature: The Synthesis Matrix

In Chapter 3, I recommended a **(Literature) Synthesis Matrix** as a useful organizing tool for the findings of your literature. This tool is a table that you can draw by hand and add rows and columns as your literature expands. If your literature has subsections, you could create several sheets to organize the sources for later use. The design consists of columns for your sources. You could label them by author name and date of publication at the top.

The rows represent main points, arguments, or dimensions of the literature. Looking across a row, you will see similarities and disagreements among authors. You will also find empty spaces where an author who produced a definition, argument, or contribution on one issue has nothing to say on another. You will have impressions about the comprehensiveness of your search: do the blanks represent more work or are there gaps in the literature?[18] Exhibit 9.8 describes only two aspects of the literature on the Delphi Method: definitions and applications/controls. It has been separated into two pages to accommodate its width.

EXHIBIT 9.5 ■ Literature With an Accompanying Hypothesis (Love of Money Study)

Machiavellianism

Christie and Geis (1970) developed a personality trait they called "Machiavellianism" based on studying religious and political leaders who manipulated their subordinates for their own self-interest. This trait suggests a calculating rationality little influenced by emotions, interpersonal attachments or empathy (Wastell and Booth, 2003). Christie and Geis (1970) identified several characteristics of high Machiavellianism such as a willingness to use manipulative tactics and endorsement of a cynical, untrustworthy view of human nature.

The Machiavellian boss is exploitative, cynical, and selfish. This value system is thought of as a clinical condition that underlies dysfunctional behavior. With little concern for morality, Machiavellians break alliances, promises, and lie with impunity. They are high on blame and low on empathy. Ironically, some corporate cultures reward them because they do well in stressful and competitive environments.

Significant research has investigated the consequences of possessing a Machiavellian personality. High Machs engaged in influence tactics such as building political connections and intimidation (Harrell, 1980), had little job satisfaction (Gabel and Topol, 1987), chose management or legal careers (Chonko, 1982) and were less likely to help others when an accident occurred (Wolfson, 1981). In addition, Machiavellians tended to be disagreeable (Elfenbein et al., 2008), uncooperative (Paal and Bereczkei, 2007), and exploitive in relationships (Mullins and Kopelman, 1988). In a business context, Machiavellianism was positively associated with choosing financial success as a primary goal in life, rather than self-actualization, family or community (McHoskey, 1995). Sakalaki et al. (2009) found that Machiavellianism was positively correlated with economic locus of control. Ross and Robertson (2003) reported that Machiavellians believed that bribes produced good customer relations and Tziner et al. (1996) found them to believe that performance appraisals may need to be falsified for political reasons. In a study of undergraduate students, Malinowski (2009) found that students high in Machiavellianism were less likely to believe questionable actions were wrong and did not anticipate guilt if they engaged in such action. Based on the previous research, it is reasonable to assume that students high in Machiavellianism would have a higher love of money and therefore H_1 is tested in the current study:

H_1: Business students scoring higher on Machiavellianism will have a higher love of money than those scoring low on the Machiavellianism scale.

EXHIBIT 9.6 ■ Literature Summary With Multiple Hypotheses (Apparel Products Study)

Especially for online reviews, usefulness refers "to the degree to which consumers believe that online reviews would facilitate their purchase decision-making process" (Park & Lee, 2009, p. 334). Online review usefulness is considered a main factor that induces consumers to read online reviews (Willemsen et al., 2011). Thus, information seekers may turn to online reviews to access product information before purchasing clothes online. Usefulness of online reviews was also found to predict whether readers would follow the online review (Cheung et al., 2008; Park & Lee, 2009). In addition, Cheung et al. (2008) suggest that queue quality of online reviews has a positive impact on the consumer decision-making process.

We argue that in the process of information adoption behavioral beliefs are formed by information quality and source credibility. Gunawan & Huarng (2015) in their study of viral effects of social media on purchasing intensions combined the Information Adoption Model (IAM) and the Theory of Reasoned Action (TRA). They argued that quality and source credibility both have a positive effect on attitude toward information usefulness (Gunawan & Huarng, 2015, p. 2240). Therefore, we propose that information quality has a positive impact on attitude toward using an information source. Information quality is measured by relevance, accuracy, and comprehensiveness. Therefore, based on the discussion of IAM and TRA, we develop the following hypotheses:

(Continued)

EXHIBIT 9.6   ■   (Continued)

H$_1$: Relevance of information, provided by a) retailer source; b) eWOM source; c) neutral source has a positive effect on attitude toward using a) retailer source; b) eWOM source; c) neutral source.

H$_2$: Accuracy of information, provided by a) retailer source; b) eWOM source; c) neutral source has a positive effect on attitude toward using a) retailer source; b) eWOM source; c) neutral source.

H$_3$: Comprehensiveness of information, provided by a) retailer source; b) eWOM source; c) neutral source has a positive effect on attitude toward using a) retailer source; b) eWOM source; c) neutral source.

EXHIBIT 9.7   ■   Conceptual Model With Multiple Hypotheses (Apparel Products Study)

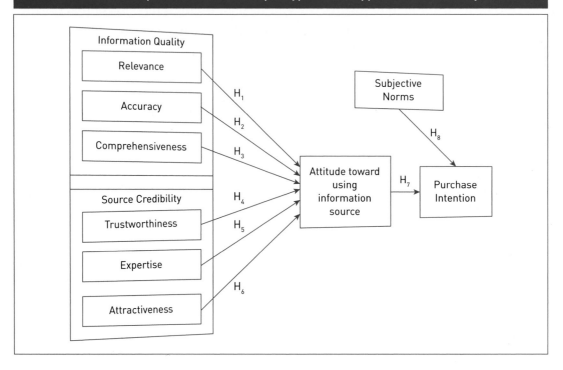

The model is applied to three online information sources: retailer source, eWOM source (electronic Word-of-Mouth source), and neutral source.

H_4: Trustworthiness of a) retailer source; b) eWOM source; c) neutral source has a positive effect on attitude toward using a) retailer source; b) eWOM source; c) neutral source.

H_5: Expertise of a) retailer source; b) eWOM source; c) neutral source has a positive effect on attitude toward using a) retailer source; b) eWOM source; c) neutral source.

H_6: Attractiveness of a) retailer source; b) eWOM source; c) neutral source has a positive effect on attitude toward using a) retailer source; b) eWOM source; c) neutral source.

H_7: Attitude toward using a) retailer source; b) eWOM source; c) neutral source has a positive effect on purchase intention.

H_8: Subjective norms of using information from a) retailer source; b) eWOM source; c) neutral source have a positive effect on purchase intentions.

Bibliographic Software

There are numerous bibliographic software programs that can help you connect the citations in your matrix with footnotes or the bibliography/references list. Be sure to check the software for compatibility with the style manual you are assigned. Consider free online resources such as EasyBib, BibMe, Citation Machine, Citavi, Citefast, Citelighter, Docear, and OttoBib (book citations). Other popular citation management programs include Zotero, Mendeley, and EndNote, which all work with Windows or Mac operating systems (compare them here: https://subjectguides.library.american.edu/c.php?g=175008&p=3205957).

How does one extract information and use the material in the review? The following draft synthesis integrates the two categories covered by the matrix. You would need to insert citations from the matrix or use the software to cite them at the appropriate points.

Delphi is a method for the systematic structuring of a group communication process that solicits and collates judgments from experts. It is applied to perplexing problems, idea generation, normative forecasts, consensus building, and inventive

EXHIBIT 9.8 ■ The Literature Synthesis Matrix

	Linstone & Turoff	Delbecq, Van de Ven & Gustafson	Dalkey & Helmer	Helmer		Helmer	Strauss & Zeigler	
Definitions	A method for structuring a group communication process so that the process is effective in allowing a group of individuals as a whole to deal with a complex problem (p. 3).	A method for systematic solicitation and collation of judgments on a particular topic through a set of carefully designed sequential questionnaires interspersed with summarized information and feedback of opinions derived from earlier responses. Optimum size is 30 well-chosen, notable experts.	The most reliable consensus of opinion of a group of experts by series of intensive questionnaires interspersed with controlled opinion feedback (p. 458).	Originally creat... technological fe... ...sus procedure for ... by Rand Corpor... estimates of an... U.S. industrial... ...led system from th... perspective of a... strategic plann... has far-reachin... applications inc... provision of "ju... input data for d... studies in the s... science area, i... hard data are t... were too costl... (p. xx).		Originally created as a technological forecasting procedure for the Air Force by Rand Corporation (for estimates of an optimal U.S. industrial target system from the perspective of a Soviet strategic planner) it now has far-reaching applications including the provision of "judgmental input data for use in studies in the social science area, in cases were hard data are unavailable were too costly to obtain" (p. xx).	Numeric: to specify a single range of numeric estimates or forecast on a problem. Policy: to define a range of answers or alternatives to a current or anticipated policy problem. Historic: to explain the range of issues that fostered a specific decision or the identification of the range of possible alternatives that could have been poised against a certain past decision (p. 253).	Definitions
Application and Controls	Turoff: a general purpose method for human communication and consensus group problem-solving and policy formation.	Evidence favors Nominal Group Technique and Delphi approaches to idea or estimate generation, interaction for purposes of clarification, and mathematical voting in the form of rank-ordering or rating for aggregated group judgments (p. 35).	Dalkey: Anonymity . . . questionnaires or online computer communication reduces the effect of dominant individuals. Controlled feedback: a sequence of rounds with a summary of results from previous rounds are conveyed to participants is a device for reducing noise. Statistical group response [reduces] group pressure for conformity . . . assures that the every member's opinion is repre- sented in the final response (p.21).	It has been use... other contexts... judgmental inf... indispensable. ... include normat... forecasts; the... ascertainment... and preference... concerning the... life; simulated... decision makin... may be called "... planning (p. x... ...h a ...om ...nts is ...pise. ...for ...at ...on ...nal		It has been used in many other contexts in which judgmental information is indispensable. These include normative forecasts; the ascertainment of values and preferences; estimates concerning the quality of life; simulated and real decision making; and what may be called inventive planning (p. xix).	Appropriate for general theoretical research in the humanities and social sciences (p.188).	Application and Controls

planning. It uses carefully designed, self-administered questionnaires distributed to approximately 30 participants by mail or accessed on a host website. Each round of questionnaires is interspersed with summarized information and feedback of opinions from participants, thereby narrowing the distance between original estimates or judgments. Control is maintained through anonymity, controlled feedback, and statistical group response. Delphi may collect qualitative or quantitative assessments through mathematical voting (rank-ordering or rating) to achieve aggregated group judgments; and it documents consensus to compare with the views of outliers. The method is valuable for securing information where hard data are unavailable, too costly to obtain; or, when logistical, problem-specific, or respondent-centered factors inhibit the use of conventional methods.

Appendix G contains another approach for organizing your literature. By way of preview, Adriano Ferrari's powerful but unassuming software program called *Gingko* (gingkoapp.com) is an outlining and writing tool that organizes information using a hierarchical card system, metaphorically like the branches and leaves of a tree. (Its name is spelled differently than the tree.) Gingko is a wonderful technique for visual or spatial thinkers who will love using it for arranging their literature review. Author quotes, literature summaries, citations, and your notes may be placed on "cards" that you can move or reorder to other columns and rows. You can see connected sibling cards with more specific information, and drop in screenshots and images of preformatted figures and tables before assembling any section of your paper.

Creating a Research Space (CARS)

Not all business fields embrace APA's basic approach to organizing and writing, as seen in the manuscript requirements for different journals. Some encourage optional templates embedded within IMRAD that are more versatile for their readers' needs. A strategy for the Introduction was developed by Swales, who analyzed writing practices from 48 journal articles across the natural and social sciences.[19] The **CARS model** creates a rhetorical space and attracts readers into that space. It consists of "moves" and "steps." The three moves are *establishing a territory* (the situation), *establishing a niche* (the problem), and *occupying the niche* (the solution). The "moves" build an outline for action, and the "steps" provide specific ideas for writing the sections. Together they form a template for a logical introduction.

The *territory* involves a claim of centrality, topic generalization, or previous research regarding the problem's importance, relevance, or interest—along with supporting evidence—and it may assess gaps in prior research or the inadequacy of remedies for the research problem. This is comparable to a general background and a preview of where your topic fits in the field.[20] It often contains a topic sentence, as shown in the following examples:

- *Centrality*: "Recently, there has been extensive interest in genuine inclusion and gender parity in organizations." "The study of company transparency has become an important aspect of annual reporting."

- *Generalization*: "It is accepted that one reason for brand switching is insufficient value offered by the brand versus the price required of the consumer." "Many job satisfaction measures are unable to distinguish between work factors and job satisfaction when comparisons are made across countries and cultures."

- *Previous Research*: "Collins (2012) concluded that . . ." "Peterson (2005) argued that . . ." "Mason (2014) found definitive evidence that . . ."

The *niche* develops a small role within the larger field that you have staked out. It involves creating a persuasive argument for your research by challenging assumptions, proving counter-claims, questioning, or expanding traditional evidence. Examples follow, respectively:

- "This view is challenged by recent data . . ." "No group matching or equalization of participants was used in the three most frequently cited field experiments on this topic."

- "Despite previous claims, 70% of employees do not trust management."

- "There are no clear findings of whether company success with allowing employees to work remotely is influenced by the company's business sector."

- "It is important to establish a new perspective on workplace violence from managerial bullying to sexual harassment." "Additional studies are needed to determine if aggressive managers who blame others for their failures are more likely to be promoted than those who accept responsibility for themselves and their group."

Occupying the niche reveals your intended contributions to knowledge or presents a new understanding of prior research. Depending on your academic custom, this can be stated in *present* or *past tense* or *by an animate actor* or *inanimate acted-upon element*. Often the section concludes with your research question and a briefly stated summary of where you intend to take the reader. Examples are, respectively:

- "The purpose of this paper <u>is</u> to describe the ROI of company training . . ."

- "Our aim <u>was</u> to present operational strategies that reduce resistance to new ideas."

- "In this study, <u>we</u> (I) propose to show how innovative companies transform their failures."

- "This <u>project</u> aims to document executives' reactions when personally dealing with their call centers."

Expanding the Headings: The Problem and Its Setting

Chapter 5 outlined an adaptation to IMRAD that is appropriate for class projects, theses, and some dissertations, which is referred to as the **Problem and Its Setting module**. It is another way to modify the Introduction with specific headings that APA does not include. This approach provides structural clarity and creates signposts that the reader uses to follow the direction of your arguments. The module contains the following elements:

- Background of the Problem

- Statement of the Problem (Research and Investigative Questions)

- Literature (optionally positioned here)

- Hypotheses (if appropriate for the design)

- Assumptions

- Delimitations

- Definition of Terms

- Importance and Benefits of the Research

The Review of Related Literature occupies its own space in this configuration and may be composed as a chapter (usually in a thesis, where it follows the Introduction and precedes the Method section) or as a separate section in the Introduction of a class paper with its own heading. Your choices for placement are flexible. For example, you could position the Literature Review after the Statement of the Problem and before the Hypotheses. This alternative uses the research question(s) as an organizing tool for the literature, shows the relationship of your problem and the arguments for the studies you reviewed, and sets up the hypothesis to test specific findings or gaps in the literature.

In the explanatory study of radiation affecting flight crews in Chapter 1 (see references 29 through 35 in that chapter), "Assumptions" are facts that bear directly on the problem and without which there would be no point in studying the phenomena. Some examples are as follows: (1) flight crews are occupationally exposed to radiation, (2) dosage rates exceed those of workers in the regulated nuclear industry, (3) the FAA recommends education but sets no dosage levels, and (4) cancer and other health risks resulting from different forms of radiation are researched by the CDC.

If the focus of the study is commercial flight crews and their exposure to radiation, "Delimitations" are the boundaries for the study. Boundaries mark what the research does not contain. They would exclude the planetary (space) research of NASA as well as the spaceflight programs of Europe, Russia, and China, along with the space activities of 70 other countries. Delimitations exclude everything but the target of your research, regardless of how interesting peripheral aspects may be. While higher doses of radiation are prevalent at altitudes above 45,000 feet, your research would restrict its scope to commercial cruising

Gary Waters/Alamy Stock Photo

A limitation in a study's design or instrument is the systematic bias that the researcher did not or could not control and which could inappropriately affect the results. Authors who do not include the limitations or include only some of the limitations of their study may cause less informed consumers of research to place more credit on a study's findings than warranted.

Source: Price, James H., and Judy Murnan, "Research Limitations and the Necessity of Reporting Them," *American Journal of Health Education* 35 (2004): 66–67.

altitudes of 28,000–35,000 feet. Only the Concorde was certified for 60,000 feet, and it went out of service in 2003. Delimitations of the research often precede the "Definition of Terms," but you may reorganize them in a way that makes sense for your research problem. For example, it may be desirable to position definitions closer to the hypotheses so that each variable is first defined operationally before it is placed into a hypothesis.

In contrast to delimitations, "Limitations" (also discussed in Chapter 1) are the anticipated or actual weaknesses of the design or methodology that could flaw a study's conclusion. Some are known in advance; others are discovered after the study concludes. You typically state them in the Discussion section where the reader can put your findings into perspective. Weaknesses include problems with sampling, inadequate controls or flawed comparison groups, questionable self-reporting, various known sources of bias, confounding variables, measurement error, attrition of participants, inappropriate statistical tests, and others.

A clear direction for the study is established in the reader's mind when the writer uses the flexible Problem and Its Setting module. A student example illustrates the template as shown in Exhibit 9.9.

The Review of Literature can be difficult to organize and position. So much of the organizing depends on the requirement of your academic paper or company report and the style manual required by your professor, college, or graduate school. In the last few sections, we looked at the Synthesis Matrix, CARS, and expanding the headings but that discussion did not get into the low-level mechanics of organizing. Appendix G contains a productivity aid, Gingko, that is effective for creating outlines and lets you connect different parts of your writing and visualize the structure.

Earlier in this chapter, we compared the abstract of an academic report to the executive summary of a business report and showed their different emphases for managers (Exhibit 9.2). Exhibit 9.10 compares the two types of introductions, one for the academic report and the other for the business report.

METHOD

The Method section directly follows the introduction, with the heading centered in bold uppercase and lowercase letters. The **Method section** is tied to your research problem and shows the process by which the research question was answered or hypotheses were tested. It describes how the study was conducted (see APA 2.06) and gives a justification and detailed description of the method(s) you have chosen. The Method section should contain sufficient detail to convince the reader that your design, method, sampling, participants, instruments, and procedures were selected to produce the highest degree of reliability and validity given the constraints of the study. This section has a tendency to "grow" on its own when you supply more detail on common, simple procedures that are already known

EXHIBIT 9.9 ■ The Problem and Its Setting (an Excerpt From a Student Health Management Study)

Background of the Problem

Since its inception then the Napico County Health Department, as part of the state public health system, has provided outpatient care to residents and visitors of the county. The health department currently operates several clinics that offer specialized outpatient services located in city and rural areas. The Nursing Director administrates operational policies for all clinics. Nursing supervisors manage individual clinics and are accountable for having the clinics' staff implement those policies. Recent trends have an impact on county outpatient services including (1) the coverage of more people affects the limited number of healthcare funds available; (2) revenues for Medicare and commercial payers have decreased in the current legislative environment; (3) the appeal to doctors of independent county medical practice has declined because of entrepreneurial business opportunities; and (4) management of county services is not of the caliber of thriving, private physician-driven outpatient facilities.

The Napico County is located near the coast. According to the U.S. Census Bureau, the county has a total of 700 mi.^{2} and is the 10th largest county by land area. The population in 2010 was 180,000 and is unevenly distributed hindering location decisions for clinics. The racial composition is 71% white, 2% African-American, 7% Asian, 0.8% Native American, 0.2% Pacific Islander, 15% other races, and 4% from two or more races. Latino and Hispanic of any race were 32%. Significant economic disparities exist between various population groups and their service needs.

Problem Statement

Appointment noncompliance is a serious administrative issue for the Napico County Health Department clinics. The Nursing Director perceives no-shows as adversely impacting practice efficiency by disrupting schedules, causing poor utilization of resources, increasing staff and physician workloads, and decreasing revenues from third-party reimbursement. The Health Department administration seeks to decrease

(Continued)

EXHIBIT 9.9 ■ (Continued)

missed appointments through data-driven changes in clinic operations. The purpose of this research is to examine clinic operations related to field appointments. The research question is: What changes in clinic operations are likely to reduce missed appointments? Investigative questions include:

- What are the current appointment-related operational practices for the county clinics?

- What are the clinic managers and staff perceptions regarding missed appointments?

Delimitations

1. Clinic operations and client characteristics explored are limited to Adult Medical, Family Planning, Pediatric, and Prenatal clinics. HIV/AIDS and Communicable Diseases are not included because of confidentiality issues associated with state laws.

2. The study is limited to the identification of operational problems, client characteristics, and staff perceptions. Operational changes implemented from this study will be tested for efficacy at a future time.

3. Baseline rates represent a short period and should not be generalized as "year-round" rates of noncompliance. Generalization is affected by seasonal variation in appointment compliance as well as holiday periods. An extended study is needed to establish reliable baselines.

Definition of Terms

- *Appointment noncompliance* is defined as a client failing to attend a scheduled appointment without providing advanced notice of cancellation. It is synonymous with no-show and missed appointment.

- *Clients* or patients are limited to persons external to the facility receiving health services from one or more facilities. Internal clients, such as employees, are not clients unless they are also patients.

- *Clinic operations* are processes involved in clinic management (policy making, organizing, planning, controlling, and directing) that may or may not affect client satisfaction.

- *Clinic staff* includes doctors, nurses, nursing assistants, lab technicians, front desk and telephone receptionists, or other employees under the control of the Clinic Manager.

Benefits of the Research

By exploring clinic operations, staff perceptions, and client characteristics, the Nursing Director can use the findings to make changes that improve appointment compliance. Better procedures will improve client behaviors that currently set back practice efficiency. Client satisfaction may also improve as a byproduct of the new structure and staff services. The project will develop a system for monitoring appointment compliance so that future benchmarking will be possible. The results of the study will contribute to a uniform approach to appointment-setting, telephone reminders, and follow up. Data collection will be ongoing and exceed the scope of this work.

Source: Proposal created by Jeff Stevens for a master's research methods class assignment. Dr. Stevens is currently the Chief of Planning and Evaluation in the Division of Vocational Rehabilitation Services, North Carolina Department of Health and Human Services.

to your readers. Therefore, strive for economy of expression while balancing the need for clarity and a level of specificity that skilled researchers can use to repeat your work.

The degree of detail is sometimes puzzling for students. Errors of omission leave questions about skipped steps, and errors of commission are burdensome because the writer overcompensates with extraneous information. Keep two questions in mind when deciding what details to include: "(1) are they important to the outcome of the study, and (2) are they necessary for understanding or for replicating the study?"[21]

Subsections of the Method section differ in the way they are labeled as well as their order of appearance based on the design and complexity of the study. The title of a subsection appears as a flush-left, bold, uppercase and lowercase heading (see APA 3.03). Traditionally, the APA format included four subsections: Participants, Materials/Apparatus, Design, and Procedure. These were sometimes combined (e.g., Design and Procedure or Materials and Procedure) if a study lacked complexity and the reporting could be better accomplished by merging information into a few paragraphs. Currently, APA suggests the inclusion of the following labeled subsections:

EXHIBIT 9.10 ■ A Comparison of the Introduction in Academic and Business Reports	
Academic Report	**Business Report**
Introduction	**Introduction**
The introduction of an academic report consists of most or all of the following points: • An introduction presenting the problem being studied and the strategy for conducting the research • The background or issue, history, or status • An exploration of the problem's importance and why the question is interesting, important, and worthy of new research • A discussion and critical evaluation of the related literature, especially the most pertinent studies bearing on the problem that establishes its relevance • A statement of the hypotheses and how they reflect the literature that your argument developed; or instead, an explanation of and justification for the research question(s) and its position • A statement of scope: any limits on the time, place, group, or aspect of the issue being studied • A preview of the main parts of the paper to follow The introduction and literature review may be combined or separated as appropriate. A lengthy literature review will require its own section, but this usually applies to major reports or if a literature review *is* the purpose of the report.	The introduction of a business report usually covers: • The background/impetus for the study; the problem statement and its significance • The purpose or objective of writing the report • A careful discussion of the problem • A brief history of the context of topic or problem • A concise review of associated theory or available secondary sources bearing on the problem • The definition of key terms, when necessary • Any assumptions that were made and any limitations placed on the material, scope, or process of the research • The size or extent of study, methods of collecting primary data, its amount, time frames, and unit of analysis (a department or whole organization) • An overview of the framework or logical structure that the reader should expect to find in the remainder of the report

Source: Kimberley, Nell, and Glenda Crosling, *Q Manual: A Student Guide for Producing Quality Work on Time*, 5th ed. (Victoria, Australia: Faculty of Business and Economics, Monash University, 2012). Figure 7-20 adapted by permission of Nell Kimberley.

These usually include a section with descriptions of the *participants* or subjects and a section describing the *procedures* used in the study. The latter section often includes description of (a) any experimental manipulations or interventions used and how they were delivered—for example, any mechanical apparatus used to deliver them; (b) sampling procedures and sample size and precision; (c) measurement approaches (including the psychometric properties of the instruments used); and (d) the research design.[22]

Remember, the APA manual was created for the discipline of psychology and often must be adapted for business studies when experiments are not the chosen design. Otherwise, business researchers find themselves force-fitting descriptions of their methods and procedures into prelabeled subsections that do not reflect the content. Design, for APA and also IMRAD, is often defined by how participants were randomly or nonrandomly assigned to experimental groups, conditions, the design type (e.g., a 2×2 between-subjects factorial), the (named) independent variables and their levels, and the (named) dependent measures. In other words, it is assumed that the design is a type of experiment.

Breaking the Rules: Reorganizing for a Business Study

Just as the flexible Problem and Its Setting module and other suggestions were proposed as alternative strategies for organizing the Introduction of the report, the APA format for the Method section is not always ideal. It is possible, however, to include many of the necessary components by reorganizing the subsections. APA 2.06 and APA Appendix Tables 1–4[23] include suggestions that might be useful for the business researcher. The following subsections are proposed for the Method section, in order of appearance:

- Design
  - Method(s)
- Sampling Procedures
  - Sample Size, Power, and Effect Size
- Participants
- Instruments (or Materials, Tests, Measures, Questionnaires)
- Procedure

Design

The **Design subsection** follows the opening and overview statements of the Method section. Its priority emphasizes that design is at the apex of the logical hierarchy for answering the research question and establishes the study's purpose. Leedy and Ormrod also stress the importance of establishing the design at the outset:

> The general *design* of the study should be clear early in the report. In particular, the researcher should state whether qualitative or quantitative methods (or both) were used and what particular research traditions were followed—for example, whether the study was a longitudinal study, . . . a single-group time-series study, a 2-by-2 factorial design, an ethnography, a grounded theory study, or some combination of approaches.[24]

You might consider describing your design according to the typology presented in Chapter 6 (Exhibit 6.3) as experimental, nonexperimental, or mixed. If the design was experimental, was it a pretest-posttest control group design—or some variation of a true experiment, repeated-measures, covariance, factorial, blocking, or quasi-experiment?

If the design was nonexperimental, was it quantitative or qualitative? If quantitative, was the primary *purpose or research objective* to describe, explain, or predict? Which *time dimension* best characterized the data collection: cross-sectional, retrospective, or longitudinal (including the variations of trend, cohort, or panel)?

If qualitative, did you use narrative, ethnography, phenomenology, case, grounded theory, or another design? Finally, if a mixed design was used, which study was dominant or were they of equal weight in contributing to the research effort; and were the studies conducted concurrently or sequentially? (See Chapter 7 for more details on mixed design.)

In the study of source credibility and information quality on attitudes and purchase intentions (the online shopping research of apparel products), Fanoberova and Kuczkowska describe their design and the rationale for its use. Exhibit 9.11 presents their example.

Method(s)

The design is followed by a description of a specific **method of data collection** that implements the design using accepted standards or, sometimes, tailored procedures. In Chapter 4, Process Phase 3 outlined the three primary modes of the survey method, its distributional modes or logistics, and techniques for data collection. The observational method and three types of observational studies and their data collection techniques were also explained. If you have chosen an experimental design, the design characteristics and protocols could be rolled into the Design section, thereby eliminating the method(s) subset.

After their example in Exhibit 9.11, the authors continue their design discussion by describing their *method* for data collection and the reasons for choosing the survey method in the form of a noninteractive, self-administered questionnaire distributed on the Internet. Exhibit 9.12 provides *excerpts* from their study.

Sampling Procedures

A description of the **sampling plan and procedures** should follow the method and precede the description of the participants (sample elements). In the APA manual, sampling is subsumed under Procedures and comes last. To some, this organization is counterintuitive because sampling procedures are responsible for the selection of individual participants; and chronologically, the participants' characteristics are ordinarily unknown until the demographics are collected and analyzed. Describing your rationale for selecting a sampling plan is of particular importance when a probability sampling

EXHIBIT 9.11   ■   Design Subsection (Apparel Products Study)

Research design serves as a framework for the collection and analysis of data (Bryman & Bell, 2011, p. 40) . . .While the descriptive study only observes and describes the phenomenon, [the] explanatory study goes beyond simple description and attempts to explain the reasons for the phenomenon (Cooper & Schindler, 2011, p. 19). Our research can be classified as an explanatory study. Furthermore, we do not only describe a studied phenomenon but also try to explain the factors that caused this phenomenon to occur. The purpose of our study is to explain relationships between independent variables, such as information quality, source credibility and subjective norms and dependent variables, attitude toward using an information source and purchase intention.

For our study, we have chosen a cross-sectional design, which can be implemented in the form of survey research. Cross-sectional designs allow collection of data on more than one case at a single point in time to collect quantitative or qualitative data in connection with two or more variables, which are used to identify patterns in associations (Bryman & Bell, 2011, p. 53). This design fits our research purpose as it gives an opportunity to examine relationships between variables and to identify common patterns in online purchases of clothes.

strategy facilitates your execution of the method. The selection of one of several probability plans is integral to generalizing the findings. The discussion of why the plan you selected best meets the study's purpose may also alert readers to compare participants' characteristics to known proportions in the population. In Chapter 4, five types of probability sampling plans and 11 nonprobability plans are described.

Select specific materials to cover that are appropriate to your type of sample. They may only require a sentence or two, but a paragraph should suffice when a criterion requires a more detailed explanation. Here are some of the relevant criteria:

- The sampling method (probability, nonprobability) and type

- Intended sample size

- How sample size was determined, including predicted attrition

- Actual sample size, if different from intended sample size

EXHIBIT 9.12 ■ Methods (Apparel Products Study)

We chose the survey method to gather primary data. Surveys allow collecting a large amount of data from a sizeable population at a low cost (Saunders et al., 2009, p. 144). The survey method can be implemented using different types of questionnaires (Saunders et al., 2009, p. 363) . . . [The] self-administered questionnaire was chosen for this study as a data collection method since we think it is more beneficial compared to other types of questionnaires. However, our research purpose is to explain relationships between variables and [not] to develop a deep understanding of online purchases of apparel products. Therefore, our research does not require more complex or open-ended questions. We chose to distribute our questionnaire online for a number of reasons. First, it is easy for people to participate in this research as online questionnaires can be [completed] at any place that has access to the Internet. Secondly, it is less costly compared to telephone and mail distribution (Cooper & Schindler, 2011, p. 250). Thirdly, our survey is devoted to the topic of online purchases of clothes, and it is logical to contact people who shop online with [an] online questionnaire, as they are web-literate.

- Eligibility and inclusion criteria for selection

- Enrollment: excluded, did not meet inclusion criteria, refused to participate, or other

- Percentage of sample approached that participated

- Self-selection (either by individuals or units, such as work teams or departments)

- Settings and locations of the sampled data

- Agreements and payments: volunteers or participation by receiving incentives

- Student participants: class requirement or class credit/extra credit

- IRB agreements, ethical standards met, informed consent, safety monitoring[25]

Power Analysis and Precision

Sample size estimation is an important consideration for researchers. It is not just using the most acceptable formula or a sample size calculator *and then estimating attrition* before establishing the size; it is qualifying the results that are statistically tested with estimates of the test's power and effect size, which reveal how reasonable it is to reject a null hypothesis. An exact sample size may be computed (from formulas in research methods and statistics textbooks, software, and websites). Without sufficient information, researchers do not know if their study is underpowered (too few participants) or overpowered (too many participants). This situation results in serious consequences:

> Studies should be designed to include a sufficient number of participants to adequately address the research question. Studies that have either an inadequate number of participants or an excessively large number of participants are both wasteful in terms of participant and investigator time, resources to conduct the assessments, analytic efforts and so on. These situations can also be viewed as unethical as participants may have been put at risk as part of a study that was unable to answer an important question.[26]

Sample size, power, and effect size (magnitude of the difference) should be included in your report. The accuracy of reporting your rejection of a null hypothesis depends on these factors. We discussed significance levels and p-values in Chapter 5 under "Steps for Statistical Testing." As a quick review, the *significance level* is the cutoff (conventionally .05 or .01) that guards against accidentally rejecting the null hypothesis when it is true. **Statistical power** is the probability (typically set at not less than 80%) of rejecting the null hypothesis when the alternative hypothesis is, in fact, true. It is the power of the selected test to reject the null hypothesis when it ought to be rejected. Thus, at 80%, there is an 8 in 10 chance of identifying a difference of the specified effect size.

For example, a student researching whether ethnic groups differed on attitudes toward animals' rights used a questionnaire with good psychometric properties. Her IRB requested that she use a power analysis to determine how many respondents she would need to recruit for her project. Her research mentor responded in Exhibit 9.13.

Graduate students and others working with IRBs should note that power analyses should be conducted *in advance* "as part of the planning of the research, when determining how many cases need be sampled to have a reasonable chance of detecting an effect of a specified size."[27]

Effect size is the size or magnitude of the difference between *groups* (although there are formulas for correlation analysis and regression coefficients as well).

> The effect size is the main finding of a quantitative study. While a *P* value can inform the reader whether an effect exists, the *P* value will not reveal the size of the effect. In reporting and interpreting studies, both the substantive significance (effect size) and statistical significance (*P* value) are essential results to be reported.[28]

EXHIBIT 9.13 ■ Sample Size and Power

"The more subjects you have, the greater your power. Power is the probability that you will find a difference, assuming that one really exists. Power is also a function of the magnitude of the difference you seek to detect. If the difference is, in fact, large, then you don't need many subjects to have a good chance of detecting it. If it is small, then you do. Of course, you don't really know how large the difference between ethnic groups is, so that makes it hard to plan. We assume that you will be satisfied if your power is 80%. That is, if there really is a difference, you have an 80% chance of detecting it statistically. Put another way, the odds of your finding the difference are 4 to 1 in your favor. We also assume that you will be using the traditional 5% criterion (alpha) of statistical significance.

If the difference between two ethnic groups were small (defined by Cohen as differing by 1/5 of a standard deviation) [.2], then to have 80% power you would need to have 393 subjects in each ethnic group. If the difference is of medium size (1/2 of a standard deviation) [.5], then you need only 64 subjects in each ethnic group. If the difference is large (4/5 of a standard deviation) [.8], then you only need 26 subjects per ethnic group." [These differences are called *effect size*.]

Source: Wuensch, Karl L., "Examples of the Use of Power Analysis in Actual Research Projects," Karl Wunsch's Statistics Lessons, East Carolina University, last modified December 2007, http://core.ecu.edu/psyc/wuenschk/StatsLessons.htm.

Recall the example in Chapter 5 of the two pilot training programs for commercial aviation being compared to reduce flight takeoff accidents. Statistical significance told us if there was a difference between the two programs. However, also recall that the first study's p-value was .048 and the second was .052. What was needed in that case was an indication of the magnitude or size of the mean group differences (i.e., *how much more effective* was one pilot training program over the other). While absolute differences are used, standardizing the difference allows them to be compared to 0. Cohen's *d* is often reported as an effect size statistic in which .2 is low, .5 is medium, and .8 has large *practical* significance. Cohen qualified his advice by saying "there is a certain risk inherent in offering conventional operational definitions for those terms for use in power analysis in as diverse a field of inquiry as behavioral science."[29] Effect size statistics include Hedges's *g*, Glass's delta, and effect size correlation, among others. Software packages for sample size, power, and effect size are available at this reference.[30]

Here is an example of calculating sample size with SAS software to achieve 80% power:

A survey claims that 9 out of 10 dentists recommend a particular brand of toothpaste for their patients suffering from sensitive teeth. A researcher decides to test this claim by taking a random sample of 80 dentists but wants first to find out if this sample size is large enough to achieve 80% power.[31]

The SAS output shows that the power is only 65.4% when the sample size is 80. To obtain power of 74%, the researcher needs a sample of 90; for 80% power, the researcher needs 100 respondents. Thus, the researcher needs 100 dentists for the sample.

Another example looks at precision in reporting and what it means:

> There was no significant difference between the mean biases of experts and novices, $t(78) = -.149$, $p = .882$, Cohen's $d = .03$. [Note that d is far less than what Cohen states is a low effect size and quite close to zero.] Power analysis revealed that in order for an effect of this size to be detected (80% chance) as significant at the 5% level, a sample of 34,886 participants would be required.[32]

It is clear that a researcher is not going to find a statistically significant difference between the expert and novice groups being compared. To do so would require an unreasonably large sample size—nearly 35,000 respondents—and that is larger than the *populations* in many studies. Virtually no discipline would find fault with this argument and how it describes a nonsignificant result.[33]

Participants

To write the **Participants subsection**, you may wish to review the section in Chapter 4 on recruiting research participants ethically, which mentions specifying eligibility and exclusion criteria as well as complying with restrictions. This section will remind you of IRB-related requirements for securing and retaining participants for your study.

This subsection is used to describe the study's demographic characteristics. At a minimum, it includes information that may affect the interpretation of results and their generalizability to the population. It will contain as many of the following items as

Shutterstock/Rawpixel.com

"The term demographics refers to particular characteristics of a population. The word is derived from the Greek words for people (demos) and picture (graphy). Examples of demographic characteristics include age, race, gender, ethnicity, religion, income, education, home ownership, sexual orientation, marital status, family size, health and disability status, and psychiatric diagnosis."—Neil J. Salkind

Source: Salkind, Neil J., "Demographics," in *Encyclopedia of Research Design*, vol. 3, ed. Neil J. Salkind (Thousand Oaks, CA: SAGE, 2010), 346–347.

necessary for your study to produce a profile of the participants for external validity considerations (types of external validity are described in Chapter 8):

- Age or age range

- Gender identity

- Ethnic and/or racial group

- Language preference

- Educational level

- Geographic area

- Socioeconomic, generational, or immigrant status

- Disability

- Attrition rate and reasons

- Reasons for exclusion of participants' data from the analysis[34]

In the research study on online shopping for apparel products, Fanoberova and Kuczkowska provided information on participant demographics as well as a rationale for why their findings on respondent characteristics offer some evidence for representativeness despite a self-selecting, nonprobability online survey. Exhibit 9.14 presents their example.

Two additional examples show different ways to describe the participants' profiles:

Twenty-seven students from the University of Calgary (12 women and 15 men) ranging in age from 17 to 43 years old voluntarily participated in this experiment. There were 9 participants randomly assigned to each of the three probe type conditions. Informed consent was obtained from all participants.

We recruited 29 subjects (17 male, 12 female) from two introductory psychology classes. They were given a choice of extra course credit or $5.00 for their participation. Subjects selected had taken Pettigrew's Category Width Scale on the first day of class and scored among the top or bottom 10% for their sex in their respective classes. Selected subjects were unaware of why they, in particular, were being asked to participate. All Ss were assigned to perform the same task. For the final data analysis, the 20 subjects with the fewest missed responses in the experimental tasks were used.[35]

Instruments (or Materials, Tests, Measures, or Questionnaires)

The **Instruments subsection** is referred to as Materials/Apparatus under APA guidelines, but you may name it to describe best the mechanisms that you used for data collection. Because true experiments are used less in business research, there would not likely

EXHIBIT 9.14 ■ Participants (Apparel Products Study)

The demographic section was comprised of questions about respondents' gender, age, education, and occupation. The questionnaire was distributed online, and 180 people participated. The respondents who took the survey answered every question, meaning that we do not have data loss. In total, 65 % of participants were female, and 35% of them were male. Watchravesringkan & Shim (2003) provide empirical evidence for significant relationships between gender and Internet information search intention. Results of their study showed that "female respondents were more likely to search for apparel information online than males" (Watchravesringkan & Shim, 2003, p. 4). As the majority of respondents in this sample were female, it is likely that they searched for online product information before purchase and, therefore, provided viable opinions about online information sources.

Regarding the age group, the majority of respondents (67.8%) were between 18 and 25 years old. The second largest group (26.1%) was comprised of people from 26 to 35 years old. The number of people representing other age groups was considerably smaller. Previous studies often involve young people in surveys about online shopping because online consumers are younger and more highly educated than conventional consumers (McKnight et al., 2002).

The next demographic . . . deals with the level of education. There were two groups prevailing in the sample, people who held Bachelor's degrees (41.7%) and those who held Master's degrees (40.6%). Two other groups, people who had high school education (7.8%) and post-graduates (10%) were considerably smaller.

Respondents were asked about their occupation. The student group dominated in the sample (76.7%), while other groups were much smaller in size. These results were predictable because the questionnaire was posted online on discussion forums and different Facebook groups. Because young people, and particularly students, spend considerable time on Facebook, they had access to the survey. However, this sample was representative for this survey, because previous studies show that young people use the Internet considerably to purchase clothes and, therefore, often constitute samples in similar studies (Xu & Paulins, 2005; Belleau et al., 2007; Kang & Kim, 2012).

be a description of apparatus (e.g., special laboratory equipment or electronic devices). Instead, you would describe instruments, tests, measures, questionnaires, interview schedules, checklists, scripts, projective and completion techniques, Q methods, biophysiologic measures, or perhaps content analysis procedures for textual data from qualitative studies or open-ended questions from questionnaires and interviews. These various means of collection are the source of your data. It is important for the reader to judge whether they accomplish the research purpose and provide validity and reliability as a function of sound psychometric properties. The description of the measure(s) should include the following:

- The variables being measured

- The name of the measure

- A citation for the measure, if it is published

- The number of total items and a few sample items

- How items are scored (including those recoded or reverse scored)

- What higher or lower scores mean

- Any special instructions given

- Research or data that support the reliability and validity of the measure (if available)

- The reliability of the instrument for *your* sample (e.g., Cronbach's alpha)[36]

The questionnaire is only one technique for data collection among many. You may use tests, interview schedules, checklists, scripts, or projective and completion techniques. Regardless, your method and technique are the sources of your data; thus, it is important for the reader to judge whether they accomplish the research purpose and provide reliability and validity as a function of sound psychometric properties.

Exhibit 9.15 describes one of the three scales used in Elias's study on business students' love of money (the Machiavellianism scale).

The online shopping study of apparel products had a more complicated description. The study included question samples not shown here. This example (Exhibit 9.16) has been abridged to avoid the impression of a green light for too much detail in term project reports.

The authors of the online apparel products shopping study also tested their instrument for reliability using Cronbach's alpha coefficient. The reliability of the model was .89 for the eWOM source, .90 for the neutral source, and .78 for the retailer source. The calculated coefficients were above the minimum threshold (.70), suggesting that the model had internal consistency with this scale.

EXHIBIT 9.15 ■ A Measuring Instrument (Love of Money Study)

In order to measure Machiavellianism, the scale developed by Dahling et al. (2009) [the Machiavellianism Personality Scale] was used. The scale developed by Christie and Geis (1970) has been extensively used in the literature to measure Machiavellianism. However, recent research found several problems with this scale such as inconsistent reliability, an ambiguous factor structure and the inclusion of several poor items (Dahling et al. 2009). On the other hand, the scale developed by Dahling et al. (2009) had excellent reliability of .84 and consisted of 16 statements. [It was also found to produce evidence for convergent, divergent, and criterion-related validity.] The respondent recorded his/her agreement with each statement on a seven-point scale ranging from 1 (strongly disagree) to 7 (strongly agree). Higher scores indicated higher Machiavellianism. The scale yielded four factors: amorality (the lack of ethics vision in different situations); desire for control (the desire to manipulate others for a person's self-interest); desire for status (the desire to show wealth and power); and distrust of others (the constant suspicion of others' intent). [Examples of items for each factor are, in order: *"I am willing to sabotage the efforts of other people if they threaten my own goals"; "Accumulating wealth is an important goal for me"; "I enjoy being able to control the situation"; and, "If I show any weakness at work, other people will take advantage of it".*]

Source: Inserts are from Dahling, Jason J., Brian G. Whitaker, and Paul E. Levy, "The Development and Validation of a New Machiavellianism Scale," *Journal of Management* 35, no. 2 (April 2009): 237, 246. http://dahling.pages.tcnj.edu/files/2013/06/dahling-et-al-2009.pdf.

Procedure

In the **Procedure subsection**, the reader learns how the data were collected and the study was carried out. This section, written in the past tense because the research has already occurred, includes

- Any pilot testing or pretesting that occurred

- What the participants were told about the research

- Where the data were collected and the nature of the environment

- The chronology of the process as it unfolded and the time required

EXHIBIT 9.16 ■ Questionnaire Information (Apparel Products Study)

We divided the questionnaire into sections . . . to make it easier to follow. The first section comprised of general questions about online shopping. [Followed by] . . .general questions about fashion retailers, [then] more specific questions about information provided by fashion retailers. The same logic was applied to fashion bloggers and professional stylists. The last section included [demographic] questions about respondents. According to Collins & Hussey (2014, p. 211), it is recommended to place classification questions at the end of the survey . . . so that respondents are less likely to refuse to answer them due to fatigue (Peterson, 2000, p. 84).

Moreover, we tried to make the questionnaire as clear as possible [by providing] definitions (such as online product information, fashion retailer, fashion blogger and professional stylist).

To measure concepts included in our conceptual model we used [eighteen] questions adapted from previous research. According to Bryman & Bell (2011, p. 263) using existing questions allows comparison with previous studies and increases reliability and validity of research. All questions, except for general questions and demographics, were formulated using 5-point Likert scales. [A] Likert scale is a rating scale often used in multiple-item measures of attitudes (Collis & Hussey, 2014, p. 215). Items [on the] scales were labeled as 1–Strongly disagree, 2–Disagree, 3–Neither agree nor disagree, 4–Agree, 5–Strongly agree.

To measure attitude towards usefulness of particular online information source, we adapted questions from Moon & Kim (2000). [For] the influence of subjective norms on purchase intention we used three items adapted from Liang & Lim (2011). Three items were adapted from Limbu et al. (2012) to measure purchase intention. Perceived information quality was assessed with items adapted from Rabjohn et al. (2008).

The concept of source credibility includes three dimensions, namely trustworthiness, expertise, and attractiveness. We used items adapted from Ohanian (1990) to measure perceived trustworthiness and perceived expertise. To assess perceived attractiveness, we used items adapted from Reysen (2005) and Gefen (2000).

- Any special instructions to given to participants

- An identification of independent, dependent, and control variables

- Any mode of administration used to present the instrument or stimuli

- The task for the participants and how they fulfilled it

- Who was responsible for collecting the data (special training, etc.)

- Characteristics of the collectors that may have affected respondent perceptions

Earlier in this chapter, you were introduced to the Delphi Method in a literature example describing the Synthesis Matrix. You recall that Delphi uses sequential questionnaires distributed through mail or accessed through a host website. Each round of questionnaires is interspersed with summarized information and feedback of opinions to the participants from the panel's earlier responses, thereby narrowing the distance between original estimates or judgments.

Studies show that the most improvement in the accuracy of expert estimates occurs after the second round and many iterations lead to a fatigue-driven attrition rate. The RAND Corporation, who developed Delphi, found that three rounds were common. As for size, Turoff, an authority on Delphi (1970, p. 153), recommended a panel of 10 to 50 participants for Policy Delphi. While there is no upper limit on participants (e.g., a 1996 national Delphi in Japan had 4,196 respondents; NISTEP, 1997, p. 3); the manageability of large samples requires substantial resources. Thus, panel size is a trade-off between decision quality and manageability.[37] Delbecq et al.[38] found that with a homogeneous sample, fewer new ideas are generated when the size exceeds 30 well-chosen individuals. Homogeneous samples help to maximize areas of agreement. When the goal of the research is to explore all aspects of the study—including controversial ones—a heterogeneous panel is most frequently used.[39] The characteristics of homogeneous and heterogeneous nonprobability samples are described in Chapter 4.

Exhibit 9.17 provides an example of the Procedure section. The study example involved three-round Delphi questionnaires on priority societal problems and the resources needed to solve them. Because surveys and self-administered questionnaires are common in business, the administration of the study should seem familiar. Participants were selected using the Nominal Group Technique (NGT)[40] and on the criteria of being well-known and well-informed professionals in various academic specialties. They also (1) represented interest groups or divergent points of view; (2) were visionaries, lateral thinkers, or facilitators; (3) were well informed about societal problems in general and resources in particular; and (4) would consider the results relevant to their knowledge, thus ensuring cooperation and motivation. The NGT panelists, who were experts themselves, nominated participants (n=114) and then reduced the sample to 45 using NGT procedures. Thirty-three nominees agreed to participate.

EXHIBIT 9.17 ■ The Procedure Section of a Delphi Study

Procedure

Advanced notices announced the study. Prospective respondents were sent a personalized cover letter inviting them to participate and explaining why they were selected. An accompanying research fact sheet contained the study's rationale, methodology, expected outcomes, and an estimate of the time required for each round's activities. The participation was voluntary, and no incentives were provided.

The first-round questionnaire sought to produce a comprehensive inventory of contemporary and future societal problems. It was seeded, according to Delphi criteria, with 50 societal problems across seven categories defined in the literature. The instructions stated that respondents could accept the list as complete, make additions to it, or flag problems as inaccurate or biased according to the instructions. They could not unilaterally delete a problem because that was done collectively in the second round. The packet consisted of a cover letter, the original list of respondents, instructions, the problem inventory questionnaire, societal problem criteria, and a return envelope with first class postage affixed. Colleagues reviewed the materials for clarity and graphic design quality.

The second-round questionnaire and feedback contained 75 problems in nine categories as enlarged by 29 respondents (88%). This questionnaire's purpose was to prioritize the problems of the refined inventory according to their importance. A 5-point importance scale with verbal anchors (Turoff, 1970) was used. The packet contained the response improvement techniques employed in the first round so as to maintain cooperation.

The third-round questionnaire contained nine problems (down from 75), which the respondents reduced using the importance scale in the second round. This questionnaire was constructed to reveal the nature of interdependent relationships among priority societal problems using a Cross-Impact Analysis matrix and to determine which resources (current or future) could be applied toward solutions. Instructions covered all phases of each task and response improvement techniques were once again used. Following the analysis, participants (77% of the original panel) received a letter of appreciation, summary of the third round, and synopsis of the study.

EXHIBIT 9.18 ■ A Comparison of the Method Section in Academic and Business Reports

Academic Report	Business Report
Method	**Method**
The method section of an academic report usually covers:	The method of a business report is usually more succinct because of the audience and includes:
• The design (experimental, nonexperimental, mixed), the time dimension of the design (cross-sectional, retrospective, longitudinal) and method to collect information (survey, observation, case study, etc.) with the technique (media and distributional approach) appropriate for the method, and a justification of why the method achieved the purpose of the research	• The kind of data used and its source(s) • How the data were collected. If from a company database or another vendor's study, which variables were selected and why secondary data were appropriate for answering the question
• The probability or nonprobability sampling plan and procedures to enlist and retain participants; the sample size, power, and effect size	• If primary data were used, reasons for choosing the method and instrumentation to solve the problem. Why this particular way? Why was it preferable to another method?
• The instruments, apparatus, materials, tests, measures, or questionnaires used to collect the data, including pretests or pilot studies	• Sampling of participants, size, and the process of selection, ethical issues, and procedures
• The chronology of the procedures for collection, how, when, where, required time, instructions, participant tasks, data collectors, and processes	• Any extra information or observations, such as changes produced to refine the method or procedures resulting from a pilot study • The use of the past tense, since the author describes what was done (the focus of this section is on what was done rather than who did it)

Source: Kimberley, Nell, and Glenda Crosling, *Q Manual: A Student Guide for Producing Quality Work on Time*, 5th ed. (Victoria, Australia: Faculty of Business and Economics, Monash University, 2012). Figure 7-21 adapted by permission of Nell Kimberley.

To conclude the discussion of the Method section of the report, Exhibit 9.18 compares the Method section of an academic report to that of a business report.

RESULTS

The purpose of the **Results section** (APA 2.07) is to present your results in a sequence that reflects the order of your research and investigative questions and, ideally, the order of your hypotheses. Some sources recommend a chronological order or sequencing from the most to least important results. This suggestion unscrambles the puzzle that you have previously solved for the reader with arguments about the research purpose and the order of the literature that supports your investigative questions and hypotheses; don't disrupt it.

Your presentation does not include interpretation of the reported findings, which is accomplished in the Discussion section. The analytical report is organized with textual and graphic materials—the latter in the form of tables and figures, which you explain to the reader. You begin with text and refer to findings in the tables and figures as you progress.

Characteristics of the Results section include the following:

- An overview of primary sections of the Results

- An objective presentation of key finding without interpretation

- The researcher's best judgment about the medium to convey the findings: text, tables, figures, or graphs where the presentation is text dominant and the graphics complement but do not repeat the text

- An integration of the results text with tables and figures (if you are unsure, use an example from a journal article recommended by your professor)

- The level set for statistical significance before testing (usually .05 or .01)

- A summary of the data using descriptive statistics (means, standard deviations, percentages, EDA graphics, etc.) and not raw values

- A description of missing data

- A report of how the data met the assumptions for the selected statistic(s)

- Statistical test names or common symbols, calculated values, degrees of freedom, confidence intervals, and p-values

- Effect size and power of the test (these add credibility to the magnitude of the finding and are required in many reports and recommended by APA to be used whenever possible)

- An account of negative or nonstatistically significant results as they make an important statement about the hypothesis (the possible reasons are interpreted in your Discussion)

- Headings for your graphics numbered consequently from the beginning of your report through the Results and Discussion

- The use of past tense, since the analysis has already occurred; while passive voice is most likely employed, strive for active voice (to note: avoid overuse of the word "significant," as it has a statistical meaning in this section)[41]

Results Example With Statistical Interpretation

A sample study will illustrate a strategy for reporting your results by connecting the problem, literature, research question, hypothesis, and statistical hypothesis with the test results. The research problem below deals with organizational assessment as it pertains to hiring decisions. The literature suggests the following:

> About 76% of organizations with more than 100 employees rely on assessment tools such as aptitude and personality tests for external hiring. That figure is expected to climb to 88% over the next few years. . . . The more senior the role, the more likely the employer is to use assessments to identify candidates with the right traits and abilities. Global estimates suggest that tests are used for 72% of middle management positions and up to 80% of senior roles, compared with 59% of entry-level positions.[42]

Although companies use résumés, interviews, and reference checks, they expand their information about candidates through testing. Those tests include (1) *competence* (measured by IQ and aptitude tests which reveal reasoning and learning skills as well as situational judgment tests that tap practical knowledge in a job role), (2) *work ethic* (ambition, reliability, and trustworthiness), and (3) *emotional intelligence* or EI (linked to job performance, entrepreneurial potential, and leadership talent). The latter can identify empathy, self-awareness, interpersonal skills, and team collaboration skills.[43] For this example, the focus of your study is leadership skill in team collaboration.

You know of a widely used EI index to identify this leadership skill, and it has good psychometric properties. From previous studies, middle managers that attain a score of 4.0 have an "average" level of team collaboration skills. Lower scores indicate a lower skill level and higher scores show a higher aptitude for team collaboration. This tells you that you are making a comparison to a criterion measure.

The organization you are researching wanted to adopt this instrument but made their hiring decisions through the interview process and now seeks to know if the middle managers they hired in the past month met or exceeded the published testing criteria for an average skill level.

Exhibit 9.19 spans several pages and demonstrates hypothesis testing for this study and ways of reporting the findings.

Exhibit 9.20 compares two types of Results sections for an academic report and a business report.

DISCUSSION

The **Discussion section** follows the Results and is the last major component of the report. "The discussion section is very important to readers but extremely challenging for authors, given the need for a focused synthesis and interpretation of findings."[44] The findings presented in the Results section put you in a position "to evaluate and interpret their implications, especially with respect to your original hypotheses. Here you will examine, interpret, and qualify the results and draw inferences and conclusions from them."[45] In this regard, the Discussion is connected to your Introduction because you are interpreting

EXHIBIT 9.19 ■ **An Integrated Example of Writing Results From Test Findings (Team Collaboration Skills Study)**

Research Question: Is there a difference between the mean score of new middle management hires of a company and the criterion (average) score of 4.0 on a leadership skill test of team collaboration?

Research Hypothesis: There is a difference between the mean score of a random sample of new middle management hires and the criterion score of 4.0 on leadership skill in team collaboration.

The statistical **null hypothesis** is one of no difference between the sample mean and criterion score of 4.0 (H_0: $\mu = \mu_0$), where μ is the population mean estimated from the sample and μ_0 is a known or hypothesized population mean/criterion.

Since the criterion is known, the null could be stated as:

H_0: $\mu = 4.0$.

The alternative hypothesis (H_A) coincides with the research hypotheses (H_1) and is therefore:

H_A: $\mu \neq 4.0$.

To test the null hypothesis, the researcher recruited a volunteer random sample of 40 newly hired middle managers in the company to take the test. Their scores on the continuous variable, leadership-team collaboration, were recorded. Using the information in Chapter 5 ("Assumptions for Using Parametric Statistics," "Selecting a Test," and Exhibit 5.8 or a decision tree), a test was chosen.

The one-sample t-test (a) determines if the sample is representative of the population being studied or (b) compares the sample to a criterion measure. For example, is there a statistically significant difference between the sample mean and the criterion mean score ($M = 4.0$) for the test? There are four *assumptions* for the use of this test: (1) there is one dependent variable and it is measured as a continuous variable (interval/ratio); (2) the data are independent—i.e., they are not correlated or related; (3) to fit the data to the one-sample t-test model and provide a valid result, there should be no significant outliers;

and (4) the dependent variable should be *approximately* normally distributed. "Approximately" means that some violations of the normality assumption can be tolerated because the test is robust.

In this example, IBM® SPSS® Statistics software was used (see the note at the end of this exhibit) for the assumption diagnostics and the hypothesis test. Having entered the score values in the Variable View data entry, you can proceed to detect outliers. To do this, select the Explore procedure from the main menu (Analyze > Descriptive Statistics > Explore). In the Explore procedure's dialogue box, move the score variable to the Dependent List; then in the submenu Plots, select the button "Factor levels together," deselect "Stem-and-leaf," check the box "Normality plots with tests," and select the "None" button under the Levene Test and the "Plots" button under Display. This gives you boxplot output (similar to Exhibit 5.5) to look for outliers and also the Shapiro-Wilk test for normality.

The boxplot display reveals no outliers and places the median slightly under 4.0 on the y-axis. You could report this finding as:

There were no outliers in the data, as assessed by inspection of a boxplot for values greater than 1.5 box-lengths from the edge of the box.

The next step is to determine if your data are normally distributed. If you do not have experience interpreting normal Q-Q plots, the Shapiro-Wilk test is a common approach for checking normality, especially with small sample sizes (<50), and was requested for output from your Explore procedure when you checked the box "Normality plots with tests." The table presented by SPSS looks like this for your data:

Tests of Normality

	Kolmogorov-Smirnov			Shapiro-Wilk		
	Statistic	df	Sig.	Statistic	df	Sig.
team_score	.071	40	.200	.984	40	.847

(Continued)

EXHIBIT 9.19 ■ (Continued)

Under Shapiro-Wilk, the far-right column, **Sig.** (significance), shows the value .847 to be greater than .05 (p>.05), which means that the normality assumption is met. If the test is rejected, the null hypothesis (p<.05) tells you that the data are not normally distributed. You could report this finding as:

> Team collaboration scores were normally distributed, as assessed by Shapiro-Wilk's test ($p > .05$).

Given the summary nature of this example, I do not cover what to do when you have outliers, violations of normality, or transformations or if you are using alternative nonparametric tests. Therefore, moving forward from the diagnostics to testing, a one-sample t-test procedure was executed.

In the One-Sample T Test procedure's dialogue box, move the dependent variable to the Test Variable box by clicking on the arrow button. Beneath that box, change the "Test Value" from 0 to 4.0 (your criterion score). If you had another leadership variable (e.g., "team building"), you could move that variable beneath the "team collaboration" variable. However, if the Test Value (criterion) were not the same for this second variable, it would make no sense to test them at the same time.

Next, click the Options button to open the Options dialogue box. Here you set your "Confidence Interval Percentage" to 95% (the SPSS default) and under "Missing Values" select "Exclude cases analysis by analysis." Although you had no missing values, if you did, SPSS would exclude them from your data set. Selecting the "Continue" and "OK" buttons creates this output:

One-Sample Statistics

	N	Mean	Std. Deviation	Std. Error Mean
team_score	40	3.7225	.73709	.11654

The dependent variable descriptive statistics present a sample size (n=40) and a mean score for the participants of 3.72 with a standard deviation of .737. The Standard Error of the Mean is not useful here although it may be in other situations. This tells you that the mean collaboration score (3.72 ± 0.74) was lower than the criterion score of 4.0.

One-Sample Test

| | Test Value = 4.0 | | | | | |
| | t | df | Sig. (2-tailed) | Mean Difference | 95% Confidence Interval of the Difference | |
					Lower	Upper
team_score	−2.381	39	.022	−.27750	−.5132	−.0418

The top row of the One-Sample Test table shows the "Test Value" or average mean criterion for team collaboration of 4.0 to which the sample mean is being compared. The first three columns pertain to the t-test and the observed t-value of −2.381 has 39 degrees of freedom, **df** (n−1 = 39), and a p-value of .022 (p<.05). The sample mean is statistically significantly different from the criterion. Further to the right, the "Mean Difference" is −0.28 and the 95% confidence intervals (95% CI) are −0.51 (lower) to −.04 (upper). You could report these findings as:

> The team collaboration mean score was statistically significantly lower by 0.28 (95% CI, 0.04 to 0.51) than the criterion for average skill team collaboration of 4.0, $t(39) = -2.381$, $p = .022$.

In the Method section, you were introduced to effect size (see the subsection on "Sampling Procedures: Power Analysis and Precision"). To calculate the effect size using Cohen's *d:*

$$d = \frac{(|M_D|)}{SD} = \frac{.27750}{.73709} = .38$$

(Continued)

EXHIBIT 9.19 ■ (Continued)

where the absolute value of the mean difference (found in the One-Sample Test table) is divided by the standard deviation of the dependent variable, team collaboration, (found in the One-Sample Statistics table). You know from the prior discussion that interpretation of effect size according to Cohen is .2 = small, .5 = medium, and .8 = large. The calculated effect size, d, is a small effect. You could report these findings as:

> The team collaboration mean score was statistically significantly lower by 0.28 (95% CI, 0.04 to 0.51) than the mean team collaboration criterion of 4.0, $t(39) = -2.381$, $p = .022$, $d = .38$.

By adding information about the diagnostics for statistical assumptions, the tests used, and power and effect size, your results could be stated:

> A one-sample t-test was run to determine whether the team collaboration mean score in recruited subjects was different from the average leadership skill level for team collaboration in middle managers (criterion), as defined by the team collaboration mean test score of 4.0. The sample team collaboration scores were normally distributed, as shown by Shapiro-Wilk's test ($p > .05$) and there were no outliers in the data, as assessed by inspection of a boxplot. Data are mean ± standard deviation unless otherwise stated. The sample mean score (3.72 ± 0.74) was lower than the average team collaboration criterion of 4.0, a statistically significant difference of 0.28 (95% CI, 0.04 to 0.51), $t(39) = -2.381$, $p = .022$, $d = .38$. The null hypothesis was rejected but the effect size was small.

> A retrospective power analysis revealed that: (1) at $\alpha = .05$ (5% error probability) with the small effect size that was found ($d = .38$) and n = 40, the achieved power of the two-tailed one-sample test was only .65; (2) a sensitivity computation showed that to achieve a power of .80 (80%) at $\alpha = .05$ with n = 40, the effect size would need to

be $d = .45$; and (3) if the sample size had been determined *a priori*, in order for the effect size found ($d = .38$) to be detected (80% chance) as significant at the 5% level, a sample of 57 participants should have been used.[a]

Source: Laerd Statistics, "One-Sample t-test Using SPSS Statistics," *Statistical Tutorials and Software Guides*, 2015. Used by permission of Dr. Adam Lund (September 2016). © 2013 Lund Research Ltd. Retrieved from https://statistics.laerd.com/. In this example, the selection of a test, testing of the test's assumptions, IBM SPSS procedures, and reporting examples were created using the subscription version of Laerd Statistics. Laerd Statistics' guides currently include over 80 statistics in SPSS and numerous procedures in Stata.

Note: [a]G*Power, Version 3.1.9.2. Faul, F., E. Erdfelder, A.-G. Lang, and A. Buchner, "G*Power 3: A Flexible Statistical Power Analysis Program for the Social, Behavioral, and Biomedical Sciences," Behavior Research Methods 39, (2007): 175–191. http://www.gpower.hhu.de.

the results consistent with how you initially stated your research question, reviewed the literature, and derived the hypotheses to be tested. The function of your discussion is to explain what the reader now understands after considering your results; and your discussion "tells how your study has moved us forward from the place you left us at the end of the Introduction" without repeating the Introduction.[46]

The Discussion section also explains to the reader the meaning of what the study accomplished, its contribution to the field, and recommendations for next steps. This section may be written in the first person and in active voice, and it will likely require several rewrites. The Results and Discussion sections may be combined (APA 2.08) when the findings are brief and require little explanation. However, writers who are less experienced and overly enthusiastic about their findings should beware of common pitfalls: discussing findings out of sequence, introducing new findings that should have been reported in the Results, or confusing a reiteration of results with a commentary about them.

Your Discussion section, depending on the study's complexity, is arranged as follows: (1) summary of findings, (2) theoretical context and implications, (3) practical implications, (4) limitations of the research, and (5) suggestions for future research.

An Opening Summary for the Discussion

Open the discussion with a synopsis or *summary* of your findings. If there were many investigative questions or hypotheses (there were 8×3 information sources or 24 hypotheses in the online apparel products study), a summary rather than a synopsis is a better choice. Because it may require several paragraphs, you may group hypotheses by theory or literature topic as they were derived and presented in the Introduction. The grouping would parallel your sequential organization in the Results section and ensure consistency throughout your report.

Unless you have a very short study, it is unlikely that you can answer the research question in the opening summary. You will want to show all the results that answered or

EXHIBIT 9.20 ■ A Comparison of the Results Section in Academic and Business Reports	
Academic Report	**Business Report**
Results	**Results**
The results of an academic report consist of:	The results of a business report usually cover:
• An overview of the Results	• The findings adapted to the technical sophistication of the audience. Mixed audiences should have modular subdivisions (e.g., brief summaries for decision makers and more detailed sections for technical advisors). Other audiences include employees, clients, and customers
• Key findings without interpretation	
• An integration of text with figures	
• Statistical significance level set before testing (usually .05 or .01)	
• A summary of descriptive statistics	• Tables, graphs, charts, diagrams, maps, sketches, and photographs that present information visually to help explain complex findings and illustrate the results
• Missing data and remedies	
• Diagnostics for statistical assumptions	
• Statistical tests or common symbols, calculated values, degrees of freedom, confidence intervals, and p-values	• Statistical analysis as per an academic report
	• Emphasis on description, not discussion
• Effect size and power of the test	• Findings (e.g., key trends, or relationships) presented in order of importance to the problem, solution, or action to be taken
• An account of negative or nonstatistically significant results	
• The use of past tense, since the analysis has already occurred	

Source: Kimberley, Nell, and Glenda Crosling, *Q Manual: A Student Guide for Producing Quality Work on Time*, 5th ed. (Victoria, Australia: Faculty of Business and Economics, Monash University, 2012). Figures 7-22 and 23 adapted by permission of Nell Kimberley.

supported a testable hypothesis by creating a perspective for each major finding. When a hypothesis was not supported, explain what this means to your study. Beyond nonsignificant findings, interpret an unexpected finding by explaining it at the beginning of the paragraph and then describing it.[47]

"Do not waste entire sentences restating your results; if you need to remind the reader of the result to be discussed, use 'bridge sentences' that relate the result to the interpretation."[48] For example:

> The attitude toward using the retailer source is affected only by information accuracy and relevance, but not by information comprehensiveness. It means that the information should contain accurate and relevant arguments to form a positive attitude toward using the retailer source.

The writers are explaining that hypotheses H_1 and H_2 for retailer source were supported but H_3 was not (see Exhibit 9.7); they suggest a reason, which is subsequently expanded, that is consistent with attitude formation theory.

Theoretical Implications

You may wish to use a **Theoretical Implications subsection**. APA sums up how to deal with the theoretical context and implications in the discussion: "Similarities and differences between your results and the work of others should be used to contextualize, confirm, and clarify your conclusions."[49] This recommendation prompts several related questions:

- Have you emphasized sound findings while qualifying others?

- How do your results support existing theories?

- Do other studies support your interpretations? If not, does this lead to a different explanation or suggest a design flaw (yours or theirs)?

- Have you reinterpreted other's findings in light of your own?

- Have you evaluated conflicting results? Has that helped to resolve controversies?

- Have you articulated how your results and those of others might be combined to create a better understanding of the problem?

- Do readers perceive you as challenging or extending existing knowledge?

- If you are challenging knowledge, have you mounted a convincing defense for why your interpretation is superior? Have you presented both sides of the argument fairly?

- If you are extending knowledge, does it enlighten theoretical, empirical, or methodological issues in the field?[50]

Although all of these issues may not apply to your report, it is important to cover those that do and be sure to cite the interpretations from related studies to support your conclusions. Existing theories may not always help to explain a particular finding, but a plausible explanation is needed nonetheless. The amount of information in this section will determine if subheadings are necessary. And, as stated before, a logical organization avoids confusing the reader.

The example in Exhibit 9.21 from the online shopping study addresses the confirmation of eWOM (electronic word-of-mouth) hypotheses, labeled "b," and provides support for existing theories.

For the same study, Exhibit 9.22 takes us into a discussion of conflicting results in the literature, their evaluation, an attempt to resolve the controversy, and a defense for the interpretation of the study's findings.

EXHIBIT 9.21 ■ Support for Hypotheses From the Literature (Apparel Products Study)

This regression examines the influence of information quality and source credibility on the attitude toward using the eWOM source. As discussed in the theory chapter, information accuracy, information relevance, and information comprehensiveness as well as source trustworthiness, source expertise, and source attractiveness were hypothesized to influence consumers' attitude toward using eWOM source. The regression analysis revealed that only source trustworthiness ($p<0.05$), source expertise ($p<0.05$) and source attractiveness ($p<0.05$) have an impact on the attitude toward using eWOM source. As a result, hypotheses H_{4b}, H_{5b}, and H_{6b} are confirmed. These results are in line with previous research stating that source credibility plays an important role in the information adoption model (Cheung et al., 2008) and influences attitude toward the source as well as purchase intention (Huang & Chen, 2006).

Practical Implications

The theoretical implications that extend the knowledge base are essential because they address "the development of theory, methods, study designs, data analytic approaches, or identification of understudied and important content areas that require new research."[51] The **Practical Implications subsection** also provides insights for the reader when the research is oriented toward the applied side of the continuum. Here the commentary speaks to the usefulness of research for decision makers in solving real-world problems. You should note that not all studies have both types of implications sections and they may be combined, particularly when they are short.

An example of practical implications shows the relevance of the findings in an educational setting where students need to be sensitized to business ethics (Exhibit 9.23).

Limitations

Stating the limitations or weaknesses of your study reveals how flaws could affect your conclusions. Your transparency in the **Limitations subsection** strengthens the readers' confidence. Defects known at the outset occur because of compromises in design, method, sampling, or procedures. They are often caused by time or resource constraints or they may arise during the study. Time pressures are common in student projects but still must be acknowledged.

It is advantageous for authors to address the major limitations of their research and their implications rather than leaving it to readers or reviewers to identify them. An open discussion of study limitations is not only critical to scientific integrity[52] but is an effective strategy for authors: reviewers may assume that if authors do not identify key limitations of their studies they are not aware of them.[53]

EXHIBIT 9.22 ■ Conflicts and Resolution of Theoretical Interpretations (Apparel Products Study)

Previous studies show controversial results regarding influence of subjective norms on behavioral intention. Some researchers found an insignificant effect of subjective norms on behavioral intention (George, 2004; Wu & Liao, 2011). Other researchers argue that subjective norms influence purchase intention (Gunawan & Huarng, 2015, p. 2241). Empirical findings of our study show that subjective norms have positive effect on purchase intentions and respondents see them as more important determinants than attitude toward using information source. This contradicts results of other studies, confirming that attitude toward information usefulness has stronger effect than subjective norms (Gunawan & Huarng, 2015, p. 2240).

However, careful examination of TRA [Theory of Reasoned Action] helps to explain this contradiction. According to Ajzen & Fishbein (1980), for different behaviors [the] importance of subjective norms and attitudes in determining behavioral intention may vary. For some behaviors, subjective norms can be more important than attitudes, and for others, the reverse can be true (Ajzen & Fishbein, 1980, p. 58). Researchers argue that subjective norms can be a more important determinant of behavioral intention than attitudes for behavior that involves other people (Park, 2000, p. 165). In the context of apparel shopping, decisions about the product choice are often influenced by opinion of others, including imagined or perceived reactions of others (Yan et al., 2010, p. 209).

Therefore, subjective norms play an important role in predicting purchase intentions of high involvement products, such as apparel. Results of our study provide evidence that in the context of online apparel shopping for all three information sources, subjective norms have a stronger effect than attitude toward information source on purchase intention.

If, for example, instructions to participants were not sufficient to understand the task, an experimental manipulation was ineffective, the measures were imprecise,[54] debriefing revealed distrust of the researchers, sources of bias were discovered, or incentive rates played a different role than expected, then you should qualify your results. Alternatively, you may have reason to question the generalizability. This may stem from problems in sampling and questions about representativeness.

Most readers will understand that a different sample or different measures might have produced different results. Unless there is good reason to think they would

EXHIBIT 9.23 ■ Practical Implications (Love of Money Study)

The current study found significant relationships between business students' love of money and their Machiavellianism and opportunism tendencies. The great majority of students were at least money admirers (80%). These results are normal and consistent with the emphasis on "the bottom-line" in business education. However, the troubling results were that students with higher love of money tended to be Machiavellians and opportunists. These negative results are not comforting since current business students are tomorrow's business leaders and the business world has been rocked by significant scandals in the last decade. Business instructors should be aware of this relationship and work on sensitizing students to ethics in business. They should focus less on the "win-at-all-costs" mentality and instead emphasize the love of money in an ethical environment. An interesting future study can examine whether business ethics education can mediate the relationship between the love of money and Machiavellianism and opportunism.

have, however, there is no reason to mention these routine issues. Instead, pick two or three limitations that seem like they could have influenced the results, explain how . . . and suggest ways to deal with them.[55]

In Exhibit 9.24, an abridged version of an example from the online shopping study, the researchers focused on the most salient issues, suggested ways to deal with them, and were objective and factual, not apologetic.

Limitations resulting from the statistical findings in the team collaboration skills study, described in the Results section, provide a different perspective to understand statistically significant results and how the application of a more reasonable criterion score could have yielded a different finding (Exhibit 9.25).

Suggestions for Future Research

The conclusion of the Discussion section usually contains a **Suggestions for Future Research subsection**. Here, you provide recommendations for future research and "a reasoned and justifiable commentary on the importance of your findings. This concluding section may be brief or extensive provided that it is tightly reasoned, self-contained, and not overstated."[56] Depending on your study's success, there are several issues to consider before writing this section. Some may be connected to the limitations and others may transcend the niche that your study occupies. Some examples are as follows:

EXHIBIT 9.24 ■ General Limitations of the Research (Apparel Products Study)

Due to constraints of time and resources, this study has several limitations. First, it is limited to Sweden. Because of that, the study's generalizability of findings is limited due to cultural differences. Future research could expand into other countries and test our proposed conceptual model on consumers with different cultural backgrounds. A cross-cultural study examining the perceived credibility of online information sources would enrich the existing knowledge and allow comparisons among countries. Second, this study employed convenience sampling. A self-administered questionnaire was posted online on Facebook groups. The participation was voluntary, and thus, there is a risk of self-selection bias. As a consequence, it limits the generalizability of study's findings to a broader population. We recommend conducting a study including the proposed conceptual model on a random sample that would result in greater generalizability. Third . . .

EXHIBIT 9.25 ■ Limitations Related to Statistical Outcomes (Team Collaboration Skills Study)

We qualify the rejection of the null hypothesis regarding team collaboration by noting that the difference found was not large enough to be *practically* significant. First, the mean difference and the effect size were small. Secondly, the power of the test that rejected the null hypothesis ($p = .02$) was only 65% compared to the minimum sought, 80%. Thus, the sample participants were roughly equivalent to an average skill level in team collaboration. Rather than inflate the importance of a statistically significant finding for the company, practicality suggests that the hiring of middle managers during the specified time interval and through an interviewing process produced average team collaboration skills that did not differ materially from the test criterion. We suspect that management set the bar too low. If this skill is vital for managers who lead cross-functional teams in the organization, then a higher standard of performance (above the average skill level) should have been set. Then, the difference between the scores obtained through testing would likely be both significantly and practically different than the scores produced by interviews alone; and, as a result, the findings would be more credible with an acceptable sample size, effect size, and power level.

- Are there important questions related to the problem that remain unanswered?

- How do you recommend that those questions be clarified and studied in the future?

- Did your research draw attention to unanswered questions obscured in the framing of the research question?

- Did you find unanticipated results and what strategy do you suggest for pursuing them?

- Would a better research strategy (design, method, procedure) ameliorate the flaws in the study?[57]

Some writers recommend that "providing a specific agenda for future research based on the current findings is much more helpful than general suggestions."[58] In this regard, (1) would it be advantageous to examine/test your conceptual framework or model in a new context, location, or culture? (2) How would a specific study that adjusts the conceptual framework (e.g., adding new constructs) advance the field?[59]

Remember the importance of argumentation (Chapter 2) and how you employed various strategies in arguing for the importance of the problem, the logical linkages to the literature, the design's rationale and blueprint for answering the question, and the most practical or efficient method to collect the data.

> *The function of your paper's conclusion is to restate the main argument.* It reminds the reader of the strengths of your main argument(s) and reiterates the most important evidence supporting those argument(s). Do this by stating clearly the context, background, and necessity of pursuing the research problem you investigated in relation to an issue, controversy, or a gap found in the literature.[60]

In ending the discussion, some conclusions merely reiterate the interpretation of results, but others are memorable. A compelling conclusion in a broader context might:

- Warn readers of the possible consequences of not attending to the problem if your essay deals with a contemporary problem.

- Recommend a specific course or courses of action that, if adopted, could address a specific problem in practice or influence the development of new knowledge.

- Cite a relevant quotation or expert opinion already noted in your paper to lend authority to the conclusion you have reached (to note, a good place to look would be studies in your literature review).[61]

Exhibit 9.26 presents two types of discussion sections, one for the academic report and the other for the business report.

EXHIBIT 9.26 ■ A Comparison of the Discussion Section in Academic and Business Reports

Academic Report	Business Report
Discussion/Conclusions	**Discussion/Conclusions/Recommendations**
The discussion in an academic report consists of:	This section in a business report consists of:
• A clear statement of results that support or do not support your research question(s)	• Discussion that is logically drawn from the findings in the previous section
• An explanation if the results do not support the research question(s)	• Questions or unresolved issues that remain
• A comparison of your results to other studies	• Conclusions drawn directly from the results and not newly introduced material
• A description of how your results relate to theory	• Theoretical or practical consequences of the results
• The position restated in alternative words	• Discussion that does not "gloss over conclusions that are puzzling, unpleasant, incomplete, or don't seem to fit into your scheme"[a]
• Acknowledgment of the limitations of your research	
• Suggestions for future directions or a research agenda	• Possible future studies based on the discussion, if relevant
• Comments on the importance of your findings to theory, practice, or the field	• Conclusions presented in order of importance, in the same order as the report's body was organized, or as separate positive and negative conclusions

Recommendations	
	• Drawn directly from the results
	• Comprise a suggested course of action to solve a particular problem or problems
	• Written as imperative statements without detailed justification
	• Expressed in clear, specific language
	• Listed in order of importance

Source: Kimberley, Nell, and Glenda Crosling, *Q Manual: A Student Guide for Producing Quality Work on Time*, 5th ed. (Victoria, Australia: Faculty of Business and Economics, Monash University, 2012). Figures 7-24 and 25 adapted by permission of Nell Kimberley.

Note: [a]Weaver, P. C., and R. Weaver, *Persuasive Writing: A Manager's Guide to Effective Letters and Reports* (New York: The Free Press, 1977), 98.

REFERENCES

The **References section** for your manuscript begins on a new page with the heading centered at the top of the page in uppercase and lowercase letters (not bold, underlined, or in quotes). In this section, I will mention several requirements for the sources cited in your paper—not those you used for background information, which are not cited. Examples then follow. Note that this section does not explain the procedures for in-text citations of authors or many other requirements of APA style. The latter are described best in the APA manual (Chapters 6 and 7) and online resources such as APA Style Central (http://www.apastyle.org/), EasyBib (http://www.easybib.com/reference/guide/apa/general), and Purdue OWL (Purdue University's Online Writing Lab; https://owl.english.purdue.edu/owl/), which is often recommended.[62]

Your reference list gives your readers the tools to

Acknowledge the work of previous scholars and provide a reliable way to locate it. References are used to document statements made about the literature, just as data in the manuscript support interpretations and conclusions. The references cited in the manuscript do not need to be exhaustive but should be sufficient to support the need for your research and to ensure that readers can place it in the context of previous research and theorizing.[63]

Consider these instructions when building a reference list:

- Double-space all reference entries.

- Check for corresponding citations in-text for all items you list.

- Format references with a hanging indent—that is, the first line of each reference is set to flush left (fully left justified) and subsequent lines are indented ½ inch from the left margin or five to seven spaces.

- There is no blank line between entries; the hanging indent is adequate.

- Entries are listed alphabetically by the last name of the first author.

- Authors' names are inverted (last name first); use the last name and initials for all authors of a work up to and including seven authors. If more than seven authors, list the first six authors and use ellipses after the sixth author's name. After the ellipses, list the last author's name of the work.

- When a source has no author, and the title is used instead, list the first significant word in the title (i.e., ignore "The", "A", "An"). Also, note the use of "Anonymous" when the author is unknown.

- When there are two sources with the same author(s) and date, order them alphabetically by title and assign a suffix (a, b, c) to each date.

- If the same author is cited for works from different years, list the references from the earliest publication date to the present.

- List the journal's full title with its punctuation and capitalization.

- Capitalize all major words in journal titles.

- Italicize titles of works such as books and journals.

- Do not italicize, underline, or put quotes around the titles of shorter works such as journal articles or essays *in edited collections.*

- For books, chapters, articles, or web pages, capitalize only the first letter of the first word of a title and subtitle, the first word after a colon or a dash in the title, and proper nouns.

- Do not capitalize the first letter of the second word in a hyphenated compound word.

- Provide full names of an organization.

- The publication location shows the city and abbreviates U.S. states (e.g., Thousand Oaks, CA: SAGE).[64]

Because this coverage is not exhaustive (especially the reference instruction list or examples), please refer to the APA manual for more information on how to cite sources. If you find a source is not covered by a conventional format, "APA suggests that you find the example that is most similar to your source and use that format."[65] Also, consult the APA Style Blog (http://blog.apastyle.org). For instance, see the McAdoo reference (with an APA Blog reference) in the following Example References list.

Example References

Ajzen, I. (2011). The theory of planned behaviour: Reactions and reflections. *Psychology & Health, 26*(9),

1113–1127. **(Journal article, one author)**

Brownlie, D. (2007). Toward effective poster presentations: An annotated bibliography. *European Journal of Marketing,*

41, 1245–1283. doi:10.1108/03090560710821161 **(Journal article online, one author, with DOI)**

Chevalier, J. A., & Mayzlin, D. (2006). The effect of word of mouth on sales: Online book reviews. *Journal*

of Marketing Research, 43(3), 345–354. **(Journal article, two authors)**

Cooper, D. R. (2019). *Business research: A guide to planning, conducting, and reporting your study.* Thousand Oaks, CA: SAGE. **(Book, one author)**

Creswell, J. W., & Plano Clark, V. L. (2018). *Designing and conducting mixed methods research* (3rd ed.). Thousand Oaks, CA: SAGE. **(Book, two authors, and edition)**

Fanoberova, A., & Kuczkowska, H. (2016). Effects of source credibility and information quality on attitudes and purchase intentions of apparel products: A quantitative study of online shopping among consumers in Sweden (Unpublished master's thesis). Umeå University, Umeå, Sweden. **(Unpublished doctoral dissertation or master's thesis)**

Hill, K. (2012, March 15) What is a good study? Guidelines for evaluating scientific studies. Retrieved from https://sciencebasedlife.wordpress.com/resources-2/what-is-a-good-study-guidelines-for-evaluating-scientific-studies **(Website)**

Jaeger, J. (2010, August). Social media use in the financial industry. *Compliance Week,* 54. **(Magazine article in print)**

Marchau, V., & van de Linde, E. (2016). The Delphi method. In P. van der Duin (Ed.), *Foresight in organizations: Methods and tools* (pp. 59–79). New York, NY: Routledge. **(Article or chapter in edited book)**

McAdoo, T. (2016, April 5). How to cite a blog post in APA style [blog post]. Retrieved from http://blog.apastyle.org/apastyle/2016/04/how-to-cite-a-blog-post-in-apa-style.html **(Article in a blog)**

McDonald, D. (2015, April 7). M.B.A. programs that get you where you want to go. *The New York Times.* Retrieved from http://www.nytimes.com/2015/04/12/edlife/mba-programs-that-get-you-where-you-want-to-go.html?_r=0 **(Newspaper online with URL)**

Nasar, S., & Gruber, D. (2006, August 28). Manifold destiny: A legendary problem and the battle over who solved it. *The New Yorker.* Retrieved from http://www.newyorker.com/magazine/2006/08/28/manifold-destiny **(Magazine online with URL)**

Smith, R. (2016, July 7). SEC looks at how insiders use exchange funds. *The Wall Street Journal,* A1. **(Newspaper with pagination)**

APPENDICES

Some sources are equivocal about the importance of **Appendices** at the end of your manuscript, but this is an excellent place for supplemental material that would otherwise interfere with the continuity of the report if it were presented within *any* of the report's sections. If your report has only one appendix, it should be labeled "Appendix" and centered at the top of a new page in uppercase and lowercase letters. When you have more than one, each appendix starts on a new page and is identified by A, B, C, and so forth in order of appearance (e.g., Appendix B). In each instance, the text starts flush left below the heading and subsequent paragraphs are indented (see APA 2.13).

The appendices often contain questionnaires and measuring instruments, instructional scripts for participants, transcripts of interviews, computer programs created for an original analytic purpose, derivations of equations, recruiting flyers, advertisements, telephone scripts, email announcements of the study, consent forms and other IRB-required materials, letters, photographs, data collection locations (maps), census charts, or a glossary.

Chapter Summary

- This chapter addresses preparing the manuscript for your research report. The template used for describing the organization of the report reflects both IMRAD and APA—with optional modifications. The discussion centers on the Title, Abstract, Introduction, Method, Results, Discussion, References, and Appendices.

- The Title page is the first page of your manuscript, and it is separate. It summarizes the main idea of your study by identifying variables and theoretical issues. APA recommends no more than 12 words because a shorter topic captures the readers' interest faster than a complex one that tries to squeeze the research question, variables, and background into one sentence.

- The Abstract is important because it determines whether a reader will continue to read the paper or skip it. Ideally, it is a summary of the study's contents with at least a sentence each on the background, problem, sample and participants, design, method, procedures, results, and principal conclusions.

- Your manuscript begins with an Introduction of the problem, an exploration of its importance, a discussion of the related literature, and a statement of the hypotheses and how they reflect the literature that your argument developed. In some research designs, you may have one or more research and investigative questions rather than a hypothesis. A synthesis matrix was recommended as a useful organizing tool for your literature. Optional organizing techniques included the CARS model, which creates a rhetorical space and attracts readers into that space, and a discussion of the "Problem and Its Setting," an eight-point option for reorganizing the Introduction.

- The Method section is tied to your research problem and shows the process by which the research question was answered or hypotheses were tested. It describes how the study was conducted and gives a justification and detailed description of the method(s) you have chosen.

It should contain sufficient detail to convince the reader that your design, method, sampling, participants, instruments, and procedures were selected to produce the highest degree of reliability and validity.

- The purpose of the Results section is to present your major findings in a sequence that reflects the order of your research and investigative questions and, ideally, the order of your hypotheses. Your presentation does not include interpretation of the reported findings, which is accomplished in the Discussion section. The analytical report is organized with textual and graphic materials such as tables and figures. You begin with text and refer to findings in the tables and figures as you progress.

- The Discussion section explains to the reader the meaning of what the study accomplished, its contribution to the field, and recommendations for next steps. Its goal is to provide a focused synthesis and interpretation of findings. Your Discussion section, depending on the study's complexity, is arranged as follows: (1) summary of findings, (2) theoretical context and implications, (3) practical implications, (4) limitations of the research, and (5) suggestions for future research.

- Your References give your readers the tools to understand the work of cited scholars and provide a reliable way to locate their materials. References are used to document and credit authors' statements about the literature and other aspects of the study.

- The Appendices are placed at the end of your manuscript. They are used for supplemental material that would otherwise interfere with the flow of the report if it were presented within the report's sections. The appendices often contain questionnaires and measuring instruments, instructional scripts for participants, consent forms, and other IRB materials.

Key Terms

Abstract
Appendices section
CARS model
Design subsection
Discussion section
effect size
executive summary
Instruments subsection
Introduction

Limitations subsection
(Literature) Synthesis Matrix
method of data collection
Method section
Participants subsection
Practical Implications subsection
Problem and Its Setting module
Procedure subsection

References section
Results section
sampling plan and procedures
statistical power
Suggestions for Future Research subsection
Theoretical Implications subsection
Title page

Discussion Questions

1. What are the qualities of good report writing (e.g., see the Chapter 9 Overview, APA Chapter 3, Turabian Chapters 5–7, and Booth et al. Chapters 13 and 14)? Look for disparities between these examples and the illustrations provided by students and professors in each

section of this chapter. Make a list of writing suggestions for your style of expression.

2. Using different ideas for your research project, practice constructing a title that captures the reader's attention in one sentence (12–15 words) incorporating the research question, variables, and a little background. What is the reason that readers prefer a shorter title?

3. Take the title or titles you have created and transform them into amusing or allusion/proverbial titles. Does this fit your expectations for a professional-looking report? Your personal style?

4. Compare the contents and style of an academic Abstract with a business report's executive summary.

   a. Compare the Introduction's coverage in an academic and business report.

   b. What are the contents of the Method section for both reports?

   c. Describe the differences in the Results section for both reports.

   d. The Discussion/Conclusions for both reports have similarities. What are their differences?

5. In the Introduction of your report, when you introduce the problem, it should contain an argument for the problem's importance and why the research question is interesting, important, and worthy of new research. What materials are essential to meet this requirement?

6. Your literature review or contribution of relevant scholarship may occupy several paragraphs to several pages, which may be most of the content in the introduction.

   a. How should you connect relevant scholarship to your research question?

   b. When citing studies, would you start with background studies or those most pertinent to establish your problem's relevance?

   c. What is more important: being comprehensive or synthesizing your notes so you emphasize major findings, conclusions, and implications?

   d. When you group studies in sections, you summarize the previous argument for that section and connect it using a transition to the next section, so that the organization flows smoothly. These are "signposts" for your reader in the Toulmin approach. How do they resemble data, warrant, or claim?

   e. What is the difference between the "funnel approach" to your literature and simply laying out the studies as you find them or choosing the ones you find most interesting?

   f. Whether you use APA, Chicago Style/ Turabian, or MLA, where do you place your hypothesis? Would you use the same logic if it were a research question?

   g. How should the research literature be connected to your hypothesis/research question?

7. The chapter suggested organizing your literature with the Synthesis Matrix and connecting it to your draft with bibliographic software.

   a. How do you create a Synthesis Matrix? How does it work?

   b. The CARS model creates a rhetorical space and attracts readers into that space. Why would some readers be attracted to the creativity of that organizing tool?

8. Describe ways that the traditional headings of IMRAD may be expanded.

   a. What is the difference between "limitations" and "delimitations" and where do they go in your report?

   b. What is the advantage, if any, of positioning the Review of Literature after the problem's background and statement of the problem? Can you foresee any improvement in the flow of the Introduction?

9. Describe the prescribed content of the APA Method section or an alternative approach, if your professor allows you to break the organizing rules.

   a. How is the Design described and what are particular source materials to connect it to the report (see Chapters 6, 7, and 8)?

   b. Consider how much detail about the Method of data collection is sufficient yet allows another researcher to repeat your work. Describe what you would include.

   c. List and evaluate the criteria for writing the Sampling Plan.

   d. What is the connection among sample size, power, and effect size (magnitude of the difference) and what is the rationale for including this information in your report?

   e. Explain the subsection used to describe the Participants in your study. Can you think of any aspects of a 'participant profile' that were omitted?

   f. Describe the description of your measuring instruments from describing the variables to quantifying the reliability.

   g. What is included in the Procedures subsection and how much of it is necessary for the topic you have chosen?

10. What is the purpose of the Results section and its essential components?

    a. How is the Discussion section connected to your Introduction? What does this section explain?

    b. Is there a benefit organizationally for grouping the discussion of results by hypotheses/research questions, by theory, or by a sub-division of the literature?

    c. What do you absolutely want to avoid in the Discussion?

    d. Evaluate the questions regarding Theoretical Implications and explain which ones apply to your report.

    e. List three reasons why Practical Implications of your research should be featured in the Discussion.

    f. What are the different Limitations that should be acknowledged in the Discussion and what is the consequence for failing to reveal your errors?

11. Building a Reference list involves numerous considerations regarding citations, some of which are unique to the style manual you are following and many of which will be automatic if you use bibliographic software. When you review the 17 instructions for building a reference list, which ones are vital for you to consider?

12. Now that you have completed your draft, you might consider the advice of Joyce Carol Oates, who said, "The first sentence can't be written until the final sentence is written."

    a. An Abstract should contain at least a brief sentence on various content sections of your report. What are they?

    b. Ideally, how much space (by word count) should an Abstract consume?

APPENDICES

APPENDIX A

Questionnaire Design Using Google Forms

Chapter 4 discussed a recent international study that supported the contention of fading respondent engagement. The problems created by questionnaire designers and the reaction by participants in the 15-country study cast doubt on participant satisfaction; three-quarters were unhappy with their survey experience. Exhibit 4.2 presented specific problems and unique solutions for creating questionnaires especially with "mobile-first" respondents in mind. Chapter 4 also discussed the advantages of online surveys and listed several websites that provide free and fee-paid design, tabulation, and analytical services.

Chapter 9 provided examples of each part of a research report. Several illustrations consisted of excerpts from a recent thesis on the effects of source credibility and information quality on consumer attitudes and purchase intention in online apparel shopping. The authors, Anna Fanoberova and Hanna Kuczkowska of the Umeå School of Business and Economics in Sweden, adapted questions from prior research (see Exhibit 9.16) to explore their conceptual model, thereby enhancing (and later testing) question reliability and validity. Also, they gave respondents a sense of direction by dividing the questionnaire into sections, controlling question number and time to completion, and providing definitions for the major terms (such as online product information, fashion retailer, fashion blogger, and professional stylist). In this appendix, you can follow the evolution of their questionnaire, including their introduction, question placement and scale determination, and transitions between sections. Representative questions from their 22-item questionnaire are shown. The online service Google Forms (https://docs.google.com/forms) was used to design, distribute, and collect the data. This appendix takes you through many features of this software.

When you are in Google Help, start by entering a key term at the prompt. Select "Create a survey using Google Forms."

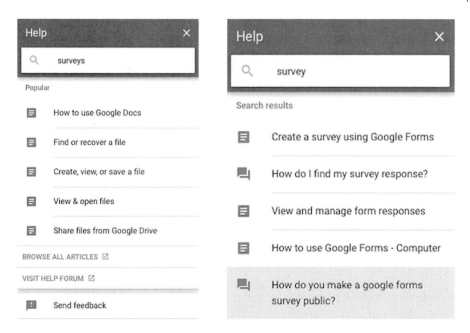

Follow the instructions in point 1 ("Go to docs.google.com/forms") or click the appropriate link to edit your form ("Learn more about editing your form").

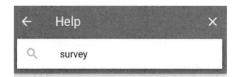

The template opens with a location for your questionnaire's title and description and shows the location of the first question. Enter your title and description or instructions for the respondents in the designated areas. The symbols labeled on the right are available options for construction.

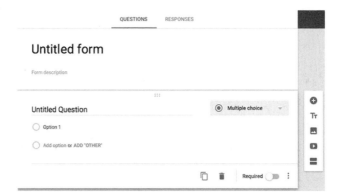

To preview the title and description or instructions you have entered, use the "eye" symbol on the top of the page. Compare the results with your notes and edit where needed. If you decide that your survey should have sections rather than be continuous, there is a provision for section breaks that then labels the section numbers at the top of the page.

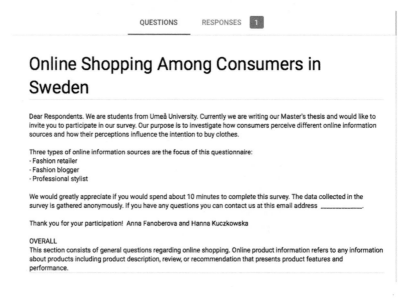

Here you see the drop-down box on the right of the "Untitled Question." This box allows you to select the desired scale that respondents will use to answer the question.

Careful planning before scale selection is essential because the nature of the scale's measurement (NOIR) determines how your data will be tabulated and analyzed. Again, statistical decisions should occur in planning your research. Note that "Multiple choice" is highlighted for Question 1.

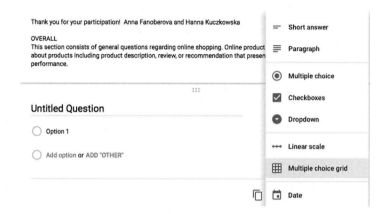

Type Question 1 into the box, choose multiple choice, select response alternatives at Option 1, and then "Add option or ADD 'OTHER'" response until finished. These questions and responses are part (as are others shown later) of the original online shopping study. This is a nominal scale in that the bubbles represent categories. Some researchers might consider this an ordinal scale in that responses are *ranked* from most to least frequent purchases. Typically, however, this would be analyzed as a nominal scale. You are viewing this question in Edit mode.

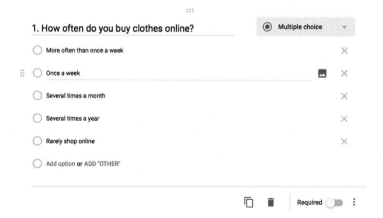

In Preview mode ("eye" symbol at the top of page), note the layout of the Title, Introduction, and Question 1.

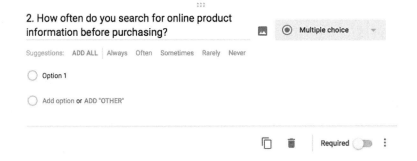

Online Shopping Among Consumers in Sweden

Dear Respondents. We are students from Umeå University. Currently we are writing our Master's thesis and would like to invite you to participate in our survey. Our purpose is to investigate how consumers perceive different online information sources and how their perceptions influence the intention to buy clothes.

Three types of online information sources are the focus of this questionnaire:
- Fashion retailer
- Fashion blogger
- Professional stylist

We would greatly appreciate if you would spend about 10 minutes to complete this survey. The data collected in the survey is gathered anonymously. If you have any questions you can contact us at this email address _____.

Thank you for your participation! Anna Fanoberova and Hanna Kuczkowska

OVERALL
This section consists of general questions regarding online shopping. Online product information refers to any information about products including product description, review, or recommendation that presents product features and performance.

1. How often do you buy clothes online?

○ More often than once a week

○ Once a week

○ Several times a month

○ Several times a year

○ Rarely shop online

SUBMIT

Google Forms provides suggestions for response options. In this case, it is suggesting levels of "how often." Of course, you may ignore the suggestions if you have decided in advance the wording you prefer for respondents' answers.

2. How often do you search for online product information before purchasing?   [Multiple choice ▾]

Suggestions: ADD ALL | Always Often Sometimes Rarely Never

○ Option 1

○ Add option or ADD "OTHER"

Required ⬤ ⋮

Clicking on the suggestions drops them in. You will note that the "Never" option was not selected.

2. How often do you search for online product information before purchasing?

[Multiple choice ▾]

Suggestions: Never

○ Always   ✕

○ Often   ✕

○ Sometimes   ✕

○ Rarely   ✕

○ Add option or ADD "OTHER"

▢ 🗑 | Required ⬤ ⋮

Now let's see the first two questions in Preview mode.

1. How often do you buy clothes online?

○ More often than once a week

○ Once a week

○ Several times a month

○ Several times a year

○ Rarely shop online

2. How often do you search for online product information before purchasing?

○ Always

○ Often

○ Sometimes

○ Rarely

Skipping to Question 8, you will see how a *Likert response format* is set up in Edit mode. This question uses the Multiple Choice Grid in the drop-down menu. It has multiple items for the respondent to evaluate concerning perceptions of the fashion retailer.

8. I perceive the fashion retailer as: (mark one per row)

Row 1. Honest   ✕

Row 2. Reliable   ✕

Row 3. Trustworthy   ✕

Row 4. Expert   ✕

Row 5. Knowledgeable   ✕

Row 6. Qualified   ✕

Row 7. Likeable   ✕

Row 8. Similar to me   ✕

Row 9. Familiar to me   ✕

Row 10. Add option

Column 1. Strongly disagree   ✕

Column 2. Disagree   ✕

Column 3. Neither agree nor disagree   ✕

Column 4. Agree   ✕

Column 5. Strongly agree   ✕

Column 6. Add option

▦ Multiple choice grid ⌄

Require a response in each row ⬤▶

Note: For more information on Likert scales and Likert response formats, see Carifio, James, and Rocco J. Perla, "Ten Common Misunderstandings, Misconceptions, Persistent Myths and Urban Legends About Likert Scales and Likert Response Formats and Their Antidotes," *Journal of Social Sciences* 3, no. 3 (2007): 106–116, http://thescipub.com/PDF/jssp.2007.106.116.pdf.

In Preview mode, the question set looks like this:

8. I perceived the fashion retailer as: (mark one per row)

	Strongly disagree	Disagree	Neither agree nor disagree	Agree	Strongly agree
Honest	○	○	○	○	○
Reliable	○	○	○	○	○
Trustworthy	○	○	○	○	○
Expert	○	○	○	○	○
Knowledgeable	○	○	○	○	○
Qualified	○	○	○	○	○
Likeable	○	○	○	○	○
Similar to me	○	○	○	○	○
Familiar to me	○	○	○	○	○

When a new section is introduced in Edit mode, fashion bloggers are defined as a different information source and thus a new section is required.

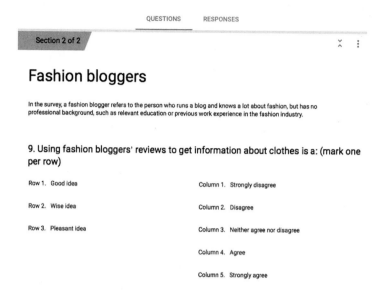

The Multiple Choice Grid for response options is used in Edit mode.

With the new section in place, the Preview shows "Fashion bloggers" highlighted and defined. Question 9 is one question in this section.

Fashion bloggers

In the survey, a fashion blogger refers to the person who runs a blog and knows a lot about fashion, but has no professional background, such as relevant education or previous work experience in the fashion industry.

9. Using fashion bloggers' reviews to get information about clothes is a: (mark one per row)

	Strongly disagree	Disagree	Neither agree nor disagree	Agree	Strongly agree
Good idea	○	○	○	○	○
Wise idea	○	○	○	○	○
Pleasant idea	○	○	○	○	○

Professional stylists are introduced as another new section with Question 15. Note that the Likert items now consist of *phrases* rather than just a stimulus *word* as in Question 8.

Professional stylists

In this survey a professional stylist refers to a person employed in the fashion industry that offers advice on clothes and other aspects of personal appearance.

15. If my friends and family knew that I checked professional stylists' reviews, I believe that they would: (mark only one per row)

	Strongly disagree	Disagree	Neither agree nor disagree	I agree	Strongly agree
Approve of me buying clothes online	○	○	○	○	○
Support my behavior of buying clothes online	○	○	○	○	○
Prefer me to buy clothes online	○	○	○	○	○

The final section, demographics, consists of four questions (age, gender, education, and occupation). The section break is created in Edit mode, and each question is set up with multiple choice options. Questions 19 and 21 are shown here.

About you

19. Age (mark only one)

○ <18

○ 18-25

○ 26-35

○ 36-45

○ >45

21. Education (mark only one)

○ High school or less

○ Bachelor's degree

○ Master's degree

○ Post graduate or above

BACK   SUBMIT

APPENDIX B

Exemption Request
(Institutional Review Board)

"Research includes evaluation of individuals using educational or cognitive tests, surveys, questionnaires, structured or open-ended interviews, or systematic observations of public behavior."—Basic Exempt Criteria 45 CFR 46.101(b)(2)

EXHIBIT B.1 ■

Tests, Surveys, Interviews, or Passive Observations of Public Behavior

Request for Exempt Determination

Principal Investigator:	
Study Title:	

Note: In some cases, individuals under 18 years of age can be evaluated with education tests only (no surveys or interviews). They can also be passively observed in public places, but only so long as researchers do not participate in the activities being observed or interact with the children.

1. Will any information from this project be submitted to the FDA? ☐ No ☐ Yes If Yes, STOP and contact us at askirb@pitt.edu

2. Check the types of measures to be used:

   ☐ Passive observation of public behavior

   ☐ Educational Tests (cognitive, diagnostic, aptitude)

   ☐ Survey

   ☐ Interview

   ☐ Focus Group

   ☐ Other (describe):

3. Describe the participants who will participate in this study:

(Continued)

(Continued)

---

4. Will participants under 18 years of age be studied? ☐ No ☐ Yes
   If Yes, address the following:

   a. Is this study limited to passive observation of public behavior and/or educational tests? ☐ No ☐ Yes   If No, STOP. This exempt category is not applicable.

      1. If Yes, describe: ▨

      2. If Yes, also address the following:

         (i) Provide a rationale for the specific age ranges of children to be studied: ▨

         (ii) Describe the expertise of the study team for dealing with children of that age range: ▨

         (iii) Describe the adequacy of the research facilities to accommodate children of that age range: ▨

         (iv) If applicable, how will parents be informed or involved in this project? ▨

5. Will you be interacting with non-English speaking participants? ☐ No ☐ Yes

   If Yes, are you fluent in the language they understand? ☐ No ☐ Yes   If No, indicate how you will communicate with participants (e.g., with interpreter - and if so, who will serve in this role): ▨

6. Address where the study will be conducted and who will collect the data: ▨

7. How often will participants be contacted and why?

8. Will information be recorded anonymously (no participant identifiers or codes that can be used to re-identify subjects will be recorded)? ☐ No ☐ Yes   If No, provide a justification for recording identifiers: ▨

9. Will sensitive information be recorded that could damage participants' reputation or employability, financial standing, or place them at risk for criminal or civil liability? ☐ No ☐ Yes If Yes, explain: ▨

10. Upload the introductory script in OSIRIS item 4.1 – a sample script is available on the HRPO website. If not applicable, explain: ▨

11. Address how the information will be obtained (e.g., face-to-face, phone, internet) and upload all interview questions, questionnaires, focus group guides, etc. into OSIRIS item 2.8: ▨

12. If data will come from, or will be sent to, another institution, you must consult with the University of Pittsburgh Office of Research regarding any necessary transfer agreements (www.research.pitt.edu). If you intend to share data, this must be addressed in OSIRIS item 5.8.

13. Additional information, clarification, or comments for IRB review: ▨

* *

Final Process: Save this document to your computer and then upload into OSIRIS item E2.0

Source: Used by permission of Michelle LeMenager, "Exempt Review," Human Research Protections Office, University of Pittsburgh, April 24, 2017, http://www.irb.pitt.edu/tests-surveys-interviews-observations. Also see "Exempt Submission: Getting Started," http://www.irb.pitt.edu/sites/default/files/exempt/Exempt_Instructions.pdf.

APPENDIX C

Sample Business Proposal

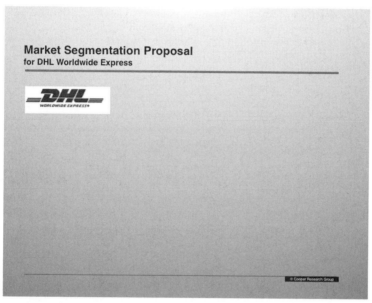

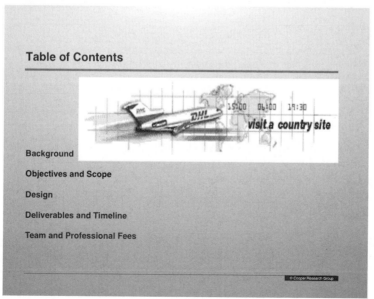

DHL INTERNATIONAL seeks to develop and implement a marketing strategy for the Southern Cone - Latin American (LA) market

Background of the Problem

DHL requires:

- A successful marketing strategy designed through an understanding of the structure of market and the patterns of competition within it.

- An identification of subgroups of customers who respond to given products/ services in a similar fashion.

- An understanding of the competitive relationship within the market: which products are true competitors and the market boundaries.

- Information to increase customer satisfaction.

- The ability to achieve and sustain competitive advantage in the Southern Cone-Latin American market (Chile, Argentina, Brazil).

© Cooper Research Group

Provide a quantitative, multivariate statistical study that analyzes collected personal interview data from enterprises using express-delivery services in Chile, Argentina, and Brazil

Project Objectives

- To identify the best structure of the fast-delivery market in the involved countries and the segments or subdivisions within that market structure.

- To profile the segments in terms of relevant collected information.

- To assess how different segments perceive DHL with respect to the competition.

- To recommend an appropriate strategy for the fast-delivery market in Latin America.

© Cooper Research Group

To obtain accurate and actionable information

Consultant Objectives

In designing the quantitative study, our key concern is to meet DHL's stated objectives to identify the structure and segments of the express- delivery market, profile the resulting segments, evaluate DHL's position in each segment, and recommend appropriate strategic actions.

This is a particularly daunting task in multi-country studies where care must be taken to ensure that each phase of the study is not be biased in terms of any one country. As outlined in this proposal, our goals are to use advanced statistical techniques to meet DHL's objectives and interpret the study findings in business terms, not just statistical analysis.

© Cooper Research Group

The Scope of the Project

- Designing and implementing a post-hoc segmentation study that will identify market segments by clustering customers and potential customers on a relevant set of characteristics (benefit, need, or attitude).
- Identifying populations for the studies (companies with more than 15 employees that presently use "express-delivery" services in Chile, Argentina, and Brazil).
- Securing representative samples stratified on geographical areas/ cities, industry, enterprise size, occupation, etc.
- Designing a data collection instrument to secure respondent impressions.
- Collecting data in the field by means of personal interviews.
- Translating and back-translating instruments.
- Coding and processing the data.
- Developing two databases: one for Chile combined with Argentina, and another for Brazil. Each database will be analyzed separately.
- Forming segments based on sorting respondents into categories via advanced statistical techniques.
- Profiling the segments on the basis of size, product use, and respondent background characteristics.
- Positioning DHL relative to the competition in each country through statistical analyses.
- Preparing recommendations for strategic and tactical marketing plans.

© Cooper Research Group

Our approach includes thorough and collaborative planning, design, pilot testing and fieldwork, data analysis, and recommendations

Approach Summary

Initiate Project Strategy Work Session	Quantitative Study Design	Fieldwork	Data Analysis	Recommend

- Identify team members
- Announce project
- Develop work plan
- Create team understanding of the priorities
- Understand linkages and logistics for DHL and the vendor
- Formulate action plans to address study objectives

- Design sample from existing DHL databases and supplemental sources
- Collaboratively prepare interview schedule/ questionnaire
- Design pretest
- Prepare data analysis including database structure

- Develop questionnaire with DHL and in-country focus groups
- Create and reproduce questionnaire
- Pretest the questionnaire
- Conduct personal interviews

- Assess instrument reliability and validity
- Perform outlier detection
- Segment the market using clustering algorithms
- Profile segments
- Position DHL relative to their competition
- Identify key drivers of customer satisfaction using multiple regression

- Provide guidelines for DHL's LA marketing strategy and resource allocation among markets and products/services.
- Develop a results-oriented program leading to increased customer satisfaction
- Present findings for implementation

Communication with client, partner, vendors

© Cooper Research Group

Sample Design

- Design the sampling frame based on DHL requirements.

- Identify populations for the studies (companies with more than 15 employees that presently use "express-delivery" services in Chile, Argentina, and Brazil).

- Acquire sample from DHL databases and supplementary acquisition from XLM or other agreed upon source.

- Secure representative samples stratified on geographical areas/ cities, industry, enterprise size, occupation, etc.

- Draw the representative sample.

© Cooper Research Group

Sample Design Specifics

We will work closely with our Latin American partners to build a sample that is representative for each country. These partners typically contribute their expertise to our research design, sampling, and questionnaire development.

For example, our Chilean partner informs us that there are only 1,200 firms with 15 or more employees in the entire country. As a result, we recommend lowering the quota for Chile to 400 interviews, and weighting the Chilean data so that it is still of equal importance to the Argentine data when the segmentation model is developed.

In each country, our partners will draw upon government information, directories and their databases to develop the sample — we expect a sampling ratio of at least 3 to 1. We also recommend that DHL provide us with current client and contact lists to supplement the sample.

© Cooper Research Group

Sample Design Specifics (continued)

- We have evaluated a minimum of two estimates per country:
  - An estimate for conducting the research in the capital cities (in Argentina and Chile) and in Brazil's two largest cities - Rio de Janeiro and Sao Paolo.

- An estimate for conducting the research in the capital city and the next largest cities.
  - Brazil - Sao Paolo, Rio de Janeiro, Brasilia, Recife, Manaus, Belen
  - Argentina - Buenos Aires, Rosario, Mendoza, and one or two others
  - Chile - Santiago, Valparaiso, and one northern city

- Half or more of all major businesses have their headquarters in Buenos Aires, Santiago, and Rio and Sao Paolo. Our partners also have their headquarters in these cities. As such, data collection will be less expensive if limited to these cities.

- The second scenario provides a national sample of businesses. This will be more expensive and we may not be able to "project costs" even though attempts are made to provide national coverage. Data for secondary cities usually is not very reliable. As such, sampling frames may not accurately represent all industry sectors in those cities.

- Decisions regarding these and other options will be made in conjunction with the client team.

© Cooper Research Group

Fieldwork Highlights

- Develop questionnaire with DHL (and in-country focus groups, if needed).
- Create and reproduce questionnaire.
- Pretest the questionnaire for appropriateness in each market.
- Conduct personal interviews.
- In-person in-language briefing and training session.
- Observation of first day/ two days' interviewing.
- Professional interviewing teams in each country.
- Thorough review of each country's first 10 interviews.
- Follow-up visits (if needed).
- Videotaped practice interview for reference purposes.
- Weekly updates from the field.

© Cooper Research Group

Questionnaire Design

- Strategy and space allocation (# questions, estimated time)-- meet with DHL.

- First rough draft of English version.

- Feedback and second draft of questionnaire -- approval by DHL.

- Translate to Portuguese and Spanish.

- Back-translate to English, settle discrepancies-- approval by DHL.

- Pretest questionnaire in the field.

- Preliminary empirical data analysis to assess reliability and validity.

- Briefings in countries.

- Interviewing.

© Cooper Research Group

Questionnaire Design Specifics

We will develop the questionnaire in conjunction with DHL. Upon approval of the English-language version of the document, we will develop initial translations in Spanish and Portuguese. The Vice President and Group Director, Latin America and Hispanic Research, will oversee the translation and back-translation process in Spanish. The Project Director in the Transportation Group, a Brazilian national, will oversee this process in Portuguese. The in-language questionnaires will then be submitted to DHL and to our Latin American partners for review.

Back-translation will be coordinated with CRG for data analysis purposes.

We expect the interview to average 30 minutes, some of which will be completed during the initial screening conducted by telephone.

© Cooper Research Group

Data Collection

- Preliminary data gathering: Brazil.
- Develop initial coding scheme.
- Briefings in Chile and Argentina.
- Interviewing: all countries.
- Data entry.
- Coding and error checking.
- Preliminary data sets to DHL.
- Data cleaned and initial tables developed.
- Data tables and final data sets delivered.

© Cooper Research Group

Data Analysis

- Perform outlier detection (clustering techniques are sensitive to the presence of outliers).
- Identify appropriate similarity or distance measures.

- Apply clustering algorithms.
- Split data and cross-replicate to assess the stability of cluster solutions.
- Meet with DHL to identify the best market structure from both statistical and practical perspectives.
- Seek additional input from country locals to gain insight into statistical results
- Profile segments in terms of characteristics of interest to DHL.
- Create three sets of positioning charts (Brazil, Chile, Argentina) .
- Develop a profile of key drivers of customer satisfaction for the express delivery market.
- Develop a results-oriented program which leads to increased customer satisfaction.
  - Present segmentation-analyzed results, positioning charts, and printouts of information by segment.
- Prepare report on strategic initiatives based on study findings.

© Cooper Research Group

Data Analysis Specifics

Use advanced statistical techniques to analyze data to meet DHL's objectives. Interpret and explain findings in business terms, not just statistics.

- We will segment the express-delivery market in Brazil and Chile/Argentina using multiple data analysis techniques. Because the market segments are not known *a priori*, we will use Cluster Analysis and Automatic Interaction Detection to partition the market into subgroups that differ in meaningful ways. Multiple discriminant analysis may also be used for sub-segment prediction. If the complexity of the market exceeds traditional multivariate methods, structural modeling will be used in the exploratory phase. Our goal is to arrive at "clusters" of customers that display small within-cluster variation relative to the between- cluster variation.

- To position DHL against the competition, we will use regression-based key driver analysis to identify strengths or weaknesses in DHL's existing customer satisfaction and recommend a results-oriented program that will lead to increased customer satisfaction.

© Cooper Research Group

Project Deliverables

- Presentation of the segmentation-analyzed results -- a presentation for the study of Chile and Argentina and another for Brazil.

- Written report of the results and recommendations from each of the two study's presentations.

- Set of profiling graphics for each market segment.

- Set of positioning charts for each country segment.

- Segment-based charts showing key characteristics of the segments.

- Tabulations by two banners of breaks per country.

- Raw data file with complete file layout in ASCI/SPSS format delivered in electronic media at half way and end points of the interviewing process.

© Cooper Research Group

Team Responsibilities

Team Responsibilities

Client Team Members	Consulting Team Members
• Demonstrate leadership and support for project objectives.	• Apply research methodology experience.
• Provide knowledge of DHL organization	• Execute the activities outlined in the approach.
• Schedule participants for workshops and interviews.	• Develop actionable recommendations.
• Collaborate on questionnaire design and segment profiling decisions.	• Communicate regularly with sponsors
• Provide adequate on-site work facilities for core and client team.	• Transfer knowledge of research concepts and techniques to client team.

© Cooper Research Group

Consultant Credentials

Our current client list includes electronics firms as well as full service consultancies -- who rely on us for advanced data analytic skills. We have completed over 100 studies for IBM alone in the last few years. Marketing research firms such as Carlson Marketing Group and Maritz Marketing Research have sought our data analytic skills. Burke, Intersearch, and Audits & Surveys provide us with their collected data to analyze for common clients. Our analysis of customer responses and credible recommendations prompted one I/T provider to change their fast-delivery vendor in one month!

Prior clients include international corporations in the computer industry, travel, heavy manufacturing, consultant services, banking, securities, and federal, state, and local government agencies.

Competitive Advantages

Experience in your marketplace. From Mexico to the Southern Cone of LA we have an extensive country and regional understanding of markets and cultural differences. We have assessed and predicted the evolution of products and services as LA markets matured.

Responsiveness. Our location provides DHL with immediate access for meetings and consultation. Our dedicated resources assigned to this engagement will exceed your expectations for quick turnaround and proactive solutions.

Integrity. Our commitment to honesty and quality work products combined with actionable research gives you confidence to move forward with data based decisions.

Competitive Costs. We pass along the benefits of our lower cost structure. Your investment in us is leveraged for optimal competitive advantage.

The Best Brains in the Business. The team includes practitioners and academics in market research, applied statistics, and organizational assessment. They possess among them some of the most respected articles, books, monographs, and consulting experiences in their fields.

Our strategic partner along with its country affiliates network, is regarded as one of the finest data collection vendors in the world. It is a full-service international marketing research supplier providing custom research to leading organizations. XLM was founded in 1960.

XLM is one of the fastest growing market research companies in the United States and has about 350 full-time employees and about 1500 part-time. The researchers, many with advanced degrees, come from many different backgrounds, including Marketing, Economics, Psychology, Sciences and Engineering. XLM has the professional staff in each discipline and the resources to execute projects from inception to analysis in-house. In the last two years, it has completed over 1000 separate research programs for clients.

Quality in survey design, execution and service has always been the key focus and the key reward for marketing research professionals. Not only our livelihoods, but our personal satisfaction has come from helping our clients to obtain and utilize the best research data and insights. At XLM, quality is both a personal and corporate commitment, supported by experience and solid procedural rules, checks, and balances.

XLM areas of expertise include information technology, telecommunications, healthcare (service providers, pharmaceuticals, bio-technology and scientific instrumentation), financial services, banking, insurance, business-to-business, and consumer packaged goods research. Types of research include new product development (from concept through launch), positioning/strategy/tactical research, segmentation studies, pricing research, customer satisfaction and quality measurement, and tracking studies.

As a member of the XLM group of companies, they use the resources of the worldwide family to meet clients' growing research needs. Whether the issue is industry, problem, or culturally specific, they can employ the expertise of 4000 professional research associates to answer questions.

XLM International is the fourth largest marketing research firm in the world. Fully integrated worldwide, it provides quality research in more than 60 offices in over 30 countries in Europe, Asia, Australia and the Americas.

Relevant Industry Experience: Strategic Partner

The following is a list of studies XLM has conducted in the industry. Although the list is not exhaustive, it is provided as an example of the broad spectrum of studies conducted in this area.

Package Distribution Industry: Studies within the European market to measure customer satisfaction, advertising testing, and corporate identity. Entailed a variety of methodological approaches including focus groups, depth interviews, and business to business interviews.

Express Delivery Market Sizing: A series of surveys have been conducted to determine potential market size for new product offerings before the products are introduced to the general public. Decisions concerning corporate direction are made based on the information gathered.

Small Business Market Potential: A telephone survey was conducted among small businesses in the US. to evaluate their interest in a new airline program. The survey identified potential small business segments to be targeted, and identified the options to be included in the program to maximize the number of potential customers.

Air Freight Focus Groups: Focus groups among distribution supervisors to determine requirements for Air Freight Services for large packages (150+ pounds).

Advertising Concept Study: Telephone interviews were conducted among air express users to test a variety of advertising campaign concepts. Four different advertising campaigns were tested before introduction.

Christmas Delivery Study: A mail survey was conducted among 5,000 air express customers to determine their interest in a Christmas delivery service.

Delivery Sweepstakes Survey: Telephone survey to measure the awareness and success of a delivery sweepstakes promotion. The carrier ran a promotion in two markets for a three week period. During that time, newspaper and radio advertising was employed. Respondents to the survey were high level corporate executives, company owners and managers.

Distribution Services Focus Groups: Focus groups among business and operations managers to determine their needs for special services for quick distribution of vital equipment.

Trucking Customer Satisfaction: Customers satisfaction survey among customers for a major common carrier to determine their satisfaction with service.

Project Costs

The cost for conducting the research is $698,600. Reimbursable expenses for travel and living away from home will be billed at cost. Project contingencies typically will not exceed 10% of proposed fees.

Terms of payment

45% at the commencement of work, 25% at midpoint, and 30% upon project completion.

The consultant and XLM will devote their best efforts to the work performed on this engagement. The findings, recommendations, and written materials we provide will represent our best professional judgment based on the information made available to us.

We require a one week period from signature of the Document of Understanding to appropriately staff the engagement before beginning work. During this time we will be available to meet with you.

Notes and Conditions

1.   It is the policy of this firm to present proposals with the *understanding that their contents are copyrighted* and that the ideas, conceptual approaches, and techniques expressed are the intellectual property of the Cooper Research Group, Inc. Fair Use applies to the limited use of author's/consultants' works for the purpose of criticism and commentary. This is a commercial document and DHL is the *only* intended recipient. As such, the company's representatives and the decision makers reviewing the contents to make a purchase decision for services may not divulge any aspect of the contents or tradecraft to a third party without the prior written permission of Cooper Research Group, Inc. Noncompliance or infringement in any form will terminate this offer and CRG will immediately initiate remedies.

2.   The concept specifications and costs will remain valid for a two month period from the date of this proposal.

3.   We acknowledge the cover logo as the trademark of DHL Worldwide Express Corporation and the property of the DHL and the DHL website.

4.   XLM is a pseudonym for an international consulting firm who was the strategic partner in this venture.

This example is the property of Cooper Research Group, Inc. Copyright, 2001, 2017. Nothing contained in this example may be used without the prior written permission of Cooper Research Group, Inc.

APPENDIX D

Statistical Decision Trees

Selecting a Descriptive Statistic

EXHIBIT D.1 ■

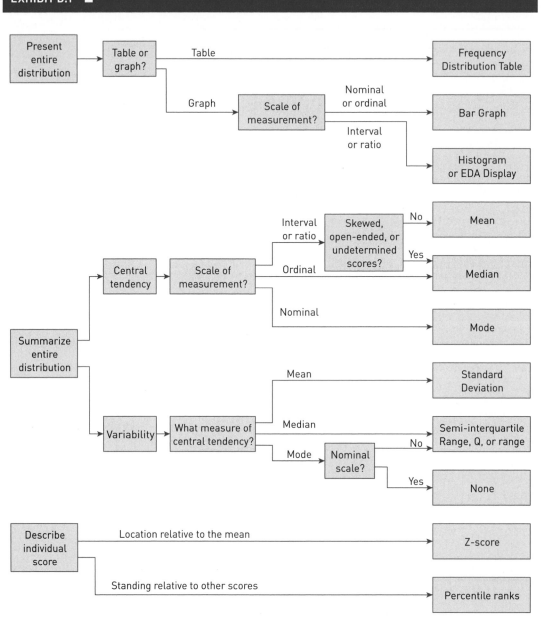

Selecting a Parametric Statistic

EXHIBIT D.2 ■

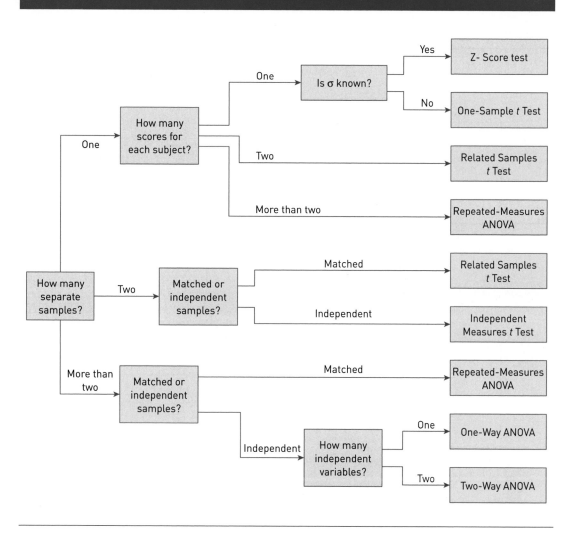

Selecting a Nonparametric Statistic

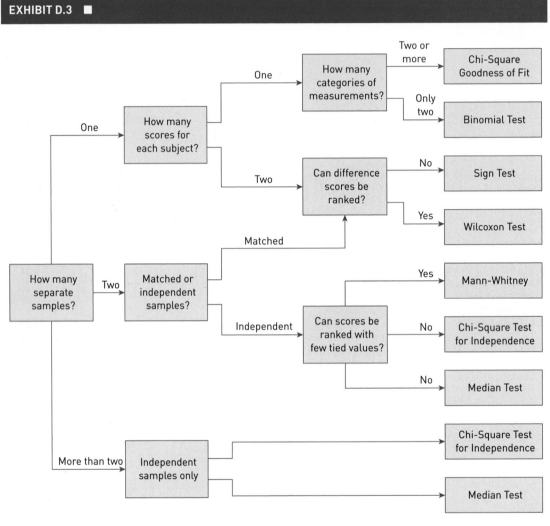

Selecting a Correlation

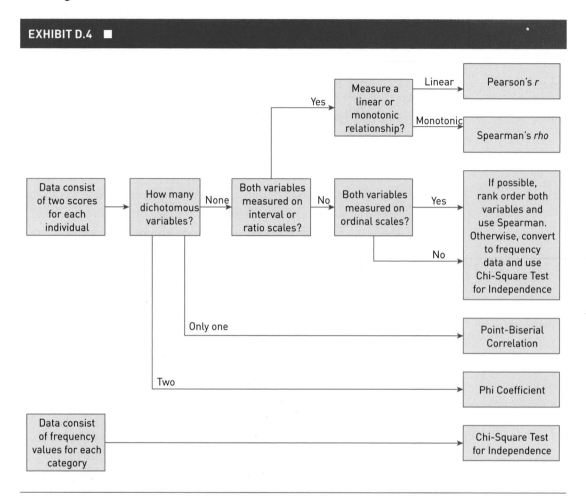

Source: Lammers, William J., and Pietro Badia, *Fundamentals of Behavioral Research* (Boston: Cengage Learning, 2004), Chapter 10, Figures 10.7–10.10. Used by permission. Copyright by William Lammers.

APPENDIX E

Results of the Quantitative Design Textbook Survey

A review of the current status of nonexperimental quantitative designs in business, social-behavioral sciences, and education used 30 contemporary research textbooks. The findings were an input for the development of a design typology for business. As noted in Chapter 6, the terms that label a design (design, method, technique, study, approach, and so forth) differ by context and are used interchangeably, producing ambiguities in definition and application.

In business research, it is well known that one of the cornerstones of design is structure. A structured design features a research question with specificity that guides the study, yet most business textbooks listed exploration as a design type. Although many designs contain elements of exploration, freestanding exploratory studies have such flexible structures that they transform themselves as they move toward *discovery* or attempt to *clarify an ambiguous situation*. Malholtra and Birks said it best by restricting the role of exploration as a way to augment or enhance a design: "Exploratory research may be the *initial step* in a research design."[1]

While useful (see Chapters 1 and 3), exploration does not fulfill any of the five design definitions and few of the design criteria. Legitimizing exploration as a design disregards the criterion of structure, the specificity that guides the study. It also undervalues design definitions, typological criteria, and the precedence of the research question. Freestanding exploratory studies have such flexible structures that they can morph into one of many forms of inquiry along their path to *discovery*. Routinely, there is no *a priori* formulation of the research question or, more importantly, a provision for answering it. For these reasons, exploration was not included as a design.

From a methodological standpoint, the finding that 70% of authors in education and social-behavioral research include correlational studies is surprising. "The term **correlational study** refers either to studies that do not employ any form of manipulation of the independent variable, or to studies that don't even identify an independent variable, because the hypothesis doesn't specify a causal relationship. So, in correlational studies we don't manipulate or select, we just measure."[2] Perhaps correlational studies have strong support because when statistical tools attempt to remove the effects of competing variables (or the "third-variable effect"), the X-Y relationship that is left often presents the *appearance* of causality. Appearance fits the maxim; correlation does not imply causation, although it is a necessary but *not sufficient condition* for causality. Gould adds, "The invalid assumption that correlation implies cause is probably among the two or three most serious and common errors of human reasoning."[3]

Most definitions of correlational *designs* are indistinguishable from *statistical techniques*. This is a remarkable finding because correlation with continuous variables is not even a robust statistic.[4] Researchers are cautious with the Pearson r when they suspect data abnormalities. It is sensitive to non-normal distributions, sample size, and is nonresistant to outliers. Pearson's r does not detect a nonlinear relationship unless a visualization tool is used to reveal it. Anscombe demonstrated this by graphing four data sets, each with *identical* summary statistics, but all with nonlinear patterns except one.[5] The confusion of design and statistical analysis was recognized over 38 years ago when Cook and Campbell stated, "The term correlational-design occurs in older methodological literature. . . We find the term correlational misleading since the mode of statistical analysis is not the crucial issue."[6]

Perhaps the best reason to suggest design status for correlation is the family of powerful statistical models associated with prediction and causal inference that use covariance/correlation matrices: advanced regression analysis, path analysis, Structural Equation Models (SEM), confirmatory factor analysis, PLS (partial least squares), PLS path and regression modeling, covariance/correlation structure models, and so forth. However, these are *statistical models* not designs.

The identification of causal-comparison studies as designs is prominent in education but also applies to business research with *ex post facto* designs. Many authors use the terms interchangeably. ***Ex post facto* studies**, because they compare pre-existing groups to some dependent variable, make after-the-fact claims of cause or consequences of pre-existing differences between two or more groups that vary on a variable of interest. Similarly, **causal-comparative studies** are said to (a) *detect associations* among variables but are principally interested in cause and effect; (b) usually start retrospectively with an observed difference between groups (an effect) and look for possible causes or consequences of this difference; (c) do not manipulate variables because that has already occurred; and (d) try to establish, after the fact, the cause or consequences of pre-existing differences between two or more groups that vary on a target variable.[7]

The *ex post facto* design (or causal-comparative) appears like a true experiment because of the way in which the groups are separated. But it is a nonexperimental design with the same drawbacks as correlational studies: direction of control and third-variable effects. Its name stems from the "assignment of participants to levels of the independent variable based on events that occurred *in the past* . . . between two or more groups of individuals with similar backgrounds who were exposed to different conditions as a result of their natural histories."[8] The dependent variable is then measured, and an inference is drawn. Sometimes, authors imply that causal relationships may be inferred from the records of historical differences. Such suggestions overlook the fact that manipulation of the independent variable or random assignment did not occur. Any inferences made do not meet the test for "strong inference" (see Chapter 1). Thus, causal conclusions are rarely justified.

As Johnson stated:

> If the primary distinction, in design, between a causal-comparative and a correlational study is the scaling of the independent variable (and not the manipulation of this variable), then, the obvious question is "Why can one supposedly make a superior causal attribution from a causal-comparative study?" The answer is that the contention is completely without basis.[9]

As with correlation, highly regarded scholars like Campbell, Stanley, Cook, Kerlinger, Pedhazur, and Schmelkin chose not to use the terms causal-comparative or *ex post facto* because of misrepresenting them as causally sound approaches for solving research problems.[10] Campbell and Stanley said that *ex post facto* was "judged to be unsatisfactory at the very best."[11] Typological usefulness (particularly mutual exclusiveness) renders these "designs" vulnerable to many criticisms.

A positive outcome from the design survey is the consensus that *description* meets the requirements for inclusion in a typology—by definition and criteria. Business, social-behavioral, and educational researchers agree on a description as a primary design objective whether using the label "descriptive" or "survey"—the latter being a *method*.

KEY TERMS

causal-comparative study   correlational study   *ex post facto* study

REFERENCES

1. Malhotra, Naresh K., and David F. Birks. *Marketing Research: An Applied Orientation.* 3rd European ed. Essex, UK: Prentice-Hall/Pearson, 2007: 65. Italics, mine.

2. Scholten, Annemarie Zand. "3.07 Experimental Designs." Lecture notes from Quantitative Methods." University of Amsterdam. https://www.coursera.org/learn/quantitative-methods/lecture/6Vdko/3-07-experimental-designs.

3. Gould, Stephen Jay. *The Mismeasure of Man.* 2nd ed. New York: W.W. Norton Publishing, 1996: 242.

4. Wilcox, Rand R. *Introduction to Robust Estimation and Hypothesis Testing.* 3rd ed. Cambridge, MA: Academic Press, 2012.

5. Anscombe, F. J. "Graphs in Statistical Analysis." *American Statistician* 27 (1973): 17–21. Cited in Chatterjee, S., and Bertram Price. *Regression Analysis by Example.* New York: John Wiley and Sons, 1977: 8.

6. Cook, T. D., and D. T. Campbell. *Quasi-Experimentation: Design and Analysis Issues for Field Settings.* Chicago: Rand McNally, 1979: 6. Emphasis in the original.

7. Fraenkel, Jack R., Norman E. Wallen, and Helen H. Hyun. *How to Design and Evaluate Research in Education.* 9th ed. New York: McGraw-Hill, 2015: Chapter 16.

8. Lammers, William J., and Pietro Badia. *Fundamentals of Behavioral Research.* Boston: Cengage Learning, 2004: 15–16. Copyright by William Lammers. http://uca.edu/psychology/fundamentals-of-behavioral-research-textbook/.

9. Johnson, Burke. "Toward a New Classification of Nonexperimental Quantitative Research." *Educational Researcher* 30, no. 2 (2001): 4.

10. Campbell, Donald T., and Julian C. Stanley. *Experimental and Quasi-Experimental Designs for Research.* New York: Houghton Mifflin (reprint), 1963; Cook, T. D., and D. T. Campbell. *Quasi-experimentation: Design and Analysis Issues in Field Settings.* Boston, MA: Houghton Mifflin, 1979; Kerlinger, F.N., and H. B. Lee. *Foundations of Behavioral Research.* 4th ed. Fort Worth, TX: Harcourt, 2000; and Pedhazur, E. J., & L. P. Schmelkin. *Measurement, Design, and Analysis: An Integrated Approach.* Hillsdale, NJ: Lawrence Erlbaum, 1991.

11. Campbell and Stanley, 64.

APPENDIX F

Brief Tutorial: Three Longitudinal Studies in One

Let's configure a hypothetical longitudinal study to compare trend, cohort, and panel studies and give you some design experience. You are interested in tracking the career performance of individuals who have served as military officers and separated from service with honorable discharges after completing their tours of duty. The time frame for military entry is from September 2001 until 2011 when Osama bin Laden was killed by U.S. forces in Pakistan. You will base the cohort date on the birth year of 1977. Officers entering the military upon commissioning at the end of university ROTC or Officers Candidate School require a 4-year bachelor's degree. But education policy experts now routinely use 6 years as a benchmark, not 4, for a bachelor's degree.[1] So you assume that the cohort will be 24 years old when they enter the military in 2001; upon discharge from duty (averaging 4 years), the cohort will be 11 years into their careers. The study ends in 2016 if one assumes no lapse in employment.

A recent study of "military CEOs" investigated the relationship between military service and future career performance in the civilian world.[2] The researchers proposed that military service makes a difference because (1) organized and sequential training creates leadership and command skills, (2) military experiences lead to better decisions under pressure or in a crisis, (3) officers advance to higher levels of authority and responsibility while at lower levels of command, and (4) military service provides a value system (duty, honor, country, dedication, and self-sacrifice) to encourage ethical behavior and company loyalty, even under adverse circumstances.

Since you are also interested in reliable measures of performance and career success, you adopt the measurements used by Ng et al., some of which were hours worked, work centrality, job tenure, organization tenure, work experience, transfer willingness, international experience, career planning, and political knowledge and skills.[3] For dependent measures, you gather data on salary level and promotion as objective measures and career satisfaction as a subjective measure. You will track the participants every 3 years using 2007 as a benchmark. You take a random sample of the officer population to be used for all three types of studies.

Your *trend study* follows the *general population of officers* who are pursuing their civilian careers, and it looks for general trends from 2007 to 2010, 2013, and 2016. Usually, the same population is used in subsequent rounds, but different samples (not resampled cases) are used, and thus there are fewer problems with attrition.

Your *cohort study* follows the *population of respondents born in 1977* who meet the sample requirements. They may be sampled randomly from the whole cohort or from a subset of the cohort (e.g., individuals from different branches of service or individuals now in certain industries, nonprofits, or NGOs) but they are not the same participants. The questioning also occurs during the prescribed intervals.

Your *panel study* is like the cohort but follows *the same individuals*. As a researcher, you must make a concerted effort to recruit the same respondents. The panel approach has the advantage of discovering differences in individual cases—which can be aggregated—but is not as successful in providing a focused picture of the changes in the overall cohort. Like the other two approaches to longitudinal studies, the panel collects data across intervals.

REFERENCES

1. Lewin, Tamar. "Most College Students Don't Earn a Degree in 4 Years, Study Finds." *The New York Times* (December 1, 2014). http://www.nytimes.com/2014/12/02/education/most-college-students-dont-earn-degree-in-4-years-study-finds.html?_r=0].

2. Benmelech, Efraim, and Carola Frydman. "Military CEOs." *Journal of Financial Economics* 117, no. 1 (2015): 43–59. http://www.nber.org/papers/w19782.pdf.

3. Ng, Thomas W. H., Lillian T. Eby, Kelly L. Sorensen, and Daniel C. Feldman. "Predictors of Objective and Subjective Career Success: A Meta-Analysis." *Personnel Psychology* 58, (2005): 367–408. http://www.psychologie.uni-mannheim.de/cip/tut/seminare_wittmann/meta_fribourg/sources/meta_obj_subj.pdf.

APPENDIX G

Tutorial: Organize Your Report With Timesaving Applications

When you browse for productivity aids and progress tracking apps, you will find many online that help you write better from sources like Entrepreneur.com, Medium, TheMuse, NYBookEditors, Lifehack, Zapier, Daily Genius, and many others. Some are complex, require significant immersion to understand their features and shortcuts, are costly, and take time away from your original goal: productivity. That's where some of the lesser known, simpler, and intuitive web apps come in. Although you may have already found a few favorites, like Grammarly, which checks grammar and style as well as keeping you from the unthinkable (plagiarism), there are other aspects of writing where you may need assistance.

After reviewing several of the offerings (one article boasted 17 apps and web tools to help you write a better research paper), I found one that may make a big difference in how you handle the details of your literature review and more. In Chapter 9, you read about different ways of structuring your presentation of the literature, but that discussion did not get into the low-level mechanics of organizing. To solve problems like this, Adriano Ferrari created a powerful but unassuming program called *Gingko* (gingkoapp.com) that was born out of his frustration while writing his doctoral dissertation.[1] The name is spelled differently than the tree.

Gingko has keyboard shortcuts, a generous FAQ, video tutorials, support staff, an online community, and more. When you have finished, you can export your results in a variety of formats, including Microsoft Word. "Gingko can be used as a writing tool, but it's equally effective for creating outlines before digging deeper into a piece of writing. [It] lets you connect different parts of your writing and visualize the structure of a piece."[2] In fact, it has mind-mapping–like features.[3]

When you are working with a long report (>30 pages), it is easy to become bogged down in the specifics and lose perspective. Gingko organizes information using a hierarchical card system, metaphorically like the branches and leaves of a tree. As the cards move to the right (three or more columns), they become more detailed. The card in the middle of Exhibit G.1 is the child of the parent card (left), and the center card underneath the child is the sibling since they are both at the same level of the hierarchy. "This horizontal approach can be really useful for planning out a big writing project. When

EXHIBIT G.1 ■ Organization Screen of the Gingko App

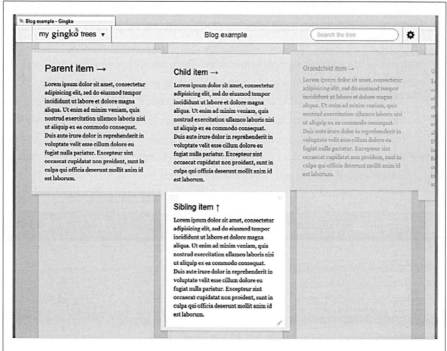

working with a vertical outline, filling out sections can make it hard to keep the overall outline visible. In Gingko you can make a single card as long as you want without losing the sense of where it fits within your horizontal tree."[4] An introductory video reveals the utility of this approach for writers (https://www.youtube.com/watch?v=egCKZHsICm8).

As an outlining and writing tool, Gingko is:

- Modular and movable: users can move or reorder cards to other columns, or click on a card to see connected siblings and their path.

- Operates in a "plain-text" environment for cross-platform applications and uses *Markdown* for syntax formatting (six levels of headings) and conversion.

- Is great for visual and spatial thinkers.

- Contains features for collaboration and presentation: users can lock cards and export them to a simple slideshow.[5]

You begin your tree as shown in the opening screen (Exhibit G.2). The illustration I will use is from Chapter 9, the study on the effects of source credibility and information quality on consumer attitudes and purchase intention in online apparel shopping. This study had an elaborate literature review that covered two main theories: the Theory of Reasoned Action and the Information Adoption Model. The authors also examined information quality, which, in the realm of online buying, refers to the product information and shopping advice provided by fellow consumers. This subtopic was divided into findings on relevance, accuracy, and comprehensiveness. Then the authors followed the research on source credibility, which included trustworthiness, expertise, and attractiveness of the information source. They concluded their review with three information sources in the online context: the retailer as a source, the interpersonal influence of electronic word-of-mouth (eWOM), and neutral sources (an expert or an independent source that provides online product recommendations from independent websites). The last aspect of their literature review is illustrated here in Exhibits G.5 and G.6.

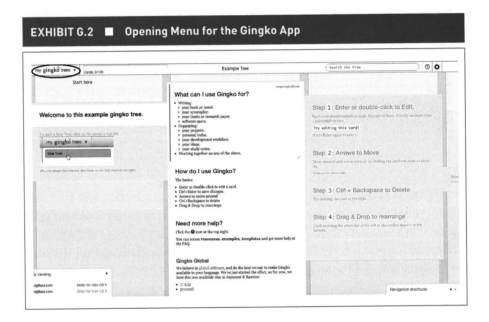

EXHIBIT G.2 ■ Opening Menu for the Gingko App

You begin your tree at the upper left corner (Exhibit G.2), which brings up a template menu (Exhibit G.3).

For this project, select Academic Paper. By selecting the Academic Template, a sample report outline—from the title through the references (Exhibit G.4)—is loaded. Spend some time reading through these examples so you can envision the possibilities for various aspects of your research (i.e., this tutorial focuses on the literature search). You can use several Gingko Trees to organize different parts of your report.

EXHIBIT G.3 ■ **Gingko Templates**

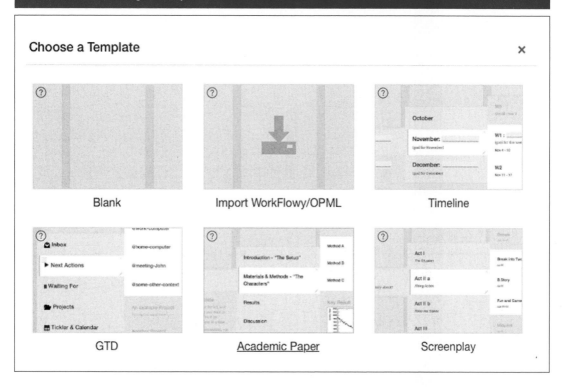

Choose a Template ✕

Blank   Import WorkFlowy/OPML   Timeline

GTD   Academic Paper   Screenplay

In the screen shown in Exhibit G.4, there are highlighted words to click for more examples and advice or you can check your current word count against your target for the section. Gingko also manages URLs and graphics.

Now, let's create an example using a portion of the online shopping study's literature on information sources: retailer, eWOM, and neutral. This tree is designed to be edited and viewed in full-screen mode; thus, it is hard to read as a screen capture.

The headings and text are as follows: Column 1 presents Online Information Sources. Column 2 presents Different Sources of Information: Retailer Source, eWOM Source, and Neutral Source. Column 3 further elaborates on each of the sources, such as Retailer Positives and Negatives, How Bloggers' Recommendations Count (eWOM), and The Nature of Neutral Sources.

To view the output in draft paragraph form, choose a format for export and the nature and size of the content (whole tree, cards, and subcards, etc.). Exhibit G.6 shows an exported file in formatted text (HTML) but the Microsoft Word version looks similar. The Word file, however, can be edited, which is more versatile for manuscript preparation.

my gingko tree ▼ | Cards: undefined/undefined

Academic Paper

search the tree

Title: Statement of your core result or finding.

Try to make your title an assertive statement, such as:

- "Changes in crystalline volume are sufficient to drive spindle scaling."

and not

- "High-performance silicon photoanodes passivated with ultrathin nickel films for water oxidation"

Rule of thumb: if your title would look weird with a period at the end, it is probably a poor title. Don't do this.

Abstract

Try to tell a story here, no matter what your field. You are writing for human beings, not computers. What's the area, what's the problem you are trying to understand. How? What have you found?

(You are summarizing your core results, not cramming them into this tiny space.)

Target: 84-151 words:
current: 43 ◎
Press v to get the word count.

How to use this template

The idea here is to start at the far left, and clarify what the core of what you want to say is first, and then expand on it by moving to the right, one column at a time.

After a couple of "passes" of expanding, you will end up with your complete, and well-structured paper on column 3, which you can export separately.

Here's a (somewhat dated) video which might help:

How to Use Gingko

Introduction – "The Setup"

[In field X, we still don't understand Y & Z.]

Write a summary of the question(s) you are trying to answer.

What is the state of the world before your research came along?

Also, answer the harsh but important question: Who cares?

In writing this, you can start general, but make sure clearly define the "before" state of the world's knowledge for the specific area this paper is addressing.

Materials & Methods – "The Characters"

[We have here method A, B, and our new method C.]

You have established that the core question(s) of your research. Now introduce the tools you are going to use to understand it.

Results

What happened? (objectively?)

Do not interpret, simply state the facts.

Let's be honest: the first thing most of us do when skimming a paper is look at the figures. If your key results can be presented in figures, then start with that, and structure your paper around that.

Discussion

Results are objective, but science isn't about listing data, it's about extracting meaning from what we observe.

What do your results tell you about the core problem you were investigating?

Conclusion

Bring it back to the big picture. How do your results fit into the current body of knowledge?

Most importantly, how can these results help you ask better questions?

References

We don't have bibliography support yet, but we do have "named links" so you can refer to specific links by name rather than repeating it each time.

"Black holes are cool." [1], and DNA is cool too [2]. But black holes are still cool, though not "absolute zero" cool [1].

primaxx: http://arxiv.org/abs/1311.7007
dnalter:
http://biorxiv.org/content/early/2015/11/07/010041

Intro – Assertive Statement 1

Here you can expand on your introduction. To guide your writing, title this card with assertive statement. Instead of "Problem Description", be direct: "The problem is that X doesn't do Y."

Intro – Assertive Statement 2

Intro – Assertive Statement 3

Method A

More details on the method, experiment design, etc. Remember that these are cards, so you can drag and drop them to rearrange if necessary.

Method B

More details on the method, experiment design, etc.

Method C

More details on the method, experiment design, etc.

If you need a checklist to make sure you address all points, go ahead:

e.g. "Mention pH of the setup?"
For how long?

Key Result

You can add figures if you'd like.

Remember these are cards so you can rearrange your results at will.
Any subcards will follow.

Conclusion (further detail)

Expand on your conclusion summary, and add more details to it.

Introduction

[You can write your actual paper here in this column. Then choosing "Export column 3" to Word or Markdown will help you move it to your final platform.]

...
...
...

Methods

Method A
...
...

Method B ...

Method C

You can keep notes & comments here.

Some other note. For example:

* xZinberg, make sure you include the voltage you used.

(the # syntax makes it easier to search for & filter comments directed at a specific person).

Notes on this reference.

Online Information Sources

In the decision-making process the information source is used by consumers to acquire the information needed to make a purchase decision (Park et al., 2011, p.22). Consumers search for product opinions to obtain the maximum of available information to reduce perceived risk associated with online purchase and product uncertainty, especially when it is impossible to evaluate a product or service on the basis of technical information (Tsao, 2014). Besides, consumers want to make an informed purchase decision, so that they collect information about product's features, prices, availability and warranties (Saxena, 2011, p.102). The common source to obtain information when shopping online is a retailer's website, which belongs to the group of marketer-controlled sources (Lee et al., 2008, p. 350).

Different Sources of Information

Literature is Contradictory

Researchers discovered that customers use different information sources in the decision making process. However, literature presents contradictory findings about which online information source they prefer. There are studies suggesting that customers lean toward customer reviews since they see other customers' opinion as more reliable and objective (Chen et al., 2016, p.468). On the other hand, there are researchers saying that information provided from anonymous people is not perceived as trustworthy (Chen et al., 2016, p.468). In order to better examine online information sources and their influence on purchase intentions, we included three information sources to our study.

Retailer Source

The fashion retailer website can provide a consumer with more detailed information about products such as product descriptions, prices, discounts, offers, ads, delivery information, after-purchase service and atmospherics cues (Chen et al., 2016, p.468). By visiting a retailer website, consumers expect to get firsthand, factual and objective information about the product or service as well as the information about the brand itself (Chen et al., 2016, p.468). Retailer's website consists of broad and up to date product information that helps a customer to make a decision (Steckel et al., 2005). Additionally, retailer's website offers various product alternatives that can be filtered in order to find the best matching product option (Chevalier & Mayzlin, 2006). Detailed product descriptions and product usage suggestions help consumers to make purchase decisions (Hye Park & Stoel, 2002, p.162).

eWOM Source

Hennig-Thurau et al. (2004, p.39), described eWOM communication as "any positive or negative statement made by potential, actual, or former customers about a product or company, which is made available to a multitude of people and institutions via the Internet". Digital WOM take place on various online platforms, such as blogs, discussion forums, review websites or social media networks, where consumers can post their opinions, comments and reviews of products (Cheung & Thadani, 2010, p.330). These new media support the information dissemination as it is almost certain for online users to encounter eWOM online review and share it further (Rabjohn, 2008, p.2). In contrast to WOM, eWOM communication has a high speed and reach of diffusion due to multiway exchanges of information on the Internet (Cheung & Thadani, 2010, p. 331), eWOM messages are more accessible and persistent as often they are archived, making them available for unlimited period of time (Hennig-Thurau et al., 2004). For the purpose of our study, bloggers were selected as being a good representative of eWOM.

Neutral Source

A neutral source is often called an expert or an independent source that provide online product recommendations from independent websites (Chen et al., 2016, p.468). Researchers claim that product reviews from independent sources are more persuasive than those from dependent sources, such as manufacturers and retailers, because they are perceived to be free from commercial influences (Alba et al., 1997). According to Chen et al. (2016, p. 468) consumers use information from neutral sources to reduce the uncertainty they feel toward information from retailers.

Retailer Positives and Negatives

Srinivasan et al. (2002) discovered that extensive retailer-related information from a retailer's source facilitates the customer's decision making process, as well as increases loyalty of a consumer who is interested in the retailer's offering. Nevertheless, research about retailer sources on consumer's attitude towards the source and purchase intention provided inconclusive findings. Some researchers argue that too vast information presented on a retailer's website confuses and overwhelms consumers making them postpone or resign from purchasing (Sismeiro & Bucklin, 2004; Steckel et al., 2005). On the contrary, other researchers state that even though information provided by a retailer might to a certain extent overwhelm potential customers, they are able to simplify information while using the website.

How Blogger's Recommendations Count

Blogs have a form of an online journals that contain a broad scope of information (Saxena, 2011, p.102). Blogs also serve as a self-representation of its authors because they often include information about the real identity of the author (Gilly & Schau, 2003). The author's background information serves as credentials showing the credibility of the blogger and the information he provides. (Zhu & Tan, 2007, p.2). The information read by consumers could be then perceived by the scope of the source, thus assigning suitable level of credibility. Published information can take a form of recommendation of a product or service what the blogger wants to share (Zhu & Tan, 2007, p.2). Thus, consumers who search for a product evaluation, could adopt his/ her opinion purchases (Hsu et al., 2013, p.71).

Nature of Neutral Sources

We use one type of neutral source, online expert reviews. In previous studies expert reviews have been compared with consumer reviews.Consumer recommendations considered as more trustworthy, but based on less expertise than expert recommendations (Huang & Chen, 2006). Expert refers to an independent established professional with expert status that could be identified through an affiliation to an independent entity or could be attributed by the consumers themselves (Plotkina & Munzel, 2016, p.2). However, we distinguish between self-proclaimed experts and professionals, who have special knowledge acquired through education or training. In this study, we use online product reviews from professional experts. As the sphere of our interest is fashion industry, we use professional stylists as experts who can provide online product reviews regarding apparel.

> ### EXHIBIT G.6 ■ Exported Literature File From Gingko
>
> **Online Information Sources**
>
> In the decision-making process the information source is used by consumers to acquire the information needed to make a purchase decision (Park et al., 2011, p.22). Consumers search for product opinions to obtain the maximum of available information to reduce perceived risk associated with online purchase and product uncertainty, especially when it is impossible to evaluate a product or service on the basis of technical information (Tsao, 2014). Besides, consumers want to make an informed purchase decision, so that they collect information about product's features, prices, availability and warranties (Saxena, 2011, p.102). The common source to obtain information when shopping online is a retailer's website, which belongs to the group of marketer-controlled sources (Lee et al., 2008, p. 350).
>
> **Different Sources of Information**
>
> *Literature is Contradictory*
>
> Researchers discovered that customers use different information sources in the decision making process. However, literature presents contradictory findings about which online information source they prefer. There are studies suggesting that customers lean toward customer reviews since they see other customers' opinion as more reliable and objective (Chen et al., 2016, p.468). On the other hand, there are researchers saying that information provided from anonymous people is not perceived as trustworthy (Chen et al., 2016, p.468). In order to better examine online information sources and their influence on purchase intentions, we included three information sources to our study.
>
> **Retailer Positives and Negatives**
>
> Srinivasan et al. (2002) discovered that extensive retailer-related information from a retailer's source facilitates the customer's decision making process, as well as increases loyalty of a consumer who is interested in the retailer's offering. Nevertheless, research about retailer sources on consumer's attitude towards the source and purchase intention provided inconclusive findings. Some researchers

REFERENCES

1. Used by permission of Adriano Ferrari. Please note: in March, 2018, Gingko was upgraded to a desktop app, open source, pay-what-you-want offering. You can still use the online version if writing online suits you better. But now there is Windows, Mac, and Linux compatibility in the downloadable version.

2. Cooper, Belle Beth. "10 Unsung Apps That Help You Write Better, Organize Work and Track Progress." *Zapier* (blog), June 4, 2015. https://zapier.com/blog/writing-apps/.

3. Houston, Natalie. "Write in a New Way With Gingko." *The Chronicle of Higher Education*, *ProfHacker* (blog), October 22, 2013. http://www.chronicle.com/blogs/profhacker/write-in-a-new-way-with-gingko/52975. The reviewer stated, "This is the first digital tool that offers mind mapping-like features in what is for me a truly intuitive design. I'm going to continue using Gingko for my own work and look forward to its continued development."

4. Cooper, op. cit.

5. Houston, op. cit. Also see an extended review by Dr Andus. "Gingko Looking for Beta Testers for Its Desktop App." *Dr Andus's Toolbox* (blog), November 8, 2016. https://drandus.wordpress.com/tag/gingko-app/.

GLOSSARY

Abduction: a form of logical inference in which one chooses the hypothesis that would be the best explanation if the evidence were true.

Abstract: a synopsis of a report that helps the reader quickly determine the paper's purpose; it reports what was done and is not a complete overview of the topic.

Academic Proposal: a document required by one's professor, sponsor, or granting institution to be certain the research meets standards established by the discipline and conventional scientific practices.

Action Research: combines research of organizational systems with the dynamics of organizational change and reveals how an organizational system perceives the need for change, articulates the desired outcome, and collaboratively plans and implements how to achieve a future goal.

Alternative Hypothesis: the logical opposite of the null hypotheses; states that there *is* a difference.

Appendices Section: often contains questionnaires and measuring instruments, instructional scripts for participants, interview transcripts, computer programs created for an original analytic purpose, derivations of equations, recruiting flyers, advertisements, telephone scripts, e-mail announcements of the study, consent forms and other Institutional Review Board–required materials, letters, photographs, data collection locations (maps), census charts, or a glossary.

Applied Research: has a problem-solving emphasis but contains the element of "understanding" before knowing what to do; the results of applied research in business are most relevant to managerial decision-making.

Backing (Toulmin): support that brings credibility to a warrant's reliability or relevance; also explains the connections between the data, warrant, and claim.

Basic Research (Pure, Conceptual, or Fundamental): examines issues of a theoretical nature to expand knowledge, theory and understanding but has a deferred impact on action, performance, or policy.

Block Randomization: results in groups of equal size. Researchers determine the optimal block size for the experiment (sometimes because of the group or cell sizes required by a statistic) and then randomly choose blocks to establish participant assignment.

Blocking Design: a type of noise-reducing experimental design that divides the sample into relatively homogeneous subgroups or "blocks."

Boundary Spanner: a relevant actor that operates as a liaison with other units in an organization.

Bounded System: a system (composed of persons, groups, dynamic situations, or processes) bounded in time and place. A case, for example, can be any bounded system that is of interest (see reference 72 in Chapter 7).

Boxplot: reduces the detail of the stem-and-leaf display to provide a "boxed" image of the distribution's location (median), spread, shape, tail length, and outliers.

Bracketing: the process in which a qualitative researcher identifies "what she or he expects to discover and then deliberately puts aside these ideas" (see reference 36 in Chapter 7).

Business Proposal: is a written document sent to a prospective client (solicited or unsolicited) to obtain their business. It consists, at a minimum, of an introduction, a statement of the client's problem, value of the project to the client, proposed methods and procedures to approach the problem, schedule and budget, and conclusion. It is designed to gain organizational access, acquire resources, and convince decision-makers that what is proposed will result in useful information or practical solutions to their problems.

Business Research: a systematic and objective process that provides information to solve problems and guide business decisions.

Calculated Value: the value from a statistical formula obtained as if you calculated the formula by hand; it compares your data with what is expected under the null hypothesis.

CARS Model: stands for Creating a Research Space and creates a rhetorical space and attracts readers into that space using "moves" and "steps." The three moves are establishing a territory (the situation), establishing a niche (the problem), and occupying the niche (the solution); the "moves" build an outline for action, and the "steps" provide specific ideas for writing the sections.

Case Study: a research procedure that uses an in-depth and detailed investigation of a case (a person, group, or situation over a period of time) and the related contextual conditions; in business it entails a study within a real-life, contemporary context or setting.

Categorical or Classificatory Variable: dichotomous and polytomous (multicategory) variables that are discrete because only certain finite values (categories) are possible.

Causal-Comparative Study: a study that is said to (a) *detect associations* among variables but is principally interested in cause and effect; (b) usually starts retrospectively with an observed difference between groups (an effect) and looks for possible causes or consequences of this difference; (c) does not manipulate variables because that has already occurred; and (d) tries to establish, after the fact, the cause or consequences of pre-existing differences between two or more groups that vary on a target variable (see reference 7 in Appendix E).

Central Tendency: descriptive measures of location that include the mean, median, and mode.

Claim (Toulmin): the statement, thesis, or assertion being argued; may be fact based, value based, or policy based.

Codebook: contains each variable in the study and specifies the application of coding rules to the variables.

Coding: involves assigning numbers or other symbols to respondent answers so the responses can be grouped into a limited number of categories that streamline the analysis.

Comparison Group: acts as a comparison to other groups that are receiving a treatment or manipulation of the independent variable in an experiment.

Concept: a generalized meaning associated with particular events, objects, conditions, and situations that aggregates objects or events that have common characteristics beyond a single observation.

Confounding Variable: an extraneous variable that influences the dependent variable.

Constant Comparison: a comparison of incoming data with those already collected so that the researcher does not wait until the end of the study to accumulate all of the data.

Construct: an image or idea invented explicitly for a given research, testing, or theory-building purpose; the combining of simpler concepts when the meaning an individual wants to communicate is not directly subject to observation.

Construct Validity: reveals whether a scale or test measures the construct adequately (what it claims to measure) and corresponds to an empirically grounded theory; the construct correlates with a known measure possessing convergent and discriminant validity.

Content Analysis: applied to the "subjective interpretation of the content of text data through the systematic classification process of coding and identifying themes or patterns" (see reference 52 in Chapter 7).

Continuous Panel: a longitudinal panel of respondents used in especially lengthy studies whose size reflects the need to compensate for attrition.

Continuous Variable: a metric (interval-ratio) variable that takes on any value in an ordered set of values in an infinite range.

Control: the researcher attempts to control for all influential factors *except* those whose effects are the focus of the investigation.

Control Group: receives no treatment; the experimental stimulus is withheld, or some standard treatment is used.

Control variable: a variable that is held constant (unchanging) throughout an experiment or observation designed to test the impact of the independent variable.

Correlational Hypothesis: states that variables occur together in some specified way that establishes an association or trend.

Correlational Study: does not employ any form of manipulation of the independent variable, or may not even identify an independent variable, because the hypothesis does not specify a causal relationship.

Covariance Design: a type of noise-reducing experimental design; it adjusts posttest scores for variability on the (continuous) covariate pretest.

Covariate: a continuous variable that acts as a control; it is not manipulated but rather observed and measured; it can affect the outcome of the study.

Covariate Adaptive Randomization: an alternative to stratified randomization; assigns new participants to treatment groups involving the technique of "minimization." Minimization works toward minimizing the total imbalance for *all factors together* instead of considering mutually exclusive subgroups (see reference 36 in Chapter 8).

Criteria for Causality: (1) the cause and effect are related, (2) the cause precedes the effect, (3) the cause and effect occur together (covary) consistently, and (4) alternative explanations can be ruled out.

Criterion Variable: the Y variable in correlation-based nonexperimental study.

Cross-Sectional: collects data at one point in time (thereby producing a snapshot) or during a single short interval to make comparisons across different types of participants or variables.

Data (Toulmin): the grounds, facts, or evidence on which the claim is based; used to prove or support the claim.

Data Analysis: the process of systematically using statistics or modeling techniques to explore the data through graphical illustration, descriptive summary statistics, and inferential statistical testing, and evaluation of hypotheses.

Data Collection: the systematic process of gathering information on variables of interest related to the research question or hypothesis; occurs in various settings from small focus groups to multinational organizations.

Data Entry: transforms the coded data gathered to a medium for viewing and statistical analysis.

Decision Tree: a decision support tool often used for statistical choices that uses a tree-like graph or to model and make decisions about possible outcomes.

Deduction: a form of reasoning that claims to be conclusive; the conclusions must necessarily follow from the reasons given if the premises are valid and the form is correct.

Dependent Variable (DV): the presumed effect in an experimental study.

Descriptive Hypothesis: typically states the existence, size, form, or distribution of some variable. As a univariate hypothesis, it contains only one variable; but may also refer to several variables or groups.

Descriptive Nonexperimental Design: a design in which the researchers are primarily describing and documenting the characteristics of the phenomenon; determining what exists about the size, form, frequency, or distribution of a variable with no attempt to analyze the effects of the variable(s) on the phenomenon.

Descriptive Statistics: a focus on the characteristics of the collected observations that does not assume that the data came from a larger population; using the measures of central tendency, variability, and shape to describe a distribution.

Descriptive Study: attempts to discover answers to the questions of who, what, when, and where; does not answer the question why.

Design: a logical plan for selecting and arranging the evidence that answers the research question(s); the framework for identifying relationships among variables; and the blueprint or overall strategy for the logical structure of the inquiry.

Design Subsection: the first subsection that follows the opening and overview statements of a report's Method section; emphasizes that design is at the apex of the logical hierarchy for answering the research question and establishes the study's purpose.

Dichotomous Variable: has only two values reflecting the presence or absence of a property.

Discontinuous Panel: differs from longitudinal continuous panels because the recruited participants and the pursued information differ with each project's goals.

Discrete Variable: dichotomous or polytomous (multicategory) variables that take on a finite number of values (categories).

Discussion Section: aims to interpret the results and explain to the reader the meaning of what the study accomplished, its contribution to the field, and recommendations for next steps.

Distribution: arrays data from the lowest to the highest scores on their scales and together with the frequency of occurrence, the observations produce a distribution of values, observed or theoretical.

Editing: detects errors and omissions, corrects them when possible, and certifies the achievement of minimum data quality standards.

Effect Size: the size or magnitude of the difference between groups (although it is used with correlation analysis and regression coefficients as well).

Element: in sampling, a specific pool of cases studied; the element is the unit of analysis in a population, which can be a participant, group, or organization being measured.

Element (Research Process): reflects *activities*, tasks, and decisions that all researchers must make in "doing" research from start to finish.

Embedding: the process of integrating or nesting strands of data in a mixed methods design in which a small amount of either quantitative or qualitative data are included within a larger qualitative or quantitative study.

Empirical Testing: uses "observations and propositions based on sensory experience and/or derived from such experience by methods . . . including mathematics and statistics" to test a hypothesis (see reference 3 in Chapter 2).

Equitable Recruitment: procedures that justly distribute burdens and benefits of the research.

Ethnography: "the study of a culture or cultures that some group of people shares, using participant observation over an extended period of time" (see reference 22 in Chapter 7).

Ex Post Facto Study: compares pre-existing groups to some dependent variable and makes after-the-fact claims of cause or consequences of pre-existing differences between two or more groups that vary on a variable of interest.

Executive Summary: is placed at the beginning of the business report, either before or after the table of contents, but before the introduction and is given a Roman numeral rather than an Arabic page number. It contains no quotations and is one page in length.

Experience Survey: is conducted by interviewing people who are experienced or are experts on the topic being under investigation to seek their ideas about important topical aspects or to discover what exists across the topic's range.

Experimental Realism: creates the phenomenon in a laboratory as it occurs in nature.

Explanatory Nonexperimental Design: aims to develop or test a theory about a phenomenon to explain "how" and "why" it operates or tries to explain how the phenomenon operates by identifying the causal factors that produce a change in it.

Explanatory or Causal Hypothesis: suggests that the presence of, or a change in, one variable (IV) causes an effect to occur in the other variable (DV).

Explanatory Study (Causal Experimental and Nonexperimental): goes beyond a description of phenomena to explain *how* and *why* an event occurs, depending on the level of causal inference demanded and the degree of control exerted by the researcher.

Exploratory Data Analysis (EDA): a perspective or way of thinking about data in which tools for visualization of the data reveal insights that direct subsequent analyses.

Exploratory Study: a preliminary or discovery-oriented study that is conducted to identify, diagnose, and explore a problem.

External Information: published data collected by others for their purposes.

External Validity: a found causal relationship generalized across persons, places, and times; the validity of inferences about whether the cause-effect relationship generalizes to persons, settings, treatment variables, and measurement variables (see reference 20 in Chapter 8).

Extraneous Variable: a variable not intentionally being studied or unknown to an experimenter that may affect the outcome or introduce error.

Factor: a controlled independent variable subdivided into levels that are set by the researcher.

Factor Level: two or more levels that are different values of the independent variable or treatment condition which has been subdivided for manipulation by the researcher. When factor levels are combined, they are referred to as the treatment.

Factorial Design: a randomized experiment (completely or by blocking) using multiple factors to determine their influence on the study's objective.

Feasibility Study: used when there are concerns that the obstacles of time, cost, and resources may reduce the likelihood of completing the full-scale project.

Focus Group: an unstructured interview with six to twelve participants used in exploratory research and as a follow-up diagnostic tool.

Grounded Theory: an approach to analyzing qualitative data in which repeated ideas are identified, summarized, and grouped into conceptual categories or broader themes, and a theory is built systematically from the ground up with "grounded" inductive observations (see reference 42 in Chapter 7) and deductive approaches to theory development.

Histogram: a diagram resembling a bar chart but displaying interval-ratio data.

Hypothesis: a proposition that is constructed for empirical testing.

Ill-Defined Problem: a class of complex problems for which there are no clear goals, solution paths, or anticipated solutions.

IMRAD: an acronym for a structure emphasizing the Introduction, Methods, Results, and Discussion.

Independent Variable (IV): the variable that researchers manipulate to explain variance in the dependent variable.

Induction: draws a conclusion from one or more particulars (specific facts or pieces of evidence). The premises are intended to be strong enough that if they were true, it would be *improbable* that you would produce a false conclusion.

Inferential Statistics: data from a sample to make inferences, or estimates, about a population in contrast to the numerical summaries of descriptive statistics.

Informed Consent: the participant in the research must be competent to consent and must have information about what will happen so that he or she can consent voluntarily.

Institutional Review Board (IRB): the ethics review board that must review and approve a study that meets federal criteria for the use of human subjects.

Instruments Subsection: describes the mechanisms used for data collection (e.g., materials, tests, measures, questionnaires, etc.).

Intact Group: a department or team.

Internal Information: is information collected by an organization and used by researchers within that organization for conducting a decision-making study.

Internal Validity: discerns whether a study's findings imply cause while other explanations are ruled out.

Interpretivist/Naturalistic Worldview: a view held by qualitative researchers who believe that people construct an image of reality based on their own preferences and prejudices and their interactions with others (see reference 73 in Chapter 1).

Interquartile Range: the difference between the first and third quartiles of the distribution; also referred to as the midspread.

Interval Variable: has both order and equality of distance between points but an arbitrary origin on scales that measure continuous variables.

Intervening Variable (IVV): a conceptual mechanism through which the independent variable and moderating variable might affect the dependent variable; also known as a mediating variable.

Introduction: starts on the third page of the manuscript and contains the running head and page number; begins with an introduction to the problem, an exploration of its importance, a discussion of the related literature, and a statement of the hypotheses and how they reflect the literature that the researcher's argument developed.

Investigative Question: a facet or sub-issue of the research question that the research must answer satisfactorily to respond to the general question.

IRB Protocol: a document that covers similar components of the research process as a proposal but goes further by determining if what is proposed constitutes "research" and protects the rights and welfare of human subjects by minimizing harm or injury.

Key Informant: people most knowledgeable about the culture; used by ethnographers in interviews.

Kurtosis: a measure of a distribution's peakedness or flatness.

Limitations Subsection: the fourth section of the Discussion portion of the report; states the limitations or weaknesses of the study and reveals how these flaws could affect the conclusions.

Literature Review (Formal): a "written document that presents a logically argued case founded on a comprehensive understanding of the current state of knowledge about a topic of study. The case establishes a convincing thesis to answer the study's question" (see reference 45 in Chapter 3).

(Literature) Synthesis Matrix: a useful tool for organizing literature findings; a table that can be drawn by hand with added rows and columns as the literature expands.

Lived Experience: the kind of human experiences studied in phenomenology.

Longitudinal Cohort: a study in which a population or subpopulation includes individuals who have a common characteristic or have experienced a similar event during a fixed period (typically birth).

Longitudinal Panel: samples and tracks the same respondents (usually individuals or households) by collecting repeated measures on the same set of variables at two or more points in time.

Longitudinal (Prospective) Study: collects data from respondents (or multiple groups) at several points in time, starting in the present and going into the future.

Longitudinal Trend: samples different groups of people (but independent samples from the same general population) at various points in time but typically asks the same questions.

Managerial Question: represents a type of research question associated with business decisions that managers must make.

Manipulation: occurs when a researcher manipulates or systematically varies the levels (often called conditions) of an independent variable (IV) and then measures the outcome of interest, the dependent variable (DV).

Matching: attempts to obtain comparable groups to recreate the feature of randomization; its intent is equivalent or balanced groups.

Mean: the arithmetic average and the measure of central tendency most often used for interval-ratio data.

Measurement: occurs when a number is assigned to a characteristic of a person, object, or event, in a reliable and valid way.

Measurement Question: asks for information from the participants in the study using various instruments, scales, or devices.

Measures of Shape: refers to skewness and kurtosis, which describe departures from the symmetry of a distribution and its relative flatness (or peakedness), respectively.

Median: the value at the midpoint of the distribution so there is an equal likelihood of falling above or below it.

Method of Data Collection: implements the design using accepted techniques or, sometimes, tailored procedures.

Method Section: is tied to the research problem and reports the process by which the research question was answered or hypotheses were tested.

Missing Data: occur "when there are no data whatsoever for a respondent (non-response) or when some variables for a respondent are unknown (item non-response) because of refusal to provide or failure to collect the response" (see reference 7 in Chapter 5).

Mixed Design: integrates quantitative and qualitative designs, the methods they employ, and a *pragmatic* *relativist paradigm* into a single study that prioritizes either a quantitative or qualitative strategy as dominant or accepts them as having equal status in answering the research question.

Mode: the most frequently occurring value in a distribution.

Moderating Variable (MV): influences the relationship between two other variables and thus produces an interaction effect.

Narrative: a form of qualitative design in which the researcher focuses on how respondents impose order on the flow of experience in their lives and thus make sense of the events and actions they have experienced (see reference 54 in Chapter 7).

Naturalistic Observation: occurs within an ecology that is natural for those being studied.

Naturalistic Setting: a field setting.

Netnography: uses "ethnographic methods to study online communities developed by people with similar interests or backgrounds" (see reference 32 in Chapter 7).

Nominal Scale: used to name, categorize, or classify measurements.

Nonequivalent Groups Design: a frequently used quasi-experimental between-subjects design in which participants are not equivalent (i.e., are not randomly assigned to conditions).

Nonexperimental Design: "a systematic empirical inquiry in which the scientist does not have direct control of independent variables because their manifestations have already occurred or because they are inherently not manipulable. Inferences about relations among variables are made without direct intervention, from concomitant variations of independent and dependent variables" (see reference 8 in Chapter 6).

Nonparametric Test: has fewer and less stringent assumptions about the shape or parameters of the underlying population distribution; does not specify a normally distributed population, or equality of variance is not relevant. It is used with nominal and ordinal data.

Nonprobability Sample: is not random and provides no information about the likelihood of an element being included (i.e., the probability of selecting an element in the population is unknown).

Nonresistant Statistics: statistics that are affected by outliers in the distribution.

Null Hypothesis: a statement of no difference between the population parameter and the sampling statistic being compared to it.

Observation: "the selection, provocation, recording, and encoding of that set of behaviors and settings concerning organisms (in situ) which is consistent with empirical aims" (see reference 10 in Chapter 7).

Observational Method: the researcher's observation of behavioral patterns of people through the detailed and systematic recording of what the research subjects say and do.

One-Tailed Test: places the entire probability of rejecting the null hypotheses into the tail of the distribution specified by the direction of the alternative hypothesis.

Operational Definition: states specific operational, measurement, and testing criteria.

Ordinal (Ranking) Variable: a variable that is rank ordered or observations that involve relational comparisons, e.g., a > b, b > c, therefore a > c.

Out-of-Range Response: a response above or below the researcher's predetermined range for the variable.

Paradigm: a set of assumptions or a belief system shared by members of a scientific community.

Paradigm Weighting: a mixed methods design process in which the researcher prioritizes (equalizes, weights, or ascribes dominance) to either qualitative or quantitative designs depending on the importance placed on the "fit" of the paradigm for the research question.

Parametric Test: relies on assumptions about the population from which the sample was drawn and uses metric (interval-ratio) data.

Participant Observation: a researcher is present in a setting that is typical for the participants; the researcher interacts with participants or may join or share in the group's activities as a member.

Participant Observer: a technique of research in which a researcher gains access to a setting and observes it.

Participant Reactivity: an awareness of being observed that may result in negative, positive, or no reaction.

Participants Subsection: a section of the report used to describe the study's demographic characteristics.

Phenomenology: studies human experiences through the introspective descriptions of the people involved.

Pilot Study: a small-scale version of the larger study performed to detect weaknesses in the research design, instructions to participants, measuring instruments, non-response and attrition rates, missing data percentages, and proxy data for the final decision about a sampling plan and its size.

Polytomous (Multicategory) Variable: has several values representing different categories of group membership.

Population: the total collection of elements about which the researcher wants to make inferences.

Positivist/Post-Positivist Worldview: a view held by researchers that are preoccupied with the scientific method because it emphasizes the most objective methods to achieve the closest estimate of empirical reality.

Practical Implications Subsection: provides insights for the reader when the research is oriented toward the applied side of the continuum.

Practical Research: fits somewhere in the middle of the continuum between basic and applied research and is more common in business because the solutions tell managers "what to do." The solutions are action oriented and provide an answer to the question that helps managers know "what to do to change or fix some troublesome or at least improvable situation" (see reference 50 in Chapter 1).

Pragmatism Worldview: sidesteps the contentious issues of truth and reality, accepts, philosophically, that there are singular and multiple realities that are open to empirical inquiry and orients itself toward solving *practical* problems in the "real world" (see reference 79 in Chapter 1).

Predictive Model: any method that produces predictions, regardless of its underlying mathematical approach.

Predictive Nonexperimental Design: research that is conducted so that it can be used to predict or forecast some event or phenomenon in the future or predict a definite course of action, evaluate future values, or assess the likelihood of a future behavior, condition, or outcome with one or more DVs.

Predictive Study: attempts to anticipate future performance before it occurs, usually with regression-based statistics and advanced modeling techniques.

Predictor Variable: the X variable in correlation-based nonexperimental studies.

Pre-experiment: typically has no control group available for contrast (or an equivalent nontreatment group).

Premise: an assumption that the researcher takes tentatively to be true in reasoning.

Pretesting: the initial test given to a participant, subject, or object being observed or measured; an aspect of pilot studies in which instruments are evaluated for utility and reliability ahead of the actual study

Probability Sample: based on random selection—a controlled procedure that assures each population element is given a known nonzero chance of selection.

Problem and Its Setting Module: an eight-point option for reorganizing the Introduction of a report.

Procedure Subsection: the section of the report in which the reader learns how the data were collected and the study was carried out.

Proposal: an academic, IRB protocol, or business plan of work used to secure approval to proceed with the research study.

Proposition: makes a statement about concepts that is judged true or false if it refers to observable phenomena.

p-Value: the probability of obtaining a value of the test statistics as extreme as, or more extreme than, the actual value obtained when the null hypothesis is true.

Qualifier (Toulmin): adds limits, nuances, or specificity to the claim, providing a context under which the argument is true; helps to counter rebuttals.

Qualitative Design: aims to discover and understand individuals' experiences, perceptions, and interactions and to make sense of and interpret the derived meanings from their thoughts, actions, and events in the wider context of inquiry.

Quartile Deviation (Q): used as a measure of dispersion with the median for ordinal data.

Quasi-experimental: comprises "research that resembles experimental research but is not true experimental research" (see reference 43 in Chapter 8).

Quota Matrix: a technique based on nonprobability sampling for balancing groups often by employing nominal demographic variables to match the sample proportion to the population (e.g., if 55% of the population are female, the matrix assigns 55% of the sample's females to predetermined groups).

Random Assignment: the assignment of participants to groups (or different conditions) using a random procedure such as a random number generator.

Random Sampling: a sampling procedure to ensure that each element in the sampling frame has an equal chance of being included in the sample.

Random Selection: a controlled procedure assuring that each population element is given a known nonzero chance of selection.

Randomized-based Design: relies on random assignment to produce group equivalence, to balance treatment and control groups, or to compensate for confounding variables.

Range: the difference between the largest and smallest value in the distribution and computed from the minimum and maximum scores.

Ratio Variable: the highest measurement level with all of the powers of ranking, equal distance between scale points plus an absolute zero or point of origin.

Realism Worldview: a view embraced by some researchers that is somewhat similar to positivism in that "reality exists independent of the mind and that what a researcher's senses show her or him is the truth, although the researcher is influenced by worldviews and their own experiences" (see reference 77 in Chapter 1).

Rebuttal (Toulmin): mitigates likely objections and counter-arguments to the claim by suggesting reasons

why a counter-claim is flawed, lacks credibility, or is not reasonable or realistic.

Recruitment Plan: a plan that *follows IRB/professor approval* and should consider several activities: (a) identifying the eligible population, (b) targeting and enlisting volunteers, (c) creating an unbiased presentation of the research purpose, (d) recruiting for a sampling plan to account for an anticipated dropout rate and meeting sample size and power requirements, (e) obtaining verifiable informed consent, and (f) retaining participants (see reference 39 in Chapter 4).

References Section: lists all sources used in the report; begins on a new page with the heading centered at the top of the page in upper and lower-case letters (not bold, underlined, or in quotes).

Regression-Discontinuity Design: an underused type of experimental design with internal validity characteristics that produce inferences comparable to randomized experiments/randomized controlled trials and is stronger than nonequivalent groups designs.

Relational Hypothesis: a statement that describes the relationship between two or more variables.

Reliability: the extent to which the tool produces consistent results. Reliable instruments produce dependable results at different times under different conditions.

Reporting Study: performs the most basic purpose of research: delving into an issue or topic "to provide an account of something" (see reference 15 in Chapter 1).

Research Data: are "collected, observed, or created, for purposes of analysis to produce original research results" (see reference 1 in Chapter 5).

Research Design: a logical plan to select and arrange the evidence that answers the research question(s); a framework to specify the relationships among a study's variables; a blueprint to outline each procedure from the hypotheses to the analysis of data; a means of configuring the study to its paradigm (e.g., achieving findings that are numeric, systematic, generalizable, and replicable) or obtaining non-numerical observations that reveal and detail the experience and constructed meanings of individuals, groups, situations, or contexts); and a means to determine how to allocate limited resources of time and budget.

Research Ethics: the analysis of ethical issues raised when people are involved as research participants.

Research Hypothesis (H₁): an insightful guess, speculation, or an even more rigorous assessment of the research outcome.

Research Problem: a fact-oriented, information gathering statement of what the researcher wants to investigate or study quantitatively or qualitatively.

Research Process: consists of seven phases: exploring, planning, creating, conducting, collecting, analyzing, and writing.

Research Protocol: a detailed application describing the planned research, which IRB reviewers use to determine if regulatory requirements have been achieved.

Research Question: the single question that best states the objective of the research study in a clear and focused way.

Research Report: represents communication in which the researcher describes the nature and importance of the problem, the sources discovered to enlighten its background, the methods chosen to collect primary data, the analysis, the interpretation, and the conclusions or solutions found.

Research Topic: a broader version of the research question, which states the objective of the research study in a clear and focused way.

Resistant Statistics: statistics that are unaffected by outliers in a distribution and change only slightly with small replacements of the data set.

Results Section: presents results of the report in a sequence that reflects the order of the research and investigative questions and, ideally, the order of the hypotheses.

Retrospective Case-Control: a study that compares specific characteristics of participants or an outcome of interest with participants who do not have that outcome (controls), and looks back retrospectively to examine the frequency of exposure to a risk factor.

Retrospective Cohort: a researcher goes back in time with individuals who are alike on many dimensions but one group differs on a characteristic of interest (i.e., an event, condition, exposure, diagnosis, or outcome).

Retrospective Study: a historically oriented study that looks back to more than one period—ideally, to make comparisons or establish a trend.

Sample: a probability or nonprobability selection of the elements of a population.

Sampling: the process in which the researcher selects some of the elements of a population, so that conclusions can be drawn about the entire population.

Sampling Frame: a list of all eligible individuals in a population.

Sampling Plan and Procedures: in a report, it should follow the method and precede the description of the participants (sample elements).

Scaling: a "procedure for the assignment of numbers (or other symbols) to a property of objects in order to impart some of the characteristics of numbers to the properties in question" (see reference 16 in Chapter 4).

Scientific Method: the process of scientific inquiry in which a researcher states a problem, creates a hypothesis to explain the problem, deduces consequences and formulates several rival hypotheses, devises a decisive empirical test to exclude one or more hypotheses as the explanation, draws a conclusion, and feeds information back into the problem.

Secondary Data: are represented by two source categories: internal and external. An enterprise collects internal information for its purposes. External information is published data collected by others for their purposes.

Self-selection (to Groups): a process in which participants choose the treatment condition for themselves.

Signal Enhancer or Noise Reducer: in experimental designs, the signal is analogous to the study variable—the program or treatment being implemented. Noise introduces variability from all of the extraneous variables that confuse the strength of the signal.

Simple Randomization: involves the assignment of participants to control and treatment groups through conventional methods (coin toss, odd-even numbers in a card deck, dice, random number tables and generators).

Skewness: a measure of a distribution's deviation from symmetry.

Standard Deviation: a measure of variability and the positive square root of the variance.

Statistical Assumption: a requirement for the use of a chosen statistical test.

Statistical Conclusion Validity: the validity of inferences about the correlation (covariation) between treatment and outcome.

Statistical Null Hypothesis: a statement of "no difference" designed for statistical testing; by challenging the research hypothesis, the statistical null hypothesis states that the IV *does not make a difference* or that any observed difference is due to sampling error.

Statistical Power: the probability (typically set at not less than 80%) of rejecting the null hypothesis when the alternative hypothesis is, in fact, true.

Statistical Significance: in hypothesis testing, this is the probability associated with determining if a result is unlikely to have occurred by chance alone.

Stem-and-Leaf Display: is closely related to histograms but presents actual data values that can be inspected directly without the use of enclosed bars.

Strand: a qualitative study's component that incorporates the major processes of conducting research: posing a research question, collecting data, analyzing data, and interpreting results (see reference 93 in Chapter 7).

Stratified Randomization: focuses on controlling confounding variables (covariates) that influence the study's outcome. Researchers identify specific covariates through the literature, experience, or foreknowledge of the recruitment pool before group assignment.

Strong Inference: consists of applying the following steps to every problem in science, formally and explicitly and regularly: (1) devising alternative hypotheses, (2) devising a crucial experiment with alternative possible outcomes, and (3) carrying out the experiment so as to get a clean result.

Subject or Attribute Variable: a personal characteristic that is not changeable, such as ethnicity, personality, education, intelligence, or gender.

Suggestions for Future Research Subsection: the conclusion of discussion section of report; usually contains recommendations for future research and "a

reasoned and justifiable commentary on the importance of your findings. This concluding section may be brief or extensive provided that it is tightly reasoned, self-contained, and not overstated" (see reference 56 in Chapter 9).

Survey: a method of descriptive research used to collect primary data from people. The research question, which drives the survey, focuses on specific aspects of participants' opinions, attitudes, beliefs, motivations, and behavior. It often seeks to discover relationships among variables, not merely describe them; and a representative sample from the population is used to generalize findings back to the target population.

Systematic Assessment (IRB): evaluates the probabilities and magnitudes of possible harm and anticipated benefits.

Systematic Observation: an alternative to self-reporting (i.e., asking the participants what they do or other forms of reporting such as behavioral ratings or reports completed by asking others who draw from cumulative experience with the participant's behavior) (see reference 11 in Chapter 4).

Textual Data: can be in the form of interview transcripts, field notes from different observer and interviewer roles, diaries, journals, social media textual information, or documents (e.g., e-mails, reports, minutes of meetings, memos, and personal letters).

Theoretical Implications Subsection: the part of the report that discusses the study in relation to existing work.

Theoretical Sampling: is based on concept representativeness and consistency.

Theory: systematically *interrelates* concepts, constructs, definitions, and hypotheses to explain and predict phenomena (facts).

Time Dimension: comprises cross-sectional, longitudinal, and retrospective studies.

Time Order: refers to when studies are conducted at the same time or one after another.

Title Page: is the first page of a manuscript and it is separate; summarizes the main idea of a study by identifying variables and theoretical issues.

Toulmin Model (Reasoning/Argumentation): involves six components that evaluate the pros and cons of an argument and the effectiveness of rebuttals. The first three components follow the practice of making a claim, supporting that claim with data, and backing the data or evidence with a warrant—all are present in every argument. Three additional elements of Toulmin's model include a backing (for the warrant), rebuttals, and qualifier(s) that may be added as necessary.

Triangulation: a "process of verification that increases validity by incorporating several viewpoints and methods . . . [and] refers to the combination of two or more theories, data sources, methods or investigators in one study of a single phenomenon to converge on a single construct, and can be employed in both quantitative (validation) and qualitative (inquiry) studies" (see reference 85 in Chapter 7).

True Experiment: the strongest design for determining a cause-and-effect relationship; maximizes internal validity.

Two-Tailed Test: corresponds with a nondirectional hypothesis and splits the probability of an unlikely outcome into two regions of rejection.

Typology: a form of classification that conceptually separates a set of items on multiple characteristics and distills them into fewer generalizable dimensions, which are intended to be nonoverlapping (mutually exclusive) and exhaustive categories.

Unobtrusive Measure: refers to "data gathered by means that do not involve direct elicitation of information from research subjects. Unobtrusive measures are unique and 'non-reactive'" (see referenced 14 in Chapter 7).

Unstructured or Exploratory Literature Review: refines the research question and determines what is needed to secure answers to the proposed research. Typically, the process begins with an exploratory literature review that reveals terminology and contribution areas (books, journal articles, white papers, government documents, annual reviews, statistical databases, and annotated bibliographic sources).

Validity: the extent to which the tool measures what it claims to measure—or accuracy.

Variability: the spread or dispersion of a set of data that is described by the descriptive statistics of standard deviation, variance, range, and interquartile range.

Variable: anything that can vary (i.e., that can assume multiple values and can change or be changed, counted or scaled).

Variance: the average of the squared deviation scores from the mean; it shows how far a set of numbers are spread out from their average value.

Warrant (Toulmin): demonstrates the connection between data and claim by creating a bridge that shows why the evidence supports the claim and makes it true.

Worldview: a point of view, mindset, philosophy, or conception of the world that shapes one's view of "knowing."

REFERENCES

CHAPTER 1

1. Medawar, Peter B. *Pluto's Republic.* Oxford: Oxford University Press, 1982: 2.

2. Taylor, Paul, Kim Parker, Rich Morin, Rick Fry, Eileen Patten, and Anna Brown. "The Rising Cost of Not Going to College." *Pew Research Center: Social & Demographic Trends*, February 14, 2014. http://www.pewsocialtrends .org/2014/02/11/the-rising-cost-of-not-going-to-college/; Caumont, Andrea. "Six Key Findings About Going to College." *Pew Research Center: Fact-tank*, February 11, 2014. http://www.pewresearch.org/fact-tank/2014/02/11/6-key-findings-about-going-to-college/. Pew defined the millennial generation as those born after 1980 (which would include adults aged 18 to 32 in 2013). The report references millennial ages 25 to 32 when most survey participants have completed their formal education and entered the workforce.

3. NACE Staff. "The Top-Paid Majors for the Class of 2018." National Association of Colleges and Employers: 2018 Salary Survey. January 8, 2018; and "Top-Paid Business Majors at the Bachelor's and Master's Levels." National Association of Colleges and Employers: 2015 Salary Survey. February 18, 2015. https://www.naceweb .org/job-market/compensation/the-top-paid-majors-for-the-class-of-2018/; also see http://careers.kenne saw.edu/employers/docs/2018-nace-salary-survey-winter.pdf.

4. PayScale. "2017–2018 College Salary Report: Best Schools for Business Majors by Salary Potential." Seattle, WA: PayScale Inc., 2017. https://www.payscale. com/college-salary-report/best-schools-by-majors/ business.

5. Strauss, Karsten. "These Are the Skills Bosses Say New College Grads Do Not Have." *Forbes*, May 17, 2016. http://www.forbes.com/sites/karstenstrauss/ 2016/05/17/these-are-the-skills-bosses-say-new-college-grads-do-not-have/#5ec3e6a8596e.

6. Adams, Susan. "The 10 Skills Employers Most Want in 2015 Graduates." *Forbes*, November 12, 2014. http:// www.forbes.com/sites/susanadams/2014/11/12/the-10-skills-employers-most-want-in-2015-graduates/ #b8617c519f6f.

7. Hart Research Associates. "Falling Short? College Learning and Career Success: Selected Findings From Online Surveys of Employers and College Students Conducted on Behalf of the Association of American Colleges and Universities." Washington, DC: Hart Research, 2015: 12. https://www.aacu.org/sites/default/ files/files/LEAP/2015employerstudentsurvey.pdf.

8. Levy, Francesca, and Jonathan Rodkin. "The Bloomberg Recruiter Report: Job Skills Companies Want But Can't Get." *Bloomberg*, April 24, 2015. http://www .bloomberg.com/graphics/2015-job-skills-report/.

9. AACSB International. "Eligibility Procedures and Accreditation Standards for Business Accreditation." Updated September 22, 2017: 53. Italics, mine. http:// www.aacsb.edu/accreditation/standards (see full PDF, 2017 update).

10. Duarte, Nancy. "How to Present to Senior Executives." *Harvard Business Review*, October 4, 2012. https://hbr .org/2012/10/how-to-present-to-senior-execu.

11. Stanko, Michael A., Jonathan D. Bohlmann, and Roger J. Calantone. "Outsourcing Innovation." *The Wall Street Journal*, November 30, 2009. https://www.wsj .com/articles/SB100014240529702044883045744265 21384198990.

12. Weiss-Mayer, Amy L. "Case Study: Consulting After College." *The Crimson.Com*, November 6, 2014. http://www.thecrimson.com/article/2014/11/6/ consulting-after-harvard-fm/.

13. Valenzuela, Dan A. "All Is Fair in Love and Jobs." *The Crimson.com*, November 11, 2016. http://www.thecrimson.com/column/just-maybe-do-it/article/2016/11/11/alls-fair-love-jobs/.

14. McDonald, Duff. "M.B.A. Programs That Get You Where You Want to Go." *New York Times*, April 7, 2015. http://www.nytimes.com/2015/04/12/education/edlife/mba-programs-that-get-you-where-you-want-to-go.html?_r=0.

15. UTS Business School. *Guide to Writing Assignments*. 3.1 ed. Sydney, Australia: University of Technology, 2014: 30. http://www.uts.edu.au/node/50946/.

16. Douglas, Alex, and Brian Johnson. "Corporate Social Reporting in Irish Financial Institutions." *The TQM Magazine* 16, no. 6 (2004): 387–395. https://doi.org/10.1108/09544780410563301.

17. Chen, Stephen, and Petra Bouvain. "Is Corporate Responsibility Converging? A Comparison of Corporate Responsibility Reporting in the USA, UK, Australia, and Germany." *Journal of Business Ethics* 87, no. S1 (2009): 299–317. https://doi.org/10.1007/s10551-008-9794-0.

18. Czarniawska, Barbara. Narratives in Social Science Research: Introducing Qualitative Methods. London: SAGE, 2004.

19. Gerring, John. "What Is a Case Study and What Is It Good For?" *American Political Science Review* 98, no. 2 (May 2004): 349. http://www.jstor.org/stable/4145316.

20. Keaveney, Susan M. "Customer Switching Behavior in Service Industries: An Exploratory Study." *Journal of Marketing* 59, no. 2 (1995). https://doi.org/10.2307/1252074.

21. Platt, John R. "Strong Inference: Certain Systematic Methods of Scientific Thinking May Produce Much More Rapid Progress than Others." *Science* 146, no. 3642 (1964): 347–353. https://doi.org/10.1126/science.146.3642.347.

22. Gartner, William B. "A Conceptual Framework for Describing the Phenomenon of New Venture Creation." *Academy of Management Review* 10, no. 4 (1985): 696–706. http://www.jstor.org/stable/258039.

23. TNS/Kantar Media. "Online Copyright Infringement Tracker Latest Wave of Research (March 2017): Overview and Key Findings." Prepared for the Intellectual Property Office, July 2017. https://www.gov.uk/government/uploads/system/uploads/attachment_data/file/628704/OCI_-tracker-7th-wave.pdf

24. Shmueli, Galit. "To Explain or to Predict?" *Statistical Science* 25, no. 3 (2010): 2. https://arxiv.org/pdf/1101.0891.pdf (pages renumbered from the original [289–310] to 1–23 in the electronic reprint).

25. Ibid., 3.

26. Platt, 347.

27. "Aircrew Safety and Health: Cosmic Ionizing Radiation." National Institute for Occupational Safety and Health (NIOSH) Division of Surveillance, Hazard Evaluations and Field Studies. Atlanta, GA: Centers for Disease Control and Prevention. Last updated May 9, 2017. http://www.cdc.gov/niosh/topics/aircrew/cosmicionizingradiation.html.

28. Schauer. D. A., and O. W. Linton. *Ionizing Radiation Exposure of the Population of the United States.* Report no. 160. Bethesda, MD: National Council on Radiation Protection and Measurements, 2009. https://www.ncrppublications.org/Reports/160.

29. Bailey, Susan. "Air-Crew Radiation Exposure—An Overview." *Nuclear News*, January 2000: 38. http://www3.ans.org/pubs/magazines/nn/pdfs/2000-1-3.pdf.

30. Lynch, Patrick. "Modeling Radiation Exposure for Pilots, Crew and Passengers on Commercial Flights." NASA Langley Research Center. Last modified December 19, 2008. http://www.nasa.gov/topics/earth/features/AGU-NAIRAS.html.

31. NIOSH, op. cit.

32. Bailey, 32–40.

33. Hwang, Junga, Kyung-Chan Kim, Kyunghwan Dokgo, Enjin Choi, and Hang-Pyo Kim. "Heliocentric Potential (HCP) for Nowcast of Aviation Radiation Dose." *Journal of Astronomy and Space Sciences* 32, no. 1 (2015): 39–44. https://doi.org/10.5140/JASS.2015.32.1.39.

34. Greener, Sue. *Business Research Methods*. Frederiksberg, Denmark: Ventus, 2008: 94. http://www.msu.ac.zw/elearning/material/1332864106introduction-to-research-methods.pdf.

35. Ibid.

36. Shmueli, 3.

37. Marchau, Vincent, and Erik van de Linde. "The Delphi Method." In *Foresight in Organizations: Methods and Tools*. Edited by Patrick van der Duin. New York: Routledge, 2016.

38. Reid, Kim. "Eduventures' Student Success Ratings Are Here!" June 7, 2016. https://encoura.org/eduventures-student-success-ratings/; and "Eduventures 2016 Student Success Ratings." June 7, 2016. http://www.eduventures.com/eduventures-2016-retention-ratings/.

39. James, E. Alana, Tracesea Slater, and Alan Bucknam. *Action Research for Business, Nonprofit, & Public Administration*. Los Angeles: SAGE, 2012: 1. Italics, mine.

40. Coughlan, Paul, and David Coghlan. "Action Research for Operations Management." *International Journal of Operations & Production Management* 22, no. 2 (2002): 220. https://doi.org/10.1108/01443570210417515.

41. Blichfeldt, Bodil S., and Jesper R. Andersen. "Creating a Wider Audience for Action Research: Learning From Case-Study Research." *Journal of Research Practice* 2, no. 1 (2006): D2. http://jrp.icaap.org/index.php/jrp/article/view/23/43

42. Sankaran, Ahankar, and Tay Boon Hou. "Action Research Models in Business Research." ANZSYS69 Paper. East Lismore, Australia, Southern Cross University, 2003: 1–2.

43. Coughlan, 222–226.

44. Adapted from Auer, Christoph, and Manuela Follack. "Using Action Research for Gaining Competitive Advantage Out of the Internet's Impact on Existing Business Models." In the *Proceedings of the 15th Bled Electronic Commerce Conference— eReality: Constructing the eEconomy*. Bled, Slovenia: Bled Electronic Commerce Conference, June 17–19, 2002: 773–774; and Coughlan, 231–232.

45. Poza, Ernesto, Sandra Johnson, and Theodore Alfred. "Changing the Family Business Through Action Research." *Family Business Review* 11, no. 4 (1998): 311–323; and Boyle, Monica. "Research in Action: A Guide to Best Practice in Participatory Action Research."

Canberra, Australia: Department of Families, Housing, Community Services and Indigenous Affairs, 2012: 1–40. https://www.dss.gov.au/sites/default/files/documents/06_2012/research_in_action.pdf.

46. Quake, Stephen. "The Absurdly Artificial Divide Between Pure and Applied Research," *New York Times*, February 17, 2009. https://opinionator.blogs.nytimes.com/2009/02/17/the-absurdly-artificial-divide-between-pure-and-applied-research/comment-page-5/.

47. Hale, Jamie. "Understanding Research Methodology 5: Applied and Basic Research," *Psych Central*, May 12, 2011. http://psychcentral.com/blog/archives/2011/05/12/understanding-research-methodology-5-applied-and-basic-research/.

48. Turabian, Kate L. *A Manual for Writers of Research Papers, Theses, and Dissertations*. 8th ed. Chicago: University of Chicago Press, 2013: 1.2.2.

49. Turabian, 1.2.3.

50. Campbell, Donald T., and Julian C. Stanley. *Experimental and Quasi-Experimental Designs for Research*. Chicago: Rand McNally, 1963: 5.

51. Adapted from the following: Hill, Kyle. "What Is a Good Study? Guidelines for Evaluating Scientific Studies." *Science-Based Life*, March 15, 2012; https://sciencebasedlife.wordpress.com/resources-2/what-is-a-good-study-guidelines-for-evaluating-scientific-studies/; du Prel, Jean-Baptist, Bernd Rohrig, and Maria Blettner. "Critical Appraisal of Scientific Articles." *Deutsches Arzteblatt International* 106, no. 7 (2009): 100–105. https://doi.org/10.3238/arztebl.2009.0100; Meltzoff, J. *Critical Thinking About Research*. Washington, DC: American Psychological Association, 1998; and Cohn, Victor, Lewis Cope, with Deborah Cohn Runkle. *News and Numbers: A Writer's Guide to Statistics*. 3rd ed. West Sussex, UK: Wiley-Blackwell, 2012: Ch. 4 "What Makes a Good Study?"

52. This section was influenced by Shaughnessy, John J., Eugene B. Zechmeister, and Jeanne S. Zechmeister. *Research Methods in Psychology*. 10th ed. New York: McGraw-Hill, 2015: 59–76; and Sieber, Joan E., and Martin B. Tolich. *Planning Ethically Responsible Research*. 2nd ed. Thousand Oaks, CA: SAGE, 2013.

53. National Bioethics Advisory Commission, "Ethical Policy Issues in Research Involving Human Participants: Summary." Bethesda, MD: National Bioethics Advisory Commission, 2001: 2. https://bioethicsarchive.georgetown.edu/nbac/human/oversumm.html.

54. University of Minnesota Center for Bioethics. "A Guide to Research Ethics." Minneapolis: University of Minnesota, 2003: 6–7. http://www.ahc.umn.edu/img/assets/26104/Research_Ethics.pdf.

55. Leedy, Paul D., and Jeanne E. Ormrod. *Practical Research: Planning and Design.* 11th ed. Boston: Pearson, 2016: 37–45.

56. A very readable introduction to validity is found in Taylor, Steven, and Gordon J. G. Asmundson. "Internal and External Validity in Clinical Research." In *Handbook of Research Methods in Abnormal and Clinical Psychology.* Edited by Dean McKay. Thousand Oaks, CA: SAGE, 2008: 23–34. https://us.corwin.com/sites/default/files/upm-binaries/19352_Chapter_3.pdf.

57. Aalto University, Helsinki. "Researchers Prefer Citing Researchers of Good Reputation." *ScienceDaily,* October 7, 2014. http://www.sciencedaily.com/releases/2014/10/141007103312.htm.

58. Hoeffel, C. "Journal Impact Factors" [letter]. *Allergy* 53, no. 12 (1998): 1225. https://doi.org/10.1111/j.1398-9995.1998.tb03848.x; also see Garfield, Eugene. "The Agony and the Ecstasy— The History and Meaning of the Journal Impact Factor." Presented at the International Congress on Peer Review And Biomedical Publication, Chicago, IL, September 16, 2005. http://garfield.library.upenn.edu/papers/jifchicago2005.pdf.

59. Western Michigan University Libraries. "Citing Sources: Citation Counts and Journal Impact Factor." Last modified November 15, 2017. http://libguides.wmich.edu/citing/citationcount.

60. Arizona State University Library. "Citation Research and Impact Metrics: Citation Counts for Authors." Last modified November 8, 2017. https://libguides.asu.edu/citation/citationcountsauthors.

61. Askew, Ian, Zoe Matthews, and Rachel Partridge. "Going Beyond Research: A Key Issues Paper Raising Discussion Points Related to Dissemination, Utilization and Impact . . ." Paper presented at the Moving Beyond Research to Influence Policy Workshop, University of Southampton, UK, January 23–24, 2001: i. https://eprints.soton.ac.uk/40958/.

62. Ibid.

63. Rajapaksa, Lalini. "Beyond Research Communication . . ." *Journal of the National Science Foundation Sri Lanka* 37, no. 4 (2009): 227–228. Italics, mine.

64. Askew et al., 19.

65. Adapted from: Saunders, Mark N. K., Philip Lewis, and Adrian Thornhill. *Research Methods for Business Students.* 7th ed. Essex, UK: Pearson Education Ltd., 2016: 124. Figure 4.1

66. Bird, Alexander. "Thomas Kuhn." In *The Stanford Encyclopedia of Philosophy.* Edited by Edward N. Zalta. Fall 2013: 3, "The Concept of a Paradigm." https://plato.stanford.edu/archives/fall2013/entries/thomas-kuhn/.

67. Kuhn, Thomas. *The Structure of Scientific Revolutions.* 2nd ed. Chicago: University of Chicago Press, 1970: 38–9.

68. Greener, 34.

69. Ulin, Pricilla R., Elizabeth T. Robinson, and Elizabeth E. Tolley. *Qualitative Methods in Public Health: A Field Guide for Applied Research.* San Francisco: Jossey-Bass, 2004.

70. Bhattacherjee, Anol. *Social Science Research: Principles, Methods, and Practices.* 2nd ed. Published under CCA-Non Commercial. Tampa: University of South Florida, 2012: 8. http://scholarcommons.usf.edu/cgi/viewcontent.cgi?article=1002&context=oa_textbooks.

71. Antwi, Stephen Kwadwo, and Kasim Hamza, "Qualitative and Quantitative Research Paradigms in Business Research: A Philosophical Reflection." *European Journal of Business and Management* 7, no. 3 (2015): 217–225.

72. Ibid., 219.

73. Schutt, Russell K. *Investigating the Social World: The Process and Practice of Research.* 8th ed. Thousand Oaks, CA: SAGE, 2016: 20.

74. Denzin, N.K., and Y.S. Lincoln. "Introduction: Entering the Field of Qualitative Research." In *Handbook of Qualitative Research*. Edited by N.K. Denzin and Y.S. Lincoln. Thousand Oaks, CA: SAGE, 1994: 2.

75. Ulin, Robinson, and Tolley. *Qualitative Methods in Public Health*, 2004.

76. Silverman, David. "Introducing Qualitative Research." In *Qualitative Research*. 4th ed. Edited by David Silverman. Thousand Oaks, CA: SAGE, 2016: 36–37.

77. Saunders, Mark N. K., and Paul Tosey. "The Layers of Research Design." *Rapport*, 30 (2012): 58. https://anlp.org/files/research-onion-layers_42_357.pdf.

78. Miller, Alexander. "Realism." In *The Stanford Encyclopedia of Philosophy*. Edited by Edward N. Zalta. Winter 2016: "Introduction." https://plato.stanford.edu/archives/win2016/entries/realism/.

79. Feilzer, Martina Y. "Doing Mixed Methods Research Pragmatically: Implications for the Rediscovery of Pragmatism as a Research Paradigm." *Journal of Mixed Methods Research* 4, no. 1 (2010): 8. https://doi.org/10.1177/1558689809349691. Italics, mine.

80. Tashakkori, Abbas, and Charles Teddlie. *Handbook of Mixed Methods in Social and Behavioral Research*. Thousand Oaks, CA: SAGE, 2003: 713.

81. Feilzer, 14.

82. Tashakkori, Abbas, and Charles Teddlie. "The Past and Future of Mixed Methods Research: From Data Triangulation to Mixed Model Designs." In *Handbook of Mixed Methods in Social and Behavioral Research*. Edited by Abbas Tashakkori and Charles Teddlie. Thousand Oaks, CA: SAGE, 2003: 679.

83. Bryman, Alan, and Emma Bell. *Business Research Methods*. 4th ed. Oxford: Oxford University Press, 2015: 27.

84. Ritti, Richard R., and Steve Levy. The Ropes to Skip and the Ropes to Know: Studies in Organizational Theory and Behavior. Hoboken, NJ: John Wiley & Sons, 2010.

CHAPTER 2

1. Confucius. *The Sayings of Confucius*. Edited by Charles W. Eliot. *The Harvard Classics XV*. P.F. New York: Collier & Son, 1909–1914: 9.

2. Goldhaber, Alfred Scharff, and Michael Martin Nieto. "Photon and Graviton Mass Limits." *Reviews of Modern Physics*, 82 (2010): 939. https://doi.org/10.1103/RevModPhys.82.939.

3. Plato. *Laws*. Book I. Translated by Benjamin Jowett. Tustin, CA: Xist Publications, 2015: 626e.

4. Miller, P. M., and M. J. Wilson, Eds. *A Dictionary of Social Science Methods*. New York: Wiley, 1983: 27.

5. Hildebrand, Joel H. *Science in the Making*. New York: Columbia University Press, 1957: 8.

6. Weinberg, S. "The Methods of Science . . . and Those By Which We Live." *Academic Questions* 8, no. 2 (1995): 8. https://doi.org/10.1007/BF02683184.

7. Pearson, Karl. *The Grammar of Science*. London: Walter Scott, 1892: 8.

8. Doyle, Sir Arthur Conan. "The Science of Deduction." In *The Sign of the Four*. London: *Lippincott's Monthly Magazine*, 1890: 5–6. https://sherlock-holm.es/stories/pdf/a4/1-sided/sign.pdf.

9. IEP Staff. "Deductive and Inductive Arguments." *The Internet Encyclopedia of Philosophy*. October 2016. ISSN 2161-0002. http://www.iep.utm.edu/ded-ind/.

10. Hwang, Stephen W., Rochelle E. Martin, and Ahmed M. Bayoumi. "Methodological, Practical, and Ethical Challenges to Inner-City Health Research." In *Evidence-Based Practice Manual: Research and Outcome Measures in Health and Human Services*. Edited by Albert R. Roberts and Kenneth R. Yeager. Oxford: Oxford University Press, 2004: 117–118.

11. Blackstone, Amy. *Principles of Sociological Inquiry: Qualitative and Quantitative Methods*. Saylor, 2012: 22. http://www.saylor.org/site/textbooks/Principles%20of%20Sociological%20Inquiry.pdf.

12. The Muse (contributor). "What to Do When Your Boss Lies." *Forbes*, October 1, 2014. http://www.forbes.com/sites/dailymuse/2014/10/01/what-to-do-when-your-boss-lies/#5855d5c171c8.

13. Goldman, Alan. *Transforming Toxic Leaders*. Stanford, CA: Stanford University Press, 2009.

14. Groves, Robert M., and Mick P. Couper. *Nonresponse in Household Interview Surveys*. New York: Wiley, 1998: 6.5.1.

15. Douven, Igor. "Abduction." *The Stanford Encyclopedia of Philosophy.* Edited by Edward N. Zalta. March 2011: 1.1. http://plato.stanford.edu/archives/spr2011/entries/abduction/.

16. Peirce, C. S. *Collected Papers (1931–1958).* Vols. 1–8. Edited by C. Hartshorne, P. Weiss, and A. Burks. Cambridge, MA: Harvard University Press: 1934, Vol. 5: 90.

17. Thagard, P. *Computational Philosophy of Science.* Cambridge, MA: MIT Press, 1988: 54.

18. Paavola, Sami. "Deweyan Approaches to Abduction." In *Action, Belief and Inquiry—Perspectives on Science, Society and Religion.* Edited by Ulf Zackariasson. Nordic Studies in Pragmatism 3. Helsinki: Nordic Pragmatism Network, 2015: 231.

19. Ibid.

20. Rohr, Susanne. "Madness as a Liminal State in the American Short Story: Edgar Allan Poe's Ratiocination and Charles Sanders Peirce's Logic of Abduction." In *Liminality and the Short Story: Boundary Crossings in American, Canadian, and British Writing.* Edited by Jochen Achilles and Ina Bergmann. New York: Routledge, 2015: 179. Italics, mine.

21. Einstein, Albert. *The Expanded Quotable Einstein.* 2nd ed. Edited by Alice Calaprice. Princeton, N.J.: Princeton University Press, 2000: 22, 287, 10. Based on the series by Root-Bernstein, Michele, and Robert Bernstein. "Einstein on Creative Thinking: Music and the Intuitive Art of Scientific Imagination." *Psychology Today,* March 31, 2010. https://www.psychologytoday.com/blog/imagine/201003/einstein-creative-thinking-music-and-the-intuitive-art-scientific-imagination.

22. Patokorpi, Erkki. "What Could Abductive Reasoning Contribute to Human Computer Interaction? A Technology Domestication View." *PsychNology Journal* 7, no. 1 (2009): 115, citing Rizzi, A. "Abduzione ed Inferenza Statistica." *Statistica e Società* 2, no. 2 (2004): 15–25.

23. NASDAQ homepage: http://www.nasdaq.com.

24. Based on Krantz, Matt. "Blame These 11 Stocks for Nasdaq Nightmare." *USA Today,* February 11, 2016. http://www.usatoday.com/story/money/markets/2016/02/11/blame-these-11-stocks-nasdaq-nightmare/80233496/; and Plaehn, Tim. "What Makes Up the NASDAQ Composite?" *Zacks.* Accessed October 2016. http://finance.zacks.com/up-nasdaq-composite-2352.html.

25. Grimes, William. "Stephen Toulmin, a Philosopher and Educator, Dies at 87." *New York Times,* December 11, 2009. https://www.nytimes.com/2009/12/11/education/11toulmin.html.

26. Wilson, G. Peter, and Carolyn R. Wilson. "The Toulmin Model of Argumentation." [Original authors; modified by D. Cooper]. *NavigatingAccounting.com,* November 2016. Creative Commons BY-NC-SA. http://www.navigatingaccounting.com/sites/default/files/Posted/Common/Resources_web_book/Toulmin_Model_of_Argumentation.pdf.

27. Toulmin, Stephen E. *The Uses of Argument.* Updated ed. Cambridge: Cambridge University Press, 2003: 89–100; and Karback, Joan. "Using Toulmin's Model of Argumentation." *Journal of Teaching Writing* 6, no. 1 (1987): 81.

28. Hoover, Kenneth R. *The Elements of Social Scientific Thinking.* 5th ed. New York: St. Martin's Press, 1991: 21.

29. Hauenstein, Patrick. "How Finding and Managing Talent Shapes Organizational Culture," *OMNIview Blog,* July 15, 2015. http://www.theomniview.com/pov/blog/how-talent-management-practices-shape-organizational-culture/.

30. Rubenstein, C. "When You're Smiling." *Psychology Today.* February 1980: 18.

31. Kováč, Ladislav. "The Biology of Happiness: Chasing Pleasure and Human Destiny." *Science and Society* 13, no. 4 (2012): 297–302. https://doi.org/10.1038/embor.2012.26.

32. Rosenberg, M. *Society and the Adolescent Self-image.* Princeton, NJ: Princeton University Press, 1965.

33. For a comprehensive review of measurement theory, see Stevens, S. S. "On the Theory of Scales of Measurement." *Science* 103, no. 2684 (1946): 677–680. https://doi.org/10.1126/science.103.2684.677; and Bandalos, Deborah L. *Measurement Theory and Applications for the Social Sciences.* New York: Guilford Press, 2018.

34. Kunert, Paul. "2009 IBM: Teleworking Will Save the WORLD! 2017 IBM: Get Back to the Office

or Else." *The Register*, February 13, 2017. https://www.theregister.co.uk/2017/02/13/ibm_changes_mind_about_teleworking/.

35. Global Workplace Analytics. "2017 State of Telecommuting in the US." http://globalworkplaceanalytics.com/resources/costs-benefits.

36. Spector, Nicole. "Why Are Big Companies Calling Their Remote Workers Back to the Office?" *NBC News*, July 27, 2017. https://www.nbcnews.com/business/business-news/why-are-big-companies-calling-their-remote-workers-back-office-n787101.

37. A *research hypothesis* is a statement of what we expect or predict to happen in the study's posited relationship between two or more variables. A *null hypothesis* is a statement of "no difference" designed for statistical testing. By challenging the research hypothesis, the statistical null hypothesis states that the IV *does not make a difference* or that any observed difference is due to sampling error.

38. Tufte, Edward R. *The Cognitive Style of PowerPoint: Pitching Out Corrupts Within*. 2nd ed. Cheshire, CT: Graphics Press, 2006: 4.

39. Kerlinger, Fred N. *Foundations of Behavioral Research*. 3rd ed. New York: Holt, Rinehart, and Winston, 1986: 9.

40. Wacker, John G. "A Definition of Theory: Research Guidelines for Different Theory-building Research Methods in Operations Management." *Journal of Operations Management*, 16 (1998): 363. https://doi.org/10.1016/S0272-6963(98)00019-9.

41. Ibid., 364.

42. Christensen, Clayton M., Michael E. Raynor, and Rory McDonald. "What Is Disruptive Innovation?" *Harvard Business Review* (December 2015): 44. https://hbr.org/2015/12/what-is-disruptive-innovation.

43. Lewin, Kurt. Field Theory in Social Science: Selected Theoretical Papers by Kurt Lewin. London: Tavistock, 1952: 169.

44. Vansteenkiste, Maarten, and Kennon M. Sheldon. "There's Nothing More Practical Than a Good Theory: Integrating Motivational Interviewing and Self-Determination Theory." *British Journal of Clinical Psychology* 45, pt. 1 (2006): 63. https://doi.org/10.1348/014466505X34192.

45. Emspak, Jesse. "8 Ways You Can See Einstein's Theory of Relativity in Real Life." *Live Science*, November 26, 2014. http://www.livescience.com/48922-theory-of-relativity-in-real-life.html.

CHAPTER 3

1. Siegel, Mark. "Can We Cure Fear?" *Scientific American*, December 1, 2005: 47; Blanchard, D. Caroline, Guy Griebel, Roger Pobbe, and Robert J. Blanchard. "Risk Assessment as an Evolved Threat Detection Process." *Neuroscience & Biobehavioral Reviews* 35, no. 4 (2010): 991–998; and Yogis, Jaimal. *The Fear Project*. New York: Rodale, 2013.

2. Turabian, Kate L. *A Manual for Writers of Research Papers, Theses, and Dissertations*. 8th ed. Chicago: University of Chicago Press, 2013: 4.

3. Booth, Wayne C., Gregory G. Colomb, and Joseph M. Williams. *The Craft of Research*. 3rd ed. Chicago: Chicago Guides to Writing, Editing, and Publishing, 2008: Kindle location 156.

4. Einstein, Albert, and L. Field. *The Evolution of Physics*. New York: Simon & Schuster, 1938: 95.

5. Adapted from: Booth, Wayne C., Gregory G. Colomb, and Joseph M. Williams. *The Craft of Research*. 3rd ed. Chicago: Chicago Guides to Writing, Editing, and Publishing, 2008: Kindle locations 457–479; also see Wilson, Jonathan. *Essentials of Business Research: A Guide to Doing Your Research Project*. London: SAGE, 2014: 38–42.

6. Litoiu, Alexandru. "Well-Defined vs. Ill-Defined Problems." *Alexandru Litoiu* (blog), January 1, 2012. http://alitoiu.com/character/2012/01/01/Well-defined-vs-Ill-defined/.

7. Schacter Daniel L., D. T. Gilbert, and D. M. Wegner. *Psychology*. 2nd ed. New York: Worth Publishers, 2011: 376.

8. King, Patricia M., and Karen S. Kitchener. *Developing Reflective Judgment*. San Francisco: Jossey-Bass, 1994: 11.

9. Litoiu, Ibid.

10. Leedy, Paul D. *How to Read Research and Understand It.* New York: Macmillan, 1981: 2.

11. Wilson, 48.

12. Leedy, Paul D., and Jeanne E. Ormrod. *Practical Research: Planning and Design.* 11th ed. Boston: Pearson, 2016: 31.

13. Ibid., 36.

14. Adapted from Poggenpohl, S. H. "Constructing Knowledge of Design, Part 2: Questions—An Approach to Design Research." Paper presented at the Second Doctoral Education in Design Conference, La Clusaz, France, July 2000.

15. Yeager, Samuel J. "Where Do Research Questions Come from and How Are They Developed?" In *Handbook of Research Methods in Public Administration.* 2nd ed. Edited by Gerald J. Miller and Kaifeng Yang. Boca Raton, FL: CRC Press, 2007: 54–56.

16. Norris, Donald F., and M. Jae Moon. "Advancing e-Government at the Grassroots: Tortoise or Hare?" *Public Administration Review* 60, no. 1 (2005): 64–75. https://doi.org/10.1111/j.1540-6210.2005.00431.x.

17. Leedy and Ormrod, 37.

18. Adapted from Virginia Tech University Libraries. "Identifying When a Topic is Too Narrow or Too Broad." Last updated February 8, 2018. http://info-skills.lib.vt.edu/choosing_focusing/10.html; also see University of Arizona Libraries. "Popular vs. Scholarly Articles—Guide." http://www.library.arizona.edu/help/tutorials/scholarly/guide.html.

19. Liston, Kathleen. "Literature Review Methods: Point of Departure." http://web.stanford.edu/class/cee320/CEE320A/POD.pdf.

20. University Library, University of Illinois at Urbana-Champaign. "Writing Your Literature Review in Global Studies." https://www.library.illinois.edu/ias/cgs/class_guides/literaturereviews/.

21. Shore, Lynn M., Beth G. Chung-Herrera, Michelle A. Dean, Karen Holcombe Ehrhart, Don I. Jung, Amy E. Randel, and Gangaram Singh. "Diversity in Organizations: Where Are We Now and Where Are We Going?" *Human Resource Management Review* 19 (2009): 117–133. https://cbaweb.sdsu.edu/assets/files/iido/HRMR-Diversity.pdf.

22. Harvey, Missy. "What Is a Literature Review?" Carnegie Mellon University. October 2010. https://lib-webspace.library.cmu.edu/CS/HCI/05-771.html.

23. Grover, Rajiv, and Marco Vriens. *The Handbook of Marketing Research.* Thousand Oaks, CA: SAGE, 2006: 64.

24. Hines, Frank. *Determining Focus Group Specifications: How to Make Difficult Tradeoffs.* White Paper. York, ME: Hines & Lee, 2016.

25. Jary, Simon. "Apple's Ive Reveals Design Secrets." *Macworld U.K.*, July 2, 2009. http://www.macworld.com/article/1141509/jonathan_ive_london.html.

26. Prigg, Mark. "Sir Jonathan Ive: The iMan Cometh." *Evening Standard* (London), March 12, 2012. http://www.standard.co.uk/lifestyle/london-life/sir-jonathan-ive-the-iman-cometh-7562170.html.

27. Isaacson, Walter. *Steve Jobs.* New York: Simon & Schuster, 2011: 567.

28. National Commission for the Protection of Human Subjects of Biomedical and Behavioral Research. *The Belmont Report: Ethical Principles and Guidelines for the Protection of Human Subjects of Research.* Bethesda, MD: U.S. Department of Health and Human Services, 1979.

29. Israel, Mark. *Research Ethics and Integrity for Social Scientists: Beyond Regulatory Compliance.* 2nd ed. Thousand Oaks, CA: SAGE, 2014. Cited in Lahman, Maria K. E. *Ethics in Social Science Research: Becoming Culturally Responsive.* Thousand Oaks, CA: SAGE, 2018: 4.

30. Lahman, 8.

31. Adapted from Walton, Nancy. "What Is Research Ethics?" *Research Ethics.ca* (blog). https://researchethics.ca/what-is-research-ethics/.

32. Seedhouse, David. *Ethics: The Heart of Healthcare.* Chichester, UK: John Wiley & Sons, 1988.

33. Lovett, L. M. and D. Seedhouse. "An Innovation in Teaching Ethics to Medical Students." *Medical Education* 24 (1990): 37–41. https://doi.org/10.1111/j.1365-2923.1990.tb02435.x.

34. Seedhouse, David. *Ethics: The Heart of Healthcare.* 3rd ed. Chichester, UK: John Wiley & Sons, 2009: 174, Figure 48. The Ethical Grid is available by request from the authors, Lovett and Seedhouse.

35. Stutchbury, Kris, and Alison Fox. "Ethics in Educational Research: Introducing a Methodological Tool for Effective Ethical Analysis." *Cambridge Journal of Education* 39, no. 4 (2009): 489–504. https://doi.org/10.1080/03057640903354396.

36. Lovett and Seedhouse, 38.

37. Seedhouse, 2009, 143.

38. Ibid., 173.

39. LaCour, Michael J., and Donald P. Green. "When Contact Changes Minds: An Experiment on Transmission of Support for Gay Equality." *Science* 346, no. 1366 (2014). https://doi.org/10.1126/science.1256151.

40. McNutt, Marcia. "Editorial Retraction." *Science* 348, no. 6239 (2015): 1100. https://doi.org/10.1126/science.aac6638.

41. Bem, Daryl J. "Feeling the Future: Experimental Evidence for Anomalous Retroactive Influences on Cognition and Affect." *Journal of Personality and Social Psychology* 100, no. 3 (2011): 407–425. https://doi.org/10.1037/a0021524.

42. Jarrett, Christian. "The 10 Most Controversial Psychological Studies Ever Studied." *The British Psychological Society: Research Digest*, September 19, 2014. https://digest.bps.org.uk/2014/09/19/the-10-most-controversial-psychology-studies-ever-published/.

43. Davis, James, and Susan Madsen. "Ethics in Research Scenarios: What Would YOU Do?" The Davis-Madsen Ethical Scenarios: Scenario 1: The Data Sleuth. *The Ethicist Blog*, February 3, 2013. https://ethicist.aom.org/2013/02/ethics-in-research-scenarios-what-would-you-do/.

44. Farrimond, Hannah. "How Do You Make Sure Your Research Is Ethical?" *The Guardian*, May 20, 2014. https://www.theguardian.com/higher-education-network/blog/2014/may/20/why-research-ethics-matter.

45. Machi, Lawrence A., and Brenda T. McEvoy. *The Literature Review: Six Steps to Success*. Thousand Oaks, CA: Corwin-SAGE, 2012: 4.

46. Adapted from Machi and McEvoy, 6.

47. Levy, Yair, and Timothy J. Ellis. "A Systems Approach to Conduct an Effective Literature Review in Support of Information Systems Research." *Informing Science Journal* 9 (2006): 182. https://doi.org/10.28945/479.

48. San Jose State University Library. "Business Research Guide." https://libguides.sjsu.edu/c.php?g=230070&p=1526959.

49. Harvard College Writing Program. "Harvard Guide to Using Sources." 2016. https://writingproject.fas.harvard.edu/news/launch-updated-harvard-guide-using-source.

50. Jung, Dong I., Chee Chow, and Anne Wu. "The Role of Transformational Leadership in Enhancing Organizational Innovation: Hypotheses and Some Preliminary Findings." *The Leadership Quarterly* 14 (2003): 525–544. https://doi.org/10.1016/S1048-9843(03)00050-X.

51. Citations for the scales used in the Jung study (reference 50) are on pages 533–534 of the article.

52. Antwi, Stephen Kwadwo, and Kasim Hamza, "Qualitative and Quantitative Research Paradigms in Business Research: A Philosophical Reflection." *European Journal of Business and Management* 7, no. 3 (2015): 220.

53. Leedy and Ormrod, 83–84.

CHAPTER 4

1. Hurston, Zora Neale. *Dust Tracks on a Road: An Autobiography*. New York: Harper, 1942: 143.

2. Babin, Barry J., and William Zikmund. *Exploring Marketing Research*. 11th ed. Boston: Cengage Learning, 2016: 167–198.

3. Cooper, Donald R., and Pamela S. Schindler. *Business Research Methods*. 12th ed. New York: McGraw-Hill/Irwin, 2014: 225, 227.

4. AYTM Team. "2017 Global Respondent Engagement Study." GRIT CPR Report: Consumer Participation in Research Report. New York: GreenBook, March 2017: 3–4. https://www.greenbook.org/grit/cpr.

5. Internet World Stats. "World Internet Users and 2018 Population Stats." https://www.internetworldstats.com/stats.htm.

6. Khalaf, Simon, and Lali Kesiraju. "U.S. Consumers Time-Spent on Mobile Crosses 5 Hours a Day." *Flurry Analytics Blog*, December 2016. http://flurrymobile.tumblr.com/post/157921590345/us-consumers-time-spent-on-mobile-crosses-5.

7. Anderson, Monica. "The Demographics of Device Ownership." *Pew Research Center: Internet & Technology*,

October 29, 2015. http://www.pewinternet.org/2015/10/29/the-demographics-of-device-ownership/.

8. McDaniel, Jr., Carl, and Roger Gates. *Marketing Research*. 9th ed. New York: John Wiley & Sons, 2012: 195, citing Yalonis, Chris. "The Revolution in e-Research," *CASRO Marketing Research Journal* (1999): 131–133; "The Power of Online Research." *Quirk's Marketing Research Review* (April 2000): 46–48; MacElroy, Bill. "The Need for Speed." *Quirk's Marketing Research Review* (July–August 2002): 22–27; Mititelu, Cristina. "Internet Surveys: Limits and Beyond Limits." *Quirk's Marketing Research Review* (January 2003): 30–33; Ray, Nina. "Cybersurveys Come of Age." *Marketing Research* (Spring 2003): 32–37; "Online Market Research Booming, According to Survey." *Quirk's Marketing Research Review* (January 2005); Roger Gates, "Internet Data Collection So Far." Speech given to Kaiser Permanente (May 2005); and Gelb, Gabe. "Online Options Change Biz a Little—And a Lot." *Marketing News* (November 1, 2006): 23–24.

9. Tourangeau, Roger, Edwards, Brad, Johnson, Timothy P., Wolter, Kirk M., and Nancy Bates, eds. *Hard-to Survey Populations.* Cambridge: Cambridge University Press: 2014.

10. Babin and Zikmund, 209. Italics, mine.

11. Yoder, Paul, and Symons, Frank. *Observational Measurement of Behavior.* New York: Springer, 2010: 2. http://lghttp.48653.nexcesscdn.net/80223CF/springer-static/media/samplechapters/9780826137975/9780826137975_chapter.pdf.

12. Ibid., 3.

13. McLeod, S. A. "Observation Methods." 2015. http://www.simplypsychology.org/observation.html.

14. Ibid.

15. de Vaus, David A. *Research Design in Social Research*. Thousand Oaks, CA: SAGE, 2001: 9. http://www.nyu.edu/classes/bkg/methods/005847ch1.pdf.

16. Phillips, Bernard S. *Social Research Strategy and Tactics*. 2nd ed. New York: Macmillan, 1971: 205.

17. Citations for suggested readings are provided in Exhibit 4.3 with URLs.

18. *Tests in Print*. Edited by Anderson, Nancy, Jennifer E. Schlueter, Janet F. Carlson, and Kurt F. Geisinger. The Buros Center for Testing. Lincoln: University of Nebraska Press, 2016.

19. Bruner, Gordon C. Marketing Scales Handbook: Multi-Item Measures for Consumer Insight Research. Vol. 7. Fort Worth: GCBII Productions, 2013.

20. Fields, Dail L. Taking the Measure of Work: A Guide to Validated Scales for Organizational Research and Diagnosis. Thousand Oaks, CA: SAGE, 2002.

21. French, Jordan. "Top 20 Female Entrepreneurs to Watch in 2018." *CIO*, December 21, 2017. https://www.cio.com/article/3243995/leadership-management/top-20-female-entrepreneurs-to-watch-in-2018.html.

22. Laerd Dissertation. "Non-Probability Sampling." *Dissertation Fundamentals*. © 2012 Lund Research Ltd. Retrieved from http://dissertation.laerd.com/non-probability-sampling.php.

23. Thompson, Steven K. *Sampling*. Hoboken, NJ: John Wiley & Sons, 2012.

24. Curtis, Sarah, Wil Gesler, Glen Smith, and Sarah Washburn. "Approaches to Sampling and Case Selection in Qualitative Research: Examples in the Geography of Health." *Social Science & Medicine* 50, no. 7–8 (2000): 1002. https://doi.org/10.1016/S0277-9536(99)00350-0.

25. Jaschik, Scott. "The Sociology of IRBs." *Inside Higher Ed*, August 15, 2005. https://www.insidehighered.com/news/2005/08/15/irb.

26. American Association of University Professors. "Reports & Publications: Institutional Review Boards and Social Science Research." 2000. https://www.aaup.org/report/institutional-review-boards-and-social-science-research.

27. Hoffman, Sharona, and Jessica Wilen Berg. "The Suitability of IRB Liability." *University of Pittsburgh Law Review* 67, no. 2 (February 2005): 365, 407–408. https://doi.org/10.5195/lawreview.2005.65.

28. National Commission for the Protection of Human Subjects of Biomedical and Behavioral Research. *The Belmont Report: Ethical Principles and Guidelines for the Protection of Human Subjects of Research*. Bethesda, MD: U.S. Department of Health and Human Services (HHS), 1979. http://www.hhs.gov/ohrp/regulations-and-policy/belmont-report/.

29. APA Committee on Associate and Baccalaureate Education. "Application for Human Subjects Research

Projects." In *The Institutional Review Board (IRB): A College Planning Guide*, in the *Publication Manual of the American Psychological Association*. Washington, DC: APA, 2016 revision: Appendix D, 18–27.

30. Bell, James, John Whiton, and Sharon, Connelly. "Evaluation of NIH Implementation of Section 491 of the Public Health Service Act, Mandating a Program for Protection of Research Subjects." Arlington, VA: James Bell Associates, 1998: V–10.

31. Gerrard, Ron. "Preparing Research Proposals for the HWS Institutional Review Board: An Informal Guide for Faculty and Students." Hobart and William Smith Colleges Institutional Review Board. http://www.hws.edu/offices/oafa/pdf/research_proposal_preparation_guide.pdf.

32. 45 CFR 46, §46.101(b), HHS Office for Human Research Protections: Regulations. http://www.hhs.gov/ohrp/regulations-and-policy/regulations/45-cfr-46/.

33. Munsey, Christopher. "Balancing Risk and Research." *gradPSYCH Magazine*, September, 2007. http://www.apa.org/gradpsych/2007/09/cover-balancing.aspx.

34. Ibid.

35. Goldfarb, Norman M. "IRB Appeals." *Journal of Clinical Research Best Practices* 7, no. 11 (2011). https://firstclinical.com/journal/2011/1111_IRB_Appeals.pdf.

36. See for example Epstein, Richard A. "Defanging IRBs: Replacing Coercion with Information." *Northwestern University Law Review* 101, no. 2 (2007): 735–747. http://chicagounbound.uchicago.edu/cgi/viewcontent.cgi?article=4988&context=journal_articles; Nichols, James. "Institutional Review Boards: An Attack on Academic Freedom" (aka "The Canadian Model: A Potential Solution to Institutional Review Board Overreach"). *AAUP Journal of Academic Freedom* 6 (2015): 1–13. https://www.aaup.org/sites/default/files/Nichols.pdf; Schneider, Carl E. *The Censor's Hand: The Misregulation of Human-Subject Research*. Cambridge: MIT Press, 2015; Schrag, Zachary M. *Ethical Imperialism: Institutional Review Boards and the Social Sciences, 1965–2009*. Baltimore: Johns Hopkins University Press, 2010. https://jhupbooks.press.jhu.edu/content/ethical-imperialism.

37. Munsey, op. cit.

38. Oakes, J. Michael. "Risks and Wrongs in Social Science Research: An Evaluators Guide to the IRB." *Evaluation Review* 26, no. 5 (2002): 460. https://doi.org/10.1177/019384102236520.

39. The inability to retain participants poses threats to the internal and external validity of the research. See Chapter 8 for validity threats: attrition.

40. National Institute of Mental Health. "Points to Consider About Recruitment and Retention While Preparing a Clinical Research Study." June 2005. http://www.nimh.nih.gov/funding/grant-writing-and-application-process/recruitment-points-to-consider-6-1-05_34848.pdf.

41. Northwestern University Office for Research. "Recruitment Materials and Guidelines." 2015. https://irb.northwestern.edu/process/new-study/requirements/recruitment-materials-guidelines; also see Stanford University's guidance that even asserts font size. http://humansubjects.stanford.edu/research/documents/GuidanceAdvertisements.pdf.

42. Krathwohl, David R., and Nick L. Smith. How to Prepare a Dissertation Proposal: Suggestions for Students in Education & the Social and Behavioral Sciences. Syracuse, NY: Syracuse University Press, 2005: 5.

43. Gerrard, Ron. "IRB Chart #1, IRB Review Determination Tree." Hobart and William Smith Colleges Institutional Review Board. Revised February 12, 2008. http://www.hws.edu/pdfs/Decision_Tree.pdf.

44. Adapted from Pajares, Frank. "Elements of a Proposal." 2007. https://www.uky.edu/~eushe2/Pajares/proposal.html; Creswell, John W., and J. David Creswell. *Research Design: Qualitative, Quantitative, and Mixed Methods Approaches*. 5th ed. Thousand Oaks, CA: SAGE, 2018; Labaree, Robert V. "Organizing Your Social Science Research Paper: 5. The Literature Review." USC Libraries Research Guides, University of Southern California. Last modified May 16, 2017. http://libguides.usc.edu/writingguide; and Leedy, Paul D., and Jeanne E. Ormrod. *Practical Research: Planning and Design*. 11th ed. Boston: Pearson, 2016.

45. Wilkinson, A. M. *The Scientist's Handbook for Writing Papers and Dissertations*. Englewood Cliffs, NJ: Prentice Hall, 1991: 96.

46. Wiersma, W. *Research Methods in Education: An Introduction*. 6th ed. Boston: Allyn and Bacon, 1995: 404.

47. World Health Organization Staff. "Recommended Format for a Research Proposal: Part 1." WHO-Research Policy. 2017. http://www.who.int/rpc/research_ethics/format_rp/en/.

48. Wiersma, 409.

49. Bhattacharya, Himika. "Research Setting." In *The SAGE Encyclopedia of Qualitative Research Methods*. Edited by Lisa M. Givens. Thousand Oaks, CA: SAGE, 2008.

50. Resnick, David B. "What Is Ethics in Research & Why Is It Important?" Research Triangle Park, NC: National Institutes of Health National Institute of Environmental Health Sciences, 2015. https://www.niehs.nih.gov/research/resources/bioethics/whatis/.

51. Adapted from van Teijlingen, Edwin R., and Vanora Hundley. "The Importance of Pilot Studies." *Social Research Update* 35 (Winter 2001). http://sru.soc.surrey.ac.uk/SRU35.html; and Crossman, Ashley. "Pilot Study: An Overview." *About Education: Sociology* (March 2016). http://sociology.about.com/od/P_Index/g/Pilot-Study.htm.

52. Baker, T. L. *Doing Social Research*. 2nd ed. New York: McGraw-Hill, 1994.

53. Visser, Penny S., Jon A. Krosnick, and Paul J. Lavrakas. "Survey Research." In *Handbook of Research Methods in Social Psychology*. Edited by Harry T. Reis and Charles M. Judd. New York: Cambridge University Press, 2000: 243.

CHAPTER 5

1. Boston University Libraries, Research Data Management. "What Is Research Data?" http://www.bu.edu/dioa/data-management/.

2. Aliaga M., and B. Gunderson. *Interactive Statistics*. Thousand Oaks, CA: SAGE, 2002.

3. Muijs, Daniel. *Doing Quantitative Research in Education with SPSS*. Thousand Oaks, CA: SAGE, 2004: 2.

4. Schutt, Russell K. *Investigating the Social World: The Process and Practice of Research*. 7th ed. Thousand Oaks, CA: SAGE, 2012: 324–325.

5. Lewins, Ann, Celia Taylor, and Graham R. Gibbs. "What Is Qualitative Data Analysis (QDA)?" *Online QDA*, Updated December 1, 2010. http://onlineqda.hud.ac.uk/Intro_QDA/what_is_qda.php.

6. Fry, Richard. "Millennials Overtake Baby Boomers as America's Largest Generation." *Pew Research Center, Fact Tank*, April 25, 2016. http://www.pewresearch.org/fact-tank/2016/04/25/millennials-overtake-baby-boomers/.

7. The International Statistical Institute. "The Oxford Dictionary of Statistical Terms." Edited by Yadolah Dodge. London: Oxford University Press, 2003. https://stats.oecd.org/glossary/detail.asp?ID=6131.

8. "General Principles for Dealing With Missing Data." Edited by J.P.T. Higgins, and S. Green. *Cochrane Handbook for Systematic Reviews of Interventions*. Version 5.1.0. London: The Cochrane Collaboration, 2011: 16.1.2; also see *The Handbook of Missing Data Methodology*. Edited by Geert Molenberghs, Garrett Fitzmaurice, Michael G. Kenward, Anastasios Tsiatis, and Geert Verbeke. Boca Raton, FL: CRC Press, 2014.

9. van den Berg, Ruben Geert. "Getting Started With SPSS: Tutorials, SPSS Data Editor Window." October 2014. http://www.spss-tutorials.com/spss-data-editor-window/.

10. Wright, Daniel B. "Making Friends With Your Data: Improving How Statistics Are Conducted and Reported." *British Journal of Educational Psychology* 73, no. 1 (2003): 134. https://doi.org/10.1348/000709903762869950.

11. Tukey, John. W. *Exploratory Data Analysis*. Reading, MA: Addison-Wesley, 1977: vi.

12. This example was created by the author for Emory, C. William, and Donald R. Cooper. *Business Research Methods*. 4th ed. Homewood, IL: Irwin, 1991: 484–486.

13. Norusis, Marija J. IBM SPSS Statistics 19 Guide to Data Analysis. Boston: Pearson, 2012.

14. Andrews, Frank M., Laura Klem, Patrick M. O'Malley, Willard L. Rogers, Kathleen B. Welch, and Terrence N. Davidson. *Selecting Statistic Techniques for Social Science Data: A Guide for SAS® Users*. Cary, NC: SAS Institute, 1998. https://www.sas.com/store/books/categories/usage-and-reference/selecting-statistical-techniques-for-social-science-data-a-guide-for-sas-users/prodBK_55854_en.html.

15. McCluskey, Anthony, and Abdul Ghaaliq Lalkhen. "Statistics IV: Interpreting the Results of Statistical Tests." *Continuing Education in Anaesthesia Critical Care & Pain* 7, no. 6 (2007): 208–212. https://doi.org/10.1093/bjaceaccp/mkm042.

16. Wasserstein, Ronald L., and Nicole A. Lazar. "The ASA's Statement on p-Values: Context, Process, and Purpose," *The American Statistician* 70, no. 2 (2016): 129–133. https://doi.org/10.1080/00031305.2016.1154108.

17. Frost, Jim. "The American Statistical Association's Statement on the Use of P Values." *The Minitab Blog*, March 23, 2016. http://blog.minitab.com/blog/adventures-in-statistics-2/the-american-statistical-associations-statement-on-the-use-of-p-values; also see: Fonseca, Marisha. "The Correct Way to Report P-Values." *Editage Insights*, October 16, 2013. http://www.editage.com/insights/the-correct-way-to-report-p-values.

18. This section *updates and expands* the testing criteria found in Schindler, Pamela S. *Business Research Methods*. 13th ed. New York: McGraw-Hill, 2019: 367. It retains the influence of Siegel, Sidney. *Nonparametric Statistics for the Behavioral Sciences*. New York: McGraw-Hill, 1956: Chapter 2.

19. Tutorials are available for SPSS (http://www.spss-tutorials.com), SAS (http://support.sas.com/training/tutorial/orhttp://www.tutorialspoint.com/sas/),Minitab (https://www.minitab.com/uploadedFiles/Documents/getting-started/Minitab17_GettingStarted-en.pdf), and R (http://www.r-tutor.com/elementary-statistics).

20. Ellis, Paul. The Essential Guide to Effect Sizes: Statistical Power, Meta-Analysis, and the Interpretation of Research Results. Cambridge: Cambridge University Press, 2010: 3–42.

21. Ibid., 45–82.

22. Althouse, Norm, Shirley Rose, Laura Allan, Lawrence Gitman, and Carl McDaniel. *The Future of Business*. 3rd Canadian ed. Toronto: Nelson Education, 2011: online resources, "Business Research, Reports, andPresentations."http://www.cengage.com/cgi-wadsworth/course_products_wp.pl?fid=M20b&product_isbn_issn=0176501401&template=NELSTU.

23. Eriksson, Päivi, and Anne Kovalainen. *Qualitative Methods in Business Research*. 2nd ed. Thousand Oaks, CA: SAGE, 2016. See esp. Chap 23, "Publishing"; Price, Paul C. *Psychology Research Methods: Core Skills and Concepts*. Washington, DC: Flat World Knowledge, 2012. ("11.3 Other Presentation Formats"): 291–298. https://2012books.lardbucket.org/pdfs/psychology-research-methods-core-skills-and-concepts/s15-presenting-your-research.pdf; and, Brownson, Ross, C., Amy A. Eyler, Jenine K. Harris, Justin B. Moore, and Rachel G. Tabak. "Getting the Word Out: New Approaches for Disseminating Public Health Science." *Journal of Public Health Management and Practice* 24, no. 2 (2018): 102–111. https://doi.org/10.1097/PHH.0000000000000673.

CHAPTER 6

1. de Vaus, David A. *Research Design in Social Research*. Thousand Oaks, CA: SAGE, 2001: 2.

2. de Vaus, 2.

3. de Vaus, 9.

4. Krathwohl, David R. *Methods of Educational and Social Science Research: The Logic of Methods*. 3rd ed. Long Grove, IL: Waveland Press, 2009: 221.

5. Kerlinger, Fred N. *Foundations of Behavioral Research*. 3rd ed. New York: Holt, Rinehart & Winston, 1986: 279.

6. Phillips, Bernard S. *Social Research Strategy and Tactics*. 2nd ed. New York: Macmillan, 1971: 93. Reprinted with permission of Macmillan Publications. Copyright 1971 by Bernard S. Phillips.

7. Margolin, Victor. *The Politics of the Artificial: Essays on Design and Design Studies*. Chicago: University of Chicago Press, 2002: 225.

8. Kerlinger, 348. Italics in original.

9. Ibid., 359.

10. Lammers, William J., and Pietro Badia. *Fundamentals of Behavioral Research*. Boston: Cengage Learning, 2004: 15–2. Copyright by William Lammers. http://uca.edu/psychology/fundamentals-of-behavioral-research-textbook/

11. Adapted from Price, Paul C. *Psychology Research Methods: Core Skills and Concepts*. Washington, DC: Flat World Knowledge, 2012: 165–166. http://2012books.lardbucket.org/books/psychology-research-methods-core-skills-and-concepts/index.html; and Lammers, 15-2.

12. Price, 165–166. Italics, mine.

13. See for example Warfield, John N., and A. Roxana Cardenas. *A Handbook of Interactive Management*. Palm Harbor, FL: Ajar Publishing, 2002. https://demosophia .com/wp-content/uploads/HIM_01.pdf.

14. de Vaus, David A. *Research Design in Social Research*. Thousand Oaks, CA: SAGE, 2001: 9. http://www.nyu .edu/classes/bkg/methods/005847ch1.pdf.

15. Gorard, Stephen. "Research Design, As Independent of Methods." In *SAGE Handbook of Mixed Methods in Social and Behavioral Research*. 2nd ed. Edited by Abbas Tashakkori and Charles Teddlie. Thousand Oaks, CA: SAGE, 2010: 241.

16. de Vaus, op. cit.

17. Yin, Robert K. *Case Study Research and Applications: Design and Methods*. 6th ed. Thousand Oakes, CA: SAGE, 2018: 26.

18. de Vaus, 8-9; example adapted from: Amrutia, Jay. "Which Personal Characteristics of Architect Become Them Best? Find Out." *Kadva*, March 1, 2018. http://www .kadvacorp.com/design/personal-characteristics-of-architects/.

19. Eppler, Martin J., and Jeanne Mengis. "Drawing Distinctions: The Visualization of Classification in Qualitative Research." mcm Working Paper no. 2. St. Gallen, Switzerland: University of St. Gallen Institute for Media and Communications Management, 2011: 2. http:// www.knowledge-communication.org/pdf/Drawing %20Distinctions%20Eppler%20Mengis%20Working %20Paper%20July2011.pdf.

20. Reynolds, Paul Davidson. "Introduction." In *A Primer in Theory Construction*. Indianapolis, IN: Bobbs-Merrill Educational Publications, 1971: 4-5. http:// www.cios.org/EJCPUBLIC/004/2/004217.HTML.

21. Tiryakian, E. A. "Typologies." In *International Encyclopedia of the Social Sciences* 16. Edited by David L. Sills. New York: Macmillan, 1968: 177-186.

22. du Toit, Jacques Louis, and Johann Mouton. "A Typology of Designs for Social Research in the Built Environment." Doctoral dissertation, Stellenbosch University, Matieland, South Africa, 2010: 208. http:// www.repository.up.ac.za/bitstream/handle/2263/ 18469/dutoit_typology_2013.pdf?sequence=1.

23. See for example Neuman, W. L. Social Research Methods: Qualitative and Quantitative Approaches. Boston:

Pearson, 2006; John W., and J. David Creswell. *Research Design: Qualitative, Quantitative, and Mixed Methods Approaches*. 5th ed. Thousand Oaks, CA: SAGE, 2018; Antwi, Stephen Kwadwo, and Kasim Hamza, "Qualitative and Quantitative Research Paradigms in Business Research: A Philosophical Reflection." *European Journal of Business and Management* 7, no. 3 (2015): 217-225; and Wand, Y., and R. Weber. "On the Ontological Expressiveness of Information Systems Analysis and Design Grammars." *Journal of Information Systems* 3, no. 4 (1993). https://doi .org/10.1111/j.1365-2575.1993.tb00127.x.

24. Pedhazur, Elazar J., and Liora Pedhazur Schmelkin. *Measurement, Design, and Analysis: An Integrated Approach*. Hillsdale, NJ: Lawrence Erlbaum, 1991: 305.

25. Johnson, Burke. "Toward a New Classification of Nonexperimental Quantitative Research." *Educational Researcher* 30, no. 2 (2001): 3-13. https://doi.org/10.31 02/0013189X030002003.

26. Belli, Gabriella. "Nonexperimental Quantitative Research." In *Research Essentials: An Introduction to Designs and Practices*. Edited by Stephen D. Lapan and MaryLynn T. Quartaroli. San Francisco: Jossey-Bass, 2009: 64-65.

27. Ibid., 65. Adapted and updated to include business research authors. Johnson, 2001, 9.

28. Hempel, C. G. "Fundamentals of Concept Formation in Empirical Science." In *International Encyclopedia of United Science II*, no. 7. Edited by O. Neurath. Chicago: University of Chicago, 1952.

29. Johnson's classification is derived from answers to questions that establish the *research objective* and the *time dimension* of a study. When the three resulting research designs are crossed with the three time dimensions in which data are collected, a 3-by-3 table or matrix is obtained. Johnson's original table and commentary are found in the following citations: Johnson, 2001, 8-11; Johnson, Burke. "It's (Beyond) Time to Drop the Terms Causal-Comparative and Correlational Research in Education." Presented at the Annual Conference of the American Educational Research Association, New Orleans, LA, April 24-28, 2000: 8-10; and Johnson, R. B., and L. B. Christensen. *Educational Research: Quantitative, Qualitative, and Mixed Approaches*. 6th ed. Thousand Oaks, CA: SAGE, 2017. Chapter 14 ("Nonexperimental Quantitative Research").

30. Additional questions to establish the "primary purpose/objective of the research" were provided by

Frankfort-Nachmias, Chava, David Nachmias, and Jack DeWaard. *Research Methods in the Social Sciences.* 8th ed, Kindle ed. New York: Worth Publishers, 2015: 8–9; and the author.

31. Lai, Kee-Hung, Thilaka S. Weerakoon, and T. C. E. Cheng. "The State of Quality Management Implementation: A Cross-Sectional Study of Quality-Oriented Companies in Hong Kong." *Journal of Total Quality Management* 13, no. 1 (2002): 29–38. https://doi .org/10.1080/09544120120098546.

32. LaRiviere, Jacob, Preston McAfee, Justin Rao, Vijay K. Narayanan, and Walter Sun. "Where Predictive Analytics Is Having the Biggest Impact." *Harvard Business Review*, May 25, 2016. https://hbr .org/2016/05/where-predictive-analytics-is-having-the-biggest-impact. Italics, mine.

33. Cronin, J. Joseph Jr., Michael K. Brady, Richard R. Brand, Roscoe Hightower Jr., and Donald J. Shemwell. "A Cross-Sectional Test of the Effect and Conceptualization of Service Value." *Journal of Services Marketing* 11, no. 6 (1997): 375–391. https://doi .org/10.1108/08876049710187482.

34. Holahan, C. K., and R. R. Sears. *The Gifted Group in Later Maturity.* Stanford, CA: Stanford University Press, 1995.

35. Immerwahr, John. "Public Attitudes on Higher Education: A Trend Analysis 1993 to 2003." National Center Report No. 04-2. San Jose, CA: National Center for Public Policy and Higher Education, and Public Agenda, 2004: 1–13. http://www.highereducation.org/ reports/pubatt/intro.shtml.

36. Johnson, 2001, 10.

37. Nielsen. "Retail Measurement." http://www.nielsen .com/us/en/solutions/measurement/retail-measurement .html?gclid=CM3A5_SYlM8CFYM8gQod5nwJWA; and Tripathy, Priyanka, and Pradip Kumar Tripathy. *Fundamentals of Research: A Dissective View.* Hamburg: Anchor Academic Publications, 2015:

38. Venkatesh, Viswanath, Michael G. Morris, and Phillip L. Ackerman. "A Longitudinal Field Investigation of Gender Differences in Individual Technology Adoption Decision-Making Processes." *Organizational Behavior and Human Decision Processes* 83, no. 1 (2000): 33–60. https://doi.org/10.1006/obhd.2000.2896.

39. Benmelech, Efraim, and Carola Frydman. "Military CEOs." *Journal of Financial Economics* 117, no. 1 (2015): 43–59. http://www.kellogg.northwestern.edu/faculty/ benmelech/html/BenmelechPapers/MilitaryCEOs .pdf;

40. Johnson, 2001, 10.

41. Goodwin, John, Kamran Ahmed, and Richard A. Heaney. "The Effects of International Financial Reporting Standards on the Accounts and Accounting Quality of Australian Firms: A Retrospective Study." *Journal of Contemporary Accounting and Economics* 4, no. 2 (2008): 89–119. https://doi.org/10.1016/ S1815-5669(10)70031-X.

42. Turner, Rochelle. "Travel and Tourism: Economic Impact 2015 World." and Corporate Author. "Global Tourism Resilient to Terrorism, Brexit and Further Macroeconomic Challenges." *World Travel and Tourism Council*, August 22, 2016. https://www.wttc.org.

43. Zimmermann, Petra, Konrad Mühlethaler, Hansjakob Furrer, and Cornelia Staehelin. "Travelers Returning Ill from the Tropics – A Descriptive Retrospective Study." *Tropical Diseases, Travel Medicine and Vaccines* 2, no. 6 (2016). https://doi.org/10.1186/ s40794-016-0021-1.

44. Yen, Louis Tze-ching, Dee W. Edington, and Pamela Witting. "Prediction of Prospective Medical Claims and Absenteeism Costs for 1284 Hourly Workers From a Manufacturing Company." *Journal of Occupational and Environmental Medicine* 34, no. 4 (1992): 428–435. http://umich.edu/~hmrc/tree/pdf/1992.pdf.

45. Silver, Sharon R., Lynne E. Pinkerton, Donald A. Fleming, James H. Jones, Steven Allee, Lian Luo, and Stephen J. Bertke. "Retrospective Cohort Study of a Microelectronics and Business Machine Facility." *American Journal of Industrial Medicine* 57, no. 4 (2014): 412–424. https://doi.org/10.1002/ajim.22288.

46. Kerlinger, 348.

CHAPTER 7

1. Diriwächter, Rainer, and Jaan Valsiner. "Qualitative Developmental Research Methods in Their Historical and Epistemological Contexts." *Forum: Qualitative Social Research* 7, no. 1, Art. 8. (2006):

Part 1. Introduction. http://nbn-resolving.de/urn:nbn :de:0114-fqs060189. Authors citing Mruck, Katja, and Günter Mey. "Qualitative Forschung und das Fortleben des Phantoms der Störungsfreiheit." *Journal für Psychologie* 4, no. 3 (1996): 3–21.

2. Diriwächter and Valsiner, 6. Conclusion.

3. Turner, Mark. *The Literary Mind.* Oxford: Oxford University Press, 1996: 4–5.

4. Price, Paul C. *Psychology Research Methods: Core Skills and Concepts.* Washington, DC: Flat World Knowledge, 2012: 187. http://2012books.lardbucket.org/books/ psychology-research-methods-core-skills-and-concepts/ index.html.

5. *John Steinbeck: The Contemporary Reviews.* Edited by Joseph R. McElrath, Jr., Jesse S. Crisler, and Susan Shillinglaw. Cambridge: Cambridge University Press, 1996: 207.

6. Steinbeck, John. *The Log From the 'Sea of Cortez.'* London: Penguin Classics, 2011: 2. From the original: Steinbeck, John, and Edward F. Ricketts. *Sea of Cortez: A Leisurely Journal of Travel and Research.* New York: Viking Press, 1941.

7. Newman, Isadore, Carolyn S. Ridenour, Carole Newman, and George Mario Paul DeMarco, Jr. "A Typology of Research Purposes and Its Relationship to Mixed Methods Research." In *Handbook of Mixed Methods in Social & Behavioral Research.* Edited by Abbas M. Tashakkori and Charles B. Teddlie. Thousand Oaks, CA: SAGE, 2003: 175–177.

8. Ibid., 175.

9. Creswell, John W., and Cheryl N. Poth. *Qualitative Inquiry and Research Design: Choosing Among Five Approaches.* 4th ed. Thousand Oaks, CA: SAGE, 2018: 65–110.

10. Weick, K. E. "Systematic Observational Methods." In *Handbook of Social Psychology.* 2nd rev ed. Edited by Gardner Lindzey and Elliot Aronson. Reading, MA: Addison-Wesley, 1968: 360.

11. Blanck, Peter, and Arthur N. Turner. "Gestalt Research: Clinical-Field-Research Approaches to Studying Organizations." Methodological Strategies: Systematic Observation. In *Handbook of Organizational Behavior.* Section III Organizational Behavior and

Methodologies. Edited by Jay W. Lorsch. Englewood Cliffs, NJ: Prentice Hall, 1987.

12. Cooper, Donald R., and Pamela S. Schindler. *Marketing Research.* New York: McGraw-Hill/Irwin, 2006. Chapter 10 ("Observation Studies").

13. ATLAS.ti. "Data Collection in Qualitative Research." http://atlasti.com/data-collection/.

14. Webb, Eugene J., Donald T. Campbell, Richard C. Schwartz, Lee Sechrest, and Janet B. Grove. *Nonreactive Measures in the Social Sciences.* Dallas, TX: Houghton Mifflin, 1981. [*Unobtrusive Measures* (1966) was revised, updated and retitled.]; see also Lee, Raymond M. *Unobtrusive Methods in Social Research.* Buckingham, UK: Open University Press, 2000.

15. Webb, Eugene J., Donald Campbell, Richard Schwartz, and Lee Sechrest. *Unobtrusive Measures: Nonreactive Research in the Social Sciences.* Chicago: Rand McNally, 1966; Webb, Eugene J., Donald T. Campbell, Richard D. Schwartz, and Lee Sechrest. *Unobtrusive Measures,* rev. ed. Thousand Oaks, CA: SAGE Publishing, 2000: 2.

16. Lee, Raymond M. "Unobtrusive Measures." *Oxford Bibliographies*, October 2015. https://doi.org/10.1093/ OBO/9780199846740-0048.

17. Kellehear, Allan. *The Unobtrusive Researcher: A Guide to Methods.* St. Leonards, Australia: Allen & Unwin, 1993: 12.

18. Webb, Campbell, Schwartz, and Sechrest. *Unobtrusive Measures,* rev. ed.: 2.

19. Kellehear, 5.

20. Schutt, 321.

21. Ibid., 324–325.

22. Ibid., 333.

23. Harris, Marvin. *The Rise of Anthropological Theory: A History of Theories of Culture.* Walnut Creek, CA: AltaMira Press, 2001. (Originally published in 1968.) Quoted in Creswell, John W., and Cheryl N. Poth. *Qualitative Inquiry and Research Design: Choosing Among Five Approaches.* 4th ed. Thousand Oaks, CA: SAGE, 2018: 90.

24. Lammers, William J., and Pietro Badia. *Fundamentals of Behavioral Research.* Boston:

Cengage Learning, 2004: 15–21. Copyright by William Lammers. http://uca.edu/psychology/fundamentals-of-behavioral-research-textbook/.

25. Armstrong, Karen. "Ethnography and Audience." *The SAGE Handbook of Social Research Methods.* Edited by Pertti Alasuutari, Leonard Bickman, and Julia Brannen. Thousand Oaks, CA: SAGE, 2008: 55.

26. Myers, Michael D. *Qualitative Research in Business and Management.* 2nd ed, Kindle ed. Thousand Oaks, CA: SAGE, 2013: 92–93.

27. Ibid., 100–102.

28. Roy, Donald F. "'Banana Time,' Job Satisfaction, and Informal Interaction." *Human Organization* 18, no. 4 (1959–1960): 158. http://www.jthomasniu.org/class/377a/Readings/roy-bananatime.pdf; and "Preliminary Guide to the Don Roy Papers, 1921–1980." Duke University Libraries. Last modified by Linda Daniel, May 2004. http://library.duke.edu/rubenstein/findingaids/uaroy/#subjectheadings.

29. Gold, R. L. "Roles in Sociological Field Observation." *Social Forces* 36, no. 3, 1958: 217–223. Cited in Robert Wood Johnson Foundation, Qualitative Research Project http://www.qualres.org/HomeGold-3648.html.

30. Watson, Tony, J. In Search of Management: Culture, Chaos and Control in Managerial Work. Rev. ed. London: Thomson Learning, 2007.

31. Watson, xii.

32. James, Nakita, and Hugh Busher. *Online Interviewing.* Thousand Oaks, CA: SAGE, 2009: 34–35.

33. Johnson, R. Burke, and Larry B. Christensen. *Educational Research: Quantitative, Qualitative, and Mixed Approaches.* 5th ed. Thousand Oaks, CA: SAGE, 2014. Chapter 16 ("Phenomenology, Ethnology, and Grounded Theory"), lecture notes: 4. https://studysites.sagepub.com/bjohnson5e/study/default.htm.

34. Smith, Jonathan A., Paul Flowers, and Michael Larkin. *Interpretative Phenomenological Analysis: Theory, Method and Research.* Thousand Oaks, CA: SAGE, 2009: 3; and, Vagle, Mark D. *Crafting Phenomenological Research.* 2nd ed. New York: Routledge, 2018.

35. Lammers, 15–21.

36. Nieswiadomy, Rose Marie. *Foundations of Nursing Research.* 6th ed. New York: Pearson, 2012: 136.

37. Johnson and Christensen. Chapter 16 ("Phenomenology, Ethnology, and Grounded Theory"), lecture notes: 2–3.

38. Thompson, Craig J. "Interpreting Consumers: A Hermeneutical Framework for Deriving Marketing Insights From the Texts of Consumers' Consumption Stories." *Journal of Marketing Research* 34 (November 1997): 438–455. https://doi.org/10.2307/3151963.

39. Ibid., 447.

40. Creswell, John W., and Cheryl N. Poth. *Qualitative Inquiry and Research Design: Choosing Among Five Approaches.* 4th ed. Thousand Oaks, CA: SAGE, 2018: 77.

41. Glaser, Barney G., and Anselm L. Strauss. *The Discovery of Grounded Theory: Strategies for Qualitative Research.* Chicago, IL: Aldine, 1967.

42. Price, 7.4: Data Analysis in Qualitative Research.

43. O'Reilly, Kelley, David Paper, and Sherry Marx. "Demystifying Grounded Theory for Business Research." *Organizational Research Methods* 15, no. 2 (2012): 247–262. https://doi.org/10.1177/1094428811434559; see also Goulding, Christina. *Grounded Theory: A Practical Guide for Management, Business, and Market Researchers.* Thousand Oaks, CA: SAGE, 2005.

44. Hobbs, Walter C., and G. Lester Anderson. "The Operation of Academic Departments." *Management Science* 18 (1971): 134–144. https://doi.org/10.1287/mnsc.18.4.B134.

45. Price, 7.4: Data Analysis in Qualitative Research.

46. Nieswiadomy, 136.

47. Ibid., 136–137.

48. Starks, Helene, and Susan Brown Trinidad. "Choose Your Method: A Comparison of Phenomenology, Discourse Analysis, and Grounded Theory." *Qualitative Health Research* 17, no. 10 (2007): 4. https://doi.org/10.1177/1049732307307031.

49. Cho, Ji Young, and Eun-Hee Lee. "Reducing Confusion about Grounded Theory and Qualitative Content Analysis: Similarities and Differences." *The Qualitative Report* 19, 64 (2014): 7–8. http://www.nova.edu/ssss/QR/QR19/cho64.pdf.

50. Johnson and Christensen. Chapter 16 ("Phenomenology, Ethnology, and Grounded Theory"), lecture notes, 6.

51. Myers, 111–114.

52. Berelson, B. *Content Analysis in Communication Research*. Glencoe, IL: Free Press, 1952.

53. Hsieh, Hsiu-Fang, and Sarah E. Shannon. "Three Approaches to Qualitative Content Analysis." *Qualitative Health Research* 15, no. 9 (2005): 1278. https://doi .org/10.1177/1049732305276687; Choy and Lee, 7.

54. Schutt, 339.

55. Bailey, Patricia Hill, and Stephen Tilley. "Storytelling and the Interpretation of Meaning in Qualitative Research." *Journal of Advanced Nursing* 38, no. 6 (2002): 574–583. https://doi .org/10.1046/j.1365-2648.2000.02224.x.

56. Riessmann, Catherine Kohler. *Narrative Methods for the Human Sciences*. Thousand Oaks, CA: SAGE, 2008: 23.

57. Ibid., 24.

58. Somers, Margaret R. "The Narrative Constitution of Identity: A Relational and Network Approach." *Theory and Society* 23, no. 5 (1994): 607. http://www.jstor.org/ stable/658090.

59. Creswell, 2018: 69.

60. Kennedy, Liam. "Remembering September 11: Photography as Cultural Diplomacy." *International Affairs* 79, no. 2 (2003): 315–326. https://doi.org/ 10.1111/1468-2346.00310.

61. Keaveney, Susan M. "The Blame Game: An Attribution Theory Approach to Marketer-Engineer Conflict in High-Technology Companies." *Industrial Marketing Management* 37, no. 6 (2006): 653–663. https://doi.org/10.1016/j.indmarman.2008.04.013.

62. Reissner, Stefanie C. "Learning and Innovation: A Narrative Analysis." *Journal of Organizational Change Management* 18, no. 5 (2005): 482–494. https://doi .org/10.1108/09534810510614968. Following citations based on the downloaded reprint's numbering from https:// www.researchgate.net/profile/Stefanie_Reissner/ publication/235265388_Learning_and_innovation_a_ narrative_analysis/links/544a2b6a0cf244fe9ea6350b.pdf.

63. Ibid., 2.

64. Ibid., 5.

65. Ibid., 12.

66. Gerring, John. "What Is a Case Study and What Is It Good For?" *American Political Science Review* 98, no. 2 (May 2004): 342. http://www.jstor.org/stable/ 4145316.

67. Yin, Robert K. *Case Study Research and Applications: Design and Methods*. 6th ed. Thousand Oaks, CA: SAGE, 2018.

68. Creswell, 2018: 96.

69. Yin, 2018: 5–6.

70. Yin, Robert K. "Case Study Methods." In *Handbook of Complementary Methods in Education*. 3rd ed. Edited by Judith L. Green, Gregory Camilli, and Patricia B. Elmore. Washington, DC: American Educational Association, 2006: 115.

71. Ibid.

72. Stake, Robert E. *The Art of Case Study Research*. Thousand Oakes, CA: SAGE, 1995.

73. Myers, 86–89.

74. Adapted from Ancona, Deborah, and David Caldwell. "Chris Peterson at DSS Consulting." *MIT Management, Sloan School*, no. 10-107 (September 10, 2010): 2–8. https://mitsloan.mit.edu/LearningEdge/ CaseDocs/10-107.Chris%20Peterson%20at%20 DSS%20Consulting.Ancona.Caldwell.pdf.

75. Ibid., 8.

76. Tashakkori, Abbas, and Charles Teddlie, editors. *SAGE Handbook of Mixed Methods in Social and Behavioral Research*. 2nd ed. Thousand Oaks, CA: SAGE, 2010: 8–9.

77. Morse, Janice M. "Principles of Mixed Methods and Multimethod Research Design." In *Handbook of Mixed Methods in Social and Behavioral Research*. Edited by Abbas Tashakkori and Charles Teddlie. Thousand Oaks, CA: SAGE, 2003: 190.

78. Steinbeck, 3.

79. Johnson, 2001: 17.

80. Morse, Janice M. and Linda Niehaus. *Mixed Method Design: Principles and Procedures*. New York: Left Coast Press, 2009: 10.

81. Reiss, Albert J. "Stuff and Nonsense About Social Surveys and Participant Observation." In *Institutions and the Person: Papers in Memory of Everett C. Hughes*. Edited by Howard S. Becker, Blance Geer, David Riesman, and Robert S. Weiss. Chicago: Aldine, 1968.

82. Yeasmin, Sabina, and Khan Ferdousour Rahman. "'Triangulation' Research Method as the Tool of Social Science Research." *BUP Journal* 1, no. 1 (2012): 156. http://www.academia.edu/7019439/Triangulation_Research_Method_as_the_Tool_of_Social_Science_Research.

83. Fielding, Nigel G. "Triangulation and Mixed Methods Designs: Data Integration With New Research Technologies." *Journal of Mixed Method Research* 6, no. 2 (2012): 127. https://doi.org/10.1177/1558689812437101.

84. Mertens, Donna, Pat Bazeley, Lisa Bowleg, Nigel Fielding, Joseph Maxwell, Jose F. Molina-Azorin, and Katrin Niglas. "The Future of Mixed Methods: A Five Year Projection to 2020." MMIRA Task Force, 2016: 5. https://mmira.wildapricot.org/resources/Documents/MMIRA%20task%20force%20report%20Jan2016%20final.pdf.

85. Ibid., 6.

86. Creswell, John W., and Vicki L. Plano Clark. *Designing and Conducting Mixed Methods Research*. 2nd ed. Thousand Oaks, CA: SAGE, 2011: 56–59.

87. Ibid., 60.

88. Morse, J. M. "Approaches to Qualitative-Quantitative Methodological Triangulation." *Nursing Research*, 40, no. 2 (1991): 120–123.

89. Creswell and Plano Clark, 2011: 66.

90. Teddlie, Charles, and Abbas Tashakkori. *Foundations of Mixed Methods Research: Integrating Quantitative and Qualitative Approaches in the Social and Behavioral Sciences*. Thousand Oaks, CA: SAGE, 2009.

91. Creswell and Plano Clark, 2011: 66–68.

92. Parry, Sara, and Beata Kupiec-Teahan. "Exploring Marketing and Relationship Software SMEs: A Mixed Methods Approach." *Management Research Review* 35, no. 1 (2010): 52–68. https://doi.org/10.1108/01409171211190805.

93. Milosevic, Dragan, and Peerasit Patanakul. "Standardized Project Management May Increase Development Project Success." *International Journal of Project Management* 23, no. 3 (2005): 181–192. https://doi.org/10.1016/j.ijproman.2004.11.002.

94. Rocco, Tonette S., Linda A., Bliss, Suzanne Gallagher, and Aixa Pérez-Prado. "Mixed Methods Use in HRD and AE." In *Academy of Human Resource Development 1999 Conference Proceeding*. Edited by K. P. Kuchinke. Baton Rouge, LA: Academy of Human Resource Development 2002: 880–887; Mingers, John. "The Paucity of Multimethod Research: A Review of the Information Systems Literature." *Information Systems Journal* 13, no. 3 (2003): 233–249. https://doi.org/10.1046/j.1365-2575.2003.00143.x; Hanson, Dallas, and Martin Grimmer. "The Mix of Qualitative and Quantitative Research in Major Marketing Journals." *European Journal of Marketing* 41, no. 1–2 (2005): 58–70. https://doi.org/10.1108/03090560710718111; Bazeley, Pat. "Mixed Methods in Management Research." In *Dictionary of Qualitative Management Research*. Edited by Robin Holt and Richard Thorpe. London: SAGE Publishing, 2008: 133–136; Rocco, T. S., L. A. Bliss, S. Gallagher, and A. Perez-Prado. "Taking the Next Step: Mixed Methods Research in Organisational Systems." *Information Technology, Learning and Performance Journal* 21, no. 1 (2003): 19–29; Hurmerinta-Peltomaki, L., and N. Nummela. "Mixed Methods in International Business Research: A Value-Added Perspective." *Management International Review* 46, no. 4 (2006): 439–459; and Molina-Azorin, J. "Understanding How Mixed Methods Research Is Undertaken Within a Specific Research Community: The Case of Business Students." *International Journal of Multiple Research Approaches* 3, no. 1 (2009): 47–57. https://doi.org/10.5172/mra.455.3.1.47.

95. Cameron, Roslyn, and Jose F. Molina-Azorin. "The Use of Mixed Methods Across Seven Business and Management Fields." Paper presented at 10th International Federation of Scholarly Associations of Management, Paris France, July 8–10, 2010: 11; also see: Roslyn A. Cameron. "History and Emergent Practices of Multimethod and Mixed Methods in Business Research." In *Oxford Handbook of Multimethod and Mixed Methods Research Inquiry*. Edited by Sharlene Nagy Hesse-Biber and R. Burke Johnson. New York: Oxford University Press, 2015: 466–485.

CHAPTER 8

1. Thomke, Stefan, and Jim Manzi. "The Discipline of Business Experimentation." *Harvard Business Review* 92, no. 12 (December 2014): 70–79. https://hbr.org/2014/12/the-discipline-of-business-experimentation.

2. Ibid., 76.

3. Ibid., 79; also see Davenport, Thomas H. "How to Design Smart Business Experiments." *Harvard Business Review* 87, no. 2 (February 2009): 68–76. https://hbr.org/2009/02/how-to-design-smart-business-experiments.

4. Campbell, Donald T., and Julian C. Stanley. *Experimental and Quasi-Experimental Designs for Research*. New York: Houghton Mifflin (reprint), 1963: 6. For an expanded treatment of individual designs and further references on this topic, I refer you to Montgomery, Douglas C. *Design and Analysis of Experiments*. 8th ed. New York: Wiley, 2012; and Kirk, Roger E. *Experimental Design*. 4th ed. Thousand Oaks, CA: SAGE, 2013.

5. Sparano, Joe. http://joesparano.com.

6. Johnson, R. Burke. Chapter 2, "Quantitative, Qualitative, and Mixed Research: Experimental Research." Lecture notes from University of South Alabama and based on Johnson, R. Burke, and Larry B. Christensen. *Educational Research: Quantitative, Qualitative, and Mixed Approaches*. 2nd ed. Boston: Allyn & Bacon, 2004. https://www.southalabama.edu/coe/bset/johnson/lectures/lec2.htm.

7. Price, Paul C. *Psychology Research Methods: Core Skills and Concepts*. Washington, DC: Flat World Knowledge, 2012: 138. http://2012books.lardbucket.org/books/psychology-research-methods-core-skills-and-concepts/index.html.

8. Ibid.

9. Leedy, Paul D., and Jeanne E. Ormrod. *Practical Research: Planning and Design*. 11th ed. Boston: Pearson, 2016: 178.

10. Lammers, William J., and Pietro Badia. *Fundamentals of Behavioral Research*. Boston: Cengage Learning, 2004: 9. Copyright by William Lammers. http://uca.edu/psychology/fundamentals-of-behavioral-research-textbook/.

11. Price, 145.

12. Lammers and Badia, 9–23.

13. Goode, William J. and Paul K. Hatt. *Methods in Social Research*. New York: McGraw-Hill, 1952: 75.

14. Scholten, Annemarie Zand. "Scientific Method: Causality." Lecture notes from Quantitative Methods, University of Amsterdam. https://www.coursera.org/learn/quantitative-methods/lecture/iQqCM/2-04-causality; Johnson and Christensen, 7; and Belli, Gabriella. "Nonexperimental Quantitative Research." In *Research Essentials: An Introduction to Designs and Practices*. Edited by Stephen D. Lapan and MaryLynn T. Quartaroli. San Francisco: Jossey-Bass, 2009: 64–65, 72.

15. Based on a fish bone diagram by Professor Kaoru Ishikawa, described by Sutevski, Dragan. "Cause and Effect Analysis to Solve Business Problems." *Entrepreneurship in a Box*, November 5, 2012. http://www.entrepreneurshipinabox.com/3899/cause-and-effect-analysis-to-solve-business-problems/.

16. Example modified for business and manufacturing from Scholten, "Scientific Method: Causality," and based on production problems noted by Sutevski, op. cit.

17. Campbell and Stanley, 297.

18. Cook, Thomas D., and Donald T. Campbell. *Quasi-experimentation: Design & Analysis Issues in Field Settings*. Boston: Houghton Mifflin, 1979.

19. Shadish, William R. "Campbell and Rubin: A Primer and Comparison of Their Approaches to Causal Inference in Field Settings." *Psychological Methods* 15, no. 1 (2010): 4. https://doi.org/10.1037/a0015916; Shadish, William R., Thomas D. Cook, and Donald T. Campbell. *Experimental and Quasi-Experimental Design for Generalized Causal Inference*. Boston: Houghton Mifflin, 2002.

20. Shadish, 4.

21. Campbell and Stanley, 206; Shadish, 5.

22. Michael, Robert S. "Threats to Internal & External Validity." Presented at "Y520: Strategies for Educational Inquiry." Bloomington: Indiana University (undated). http://www.indiana.edu/~educy520/sec5982/week_9/520in_ex_validity.pdf.

23. Johnson, R. Burke. Chapter 8, "Validity of Research Results: Outcome Validity." Lecture notes from University of South Alabama and Johnson, R. Burke, and Larry B. Christensen. *Educational Research: Quantitative, Qualitative, and Mixed Approaches.* http://www.southalabama.edu/coe/bset/johnson/lectures/lec8.pdf.

24. Price, 137.

25. Campbell and Stanley, 5–6.

26. Campbell and Stanley, 6.

27. Campbell and Stanley, 13. For a comparison with the Campbell and Stanley typology, see Jadad, Alejandro R., and Murry W. Elkin. *Randomized Controlled Trials: Questions, Answers, and Musings.* 2nd ed. Oxford: Blackwell Publications, 2007: 1–28.

28. Scholten, Annemarie Zand. "Research Design: Lab vs. Field." Lecture notes from the course Solid Science: Research Methods, University of Amsterdam. https://www.coursera.org/learn/quantitative-methods/lecture/wdLk9/3-05-lab-vs-field.

29. Campbell and Stanley, 24–25.

30. Frankfort-Nachmias, Chava, David Nachmias, and Jack DeWaard. *Research Methods in the Social Sciences.* 8th ed, Kindle ed. New York: Worth Publishers, 2015: 86–93. Chapter 5, "Components of a Research Design, Control Groups."

31. Ibid.

32. Desvaux, George, Sandrine Devillard-Hoellinger, and Pascal Baumgarten. "Women Matter: Gender Diversity, A Corporate Performance Driver." New York: McKinsey & Company, 2007. http://www.raeng.org.uk/publications/other/women-matter-oct-2007.

33. Mitchell, Mark L., and Janina M. Jolley. *Research Design Explained.* 7th ed. Belmont, CA: Wadsworth, 2010: 344; and Helgeson, Vicki S. *Psychology of Gender.* 5th ed. London: Routledge, 2016: 42, Table 2.1.

34. Suresh, K. P. "An Overview of Randomization Techniques: An Unbiased Assessment of Outcome in Clinical Research." *Journal of Human Reproductive Sciences* 4, no. 1 (2011): 8–11. https://doi.org/10.4103/0974-1208.82352.

35. Ibid.

36. Scott, Neil W., Gladys C. McPherson, Craig R. Ramsay, and Marion K. Campbell. "The Method of Minimization for Allocation to Clinical Trials: A Review." *Controlled Clinical Trials* 23, no. 6 (2002): 664. https://doi.org/10.1016/S0197-2456(02)00242-8.

37. Trochim, William, James P. Donnelly, and Kanika Arora. *Research Methods: The Essential Knowledge Base.* Boston: Cengage, 2015: 236–238. Chapter 9, "Experimental Design": 229–255.

38. CEB Test Preparation and Career Center. "Assessment Advice." Updated 2016. https://www.cebglobal.com/shldirect/en-us.

39. Hall, Richard. "2x2 Between Subjects Factorial Design." *Psychology World: Experimental Psychology*, 1998. https://web.mst.edu/~psyworld/experimental.htm.

40. Trochim, William M. "Factorial Designs: Summary." In *The Research Methods Knowledge Base.* 2nd ed. Version current as of October 20, 2006. http://www.socialresearchmethods.net/kb/.

41. Ibid., "Covariance Designs" and "Randomized Block Designs."

42. Ibid., "Randomized Block Designs."

43. Price, 178.

44. Lammers, 11-10.

45. Shadish et al., 156.

46. "The Most In-Demand Programming Languages of 2016." *Coding Dojo Blog*, January 27, 2016. http://www.codingdojo.com/blog/9-most-in-demand-programming-languages-of-2016/.

47. Campbell and Stanley, 47–48.

48. Trochim, "Quasi-Experimental Design."

49. Elizabeth A. Stuart, and Donald B. Rubin. "Best Practices in Quasi-Experimental Designs: Matching Methods for Causal Inference." In *Best Practices in Quantitative Social Science.* Edited by Jason W. Osborne. Thousand Oaks, CA: SAGE, 2007: 155–176. Chapter 11.

50. Babbie, Earl R. *The Basics of Social Research.* 5th ed. New York: Cengage/Wadsworth, 2011: 252–253, Figure 8-2.

51. Rubin, Guido W., and Donald B. Imbens. *Causal Inference for Statistics, Social, and Biomedical Sciences: An Introduction.* Part II. Cambridge: Cambridge University Press, 2009: 15.6.

52. Adapted from Loman, Tony. "Matching Procedures in Field Experiments." Institute of Applied Research. 2003. The process includes: (1) Discover the matching variables for subjects in both the experimental group and the pool of potential matches. Also, decide if you can evaluate the outcome measures planned for the experimental cases along with the control cases. (2) Select the most relevant demographic, psychosocial, and program-related variables from among the set to become screening criteria, at the step shown in the diagram. The timing for securing these data requires contemporaneous and synchronized matching—immediately identify control cases. However, outcome measures based on routine stored data permit a more relaxed approach. (3) Rank or weight the variables to establish a hierarchy of importance, i.e., determine which are the most necessary for the experiment and its outcomes. (4) Collect and update these variables for recruits in the pool and existing participants of the experimental group. (5) Use a computer program to search the pool's data for the best possible matches with new cases entering the experimental group. http://capacitybuilding.net/Matching%20 Procedures%20in%20Field%20Experiments.pdf.

53. McNamee, R. "Regression Modelling and Other Methods to Control Confounding." *Occupational and Environmental Medicine* 62, no. 7 (2005): 500–506. https://doi.org/10.1136/oem.2002.001115.

54. See for example Stuart, Elizabeth. "The Why, When, and How of Propensity Score Methods for Estimating Causal Effects." Presented at a workshop for the Society for Prevention Research, May 31, 2011. http://www.preventionresearch.org/wp-content/ uploads/2011/07/SPR-Propensity-pc-workshop-slides. pdf; Stuart, Elizabeth A. "Matching Methods for Causal Inference: A Review and Look Forward." *Statistical Science* 25, no. 1 (2010): 1–21. https://doi.org/10.1214/09-STS313; Rosenbaum, Paul R., and Donald B. Rubin. "The Central Role of the Propensity Score in Observational Studies for Causal Effects." *Biometrika* 70, no. 1 (1983): 41–55. https://doi.org/10.1093/ biomet/70.1.41; and Herbert, Paul L. "A Practical Guide to Propensity Score Models." Presentation

(June 29, 2009). https://www.pdffiller.com/jsfiller-desk6/?projectId=185372791&expId=3395&expBranch= 2#599423a1549a429ea6e3612543ab7f3b.

55. Trochim, William M. *The Research Methods Knowledge Base.* 2nd ed. "Quasi-Experimental Design: The Regression-Discontinuity Design." Version current as of October 20, 2006. http://www.socialresearch-methods.net/kb/quasird.php.

56. Thistlethwaite, Donald L., and Donald T. Campbell. "Regression-Discontinuity Analysis: An Alternative to the Ex Post Facto Experiment." *Journal of Educational Psychology* 51, no. 6 (1960): 309–317. https://doi .org/10.1037/h0044319; Imbens, Guido W. and Thomas Lemieux. "Regression Discontinuity Designs: A Guide to Practice." *Journal of Econometrics* 142, no. 2 (2008): 615. https://doi.org/10.1016/j.jeconom.2007.05.001; Trochim, op. cit.; Parmar, Divya, and Manuela De Allegri. "Operationalizing Impact Evaluations: From Theory to Practice." In *A Practical Guide to Impact Assessments in Microinsurance.* Edited by Ralf Radermacher and Katja Roth. Luxembourg: Microinsurance Network & Micro Insurance Academy, 2014: 123. ISBN 978-99959-864-8-3.

CHAPTER 9

1. Ferguson, Euan. "He's All the Rage." *The Guardian*, March 17, 2002. https://www.theguardian.com/ books/2002/mar/17/crimebooks.features.

2. Handley, Ann. "9 Qualities of Good Writing." *Ann Handley.com*, November 18, 2013. http://www.annhand ley.com/2013/11/18/9-qualities-of-good-writing/.

3. American Psychological Association. *Publication Manual of the American Psychological Association.* 6th ed. 2nd printing. Washington, DC: American Psychological Association, 2010.

4. University of Chicago Press Staff. *The Chicago Manual of Style.* 16th ed. Chicago: University of Chicago Press, 2010; Turabian, Kate L. *A Manual for Writers of Research Papers, Theses, and Dissertations.* 8th ed. Chicago: University of Chicago Press, 2013.

5. Modern Language Association of America. *MLA Handbook.* 8th ed. New York: Modern Language Association of America, 2016.

6. Booth, Wayne C., Gregory G. Colomb, and Joseph M. Williams. *The Craft of Research*. 3rd ed. Chicago: University of Chicago Press, 2008. Kindle edition: 1.3.

7. Elias, Rafik Z. "The Impact of Machiavellianism and Opportunism on Business Students' Love of Money." *Southwestern Business Administration Journal* 13, no. 1–2 (2013): 1–22. Excerpts used by permission of Rafik Elias and S. Srinivasan, Editor-in-Chief of *SBAJ*. http://www.tsu.edu/academics/colleges-and-schools/jesse-h-jones-school-of-business/pdf/sbaj/sbaj-volume-13-no1and2-paper1.pdf. Machiavellianism is a duplicitous interpersonal style, displaying cynicism, disregard for morality, and an agenda of self-interest and personal gain. For more information on pathological disorders such as machiavellianism, see Jones, Daniel N., and Delroy L. Paulhus. "Machiavellianism." In *Handbook of Individual Differences in Social Behavior*. Edited by Mark R. Leary and Rick H. Hoyle. New York: Guilford Press, 2009: 257–273. Chapter 7.

8. Fanoberova, Anna, and Hanna Kuczkowska. "Effects of Source Credibility and Information Quality on Attitudes and Purchase Intentions of Apparel Products: A Quantitative Study of Online Shopping Among Consumers in Sweden." Master's thesis, Umeå University, Umeå, Sweden, 2016. Excerpts used by permission of the authors. http://www.diva-portal.org/smash/get/diva2:946730/FULLTEXT01.pdf.

9. Commentary and suggestions for manuscript elements are from American Psychological Association. *Publication Manual of the American Psychological Association*. 6th ed. Kindle ed. Washington, DC: American Psychological Association, 2013; Price, Paul C. *Psychology Research Methods: Core Skills and Concepts*. Washington, DC: Flat World Knowledge, 2012: Chapter 11, "Presenting Your Research." http://2012books.lardbucket.org/books/psychology-research-methods-core-skills-and-concepts/index.html; Lammers, William J., and Pietro Badia. *Fundamentals of Behavioral Research*. Boston: Cengage Learning, 2004: Chapter 16 ("Fundamentals of Disseminating Research"). Copyright by William Lammers. http://uca.edu/psychology/fundamentals-of-behavioral-research-textbook/; Hummel, John H., Mark A. Whatley, David M. Monetti, Deborah S. Briihl, and Katharine S Adams. "Using the Sixth Edition of the APA Manual: A Guide for Students." *Georgia Educational Researcher* 7, no. 2 (2010): 1–31. http://citeseerx.ist.psu.edu/viewdoc/download?doi=10.1.1.908.292&rep=rep1&type=pdf; and Labaree, Robert V. "Organizing Your Social Science Research Paper." USC Libraries Research Guides, University of Southern California. Last modified November 18, 2016. http://libguides.usc.edu/writingguide.

10. APA. *Publication Manual*. Kindle ed., 229.

11. Lammers, 16-5; and Price, 276.

12. Lammers, 16-5.

13. Zwaan, Rolf. "Overly Amusing Article Titles." *Zeistgeist: Psychological Experimentation, Cognition, Language, and Academia* (blog), January 12, 2013. https://rolfzwaan.blogspot.com/2013/01/overly-amusing-article-titles.html.

14. Zwaan, Rolf. "Amusing Titles in Psychological Science," *Zeistgeist* (blog), January 20, 2013. Examples from the journal *Psychological Science*. https://rolfzwaan.blogspot.com/2013/01/normal.html.

15. APA. Kindle ed., 26–27.

16. Quote by Joyce Carol Oates in Doty, Kim. "Writing the First Sentence: Thoughts on Revision." *Abbott Press* (blog), January 29, 2013. http://blog.abbottpress.com/writing-the-first-sentence/.

17. APA. Kindle ed., 28.

18. Ingram, Laura, James Hussey, Michelle Tigani, and Mary Hemmelgarn (with Stephanie Huneycutt). "Writing a Literature Review and Using a Synthesis Matrix." NC State University Writing and Speaking Tutorial Service Tutors, 2006. https://tutorial.dasa.ncsu.edu/wp-content/uploads/sites/29/2015/06/synthesis-matrix.pdf.

19. Swales, John M. *Genre Analysis: English in Academic and Research Settings*. New York: Cambridge University Press, 1990.

20. Labaree, Robert V. "The C.A.R.S. Model." USC Libraries Research Guides, University of Southern California. Last updated May 7, 2018. http://libguides.usc.edu/writingguide/CARS; and Pennington, Ken. "The Introduction Section." Helsinki University of Technology Language Centre. 2005. http://www.cs.tut.fi/kurssit/SGN-16006/academic_writing/cars_model_handout.pdf.

21. Lammers, 16-8.

22. APA 2.06. Kindle ed., 29; Appendix Tables 1–4: 247–252. Italics, mine.

23. APA. Kindle ed., 247–252.

24. Leedy, Paul D., and Jeanne E. Ormrod. *Practical Research: Planning and Design*. 11th ed. Boston: Pearson, 2016: 332.

25. Adapted from APA. Kindle ed., 30, 247–8; Lammers 16-9; and Price, 280–281.

26. Sullivan, Lisa. "Power and Sample Size Determination." Boston University School of Health. http://sphweb.bumc.bu.edu/otlt/mph-modules/bs/bs704_power/BS704_Power_print.html.

27. Wuensch, Karl L. "Retrospective (Observed) Power Analysis." Karl Wunsch's Statistics Lessons. East Carolina University. Last modified September 18, 2014. http://core.ecu.edu/psyc/wuenschk/StatHelp/Power-Retrospective.htm.

28. Sullivan, Gail M., and Richard Feinn. "Using Effect Size—or Why the *P* Value Is Not Enough." *Journal of Graduate Medical Education* 4, no. 3 (2012): 279–282. https://doi.org/10.4300/JGME-D-12-00156.1; see the section titled "Why Report Effect Sizes."

29. Cohen, J. *Statistical Power Analysis for the Behavioral Sciences*. 2nd ed. Hillsdale, NJ: Lawrence Erlbaum Associates, 1988: 25.

30. Some of the software options for sample size, power, and effect size calculations are as follows: Minitab Statistical Software (currently a 30-day trial; https://www.minitab.com/en-us/Published-Articles/Minitab-s-Power-and-Sample-Size-Tools/), PS: Power and Sample Size Calculation version 3.1.2 (2014; Department of Biostatistics, Vanderbilt University; http://biostat.mc.vanderbilt.edu/wiki/Main/PowerSampleSize), IBM SPSS SamplePower (trial download for version 3.0; https://www-01.ibm.com/marketing/iwm/iwmdocs/tnd/data/web/en_US/trial-programs/U741655I36057W80.html); and G*Power: Statistical Power Analyses for Windows and Mac (free by request and purpose of use; http://www.gpower.hhu.de).

31. Louisiana Clinical and Translational Science Center. "Overview and Examples of Power and Sample Size Determination Using SAS Proc Power." Design, Epidemiology, and Biostatistics Core, Pennington Biomedical Research Center, Baton Rouge, LA: 6. https://lacats.pbrc.edu/documents/PASS.pdf.

32. Waylen, A. E., M. S. Horswill, J. L. Alexander, and F. P. McKenna. "Do Expert Drivers Have a Reduced Illusion of Superiority?" *Transportation Research Part F* 7 (2004): 329. https://doi.org/10.1016/j.trf.2004.09.009.

33. Louis, Winnifred R. "Writing Up Power Analyses." Queensland, Australia: School of Psychology, University of Queensland, 2009. Copyright by W. R. Lewis 2009. Used by permission. https://www2.psy.uq.edu.au/~uqwloui1/.

34. Adapted from: APA. Kindle ed., 29, 247–248; Lammers 16-9; and Price, 280–281.

35. Harnish, Roger. "APA Method Section." GSSP400 Lecture Series, Rochester Institute of Technology. Used by permission.

36. Adaptation based on Frye, Alice. "Writing a Method Section: Describing Measures" [PowerPoint slide 10]. Department of Psychology, University of Massachusetts, Lowell. https://www.uml.edu/Images/Writing%20a%20Method%20Section-Measures_tcm18-117658.pptx; and Whatley, Mark M. "Paper Resources: Method." *Dr. Whatley's Experimental Psychology Homepage*. Valdosta State University. http://mypages.valdosta.edu/mwhatley/3600/.

37. All paragraph citations in APA format are found in von der Gracht, Heiko A. *The Future of Logistics: Scenarios for 2025*. Wiesbaden, Germany: Gabler-Verlag, 2008: 45–46.

38. Delbecq, Andre L., Andrew H. Van de Ven, and David H. Gustafson. *Group Techniques for Program Planning: A Guide to Nominal Group and Delphi Processes*. Middleton, WI: Greenbriar, 1986: 89.

39. von der Gracht, 44.

40. Delbecq et al.

41. Adapted from "The Structure, Format, Content, and Style of a Journal-Style Scientific Paper." Department of Biology, Bates College, Lewiston, Maine. Modified March 7, 2011. http://abacus.bates.edu/~ganderso/biology/resources/writing/HTWsections.html#results; Wright, Daniel B. "Making Friends With Your Data:

Improving How Statistics Are Conducted and Reported." *British Journal of Educational Psychology* 73, no. 1 (2003): 123–136. https://doi.org/10.1348/000709903762869950; and Drotar, Dennis. "Editorial: How to Write an Effective Results and Discussion for the Journal of Pediatric Psychology." *Journal of Pediatric Psychology* 34, no. 4 (2009): 339–343. https://doi.org/10.1093/jpepsy/jsp014.

42. Chamorro-Premuzic, Tomas. "Ace the Assessment." *Harvard Business Review* 93, no. 7/8 (July–August 2015): 118. https://hbr.org/2015/07/ace-the-assessment; and Chamorro-Premuzic, Tomas. *The Talent Delusion: Why Data, Not Intuition, Is the Key to Unlocking Human Potential*. London: Little, Brown, 2017.

43. Ibid., 118–121.

44. Drotar, 340.

45. APA. Kindle ed., 35.

46. Department of Biology, Bates College.

47. Kretchmer, Paul. "Fourteen Steps to Writing an Effective Discussion Section." *San Francisco Edit*, 2003–2008. http://www.sfedit.net.

48. Bates, op. cit.

49. APA. Kindle ed., 35.

50. Adapted from: Lammers 16-10; Price, 283; Drotar, 341; Bates, op. cit.; and Kretchmer, op. cit.

51. Drotar, op. cit.

52. Drotar, Dennis. "Editorial: Thoughts on Establishing Research Significance and Presenting Scientific Integrity." *Journal of Pediatric Psychology* 33, no. 1 (2008): 1–5. https://doi.org/10.1093/jpepsy/jsm092. https://academic.oup.com/jpepsy/article/34/4/339/1078796/Editorial-How-to-Write-an-Effective-Results-and.

53. Drotar, 2009, 341.

54. Price, 284.

55. Ibid.

56. APA. Kindle ed., 36.

57. Price, 284; Labaree, Robert V. "Organizing Your Social Science Research Paper: 8. The Discussion." USC Libraries Research Guides, University of Southern California. Last modified January 28, 2017. http://libguides.usc.edu/writingguide/discussion; Laerd Dissertation. "Research Limitations and Future Research." *Dissertation Essentials*. © 2012 Lund Research Ltd. Retrieved from http://dissertation.laerd.com/research-limitations.php; and UNC College of Arts & Sciences. "Conclusions." The Writing Center, University of North Carolina-Chapel Hill. http://writingcenter.unc.edu/handouts/conclusions/.

58. Drotar, 342.

59. Laerd Dissertation, op. cit. http://dissertation.laerd.com/research-limitations.php

60. Labaree, Robert V. "Organizing Your Social Science Research Paper: 9. The Conclusion." USC Libraries Research Guides, University of Southern California. Last modified February 7, 2017. http://libguides.usc.edu/writingguide/conclusion. Italics, mine.

61. Labaree, Ibid.

62. Portions of this section were based on Paiz, Joshua M., Elizabeth Angeli, Jodi Wagner, Elena Lawrick, Kristen Moore, Michael Anderson, Lars Soderlund, Allen Brizee, and Russell Keck. "General Format." *Purdue Online Writing Lab*, May 13, 2016. Retrieved from http://owl.english.purdue.edu/owl/resource/560/01/.

63. APA. Kindle ed., 37.

64. List compiled as modified from Paiz et al. http://owl.english.purdue.edu/owl/resource/560/05/; APA, 37; Price, 285; Lammers, 16-10/11; and Nell and Crosling, 72.

65. Paiz et al., op. cit.

INDEX